HANDBOOK ON TEACHING

EDUCATIONAL PSYCHOLOGY

EDUCATIONAL PSYCHOLOGY

Allen J. Edwards, Series Editor
Department of Psychology
Southwest Missouri State University
Springfield, Missouri

HANDBOOK ON TEACHING EDUCATIONAL PSYCHOLOGY

EDITED BY

Donald J. Treffinger

Department of Educational Psychology and Research,
University of Kansas
Lawrence, Kansas

J. Kent Davis

Departments of Psychological Sciences and Education
Purdue University
Lafayette, Indiana

Richard E. Ripple

Department of Educational Psychology
Cornell University
Ithaca, New York

ACADEMIC PRESS   New York   San Francisco   London   1977

A Subsidiary of Harcourt Brace Jovanovich, Publishers

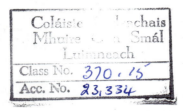
ACADEMIC PRESS, INC.
111 Fifth Avenue, New York, New York 10003

United Kingdom Edition published by
ACADEMIC PRESS, INC. (LONDON) LTD.
24/28 Oval Road, London NW1

Library of Congress Cataloging in Publication Data

Main entry under title:

Handbook on teaching educational psychology.

(Educational psychology series)
Includes bibliographies.
1. Educational psychology.   2.   Educational
psychology—Study and teaching.   I.   Treffinger, Donald J.
II.   Davis, J. Kent.   III.   Ripple, Richard E.
LB1051.H236   370.15'07   76-45989
ISBN 0−12−697750−X

Contents

7 Humanistic Psychology: Theoretical–Philosophical Framework and Implications for Teaching

DON E. HAMACHEK

PART III   SPECIFIC INSTRUCTIONAL APPROACHES

8 Mastery Learning   163

LORIN W. ANDERSON and JAMES H. BLOCK

9 Competency-Based Formats in Educational Psychology   187

ROBERT L. HOHN

PART IV SUMMARY: UNDERGRADUATE
AND GRADUATE LEVELS

List of Contributors

Numbers in parentheses indicate the pages on which the authors' contributions begin.

LORIN W. ANDERSON (163), College of Education, University of South Carolina, Columbia, South Carolina

HARVEY B. BLACK (45), Department of Instructional Science, Brigham Young University, Provo, Utah

JAMES H. BLOCK (163), Department of Education, University of California, Santa Barbara, California

HENRY P. COLE (263), Department of Educational Psychology and Counseling, College of Education, University of Kentucky, Lexington, Kentucky

RODNEY E. COPELAND (91), Psychology Department, Southwestern Missouri State University, Springfield, Missouri

JOHN P. DE CECCO (333), Department of Psychology, San Francisco University, San Francisco, California

S. FARNHAM-DIGGORY (113), Department of Educational Foundations, College of Education, University of Delaware, Newark, Delaware

JOHN FELDHUSEN (313), Departments of Psychological Sciences and Education, Purdue University, West Lafayette, Indiana

DON E. HAMACHEK (139), College of Education, Michigan State University, East Lansing, Michigan

ROBERT L. HOHN (187), Educational Psychology and Research Department, University of Kansas, Lawrence, Kansas

ROBERT E. KEYSOR (45), Department of Instructional Research Development, Brigham Young University, Provo, Utah

B. CLAUDE MATHIS (25), Center for the Teaching Professions, Northwestern University, Evanston, Illinois

JAMES H. McMILLAN (25), School of Education, University of Colorado at Denver, Denver, Colorado

ROBERT J. MENGES (25), Center for the Teaching Professions, Northwestern University, Evanston, Illinois

LOUISE S. MUSSER (263), Department of Educational Psychology and Counseling, College of Education, University of Kentucky, Lexington, Kentucky

JAMES B. OLSEN (45), Department of Instructional Research Development, Brigham Young University, Provo, Utah

ARLENE K. RICHARDS (333), Psychologist, Private practice, New York City

HERBERT J. RIETH, JR. (91), Department of Special Education and Center for Innovation in Teaching the Handicapped, Indiana University, Bloomington, Indiana

S. J. SAMUELS (67), Educational Psychology Department and Center for Research in Human Learning, University of Minnesota, Minneapolis, Minnesota

GEORGE SEMB (243), Department of Human Development, University of Kansas, Lawrence, Kansas

MONTE F. SHELLEY (45), David O. McKay Institute, Brigham Young University, Provo, Utah

ROBERT E. SPENCER (243), Department of Human Development, University of Kansas, Lawrence, Kansas

DOUGLAS J. STANWYCK (287), Department of Educational Foundations, Georgia State University, Atlanta, Georgia

ROBERT D. TENNYSON (215), Instructional Systems Laboratory, University of Minnesota, Minneapolis, Minnesota

PAMELA R. TERRY (67), Department of Special Education, Indiana University, Bloomington, Indiana

WILLIAM CLARK TROW (3), Professor Emeritus of Education and of Psychology, University of Michigan, Ann Arbor, Michigan

ADRIAN P. VAN MONDFRANS (45), David O. McKay Institute, Brigham Young University, Provo, Utah

DAVID D. WILLIAMS (45), David O. McKay Institute, Brigham Young University, Provo, Utah

Preface

During the last decade, there has been a nationwide pattern of rapidly increasing concern for the quality of postsecondary instruction. This concern has involved both the evaluation and improvement of college teaching. While it has doubtless come about through the interaction of many complex pressures or influences, the theme of "accountability" has run strong.

The discipline of educational psychology has been involved in this pattern. There have been published efforts to define goals and objectives for educational psychology, to delimit the boundaries of educational psychology in relation to other disciplines, to describe the fundamental structure and methods used by educational psychologists, and to offer "helpful hints" to teachers of educational psychology. Educational psychologists have begun to recognize that they are charged, not only with studying and improving the teaching and learning of *others,* but with looking as well at the quality of *their own* instruction.

The purposes of this *Handbook* are to provide a contemporary, wide-ranging survey of practices and problems in teaching educational psychology, and to review and evaluate in a single reference sourcebook the conceptual and methodological bases of the practices and the problems. It is a survey and review of contemporary educational psychology as it is taught, one that integrates many themes that have previously been addressed only in an isolated, fragmented way.

The *Handbook* is addressed to experienced educational psychologists and to others, both professionals and students, seeking useful information about many of the contemporary dimensions of educational psychology. It is organized in four principal sections, each containing several chapters prepared by leaders in various aspects of educational psychology.

The first section includes four chapters that provide an overview of the general problems confronted by the educational psychologists and the methods for attacking those problems. The first chapter is historical in content. Chapter 2 confronts the problems of defining the content and boundaries of educational psychology. Chapter 3 addresses the methodological tools and issues that are used by educational psychologists in studying educational problems. Chapter 4 looks toward the future to explore some emerging issues and challenges that educational psychology must face.

The second section consists of three chapters that survey the general conceptual and theoretical models that have influenced research and instructional development in educational psychology. Chapter 5 presents the behavioral analysis model, representing the behavioristic orientation. Chapter 6 presents the cognitive view point. Chapter 7 describes the humanistic model of educational psychology. These chapters provide the general conceptual framework upon which specific instructional strategies and methods are based.

The third section, comprising six chapters, surveys a variety of specific teaching approaches or strategies that are currently employed in educational psychology courses throughout the discipline. Chapter 8 describes the well-known "learning for mastery" model. Chapter 9 surveys specific problems and principles involved in educational psychology's role in competency-based teacher education programs. Chapter 10 examines the contributions of instructional technology. Chapter 11 describes the personalized system of instruction (PSI) approach. Chapter 12 addresses the applications of "process education" models to instruction at the college level. Chapter 13 reviews methods and techniques for encouraging affective development, self-awareness, and personal growth.

The final section provides a summary of some of the major issues and advances in teaching educational psychology, organized to distinguish between the undergraduate and graduate levels of instruction. Chapter 14 addresses undergraduate instruction, and Chapter 15 is concerned with graduate courses.

As we have read the chapters ourselves, we have had a sense of motion, an awareness of divergency. At first, there was a tendency to treat that as matter of stylistic differences among writers, and to seek to "edit it out" of the volume. As we continued to review and to discuss the material, however, we realized that the differences, and the sense of change, reflected the very nature of the discipline. Hence, rather than viewing this as a problem, we came to accept it as an accurate representation of our profession. Viewed in this way, we found it exciting and challenging; we hope you will also allow yourself to capture that enthusiasm.

We should also mention that we hope this *Handbook* will become a publication that contributes to the process of growth in the field. To that end, and in addition to whatever contribution the *Handbook* can make through its structure and content, we have agreed that all royalties from its sale (after payment of a token honorarium to the contributing authors) will be returned to the American Psychological Association's Division 15, for use in work for the improvement of teaching educational psychology, and to the American Educational Research Association's Special Interest Group on New Directions in Educational Psychology.

Part I

NATURE AND
ORGANIZATION OF
EDUCATIONAL PSYCHOLOGY

1

Historical Perspective

WILLIAM CLARK TROW[1]

The University of Michigan

NEW AND OLD KNOWLEDGE

In the better colleges and graduate schools it is customary to emphasize new knowledge. Recent events and discoveries are examined, and experiments are replicated, perhaps under varying conditions. Thus the new is either found wanting and discarded, or it is accepted and becomes common knowledge or is relegated to a footnote and gradually forgotten. And so the old new gives way to the new new. The next generation of students may be uncertain by which fate it has been overtaken—they may never have heard of it.

As a consequence, many students miss the fun and excitement of the disputation the old new originally engendered among fellow students and among leaders in the field. They may even have no knowledge of what it is they do not know, or of how it might be applied to current problems. This is likely to be true of the writings of the European educational philosophers and of the work of the early psychologists as well.

Pure and Applied Psychology

And in America, where the pure immured themselves with their rats in the psychology departments, and the impure with their tests in the schools of

[1] William Clark Trow is Professor Emeritus of Education and Psychology. His present address is: 931 Oakdale Road, Ann Arbor, Michigan 48105.

education, reliable knowledge, new or old, has been increasingly difficult to identify. The observation that the former have devoted themselves to experimentation, the latter to measurement and evaluation, and both to guidance (this by virtue of the happy marriage of the bench and the couch), comes nearer to the truth than we might wish. The dichotomy of the pure and the applied has always been inadequate. Yet many of the pure psychologists continued to run rats when they could well have attended to Thorndike's studies using human subjects; and many have neglected Skinner's perpetual-motion pigeons in favor of his disquisitions on school marks and on freedom and dignity.

Having outlived several swings of the pendulum I have been able to observe that the object of the game has been to determine which swing is the right one, though properly considered neither is all right or all wrong. It becomes necessary to make invidious distinctions in order to discover additional influential variables, and in other ways to avoid the either–or fallacy.

Functions of Psychology in School and College

Confusion seems to be inevitable wherever psychology is found; but when psychology strays into an educational milieu, its focus narrows somewhat and it becomes primarily concerned with those possible voluntary changes in behavior that are called learning.

As a high school subject, psychology is supposed to help the student to understand himself and his world and how to cope with it. As a college subject, its chief role has been to train prospective schoolteachers to think psychologically in teaching their pupils, to adapt their instruction to pupil needs and abilities, and to enable prospective psychological practitioners to deal with the problems of adjustment and learning of young people. The graduate school cultivates the more arcane features of the science, looking toward the revelation of further truth and to its more effective application.

Application

If these goals are to be realized more fully than has heretofore been possible, it would seem that the first requirement is a closer collaboration between the psychological and the educational specialists (despite departmental separations) than has been customary in times past, particularly in European practice. Whatever the psychologists have that can be used to help solve educational problems should be made available, providing they understand that it can probably not be transferred *in toto* from the laboratory to the schoolroom. While we would certainly have no objection to experiments designed to find out the facts (pure science) and "tell it like it is," we are dealing primarily with an applied science, seeking to improve certain processes.

Reform

The second requirement is reform—correcting the faulty practices of the past. Among these faulty practices can be listed corporal punishment, grade grouping, the marking system, and judgments of competence of high school graduates for college entrance and of candidates for teaching positions by the hours of academic credit they may have accumulated. Among possible substitutions can be listed clarification of instructional objectives, evaluations in terms of competence of performance, techniques of behavior modification, and attention to ethical and other values as well as cognitive.

Some of these topics are discussed in detail later in this volume, but before taking any of them up one at a time it would seem best to get an overview of the whole field and discover some of their origins and the patterns of their development. Even though no complete history is possible in this limited space, such a survey ought to suggest sources that might otherwise be overlooked and problems that deserve further attention.

THEORETICAL BASES

Medical—Observation

If a student has not been informed about a certain intellectual product or discovery, he is likely to think that there never was any such thing until his own generation invented it. For example, such a definition of the purpose of education as the following might seem to him to be a recent correction of narrower early views:

> The object of education and training is to bring the child into harmony with his surroundings, the home and the school, in order that in future years he may live harmoniously with whatever circumstances may surround him.

But instead of being the last word emanating from our present enlightened era, these words appear in the preface of *A Course of Lectures on the Growth and Means of Training the Mental Faculty* by Francis Warner, M.D., London, published in 1890. In it, the author notes his interest in "teaching as a profession," and his belief that schoolteachers and others concerned in education should acquire a more accurate and scientific knowledge of different kinds of children and of pupils under different conditions. To that end he gives directions for observation of children that would result in about the same kind of referral as one would be likely to find today, allowing for the more recent increases in the development of neural physiology. But he would be one of those whose methods were decried by Binet as indicating a need for measurement, for

Dr. Warner reported on the basis of his observations such items as "Defective in brain power, a big, fat, dull boy," and "Mentally defective. Could not carry a message."

Psychological—Introspection

Certainly if one is seeking historical perspective he should be quite clear about what he is looking for, noting the theoretical bases for his observations. For the psychological base, we can turn back to the year 1884 when James Sully, examiner for the moral sciences in Cambridge, published his *Outlines of Psychology with Special Reference to the Theory of Education* (p. 695). Some of its 19 chapter titles look like standard psychology; e.g., Mental Development, Attention, Sensation, Perception, Memory (including association), Conception, Judgment and Reasoning, and Feelings (preferred to affectivity).

In his Appendix A, however, Sully discusses two "methods of psychology": introspection and the objective method of observation—which Dr. Warner employed in the lectures reported above—but there is no mention of measurement or experimentation. And in his Appendix B, Sully abandons Aristotle's bipartite division of mind into thought and desire, in favor of a tripartite division—knowing (logic), feeling (esthetics), and willing (ethics).

To find the "theory of education" referred to in the title one must search more diligently. It seems that, to Sully, psychology as a whole supplies the basis of education, which aims at cultivating the three divisions of the mind. Education is construed as a practical rather than a theoretical science, and as such is concerned with things as they are, in contrast with things as we wish them to be.

And education is also an art since it is engaged in "exercising or training the faculties of the mind—memory, judgment, observation [perception], and so on." So the educator should have a knowledge of the laws of mental operations since his aim is "to call forth a faculty into exercise." This will be easily recognized as the doctrine of formal discipline, which promised students of past generations that the subjects they were required to study would "build up a reservoir of mental power." Of course, we have been taught that there are no such things as faculties; this is obviously old stuff. Still, we should note that this process is here translated, "bring about a particular mental result," a consummation now likely to be masked as behavior. We are no doubt better off for our concern with definitely observable phenomena, though in our preoccupation with the overt we may well have erred by neglecting the covert, and we would certainly do well not to think of either phenomenon as causing the behavior that follows.

Education—Philosophy

To find the psychological base for the educational contribution we turn back another 5 years to 1879, to the publication of *Lectures on Pedagogy—Theoretical and Practical* by Professor Gabriel Compayré or to its translation by W. H.

Payne (1887, p. 491). According to the author's statement in the Preface, this is an elementary manual of teaching. Compayré divided his treatise into two quite distinct parts. In the first, "Theoretical Pedagogy," he dealt with the study of the child in himself, in his natural development, and in the formal culture of his faculties. (Here we are on familiar ground.) In Part II, "Practical Pedagogy," he set forth the methods of instruction and the principles and rules of discipline. Education was still viewed as a science and an art (skill embodied in practice), while the term pedagogy was reserved for educational theory.

In fact, however, Compayré was one of the first to be concerned with the role· of education in fostering the psychological development of the growing child. What this should consist of was indicated in Part I, which includes chapters on physical, intellectual, and moral, esthetic, and religious education; the culture of the attention; the memory; the imagination; the feelings; and the faculties of reflection, judgment, abstraction, and reasoning; and a chapter on will, liberty, and habit. Part II consists of what we would call methods courses, and besides covering the common school subjects it includes chapters on methods in general, object lessons, morals, and civic instruction, rewards and punishments.

It may readily be seen that except for a smattering of what we might think of as quaint terminology, the present-day educational psychologist would feel quite at home here. And yet, in the quest of this chapter for the historical beginnings of educational psychology, we note here little more than a juxtaposition of two ingredients—a few chapters on psychology followed by a few on education. This juxtaposition, valuable as it was at the time, is not exactly what we seek. Our current interest is in finding ways in which psychological knowledge can help to educate the individuals of the present and oncoming generations. What seems to be needed is not the structuring of two disciplines so much as a more complete knowledge of the learning and the teaching processes.

We have noted two related methods of obtaining knowledge—observation (of the overt) and introspection (of the covert). But during the nineteenth century, a third, the method of experimental science, pressed for attention. Before psychologists could make more than sporadic use of this new method, however, problems had to be formulated, theoretical considerations examined, and hypothetical solutions arrived at. By the late 1800s the "new" psychology was aborning (Boring, 1929).

THE PSYCHOLOGICAL THEORISTS

The British Associationists[2]

Some of the philosophical base bears such a direct relation to educational psychology that it calls for specific mention. The earlier philosophers, who took

[2] See Rand (1912).

all knowledge for their province, often read a paper or wrote a book setting forth their views on the nature of man; but to trace their ideas about education, beginning with Plato and Aristotle, would be far beyond the scope of this chapter, except for mention of Aristotle's delineation of the laws of association—similarity and contrast, and contiguity in space and time (succession). Later, a remarkable group of philosophers, usually referred to as the British associationists, dominated the field; among them Locke, Hume, Hartley, the Mills, and Bain are perhaps the best known. They elaborated the older laws or principles of association, holding that the mind is like a wax tablet (*tabula rasa*) upon which experiences write the content of the mind depending on the relation of these experiences as influenced by pleasantness and unpleasantness (P and U). Without experimenting themselves they established what I like to think of as the main line of psychological development, that of the experimentalists.

The Continental Theorists

Meanwhile, on the Continent, three philosophers produced important changes in matters of interest to educational psychologists. The first of these was Pestalozzi (1746–1827) who has been called the "father of modern pedagogy." Early influenced by Rousseau's brainchild, Émile, whose education was based on the "return to nature" idea, Pestalozzi later concluded that reform of the environment alone is not enough; educational effort is necessary. He held that there should be instruction for teachers in how to teach—which was then a new idea—and for parents in how to bring up their children. The spread of the Pestalozzian movement in this country as well as abroad can be traced in the increasing number of normal schools that were founded to prepare elementary schoolteachers for their work.

Earlier, the universities in the medieval period had prepared their doctoral graduates for disputation, and later, universities added educational theory as it related to the secondary school period. The courses were in what was termed the science and art of teaching. The general lack of concern for the elementary school years led to the spread of normal schools which assumed varied forms, sometimes following the ideas of one or another of the educational theorists and sometimes following an eclectic pattern.

As these normal schools, referred to as experimental or demonstration schools, were gradually absorbed by the universities, they gave relatively different amounts of time to educational history and to social and psychological theory on the one hand and to practice teaching on the other. Methods ranged from having each student teach a class of children on a stage while being observed by classmates—a traumatic experience for many—to current supplementary schemes using brief periods (modules) or TV practice units.

The second of the three continental theorists was Herbart (1776–1841), who was a more orthodox philosopher than either of the other two, and who succeeded to Kant's chair at Königsberg. But he, like the others, arranged for experimental groups on which to try out his theories as did Dewey later at Chicago. Herbart enunciated the doctrine of apperception, insisting that ideas do not develop by a kind of chance association, laws or no laws, but instead, new ideas are brought into consciousness by those already present (the apperceptive mass). Education, therefore, must prepare and present the new in such a way that it will be assimilated and become a part of the mental content. The "Herbartian movement" resulted in notable changes in educational methods, especially that of handling the recitation.

The third of the three educational philosophers was Froebel (1782–1852), who perhaps had the widest influence. He invented the kindergarten, of which even the naming was a stroke of genius. Other more descriptive but less succinct titles had preceded it—*Anstalt für Kleinkinderpflege* (Institution for the Care of Little Children) and *Kleinkinder Beschäftigungs Anstalt* (Little Children's Activity Institution). Froebel spent several months visiting Pestalozzi and observing his methods. The catch phrases descriptive of Froebelian psychology have become so familiar that their source is often forgotten, e.g., self-activity, physical and mental growth and development, continuity, self-expression, and creativity. Much to the dismay of some traditionalists, these ideas have pushed their way up from the kindergarten and into the elementary and high school so that the to-be-expected reaction soon appeared in various forms, among them the doctrine of essentialism which, in turn, has been accused of following the directive, "Find out what the pupils don't want and then give them plenty of it."

Two other more recent philosophers should be added, Thomas Huxley (1825–1895), who introduced the evolutionary viewpoint, and Eduard Spranger (1882–1963), who represented the *Geisteswissenschaft* (cultural science) view which fathered the Gestalt psychology of Wertheimer and others, and whose ideal types (Spranger, 1925) were the source of the Allport–Vernon scale of values.

Studies of Growth and Development

A new pattern of psychological inquiry began to take shape around the turn of the century that has held the continuing interest of educators. It was prompted by a desire to know more of the physical and mental characteristics of children and youth and also of the transition from one period to the next. Adolescence, which was known as a marginal period, was of primary interest and was explored by G. Stanley Hall (1904), who employed the questionnaire method. Later, Arnold Gesell (1940) explored the first years of life, recording his observations on motion picture film. Unfortunately, disagreement of data with his norms was sometimes interpreted by disturbed parents as abnormality.

Jean Piaget (1952) carried the inquiry to cognitive development of the elementary school period, and Williard Olson (1949) to the parallelism between physiological and mental growth.

The American Philosophers

The philosophical method eventually escaped its theological bondage in America and was best represented by William James (1842–1910), who was more psychologist than educator. But his two volume *Principles of Psychology* (1890) exerted a wide influence with its neurological inclination which included his well-known theory (shared with Lange) of the nature of emotion. In contrast was his *Talks to Teachers* (1899), a slender volume that revealed the pragmatism of which he and C. S. Peirce were the founders.

Later John Dewey (1859–1952) and his followers elaborated this view which, briefly stated, is that the meaning of an idea consists in the conduct it designates (or more broadly, in its practical consequences); hence these are the test of truth. Educationally, the pragmatist views the child as a changing, growing personality; and learning and teaching serve to promote the "reconstruction of experience." This latter will perhaps be recognized as a descendant of Herbart's assimilation of ideas by the apperceptive mass. Allied with the pragmatic view was the utilitarian, which for ethical judgments adopted the formula of the greatest happiness of the greatest number, and, for other values, made practical usefulness the criterion.

Translated into psycho-educational terms, these views were basic to functionalism, which was spelled out by Dewey in his experimental school at the University of Chicago. Functionalism differed from structuralism in its view of psychological content, for instead of seeking an answer to a question by asking "What is it?" it asked, "What is it for?" That is, what is its function? It is interesting that in his presidential address on "Psychology and Social Practice," before the American Psychological Association in 1900, Dewey made a plea for a program for educational psychology.

The Experimentalists[3]

A change came during the last years of the nineteenth century. Psychological and educational problems began to receive the kind of attention that those of the older sciences had been accorded for a couple of hundred years or more. In archaic slang this idea was to "try it out on the dog."

More properly speaking, it was to set up a situation in which the significant conditions were similar to those usually found, except that they were subject to

[3] See Boring (1929).

the experimenter's control. Thus it was an analogy in which all significant parts (variables) were held constant, with the expectation that each time it was repeated the same results would follow. Or a single variable might be introduced or withdrawn, following which any change in the consequences would be considered to be an effect caused by that variable. Since such change would depend on the presence or absence of this factor it became referred to as the dependent variable. It seems strange that it took so long for this comparatively simple idea to occur to people during the million or more years that this planet has been occupied by genus *Homo.*

But we know that as a consequence of its use enormous advances have been made in physics, chemistry, and biology in both the pure and the applied fields. However, owing to the elusive nature of psychological phenomena, it has been more difficult to apply to the social and behavioral sciences.

Wundt (Structuralism)

The first psychological laboratory was founded in 1879 by Wilhelm Wundt (1832–1920) at Leipzig, though William James at Harvard had a room set apart for psychological experimentation 4 or 5 years earlier (Boring, 1929, p. 318). As the number of laboratories increased, by the careful observation of overt and covert (introspection) phenomena, Wundt and others, including Titchener (1919) in America, were able to describe sensation, perception, P and U, feeling and imagery, i.e., the content of consciousness generally.

Thorndike (Connectionism)

It was Thorndike (1874–1949) who, at the turn of the century, probably did more than any other to take psychology out of its "armchair" and rescue it from its dependence on introspection. In a sense, therefore, Thorndike (1913, 1914) became the first educational psychologist. He joined the associationist principle of contiguity to those of P and U (renamed satisfiers and annoyers) and in situations analagous to those found in the behavior of chicks and kittens, used the maze and the puzzle box, which he invented, and recorded his observations. From them he promulgated the empirical laws of exercise (repetition of a connection strengthens it, i.e., under similar conditions makes the response more probable) and effect (a connection is strengthened if it is accompanied or followed by a satisfying state of affairs).

Thorndike also formulated the principle of associative shifting (if two stimuli are presented together, one will tend to substitute for the other in evoking the original response). He borrowed the concepts of frequency (use, exercise), recency, and intensity from the associationists and employed his own invention, belongingness; in so doing he paid his respects to the part–whole relationship which the Gestalt psychologists insisted on.

And perhaps most important of all, he took formal discipline out of the mystic realms of surmise and dogma, provided a new name for the phenomenon (transfer) and an explanatory hypothesis (identical elements or components), and so made it a proper object of investigation into how much and under what circumstances.

Köhler (Gestalt)

Objection to the stimulus–response connectionism came chiefly from the small band of Berlin psychologists who one by one emigrated to America. They objected to the S–R concept as being too mechanical, supposedly implying something as elemental as the reflex arc or an electric circuit. But since all parts are wholes and all wholes are parts, whether they are responses or stimulus situations, much trouble seemingly could be avoided if the speaker or writer made clear which parts and which wholes he was concerned with. Prominent among the Gestalt or configurationist psychologists was Wolfgang Köhler (1887–1967), who on the basis of his nonquantitative experiments on chimpanzees (1927) took exception to Thorndike's slowly descending curves of learning, claiming they recorded time taken to manipulate the apparatus, not to think; the latter, he asserted, involved an instantaneous "insight."

Mention should also be made of Kurt Lewin (1890–1947), the last of the original Gestalt psychologists and founder of group dynamics, which has made a creditable research record in the area of social psychology (1935), but which has not yet, in this writer's opinion, made the contribution it might to educational processes.

Pavlov (Conditioning)

Meanwhile the Russian physiologist, Ivan P. Pavlov (1849–1936), with his dog and bell, was working on the salivary reflex. From such atomistic data evolved the concept of the conditioned reflex (Pavlov, 1928). (The Russian word *ooslovny* means conditional, i.e., appearing under certain conditions.) His elaboration of what Thorndike saw as a special case of his associative shifting was highly acceptable to the pure psychologists.

J. B. Watson (Behaviorism)

Though the experiments of John B. Watson (1878–1958) were all of the narrow reflex response, they were widely publicized and provided the basis for his formulation of the principles of behaviorism (1919), which he applied broadly to emotional learning and child care. A generation or more was required to mitigate the unfortunate effects of his applications of the conditioning principle and permit the acceptance of tender loving care (TLC) as a necessary part of the child's environment.

B. F. Skinner (Operant Behaviorism)

The subsequent and more highly sophisticated operant behaviorism delineated by Skinner brought the main line development to its present terminal and is too recent to be included in this historical review. Suffice it to say that it is less closely related to Watson than it is to Thorndike. Skinner's elaboration of the principle of effect (Thorndike) or reinforcement (Pavlov) is noteworthy, as is his recognition of the educational implications of his labors.

Measurement and Testing

Paralleling the main line development of experimentation came the activity variously referred to as measurement, testing, assessment, and evaluation—Usually they involve some statistics and are commonly regarded as research.

Aptitude

Apart from the subjective marking to which student effort has been subjected for centuries, the first measurement of mental excellence was conducted by Binet and Simon (1916). Their assignment was to devise a scheme to identify the mentally retarded children in the Paris schools, one that would be more dependable than the medical type of observation then in use. Their tests, however, were not, like the school examinations, aimed at discovering how much the pupils remembered of what they had supposedly been taught, but rather how well they would be likely to do what they were going to be taught—their school aptitude. Whether or not these tests would also measure intelligence would depend on one's definition of intelligence. The criterion, then, would be ability to perform future schoolwork and nothing else. Familiar as this distinction is today, there are still many, who should know better, who are critical of the aptitude tests because they do not measure what they are not intended to measure. Binet's pioneering contribution was the concept of mental age. Others have made additions—Stern the ratio of mental to chronological age, Spearman g and s, Terman the IQ, and others the group test, developed for the U.S. Army in World War I. The so-called Alpha test was for literates and the Beta for illiterates, roughly those who had not passed beyond the fourth grade. Variations of these tests were widely developed for routine testing in the schools.

Achievement

The scheme of using short items as employed in the aptitude tests was tried out early for achievement testing and has been extensively used, often along with the familiar essay-type examination. But the idea that the achievement tests should measure the success of the students in attaining the course objectives has been slow to be adopted, largely because of lack of agreement on what the objectives of any course really are. Granting this agreement, however, it is significant that a new view of standard performance for marking is beginning to be recognized—not only the average performance of the group being tested (or a similar group), referred to as the "norm-referenced" mark, but also the excellence of the performance of the student no matter what others do, the "criterion-referenced" mark.

Personality

Measures other than those of cognitive content should also be mentioned— questionnaires, rating scales, and especially projection tests of which the work of Hermann Rorschach (1884–1922) using inkblots is the prime example. (Rorschach tests, of course, are not tests at all but observational instruments which presumably reveal deep-seated emotional characteristics.)

The Psychiatric Approach: Mental Hygiene and Guidance

Abnormal Psychology[4]

Parallel with the main line development and measurement, and branching off from the medical method of observation, came the psychiatric approach that gradually attracted the attention of psychologists; and the possibilities of its use with children aroused the interest of psychiatrists who formerly had been primarily concerned with adults. Naturally the psychologists were confronted by educational problems and particularly those of pupil adjustment to school and family. At first, as a rule, money was available only for Binet's problem of school retardation, for which the Terman revision of the Binet tests and the Wechsler tests were widely used. On this basis, the school psychologist (or examiner or diagnostician as he was variously called) merely measured and made recommendations to a faculty screening committee which then disposed of the case as it saw fit. This minor role as a technician was far from satisfying. Not only were the referred maladjusted children often not in the least retarded, but in any case some other type of followthrough and treatment was usually desirable beyond what was often not a very satisfactory change in school placement.

The dispute which followed over who should be legally responsible for the diagnosis and treatment of the maladjusted was to the credit of neither the medically trained psychiatrists, who were gradually moving over into the juvenile field, nor to that of the clinical psychologists, who were gradually becoming concerned with parents and other adults as well as with school children. These cases ranged from slight personality disorders through the relatively mild neu-

---

[4] See Murphy (1929).

roses to psychoses so severe that the client, or patient, was judged irresponsible. The psychiatrists seemed to think the psychologists were not adequately trained to deal with such cases, and unfortunately this was sometimes true. And sometimes the psychologists were not adequately trained educationally to deal with the school age youngsters, especially in group therapy situations. Certainly the school budgets were not such that the prolonged individual psychiatric treatment required could be provided, though referrals could be recommended to the family. The same was true of the Freudians whose training consisted of being psychoanalyzed. Since the number of psychiatrists, Freudians or other, was and is too small to deal with the total abnormal population, an amicable system of referrals and treatment has evolved in many places, as have training programs providing for both psychological and educational practice.

Freud (Psychoanalysis)

The genius of the period was, of course, Sigmund Freud (1856–1939) whose concept of the unconscious mind and revolutionary theories seemed able to explain all mental regularities and deviations. For the neuroses and psychoses, however, cures were another matter. The interest of Freud (1920) in maladjustment problems derived in part from his medical training, though he never practiced medicine; from the work of Charcot, the French psychiatrist whose demonstrations of hypnosis were attracting wide attention; and partly from the British associationists, some of whose work Freud translated. The free association which he employed in his analysis reveals this early affiliation, and his concept of displacement bears a striking resemblance to Thorndike's transfer.

Many of Freud's original supporters and fellow psychoanalysts eventually rejected his leadership, largely because of his preoccupation with sex and his doctrinaire attitude. This was the case with Alfred Adler who promoted what he termed "individual psychology," which emphasized the power goal and feelings of inferiority over failure to attain it. And this was true also of Carl Jung who promoted the mythical idea of an inherited, collective unconscious as a source of dreams and neurotic symptoms. His type psychology (introversion and extraversion) achieved wide popularity.

The Neo-Freudians

Freud's orthodoxy came to be more and more frequently challenged. Carl Rogers developed his "nondirective" or "client-centered" therapy as an interview method, and Erik Erikson elaborated his concepts of autonomy and identity. Others have emphasized the importance of social and other environmental influences, especially during the childhood years.

What seems to many to be an aberrant form of group therapy, one with sociological complications, has followed from the group dynamics exercises at Bethel, Maine. Now known as the Esalen Institute, with branches in Big Sur and

San Francisco, California, it has begun to set up university-connected conferences with a $50 admission fee, to explore "those trends in the behavioral sciences, religion, education, sports, and philosophy which emphasize the potentialities and values of human existence [Esalen Institute flier] ."

Other closely related forms of group interaction in therapy are known as sensitivity training, T-groups, and encounter and confrontation groups. What is called gestalt seems to have no particular relation to the *Gestalt* of Wertheimer, Köhler, Koffka, and Lewin. A more orthodox movement, referred to as humanistic psychology but having no particular relation to scientific or religious Humanism, employs mental hygiene principles and behavior modification processes. It not only favors individual therapy, but also efforts to improve man by improving his environment. Its supporters (Mahoney, 1975) recognize that organic evolution aims at no utopian goal, and that physical aggression and sexual fertility no longer have their old survival value. So for a good life, such other goals as individual responsibility, personal freedom, and social sensitivity, as well as delayed satisfaction and even limited aspiration, should be sought.

While educational psychology has historically been aimed at children and youth, these recent developments point to an increasing concern with problems of adult adjustment and group enterprise.

THE PAST AS GUIDE

In his "Give me liberty or give me death" speech, Patrick Henry proclaimed that he knew no way of judging the future but by the past. And neither does anyone else. Rough judgments may be made based on the individual's experiences, but empirical truths are established by the consequences of carefully observed past events, and controlled experiments are undertaken seeking to test and perhaps confirm preestablished theories. But scientists, as well as people generally, sometimes make terrible mistakes because of their failure to reckon with certain large or small differences in the conditions then and now—what we have come to call variables.

To deal with this problem, scientists go to great lengths to determine the nature and operation of these variables and to analyze their effects on any given situation. People often use what they call "common sense," which is really no more than the process of taking into account certain neglected variables. Such variables frequently include the quality of the phenomena under study, the nature of the individuals (subjects) involved, or the culture within which the operations were or are to be carried on. And besides these are the errors of design and of procedure and the fallacious conclusions which may not follow logically from the experimental data. If we are to avoid some of the errors of the past, we should advantageously use other past events, so briefly recounted here, to suggest some of the changes in our schools that may be promoted through the agency of educational psychologists. Here, then, are a few lessons that "history teaches"—or might if we were better learners.

Bias—Universality

No one single person or group of persons is to be trusted to determine curricular content or educational method, neither philosophers nor scientists, practical educators nor subject matter specialists. Any such group may be right, or it may be sadly out of line with present needs or future trends.

The philosophers are likely to be biased in favor of some theory, perhaps being overcommitted to Nature as a guide, to associationism, or to patterns or structure; the scientists to the covert or the overt, to introspection or behavior; the practical school administrators to what they think can or cannot be done; and the subject matter specialists to what they know. On the other hand, any one of these individuals or groups may be very right, deserving to be heard and to have their advice followed. Who shall decide?

Either—or Fallacy—Nonacceptability

The usual practice, whatever it may be, requires continuous study and revision so that its position in the swing of the pendulum may be determined and corrections made. Some people tend to favor the status quo as a matter of principle, and others favor change. But care must be taken to avoid the either—or fallacy, the tendency to simplify decision making on the assumption that a choice can and should be made of one of two alternatives, say, as directive or nondirective therapy, heredity or environment, learning by saying or by doing, word recognition or phonics, rewards or punishments, and open or closed schools.

Both are often needed. For some students, clay modeling, the new math, or more freedom may be just what the doctor ordered, but for others, one or another might produce a negative reaction. Television, if it has done nothing else, should by this time have taught the great American public to recognize a sales pitch when they see it, to realize that the purchase so vigorously advocated may not always be in the best interest of the individual prospects, and to be wary of the practices of venality. It might be a good idea to listen to both sides of the argument, for example, to the open schools enthusiast and also to the pupil who wants, above all else, a quiet place to study.

But besides such general cautions, it should be possible to identify some more positive suggestions. I find it convenient to divide them into two major groups: teaching modes and values or objectives, five of each. I am indebted for the modes to what Bank (1975) calls models and which could advantageously be served up as modules. Hers is a good working list, although I would prefer such modifications as the following:

TEACHING MODES

Knowledge Transmission

I have chosen the general name of knowledge transmission to cover the traditional school practice usually referred to when used orally as the lecture method. (Other titles that have been suggested for precollege levels such as lecturette have not caught on.) When supplemented by audiovisual aids, the formula (model) *tell–show–question* would be descriptive, especially when the teacher's questions are supplemented by those of the pupils. With assigned readings, it becomes the recitation. For both, the formula becomes *present–assign–quiz*. It is doubtful if the lecture segment has been improved as much in recent years as have the textbooks and supplementary readings. In any case, this is the teaching mode which, though highly convenient and reasonably efficient owing largely to its use of the contiguity principle and built-in sanctions, has been the object of considerable adverse criticism by philosophers and others. But it may be that the criticism has been too effective. Perhaps more attention should be given to improving the oral presentations with more carefully prepared technological aids made more easily available. And there should be more emphasis on clarifying percepts and concepts thus enabling pupils to discriminate and identify the objects of their environment and to build a knowledge foundation on which judgments can be based.

Behavior Modification

The currently popular concept of behavior modification is similar to the mode just discussed, except that it is not so exclusively cognitive and is based more on the reinforcement principle and the detailed use of progressive approximation as a consequence of the Skinnerian influence. Behavior modification can be widely used in a variety of learning situations and at present seems to be in an active exploratory stage in spite of the recently reported affirmation by the president of the American Psychological Association that Skinner is an anachronism.

Counseling

Called tutoring in the cognitive area, counseling usually refers to individual instruction in social behavior, though group counseling has the advantage of

economy of time. It is sometimes not successful in the hands of the psychologically trained, who have reported disciplinary problems instead of the mutual
help it is intended to provide. Counseling derives from the psychiatrists in
general and the psychoanalysts in particular in dealing, in part at least, with
subjective or covert phenomena. It may not be on the backswing of the
pendulum, orthodoxy being less exacting than formerly as sex interests tend to
be superseded by problems of development—autonomy, identification, integrity,
and other healthful attitudes.

Counseling is recognized as having a different function from that of teaching,
for its aim is usually to teach social behavior while teaching, as such, involves
keeping social behavior under control so as to be able to teach other content.

Role Playing

A teaching mode that is more restricted in its use, role playing may be
thought of as a special case of group counseling. Developed by J. L. Moreno
(1934), inventor of sociometry and the sociogram, the name sidesteps his nice
distinction between sociodrama and psychodrama. It aims to teach acceptable
interpersonal behavior by using unrehearsed dramatic presentations to help the
learner better to understand the attitudes and behavior of others, and incidentally his own.

Permissiveness

Whether permissiveness is a mode of teaching is a matter of definition, at least
in its extreme forms like Neill's Summerhill, which some have said is not a
school at all. Nearer the center of the swing of the pendulum was Maria
Montessori, who visited this country in 1915, whose influence accounted for
increased attention to sense training, object teaching, and individualized instruction, particularly in the Winnetka and Dalton school experiments. Furthermore,
the Montessori method encouraged pupil choice in decision making, but within
certain environmental limits: e.g., "You can have whatever you want for des-
sert—there are oranges and bananas." A good deal can be said for this approach
since it accustoms children to a world that sets limits to the satisfaction of
desires.

Set in motion by the psychiatric guidance people, the permissiveness pendulum is currently at different positions in different schools. In general, the far
right position is illustrated by the school with a prescribed curriculum, a
rulebook, and the same requirements for all students. Difficulties arise at all
points and especially during periods of rapid social change. The best solution
seems to be in participation in decision making.

VALUES AND OBJECTIVES

Each of the teaching modes described previously is employable in many kinds of situations, and it is chiefly the responsibility of the educational psychologist to determine what educational content can best be taught to whom and by which mode. This would not be too difficult if each major educational objective had its own mode, or if one mode was used for all, which is very nearly what happened earlier for knowledge transmission.

A similar danger hangs above the head of the educator in allowing a like reduction to take place in his educational objectives. A brief survey of major objectives may help to avoid this possibility (Trow, 1971, 1975).

Cognitive Values

It has often been said that the schools should teach their students to think, a highly commendable objective which in the old days was supposedly attained more or less automatically according to the principle of formal discipline. The unfortunately thing about this kind of laissez-faire procedure was that the students were taught the facts, or some of them at least, but often quizzed on thinking. Nowadays it is becoming customary to examine students, i.e., to measure their competence, in what they have supposedly been taught or trained to do—in this case, perhaps, to think like John Dewey. The nature of thinking has been more recently analyzed by Bloom (1956) and others, and practice has been provided in individual and small-group problem solving—a frequent committee activity in a democratic society. Also a particular style of solution, referred to as creative, has been analyzed. These matters have been receiving some recent attention and might properly receive more.

Health Values

Both physical and mental health have also recently been given special attention, partly on the verbal knowledge level and partly on the problem-solving performance level. This can well be continued, though it is sometimes difficult to draw the line between education and treatment.

Performance Values

Much has been made of the Dewey aphorism, "learning by doing," but in some quarters it could well be reversed to read, "doing by learning." The doing starts early and continues throughout the school years and perhaps later, with learning to read, spell, write, and compute—what schools were originally set up for—but now permitting so-called students to pass through them without acquiring these skills. In some places the pendulum has begun to swing back, but with an important change—the young people are not "failed" for what they have not been taught; they are given more time until an agreed-on level of competence is reached.

But merely providing more instructional time is not enough as Rice (1893) so dramatically showed in the time given to the teaching of spelling, for this variable bore no relation to the competence of the pupils. Nor is such experimental revelation enough, for educators paid practically no attention to his findings.

Applicable in athletics, music, and art, in vocational training, and social usage, the performance objectives in the past have been sadly neglected, sometimes even thought of as not being quite respectable, and those who fought for them had an uphill struggle. An analysis of the needs here is a must, to be followed by an intelligent program in all areas. But care must be taken not to let the pendulum swing too far.

Esthetic Values[5]

The quest for beauty with its epicurean reverberations has had a troubled past in the schools. There was a time, and it may yet come again, when perversion was not considered a necessary ingredient of the arts as it seems to be today. If we set our minds to it, we may be able to broaden the concept of esthetic values to include not only art and literature but also the beauty of nature and of life activity.

Socio-ethical Values

Perhaps what we most need to do is to supplement the self-fulfillment ideal of becoming all one is capable of becoming with social purpose, and somehow to teach young people to participate in helpful rather than in aggressive and destructive behavior. But this will not be easy in a country where looters move in on the trail of a tornado to profit from the misfortunes of others, and where, at least in one state, a law is thought to be necessary to penalize elected officials for lying to their constituents. In such a land, one should not be surprised that children vandalize the schools and become highly competent lawbreakers.

Perhaps a permanent educational psychology think tank with a slowly revolving membership of invited participants from various fields of interest should be

---

[5] See Krathwohl, Bloom, and Masia (1964).

established to make some of the necessary choices for research emphasis among the teaching modes and values. (See Allen, 1975, for a possible starting point.) With a familiarity with past ideas and ideals, and with past failures and successes, an approach could be made to establishing policies on a national level that would help to concentrate efforts and produce some of the needed changes.

PROFESSIONAL ORGANIZATION: DEVELOPMENT AND PUBLICATIONS

Meanwhile, organizational needs and the demands for publication call for continued development (see R. L. Watson, 1961, and also R. E. Grinder, 1967). The American Psychological Association was founded in 1892. Among the founding fathers (Dennis & Boring, 1952) with more or less educational interest were the following: G. Stanley Hall at Clark, William James at Harvard, James McK. Cattell at Columbia, W. L. Bryan at Indiana, and John Dewey at Michigan.

Continuity of interest and effort was probably maintained as much by H. E. Buchholz, original owner and managing editor of the *Journal of Educational Psychology* (from 1910 to 1952) as by any other individual, with the exception of E. L. Thorndike who was an early contributer. In 1951, Buchholz transferred editorial control of the *Journal* to a committee of three appointed by the Association to serve as a board of editors. The Board was composed of Corey, Stroud, and Trow, with Corey first in the rotating chairmanship. In 1957, the *Journal* was sold to the APA and a permanent editor appointed.

The two pertinent sections of the American Association for the Advancement of Science, Psychology and Education (named *I* and *Q* but purely coincidentally), made for both separation and union. However, unitary qualities were promoted by the Educational Psychology Section of the newly founded (1937) American Association of Applied Psychology, and later, after the two were merged (1945), by Division 15 of the American Psychological Association. Since 1963 the Division has published its own journal, the *Educational Psychologist,* which developed from its *Newsletter* (Feldhusen, 1976). Division 16, School Psychology, and other divisions and groups proliferated, as did the journals, including *Psychology in the Schools, Journal of School Psychology, Journal of Educational Technology,* and others, e.g., the Society of Professors of Education (formerly the American Association of College Teachers of Education) and the American Educational Research Association. The journals and annual meetings of these groups have tended to focus attention on the psychological aspects of teaching, as for example, the work of the first three presidents of Division 15: Brownell in arithmetic, Symonds chiefly in personality factors, Gates in reading, and others who followed down to the present day.

CONCLUSION

This brief sketch of the forces that have produced educational psychology, if it does nothing else, should serve to reveal some of the riches upon which we are now free to draw and some of the errors we should attempt to avoid. At present, however, educational psychology is more of an inchoate mass than a unified discipline. It is like a large rural area, some parts of which have been cultivated with great care, some parts have been planted and then left uncultivated, while others have been neglected and left to return to weeds and underbrush.

In this writer's view, what we need to do is to make a careful survey of the whole area to discover what parts can be used and what they can best produce, and we must set to work to grow what is most needed. We can continue, as in the past, to observe both overt and covert data, to theorize, to experiment, measure, and interview. We can direct our attention to the practice of education and adapt available teaching models more closely to our objectives not only to improve the usual cognitive and performance skills but also those that have been neglected—particularly those related to the esthetic and social values.

But we must not be content just to write to each other. We must also write and talk not only to practitioners—teachers and administrators, but we must learn to promote and finance communication to laymen—to parents, board members, congressmen, and everyday citizens. For without their cooperation and their votes few important changes will be made. There will be no one to buy our wares. Then after informing ourselves and others we must see that, as in the past, experimental schools are developed in which to demonstrate the procedures we advocate; and with the help of the practitioners and the pupils work out the ways in which our recommendations can best be implemented.

REFERENCES

Adler, A. *Understanding human nature.* New York: Greenberg, 1927.

Allen, D. W. A baker's dozen educational alternatives. *Phi Delta Kappan,* 1975, *57,* 33–36.

Bank, A. The uses of teaching models in planning and evaluation. *Journal of Educational Evaluation—Evaluation and Comment.* Center for the Study of Evaluation, California at Los Angeles 1975, *5,* 5–7.

Binet, A., & Simon, T. *The development of intelligence in children.* (E. S. Kits, trans.) Vineland, New Jersey: Training School, 1916.

Bloom, B. S. (Ed.). Taxonomy of educational objectives. The classification of educational goals. *Handbook I: Cognitive domain.* New York: Longmans, Green, 1956.

Boring, E. G. *A history of experimental psychology.* New York: Century, 1929.

Compayré, G. *Lectures on pedagogy, theoretical and practical.* (Translated by W. H. Payne with an introduction, notes, and an appendix). Boston: D. C. Heath, 1887. (Originally published, 1879.)

Dennis, W., & Boring, E. G. The founding of the APA. *American Psychologist, 7,* 1952, 95–97.

Erikson, E. H. *Childhood and society.* New York: Norton, 1950.

Freud, S. *A general introduction to psychoanalysis.* New York: Boni & Liveright, 1920.

Feldhusen, J. F. Educational psychology and all is well. *Educational Psychologist,* 1976, *12,* 1–13.

Gesell, A. *The first years of life.* New York: Harper, 1940.

Grinder, R. E. The growth of educational psychology as reflected in the history of Division 15. *Educational Psychologist,* 1967, *4,* 12–35.

Hall, G. S. *Adolescence.* New York: Appleton, 1904.

James, W. *Principles of psychology.* New York: Holt, 1890.

James, W. *Talks to teachers on psychology; and to students on some of life's ideals.* New York: Holt, 1899.

Jung, C. G. *Psychological Types.* New York: Harcourt, Brace, 1923.

Jung, C. G. *Contributions to analytical psychology.* New York: Harcourt, Brace, 1928.

Köhler, W. *The mentality of apes.* New York: Harcourt, Brace, 1927.

Krathwohl, D. R., Bloom, B. S., & Masia, B. B. Taxonomy of educational objectives—a classification of educational goals. *Handbook II, Affective domain.* New York: David McKay, 1964.

Lewin, K. *A dynamic theory of personality: Selected papers.* (D. Adams & K. E. Zener, trans.). New York: McGraw-Hill, 1935.

Mahoney, M. J. The sensitive scientist in empirical humanism. *American psychologist,* 1975, *30,* 864–867.

Moreno, J. L. *Who shall survive? A new approach to the problem of human relations.* Washington, D.C.: Nervous and Mental Diseases Publishing, 1934.

Murphy, G. *Historical introduction to modern psychology.* New York: Harcourt, Brace, 1929, 1949, 1972.

Olson, W. C. *Child development.* Boston: Heath, 1949.

Pavlov, I. P. *Lectures on conditioned reflexes.* (W. H. Gantt, trans.) New York: International, 1928.

Piaget, J. *Origin of intelligence in children.* New York: International Universities, 1952.

Rand, B. *The classical psychologists.* Boston: Houghton Mifflin, 1912.

Rice, J. M. *The public school system of the United States.* New York: Century, 1893.

Rogers, C. R. *On becoming a person.* Boston: Houghton Mifflin, 1961.

Spranger, E. *Psychologie des jugendalters.* Leipzig: Quelle & Meyer, 1925.

Spranger, E. *Types of men.* Halle: Niemeyer, 1928.

Sully, J. *Outlines of psychology with special reference to the theory of education.* New York: D. Appleton, 1884.

Thorndike, E. L. *Educational psychology* (3 Vols.). New York: Teachers College, Columbia University, 1913, 1914.

Titchener, E. B. *A textbook of psychology.* New York: Macmillan, 1919.

Trow, W. C. *Paths to educational reform.* Englewood Cliffs, New Jersey: Educational Technology Publications, 1971, Chaps. 4, 18, 25, 27.

Trow, W. C. *Gulliver's visit to Walden III—A report on values in education.* West Lafayette, Indiana: Kappa Delta Pi Press, 1976.

Warner, F. *A course of lectures on the growth and means of training the mental faculty.* Cambridge: Cambridge University Press, 1890.

Watson, J. B. *Psychology from the standpoint of a behaviorist.* Philadelphia: J. B. Lippincott, 1919.

Watson, R. I. A brief history of educational psychology. *The Psychological Record,* 1961, *11,* 209–242.

2

Content and Boundaries
of Educational Psychology

B. CLAUDE MATHIS
ROBERT J. MENGES
Northwestern University
and
JAMES H. McMILLAN
University of Colorado at Denver

> "When *I* use a word," Humpty Dumpty said, in rather a scornful tone, "it means just what I choose it to mean—neither more nor less."
>
> "The question is," said Alice, "whether you *can* make words mean so many different things."
>
> "The question is," said Humpty Dumpty, "which is to be master—that's all."
> [Lewis Carroll, *Through the Looking-Glass,* p. 163]

Educational psychologists, in attempting to establish a professional and conceptual identity for their discipline, might give some thought to providing Humpty Dumpty with an honorary membership in their guild. Lewis Carroll's statement about meaning, delivered through Alice's querulous companion, reflects much of what the history of our discipline says about the words "educational psychology" and "educational psychologist." Meaning is to be found more in the opinions of those who search than in the place where it should reside—a conceptual structure with logical relationships to external categories, to performance criteria, or to consensus about the ownership of a territory for scholarship and research.

Education psychologists have a history of concern about the content and boundaries of their discipline. Unlike many of the fields of study found in the curriculum of higher education, educational psychology is identified with two disciplines which in themselves are separate fields of study—education and psychology. This problem of identity is further compounded today by including as "education" much that is not schooling, as we have traditionally known it, and by the application of content to the study of education, broadly defined, that is derived from sources other than psychology; for example, sociology, anthropology, and even biology.

Adding to this issue of amorphous content—content that is as much derived from research in other fields as from the research contributions of educational psychologists themselves—is the additional issue of the applied nature of educational psychology. The lack of consensus among educational psychologists about a definition of the discipline derives in no small part from a lack of conceptual ownership for much of what the educational psychologist attempts to apply. Most academic disciplines, particularly the physical and biological sciences, are able to define a content with a sense of agreement far beyond that found in educational psychology because those who disseminate the content of the discipline also participate in the creation of it. In addition, their research is usually thought of as being basic rather than applied. The relative neatness of content boundaries in the physical and biological sciences begins to disappear when that content is dealt with in the context of the engineering sciences. The discordant nature of educational psychology results from a lack of the very things which make these other disciplines appear to have a conceptual clarity. Educational psychology is a discipline that legitimately depends heavily on scholarship contributed by others who are not themselves educational psychologists; and educational psychology is enough of an engineering science to lack the concord of both method and content found more frequently, sui generis, in the basic research disciplines. Little wonder, then, that attempts to define educational psychology by laying claim to a particular content, or by attempting to limit the boundaries of application to narrow definitions of education, have not resulted in either an elevated status in the hierarchy of the behavioral sciences, or a definition of educational psychology that clearly indicates the parameters of inclusion and exclusion for participants as well as content.

HISTORICAL ANTECEDENTS

Perhaps if Edward L. Thorndike had had his way when he charted the early course of educational psychology with the publication of a series of textbooks between 1903 and 1914 we would have a discipline based, for the most part, on original investigations done by educational psychologists. Watson (1961), in his history of educational psychology, quotes from Thorndike's first educational psychology textbook as follows: "This book attempts to apply to a number of educational problems the methods of exact science. I have therefore paid no attention to speculative opinions and very little attention to the conclusions of students who present data in so rough and incomplete a form that accurate quantitative treatment is impossible [Watson, 1961, p. 222] ." When Thorndike published his expanded text on educational psychology in 1914, it had grown to three volumes and contained experimental studies which, for the most part, were the results of his and his students' efforts (Thorndike, 1914). Unfortunately, those who followed in the years after Thorndike did not all produce the same quantity and quality in their research efforts. In addition, while Thorndike's view of learning, intelligence, and individual differences is still a significant influence in educational psychology today, other points of view demanded to be heard. By the time that Symonds (1958) made his contribution to a content for educational psychology in the mid-1950s, Thorndike's name had become one among many who were not themselves educational psychologists.

Thorndike charted the broad parameters for a content in educational psychology. He saw learning, particularly learning in the verbal ambiance of a classroom, as a central concern for the educational psychologist. Individual differences, particularly in intelligence, were important, especially in relationship to school achievement. His interest in the testing of achievement, and in mental testing generally, along with Cattell, brought measurement and evaluation into an early prominence as appropriate content for the field of educational psychology.

A frequently cited article by Hall-Quest (1915) provides an early empirical basis for the content of educational psychology as well as some suggestions for the boundaries of the discipline. He points out that:

> To call educational psychology a distinct discipline or science is . . . looked upon by many as arrogant presumption. . . . But the fact that education forms one of the many fields of specific application of psychological truth and one of the most significant in the life of individuals and nations is reason enough to emphasize educational psychology as worthy of a distinct title. For this particular phase of the "science of mind" or of "behavior" deals with a select group of processes, and specialization is necessary, for the sake of economy of time at least, to investigate and organize the data here available. It is fundamentally important that experiments be made throughout the entire field of education. The problems of the school room and of the learner are peculiar to these phases of society. Experimental pedagogy is just as important and just as possible as experimental farming. . . . Educational Psychology is distinct from general psychology, biology, history, and philosophy but it uses data from all of these departments of learning and in addition seeks to demonstrate in mathematical terms or graphs the results of investigations carried on in the school or under conditions similar to the school. The task is indeed herculean [Hall-Quest, 1915, p. 602].

This early statement by Hall-Quest has a contemporary ring to it. Educational psychologists still are thought by some to be presumptuous in their scientific aspirations. Hall-Quest and his contemporaries readily recognized the eclectic nature of educational psychology and the need to establish a quantitative basis for its modes of inquiry.

The data generated in Hall-Quest's study prompted him to conclude that there "does not seem to be a general agreement as to [the contents of educational psychology] as over against the delimitations of psychology in general [Hall-Quest, 1915, p. 602]." He asked those members of the Society of College Teachers of Education who taught educational psychology to respond to a questionnaire about their courses. From 53 replies he concluded that the learning process and memory were the most frequent topics taught, with individual differences, association, perception, attention, thinking, and reasoning all ranking high in terms of the importance attributed to the topic by many of the professors who responded. He concluded his analysis with a number of observations about educational psychology as taught in 1915, including the following comment about content:

> In general, courses include the study of the learning process with special attention to instincts, habit formation, imaging with special reference to memory, association, thinking. School subjects are being analyzed psychologically. "Individual differences" are receiving much attention in connection with the study of exceptional children and the problem of retardation. The science of measurement is included as the sine qua non of accuracy in experimentation and investigation [Hall-Quest, 1915, p. 613].

The diffuse nature of the content and boundaries of educational psychology has long been recognized by authorities in the field. In an early edition of the *Encyclopedia of Educational Research,* Hendrickson and Blair (1950, pp. 346–352) discuss the difficulty of making any sharp distinctions between general psychology and educational psychology. To illustrate the problems of classifying content in psychology, these authors report that in two studies done in 1930, which attempted to classify the number of psychological publications which were devoted to educational psychology, one investigator reported 12% while the other reported 25%. The difference was clearly one of the criteria used for the classification. Hendrickson and Blair (1950) indicate that, in addition to the many content areas which educational psychology shares with general psychology, fields other than psychology, such as medicine, psychiatry, sociology, and cultural anthropology, have contributed content to educational psychology. They acknowledge that educational psychologists have been active in developing areas of research that are indigenous. Research on such topics as instructional methods, teacher–pupil interactions, exceptional children and special learning problems, the use of technology in teaching, and the measurement of learning outcomes, among others, were at one time all areas of inquiry that educational psychologists viewed as their own. Much of this autochthonous content has now bred subfields, such as special education, school psychology, and measurement and evaluation. This development further compounds the difficulties of establishing the contemporary parameters of educational psychology.

Seagoe (1960, pp. 403–407), in her survey of the field for a later edition of the *Encyclopedia of Educational Research,* defines educational psychology as follows:

> Educational psychology is concerned with the human factor in learning. It is a field in which concepts derived from experimental work in psychological laboratories are applied to education, but it is also a field in which experimentation is carried out to test the applicability of such concepts to education and to round out the study of topics of crucial interest to teachers. It is the study of the learning–teaching process in its various ramifications [p. 403].

Note that the author does not provide a definition of educational psychology which is either inclusive or exclusive of either its own content or that of other areas of psychology. The emphasis is on one boundary—education—and a primary function—that of experimentation and application. Seagoe (1960) provides extensive documentation for her statement that apparent confusion exists in the minds of educational psychologists about the "scope of the field and the diversity of its relationships [p. 403]." She attributes the apparent confusion to the following:

1. The increased complexity of psychology on the one hand and changing educational objectives on the other
2. The splitting-off of certain rapidly developing areas of investigation formerly central in educational psychology as disciplines in their own right, such as learning and developmental psychology
3. The recent shift in emphasis in educational psychology from the learning process itself to the study of the learner; and
4. The apparent conflict between educational psychology as the application of particular psychological concepts, and educational psychology as an integrative and independent area of research concerned with specific educational problems (Seagoe, 1960, p. 403).

Travers (1969) summarizes the activities of educational psychologists in their attempts to examine their field to seek a common framework for the discipline. A brief history of the profession's several excursions into the complexities of self-analysis is contained in the product of one of these groups, the *Handbook for Instructors of Educational Psychology* (1965). Blair's analysis of technical vocabulary used in a sample of educational psychology texts was reported in 1941 (Travers, 1969, pp. 413–419). He found a lack of overlap which supported, "the commonly voiced opinion that there is little agreement on the areas of research in psychology that have maximum potential for educational application [p. 415] ."

Two professional groups examined educational psychology in 1946. Division 15 of the American Psychological Association and the National Society of Colleges of Teacher Education (NSCTE) both appointed committees to investigate the professional activities of educational psychologists and the content of educational psychology. The publications of the NSCTE underscored the eclectic and broad nature of the discipline relative to content dimensions. The committee of Division 15 was more restricted in its examination of content. It defined educational psychology in terms of the application to education of research findings from the areas of learning, personalty and adjustment, human growth and development, measurement and evaluation, and techniques and special methods of educational psychology (Travers, 1969, pp. 413–419).

The *Handbook for Instructors of Educational Psychology* (1965) was written by another committee of Division 15. This group concluded that the proper content of educational psychology was so diffuse that a descriptive summary of the field would be of little value. The handbook which resulted places major emphasis on methods which might be used to teach educational psychology (Travers, 1969).

EDUCATIONAL PSYCHOLOGY TEXTBOOKS

Logic suggests that one of the most useful sources for information about the content of a discipline would be the textbooks which are written by the academic representatives of that discipline for use in courses. Hendrickson and Blair (1950, pp. 346–352) report on the content of selected textbooks in educational psychology published during the period 1940–1946 by summarizing an unpublished study done by Blair and Nelson at the University of Illinois. Like earlier analysts, Hendrickson and Blair concluded that the textbooks examined varied widely with respect to both emphasis and topic.

Blair (1949) reported a study which involved a detailed examination of five textbooks published during 1948. Twenty-six topics were identified from the index of each book. The contents of the five texts were then analyzed page by page to determine the presence of absence of material relating to one or more of the topics. Lack of agreement among the texts with respect to the emphasis given each topic was apparent. These differences became even greater when the topics were grouped under four broad headings: developmental, learning, personality and adjustment, and tests and measurements. For example, one text devoted only 8% of its space to developmental psychology, while another text gave 26% of its space to the same topic. Blair (1949) concluded that the content of educational psychology textbooks varies widely; and, that this content overlaps to a great extent the content of other courses in psychology. He also found that the most common content related to the topics of learning, growth and development, adjustment, and evaluation.

One paragraph from the summary of this study clearly focuses on problems introduced earlier in this chapter. According to Blair (1949):

> The overlapping of the content of educational psychology with general psychology, child psychology, and other courses in psychology is inevitable. Educational psychology must draw heavily from these areas. The orientation and emphasis of the educational psychology text should, however, be decidedly different from that of courses or texts in the general field. The educational psychology text should illustrate the principles of general and child psychology in the work of the teacher. The educational psychology text should be an engineering manual that bridges the gap between psychological theory and the practice of teaching [p. 274].

During March 1970, a symposium was presented at the annual meeting of the American Educational Research Association entitled "The Crisis of Content in Educational Psychology Courses." This symposium was important not only for the breadth of the commentary but also because it represented yet another public recognition of the lack of consensus within the profession about a common identity. At that symposium, Yee (1970) reviewed his analysis of a sample of books of readings in educational psychology. Diversity was the major characteristic. Yee (1970) states that a "plausible reason for the variance is that there are many spokesmen and little agreement on what content is most relevant for the area. Support for this explanation increases when one examines the selections and sees the wide range of theoretical and methodological content considered significant and contemporary. Certainly there are few authors who are recognized as universal spokesmen for educational psychology [p. 5]."

Yee's conclusions have most recently been supported by Englander (1976) who asked a sample of teachers of educational psychology to indicate how fundamental they thought 75 contemporary concepts in psychology were for their courses. From these 75, only behavior modification received a unanimous rating as a fundamental concept. After behavior modification, those concepts receiving the most attention were readiness, Piagetian stages, intrinsic–extrinsic motivation, self-concept, and level of aspiration, all in the domain of development. In the area of the teaching–learning process, both operant conditioning and discovery learning had high agreement among respondents. Performance objectives and learning for mastery were high agreement concepts in measurement, as were behavior modification and interpersonal communication in the area of classroom management (Englander, 1976).

In addition, educational psychology textbooks have been examined from perspectives other than content analysis. Hofmann and Vyhonsky (1975) reviewed 36 educational psychology texts published since 1969 to assess human interest and reading ease as determined by procedures established by Flesch

(1951). Flesch's definition of reading ease involved seven categories ranging from least difficult to most difficult. All of the texts used in the study had reading ease scores in the three most difficult categories. Eight of the texts were in the highest category of difficulty. Flesch defined five categories of human interest, and the texts studied all fell into the two lowest categories. Thirty-two were judged to be dull and four to be mildly interesting. One of the authors of this chapter contributed to a text in educational psychology that was judged by Flesch's criteria to be completely devoid of human interest (Mathis, Cotton, & Sechrest, 1970). Hofmann and Vyhonsky (1975) point out that the correlation of .47 between reading ease scores and human interest scores suggests that the more readable textbook in educational psychology also tends to be the most interesting. In comparing this study with similar studies done with introductory psychology texts, the authors conclude that, "educational psychology texts, on the basis of the sample used in this article, have a greater probability of being classified as dull and very difficult than do introductory psychology texts ... [Hofmann & Vyhonsky, 1975, p. 791]."

A rebuttal to this interesting finding was published in the "comment" section of the *American Psychologist* (Eson, 1976). The critic indicated that the Flesch index of reading ease would predict the range of scores obtained by Hofmann and Vyhonsky (1975) if the texts were written for the grade level at which introductory college courses are offered. The finding concerning the human interest value of the texts was also challenged. The books in the "dull" category were all in the classification of scientific and professional writing, as defined by Flesch. Eson (1976) points out that the results of the text analyses indicate that the books were written for the intended readers—college undergraduates at the 13th to 16th grade levels.

One conclusion which can be made from this exchange is that, whether appropriate or inappropriate, the variable content of contemporary educational psychology textbooks is presented in a complex manner through the use of a scientific writing style involving a level of reading difficulty somewhat beyond that of introductory psychology textbooks. This raises the question of whether textbook authors in educational psychology write for students or for each other. If students are the reference, then the types of students whom Cross (1971) suggests will appear more frequently in our classrooms may not be prepared to assimilate the level of difficulty presented by most educational psychology texts. Neither will they be attracted by the variable, wide, and sometimes confusing logic of the content included in these texts.

An examination of the stated purposes of a sample of recently published textbooks of educational psychology confirms the diffuse nature of the boundaries of the discipline from the definitions of educational psychology which are implicit in an author's statement of objectives. For example, Ausubel (1968) emphasizes that educational psychology is "primarily concerned with the

nature, conditions, outcomes, and evaluation of classroom learning (p. vii)."
Blair, Jones, and Simpson (1975) direct their textbook at a much broader
purpose with the following statement:

> Learning how to make judgments and to take decisive action . . . require the teacher
> to understand himself, his pupils, and the processes of learning and intellectual
> development. These understandings are essential parts of educational psychology,
> which selects from the total field of psychology those facts and principles that have a
> direct bearing on the growth, learning, and adjustment processes [Blair, Jones, &
> Simpson, 1975, p. 15].

Klausmeier and Goodwin (1966) emphasize human learning, instructional conditions, and the improvement of educational practice, while Charles (1972) defines
educational psychology as the study of the conditions which facilitate and
inhibit desired learnings. Educational psychology "is important to teachers only
insofar as it helps them do their jobs better [Charles, 1972, p. 350]." Gage and
Berliner (1975), Schwartz (1972), and Sprinthall and Sprinthall (1974) point
out the importance of the relationship between theory and practice.

Using introductory textbooks as an index of the content parameters of the
discipline is subject to errors of sampling and interpretation. The studies reviewed here, and others (for example, Nunney, 1964) that have analyzed the
content of courses and textbooks in educational psychology have consistently
demonstrated the idiosyncratic nature of content selection for texts and courses.
This diffusion of content has a clear historical continuity with the several major
attempts to define the discipline already described (for example, Hendrickson &
Blair, 1950; Seagoe, 1960; Travers, 1969).

EDUCATIONAL PSYCHOLOGY AND BOUNDARIES

The issue of basic versus applied research in educational psychology may
seem to be spurious as long as the research which gets done is done well.
However, in any scientific discipline there are subtle differences between the
concepts of basic and applied. These differences influence the manner in which
future practitioners are trained and the kinds of problems and tasks which are
studied. For example, if the boundaries of educational psychology were largely
stabilized around a concept of engineering application, much of the basic
research relevant to the discipline would be done by other subfields in the
behavioral sciences, and educational psychologists would then involve themselves
more frequently in establishing a scientific basis for application of the facts
derived from outside the boundaries of their field. On the other hand, if
educational psychologists adopted the position that they should be the ones to
establish the basic research programs in their field and that basic research should
be their major concern, then they would risk the possibility of alienation from

the very laboratory so essential to basic research efforts—schools and the pupils who attend them—since schools evaluate educational research in terms of what impact it has on pupil performance.

Unfortunately, our scientific tradition defines pure, or basic, research as best, while relegating the applied researcher to the lower, or not quite respectable, end of the hierarchy. Not infrequently, applied research is considered to be another term for development. Given the uncertain status of educational psychology in its own professional organization (Grinder, 1967; Feldhusen, 1976) one should not be surprised at the undercurrents of dissonance in the discipline which frequently produce a statement about research in educational psychology. For example, Haggard (1954) represents the view of many educational psychologists in his call for educational psychologists to depend less on other areas of psychology for the content of their discipline and to assume responsibility for the development of their own theoretical structures to support systematic research.

Another popular position, exemplified by Wittrock (1967), is that research in educational psychology represents more than unrelated facts about instruction and teaching. The development of the discipline, he believes, is now at a stage where educational psychologists should begin to be more liberal and less restrictive in conceptualizing the role of the educational psychologist. The educational psychologist should not think of himself or herself only as someone who applies psychological principles to education. Wittrock (1967) emphasizes what many feel to be a future trend in educational psychology in his statement that, "It is time for us to practice a liberal conceptualization of educational psychology as the scientific study of human behaviors in educational settings. As scientists we should attempt to describe, understand, predict, and control behavior in education [p. 17]."

Others have called for a greater independence of the research mission in educational psychology. Bruner (1966) has this to say about the problem:

> Something happened to educational psychology a few decades ago . . . the circumstances need not concern us save in one respect. Part of the failure of educational psychology was its failure to grasp the full scope of its mission. It has too readily assumed that its central task was the application of personality theory or of group dynamics or whatnot. In fact none of these efforts produced a major contribution to educational practice largely because the task was not really one of application in any obvious sense, but of formulation. Learning theory, for example, is distilled from descriptions of behavior in situations where the environment has been arranged either for the convenience of observing learning behavior or out of a theoretical interest in some special aspect of learning. . . . But a theory of instruction, which must be at the heart of educational psychology, is principally concerned with how to arrange environments to optimize learning according to various criteria [p. 103].

Bruner's statement calls for application, but application growing from the development of a systematic conceptualization of education—a theory of instruction—which would commit the educational psychologist to basic programmatic research necessary to test the theory.

Haggard (1954) criticizes educational psychologists for their reliance on "hand-me-downs" in their use of research from other subfields within psychology, and from other disciplines. This leads, in his opinion, to textbooks that are cluttered with irrelevant "facts," assertions about theory and research results which are often distorted, if not misstated, and that are applied to educational practice in a manner not justified by the context within which the data were derived. He states that:

> The core of the problem in educational psychology today, and one most in need of attention, is failure of many persons to do their own basic research, and, secondarily, their willingness to take at face value the facts and theories from other disciplines so long as they appear on the surface to be relevant to the educative process [Haggard, 1954, p. 540].

Haggard (1954) calls for educational psychologists to determine the problems appropriate for developing the methods, conceptualizations, and research programs to give educational psychology its own research base for content. This would involve an integration of theory, method, and data from other fields in the behavioral sciences into the theoretical structure that educational psychologists themselves would evolve in their study of the educative process. The crucial commitment asked of the educational psychologist is to develop theories of behavior and to conduct research programs "to test, refine, and extend such formulations, either by themselves or in collaboration with other behavioral scientists [Haggard, 1954, p. 541]."

The persons quoted represent, in varying degrees, the concept of educational psychology as an independent discipline with its own structure of knowledge generated by educational psychologists who themselves would be committed to developing this structure through a program of basic research carried on within the broadly conceived parameters of the educative process. Others have pressed for an alternate view that would define the research function more in the mode of applied research and development activities directed specifically toward educational problems in the classroom. Ausubel (1969), in a paper delivered at the American Educational Research Association, and in other publications (Ausubel, 1968), argues persuasively for this point of view. Because his approach is representative of others who have voiced this preference, we will present Ausubel's thesis in some detail.

Ausubel's Thesis

Ausubel (1969) defines educational psychology as "that special branch of psychology concerned with the nature, conditions, outcomes, and evaluation of school learning and retention [p. 232]." He states that educational psychology is an applied science which should not be concerned with general laws of learning per se, but only with "those properties of learning that can be related to efficacious ways of *deliberately* effecting stable cognitive changes which have social value [p. 232] ." Ausubel believes that the psychologist should be involved in investigating the more general aspects of learning, while the educational psychologist has as a special province the classroom and classroom learning "that is deliberately guided learning of subject matter in a social context. The subject matter of educational psychology, therefore, can be inferred directly from the problems facing the classroom teacher [1969, p. 233] ."

Ausubel states:

> My position . . . is that the principles governing the nature and conditions of school learning can be discovered only through an applied or engineering type of research that actually takes into account both the kinds of learning that occur in the classroom as well as salient characteristics of the learner [1969, p. 234].

The author discusses three kinds of research orientations which have been used extensively by applied disciplines. The first of these is basic science research which is concerned with defining general principles and laws of phenomena. Basic science research has as its purpose the advancement of knowledge as an end in itself, apart from any relationship to problems to be solved. According to Ausubel:

> Ultimately, of course, such knowledge is applicable in a very broad sense to practical problems; but since the research design is not oriented to the solution of these problems, this applicability is apt to be quite indirect and unsystematic, and relevant only over a time span which is too long to be meaningful in terms of the short range needs of the applied disciplines [1969, p. 235] .

The second kind of research is extrapolated research in the basic sciences. This approach is concerned with the solution of problems that are both practical and applied, but quite often does not recognize the complex nature of these problems. Because of this, the generalization from basic research to applied problems fails to recognize the two levels of generality involved. Additional research must be done to bridge the gap between the levels of applicability if this approach is to have relevance for educational problems.

The third approach to research is described as research at an applied level which involves the investigation of problems of education, in situ, at appropriate levels of complexity, thus avoiding questions of relevance or problems of extrapolation. This means of investigation allows for the data to be "*particularized* at an applied level of operations [p. 237] ."

Ausubel (1969) believes that this third research model is the most appropriate for educational psychology. To this extent his argument is similar to that of Bruner (1966) who seeks a theory of instruction as the basic organizer for research about the educational process, although one does not find in Ausubel

(1969) the quest for conceptual and theoretical sophistication that is suggested by Bruner. Also, Ausubel's emphasis on learning, especially on meaningful verbal learning, studied in the form in which it actually occurs in the classroom would give educational psychology a definition of content that others would view as restrictive. The requirement of research programs that would investigate educational problems under those conditions of classroom practice would not be entirely acceptable to those educational psychologists who are willing to compromise on the use of the three approaches to research described by Ausubel (1969) by accepting the validity of all three methods in educational psychology.

Ausubel offers the following description of the future shape of the discipline:

> I am hopeful that the educational psychology of tomorrow will be primarily concerned with the nature, conditions, outcomes, and evaluation of classroom learning, and will cease being an unstable and eclectic amalgam of rote learning theory, developmental and social psychology, the psychology of adjustment, mental hygiene, measurement, and client-centered counseling. Thus, hopefully, the new discipline will not consider such topics as child development, adolescent psychology, the psychology of adjustment, mental hygiene, personality, and group dynamics as ends in themselves but only as they bear on and are *directly* relevant to classroom learing [1969, p. 241].

Ausubel's position is reinforced by a brief commentary by Becker (1970) in which he suggests that educational psychologists may have overvalued their profession and its role in society. He feels that the discipline of educational psychology tells us more about the needs of educational psychologists than it does about the education of students. These observations are supported by Becker's argument that the emphasis placed on scientific respectability has caused us to become more concerned with the purity of our methods of investigation than with any applications of knowledge to the problems of classroom practice. Becker (1970) quotes a statement from an article by Davis which points out that the best practice is almost always ahead of the best theory. Others have questioned the role for theory development in providing knowledge about practice in education (Mathis, 1965).

Another point at which Ausubel's description of the discipline may need expansion is his specification of the classroom as the context for research and application. As one of us has argued in an educational psychology text (Menges, 1977), the "classroom" need not be only a physical place within the school but may be any place where teaching and learning are intentionally attempted. The parties to teaching and learning are not only teacher and student as conventionally defined but may also be coach and player, nurse and patient, minister and parishioner, parent and child. Thus educational psychologists should study all of these settings and should attempt to apply basic science findings to each of them. According to this view, the boundaries of educational psychology are congruent with the teaching–learning process rather than with a particular physical environment such as the classroom. Such a definition of boundaries is anticipated by recent undergraduate programs, including those at Harvard and Northwestern, for training educators to work in nonschool settings.

No consensus seems in sight about the proper concern of the educational psychologist. A review of the statements of the presidents of Division 15 (Educational Psychology) of the American Psychological Association which appears in the *Educational Psychologist* offers no clear call to agreement on either the content or the boundaries of educational psychology. Neither does the commentary of other educational psychologists (see Carroll, 1963; Glaser, 1973). The single theme which weaves its way through much of the literature is an acceptance that educational psychology represents the intersection of the study of behavior and the process of education. Beyond that point, there is dissonance present about research methods as well as the appropriate parameters for determining what is, and what is not, involved in the process of education. Agreement is possible, in general, about the central place of learning in educational psychology. Beyond that, one author's list becomes another author's exclusions. To say that the problem that educational psychology has in coming to terms with its nature is an expression, in a more specific context, of the problem which psychology has in general does not make the issue disappear. Certainly educational psychology's confusion is related to a larger quest for a disciplinary structure, but the larger issue should not be used as a rationalization to dismiss the need for educational psychologists to continue their dialogue about the content and boundaries of their field. The history of the debate about content leads one to speculate that concern for the ownership of a specific part of the body of knowledge about human behavior masks a more basic concern for an acceptable level of status within psychology generally—a status which many would agree has been achieved.

Educational Psychology: Content in the Behavioral Sciences X
Boundaries of Education X *Research Function*

The search for a definition of educational psychology will be defined more by frustration than closure as long as educational psychologists use reductionist, univariate strategies. Seeking simple answers to complex problems changes the forms of the problems and does not advance constructive solutions. Three general themes emerge from the literature about a definition for educational psychology. One theme has to do with the content of the discipline. We have seen that opinions about a proper content for educational psychology range from (*a*) any fact in any field of study (especially the behavioral sciences) which has an application to the process of education, to (*b*) specific content about verbal learning in the classroom.

The second theme relates to the research and development function within educational psychology. Here there is agreement on the general applied nature of educational psychology, but variance is clearly present on the following issues about research parameters within the field:

1. Is educational psychology an engineering science which should have as its primary concern the *application* of relevant knowledge to the process of education with its research function, for the most part, concentrated on application; or,
2. Is educational psychology an applied science which should develop its own basic research programs necessary for the creation of a body of knowledge directly relevant to the process of education and based upon sound techniques and methods of experimentation developed specifically for research in education?

The third theme concerns the boundaries for educational psychology and what is meant by the process of education. Two issues are apparent here:

1. Is educational psychology a discipline which should be concerned specifically with the instructional and performance parameters of the school classroom; or,
2. Is educational psychology a field which should include the study of the process of education both inside and outside of formal schooling and at all age levels?

One recognizes in these issues, and others not listed, the kinds of problems which any field of study becomes concerned with when the professionals in the field become secure enough to engage in self-examination. The search for identity in terms of content alone reaffirms the statement of the general semanticist that "the map is not the territory." Content, as judged from textbooks in the field, is not a reliable index, if for no other reason than the pragmatic influence on content exerted by the economics of the publishing industry. Also, whether or not an introductory general psychology course is a prerequisite for the beginning educational psychology course influences the content of texts in the field. Basic agreement about the primacy of the human learning process as a central content in educational psychology is easy to document, but the problem of boundaries attenuates this consensus since learning is basic to the understanding of *all* behavior, and the process of learning is itself influenced by factors which may not be a direct part of the immediate aspects of the process.

Content in any discipline is also influenced by the nature of the research function in the discipline. An engineering science that is primarily concerned with the application of knowledge derived from basic science will emphasize making derivative knowledge work in specific situations. All applied sciences do not follow such an approach. Many applied fields, medicine for example, also have well established research traditions which involve contributing original content to the field more than applying knowledge which originates in another field of study.

Neither should research function alone be used as the single referent for a definition of educational psychology. Consensus about the applied nature of educational psychology makes it difficult to articulate any defensible principles of inclusion and exclusion about the field based on type or method of research alone. Commitment solely to basic research would soon lead to an experimental elitism, removing the experimenter from the arena of application—the school classroom. Emphasizing only derivative applications would neglect important transitional research needed to establish the relevance of basic knowledge to some aspect of the educational process.

The avenues of those aspects of the educational process which are relevant for either content application or research investigation leave much to be desired when given primacy in defining educational psychology. Studying human learning only in an intact classroom may deprive the investigator of data vital to the understanding of performance in school and in other teaching—learning settings. On the other hand, equating all behavior with learning is to make an educational psychologist of anyone worthy of the name "psychologist."

If none of these avenues of emphasis is alone appropriate for seeking a definition of the content and boundaries of educational psychology, how shall our inquiry be ordered? Perhaps the answer lies in the interaction of content, boundaries, and the research function more than in the pursuit of significance through the emphasis on any one of these independent variables alone. The verbal equation, *"basic knowledge* $\times$ *process of education* $\times$ *research methods = educational psychology,"* represents this type of interaction. Among the issues implied in this interactive equation are the following:

1. The nature of the interaction is multiplicative and not additive. The absence of one variable renders the remainder meaningless.

2. Basic knowledge from any field should be of use in educational psychology provided it has relevance to the educational process or its relevancy can be established through transitional research done by educational psychologists.

3. Basic knowledge from any field to be used in educational psychology should meet the same standards of quality as research done within that field. This should include an emphasis on:
   a. fact over "expert" opinion;
   b. logic over intuition; and
   c. purity of research methods over speed of gaining knowledge (Mathis, Cotton, & Sechrest, 1970, p. 18).

4. Educational psychologists should be committed to contributing original knowledge *and* theory construction *and* systems development in relation-

ship to those aspects of the process of education that interest them. One foot in the laboratory and one foot in the classroom can be the most productive stance for an educational psychologist (Glaser, 1973) provided both feet are linked to a common ethic of quality in his or her research functions.

5. The parameters of "education" should be broad and flexible. Human learning becomes the common denominator for educational psychology, but the study of human learning includes much that may be conceptually removed from an immediate relationship with performance. The determination of who is called an educational psychologist should be left up to the individual, contingent upon demonstrated commitment to quality and objectivity in scholarship and research.

6. The research methods that educational psychologists use can be related to basic research, applied research, and development needs. Commonality should be sought in commitment to the standards of excellence and objectivity expected in any science. Status in the sciences is not to be found so much in the knowledge "owned" as in the quality of the efforts made both to discover and to apply knowledge.

7. Educational psychologists should be especially sensitive to the need for examining basic knowledge, whether it comes from investigations in other fields or from other educational psychologists, by engaging in "transitional research" before applying such knowledge to the solution of educational problems. This "relevancy testing" function can represent a unique role for educational psychology through the contribution of techniques and methods of experimentation not heretofore available in other applied fields.

8. The three variables should be viewed in the dimensions of a constantly changing process where new perspectives, knowledge, and methods in any one area will affect the other areas.

The process and parameters of education change through pressures from the public, governmental intervention, or other sources, thus affecting definitions of relevance. Our contemporary emphasis on the life-long learner expands the opportunities for formal educational programs far beyond the traditional years of schooling. In addition, informal education takes on a new meaning. Knowledge in some fields which was not meant to impact the educational process can be of great significance when the zeitgeist evolves to create an educational problem relevant to these data. For example, the relationship between nutrition and behavior lay dormant as an educational problem until social needs forced a recognition of this interaction.

The content and boundaries of educational psychology have changed through time. They should continue to change if educational psychology is to remain an applied branch on the tree of psychology. That branch may sprout leaves that become branches themselves, and this has already taken place with special education, school psychology, and measurement. This should be interpreted as a sign of the vitality of the field rather than as an index of conceptual confusion. Those who seek to define educational psychology through definitions of content and boundaries in as arbitrary a style as Humpty Dumpty's might better serve the discipline by accepting the changes and differences which time and discourse make inevitable. They might also seek agreement on methods of inquiry which can hold constant the quality of our facts, the logic of our conceptualizations, and the purity of our research strategies, despite transitory notions about content and boundaries of the field.

REFERENCES

Ausubel, D. P. *Educational psychology: A cognitive view*. New York: Holt, Rinehart & Winston, 1968.

Ausubel, D. P. Is there a discipline of educational psychology? *Psychology in the Schools*, 1969, *4*, 232–244.

Becker, N. The psychology of educational psychology. *Educational Psychologist*, May, 1970, *7*(3), 5–6.

Blair, G. M. The content of educational psychology. *Journal of Educational Psychology*, 1949, *40*, 267–273.

Blair, G. M., Jones, R. S., & Simpson, R. H. *Educational psychology*. New York: Macmillan, 1975.

Bruner, J. S. Education as social invention. *Saturday Review*, February 19, 1966, *49*(8), 70–72, 102–103.

Carroll, L. *Through the looking-glass*. In *Alice in wonderland*, Carroll, L., ed. by D. J. Gray. New York: W. W. Norton, 1971.

Cross, K. P. Beyond the open door: New students to higher education. San Francisco: Jossey-Bass, 1971.

Englander, M. E. Educational psychology and teacher education. *Phi Delta Kappan*, 1976, *57*, 440–442.

Eson, M. E. A critique of Hofmann and Vyhonsky's evaluation of introductory psychology textbooks. *American Psychologist*, 1976, *31*, 256.

Feldhusen, J. F. Educational psychology and all is well. *Educational Psychologist*, 1976, *12*, 1–13.

Flesch, R. *How to test readability*. New York: Harper, 1951.

Gage, N. L., & Berliner, D. C. *Educational psychology*. Chicago: Rand McNally, 1975.

Glaser, R. Educational psychology and education. *American Psychologist*, 1973, *28*, 557–566.

Grinder, R. E. The growth of educational psychology as reflected in the history of division 15. *Educational Psychologist*, March, 1967, *4*(2), 13–16.

Haggard, E. A. The proper concern of educational psychologists. *American Psychologist*, 1954, *9*, 539–543.

Hall-Quest, A. L. Present tendencies in educational psychology. *Journal of Educational Psychology*, 1915, *6*, 601–614.

Handbook for instructors of educational psychology. Urbana, Illinois: College of Education, University of Illinois, 1965.

Hendrickson, G., & Blair, G. M. Educational psychology. In W. S. Monroe (Ed.), *Encyclopedia of Educational Research.* New York: Macmillan, 1950.

Hofmann, R. J., & Vyhonsky, R. J. Readability and Human Interest Scores of thirty-six recently published introductory educational psychology texts. *American Psychologist,* 1975, *30,* 790–792.

Klausmeier, H. J., & Goodwin, W. *Learning and human abilities: Educational psychology.* New York: Harper & Row, 1966.

Mathis, B. C., Cotton, J. W., & Sechrest, L. *Psychological foundations of education.* New York: Academic Press, 1970.

Mathis, C. Is theory necessary for educational research? *Psychology in the Schools,* 1965, *2,* 10–16.

Menges, R. J. *The intentional teacher: Controller, manager, helper.* Monterey, California: Brooks/Cole, 1977.

Nunney, D. H. Trends in the content of educational psychology. *Journal of Teacher Education,* 1964, *15,* 372–377.

Schwartz, L. L. *Educational psychology: Focus on the learner.* Boston: Holbrook Press, 1972.

Seagoe, M. V. Educational psychology. In C. W. Harris (Ed.), *Encyclopedia of Educational Research.* New York: Macmillan, 1960.

Sprinthall, R. C., & Sprinthall, N. A. *Educational psychology: A developmental approach.* Reading, Massachusetts: Addison-Wesley, 1974.

Symonds, P. M. *What education has to learn from psychology.* New York: Bureau of Publications, Teachers College, Columbia University, 1958.

Thorndike, E. L. Educational psychology. New York: Lemcke & Buchner, 1903.

Thorndike, E. L. Educational psychology. New York: A. G. Seiler, 1905.

Thorndike, E. L. Educational psychology. (Three vols.) New York: Teachers College, Columbia University, 1913–1914.

Travers, R. M. W. Educational psychology. In R. L. Eble (Ed.), *Encyclopedia of Educational Research.* New York: Macmillan, 1969.

Watson, R. I. A brief history of educational psychology. *The Psychological Record,* 1961, *11,* 209–242.

Wittrock, M. Focus on educational psychology. *Educational Psychologist,* March, 1967, *4*(2), 17.

Yee, A. H. Educational psychology as seen through its textbooks. *Educational Psychologist,* November, 1970, *8*(1), 4–6.

3

Methods of Inquiry
in Educational Psychology

ADRIAN P. VAN MONDFRANS, HARVEY B. BLACK,
ROBERT E. KEYSOR, JAMES B. OLSEN, MONTE F. SHELLEY,
AND DAVID D. WILLIAMS
Brigham Young University

INTRODUCTION

Nonsignificant Differences in Educational Psychology

In trying to maximize the payoff from research on educational phenomena, educational researchers have followed methods of inquiry developed in other disciplines. After 75 years of using these borrowed approaches, what is the present condition in education? On the one hand, educational research has yielded many studies with nonsignificant differences or with significant differences which favor a given hypothesis some of the time and which contradict it some of the time. On the other hand, we have grand descriptive theories with little or no empirical support, which are also contradictory among themselves. The educational practitioner has little or nothing from theory or research to rely on when he must make specific instructional decisions.

This failure of social science laws to serve the purposes of applied social scientists, such as educators (to the same extent that physical and biological science laws served the engineers in those areas), has led to several possible explanations.

45

1. Research methodology is so poor in the social sciences that failure is not surprising. Although social science research is admittedly widely flawed, there seems to be no relationship between methodological quality and the robustness of resulting laws (Mann, 1965).

2. An engineering level of research has not been established in education as has been done in physical and biological sciences (Hilgard & Bower, 1975). This failure to develop an engineering level of research is hardly due to a lack of effort. The majority of the thousands of research studies completed each year are more easily assigned to the engineering level than to the theory-building level of research. However, these studies that attempt to establish universal laws consistently fail tests for external validity. If effects in principle are not generalizable there is no reason to make such studies except to demonstrate the absence of generalizability.

3. An analysis of complex pragmatic experiments reveals that interaction effects and confounded variables account for unstable outcomes. Such research, e.g., aptitude treatment research (Cronbach & Snow, 1969, 1975), media variable research (Lumsdaine, 1963), and classroom observation research (Rosenshine & Furst, 1973), reveals ever greater complexities, but no reliable results. Thus, the results of these studies do not help educational designers predict and control instructional outcomes.

4. A fourth proposal is that social science phenomena are influenced by variables (e.g., cognitive processes) which are extremely difficult to control and observe. Even the more radical behaviorists acknowledge attentional "precursory behaviors" (Holland, 1965, p. 78) and "covert self reinforcement" (Bandura, 1974, p. 863) to attempt to account for failures of predicted effects of overt reinforcement on instructional and even laboratory behavior.

As one reviews the progress made in the various sciences, a great deal of advancement seems to have taken place in certain subject areas, whereas other fields of inquiry have yielded minimal outcomes and seem to offer small hope for any further research. What determines the success of research in a given field of inquiry? Two critical elements account for a large portion of the final outcome of any research (Sutherland, 1973). These are (*a*) the nature of the phenomenon of interest and (*b*) the suitability of the instruments of measurement and the methodological strategy implemented by the researcher. Both of these elements will be treated in an effort to understand the present position of research in educational psychology.

The Nature of the Phenomenon

One of the chief objectives of traditional research is to *predict* the phenomenon in question through a knowledge of its properties and the variables that affect it. Implicit within any such endeavor is the assumption that the phenomenon is of a deterministic or probabilistic character. Accordingly, a thorough knowledge of the causes will provide the necessary information to predict the behavior under study, if not totally, then at least within a probabilistic range of error. If a researcher wants to predict a certain phenomenon, he can be successful only if the phenomenon is deterministic or probabilistic by nature (i.e., governed by universal laws). If, however, the phenomenon under observation is stochastic or indeterminate (i.e., only partially, if at all, governed by universal laws), then the researcher cannot successfully predict the behavior. If the phenomenon is not subject to universally generalizable laws then no amount of research will provide a basis for predicting its behavior.

A distinction should be made between phenomena that are *inherently* stochastic and those that are only *effectively* so. A phenomenon that is inherently stochastic is one that is not determined, not even in principle, by universally consistent laws, but rather by causes that cannot be predicted on a universal basis. An effectively stochastic phenomenon is one which is deterministic *in principle*, but for present purposes must be treated as stochastic due to deficiencies in (*a*) observability, (*b*) measurability, or (*c*) manipulability. If the study of a phenomenon falls short in one or more of these areas to a significant degree, the phenomenon may, for practical purposes, be considered to be something less than deterministic.

Suitability of the Methodology

Assuming the phenomenon of interest to be deterministic or probabilistic in nature, a number of methodological strategies may be employed. These include those popularly accepted in methodological literature, such as experimental, quasi-experimental, and correlational designs. These methodologies are designed to approach an understanding of universally generalizable laws applicable to contexts that are temporally, spatially, and environmentally remote or *distal* to the original context under study. Another type of methodology is also emerging, however, which does not pretend to such universal application. The chief value of such research lies in the validity of its *temporal* generalizations, whereas environmental generalization is restricted to contexts identical or *proximal* in character to the context originally studied. These methodologies may be broadly classified as "proximal research," or research in search of contextually consistent laws of "proximal" validity versus "distal research," referring to research designed to discover universally consistent laws.

John Sutherland (1973) points out that the inquiry strategy used should be a function of the nature of the phenomenon under observation. That is, a phenomenon of severely stochastic character would best be studied through proximal research, whereas a probabilistic or deterministic phenomenon if best suited to distal research.

We are thus led to the problem of determining when to employ the various methodologies. Three general guidelines may be offered in this respect:

1. *Deductive argument.* Judging from the criteria of observability, measurability, and manipulability, what is the apparent nature of the phenomenon?
2. *Inductive argument.* Reviewing prior research in the subject area, does historical evidence point to consistent, well-defined results or to weak, conflicting results?
3. *Pragmatic argument.* Do costs (i.e., time and resources) outweigh advantages gained from prior or planned research (either in terms of knowledge gained or relevance of that knowledge as interpreted by the sponsor of the research)?

If performance under these criteria is weak, there is a good chance that the methods of inquiry previously used (or being considered) assume a greater degree of determinancy in the phenomenon than is actually the case. Under such conditions, a proximal research design rather than a distal research design would usually be recommended.

An important facet of this argument needs to be stressed at this point. *Inherently* stochastic or indeterminate phenomena are restricted to proximal research indefinitely, and only limited generalizations can ever be attempted. However, phenomena which are only *effectively* stochastic (i.e., deterministic or probabilistic in principle) would gradually become more amenable to distal research. Hopefully, through successful proximal research, the door may be opened to eventual distal research, assuming the phenomenon to be, in principle, predictable.

Application to Educational Psychology

The Need for Proximal Research

Following the general argument stated above, educational psychology may yield more efficient results by shifting focus from distal research to proximal research. This position may be defended on all three grounds stated previously (i.e., deductive, inductive, and pragmatic arguments).

From a theoretical viewpoint, one would suspect a good portion of the subject matter of educational psychology to be stochastic or indeterminate in character. Certain attributes of the phenomena of educational psychology lend support to the notion that this stochasticity is inherent. One is the dominant *teleological* character of the educational process. Human beings are capable of "strategic behavior" (Sutherland, 1973, p. 99), which is to say they often have goals and objectives which may conflict with those of the researcher. Another attribute of educational phenomena is the *reactivity* of the actors. Experimental manipulation or intervention (even the mere presence of an observer in a classroom situation) may alter or distort the very phenomenon intended to be measured. A third attribute is the *idiosyncratic* cognitive representations of experience by the actors which become prominent, if not dominant, elements in influencing the actors' behavior. All these attributes cause educational phenomena to be refractory to empirical investigation and give evidence to support the belief that many of the phenomena of educational psychology are inherently stochastic in nature. Furthermore, many educational variables are only partially observable, difficult to measure accurately, and resistant to experimental control and manipulation. This would suggest that the phenomena are at least effectively stochastic, if not inherently stochastic, and thus best suited to proximal research.

From an inductive point of view, historical evidence in the field of educational psychology shows little or no substantive progress in discovering universally applicable laws. Indeed, perhaps the most consistently supported generalization to emerge from educational research is that *no* educational phenomenon seems to generalize beyond a proximate set of educational settings. Further support is given, then, to the position that proximal research strategies should play a greater role in educational research.

Finally, from a pragmatic viewpoint, tremendous amounts of resources and time have been invested in educational research with, as has been stated, little or no substantive results. On a narrower scope, many patrons of educational research (e.g., federal and state governments, universities and school districts, etc.) are becoming more concerned with seeing profitable outcomes in return for their investments. Consequently, the need to produce worthwhile results has risen in importance among both researchers and practitioners.

The authors believe that a shift in methods of inquiry is indeed appropriate in educational psychology. In doing so, the educational psychologist is not necessarily "giving up" his search for universal laws. On the contrary, it may be that by beginning at the proximal level of research a foundation can be built which will eventually lead to the discovery of some universally applicable laws. To the extent, however, that educational phenomena are inherently stochastic and indeterminate, the educational researcher must be content to make contextually valid predictions indefinitely.

Suggested Relationship of Distal and Proximal Research

The emphasis of this argument has been on proximal research. There is, however, a valid and important place for distal research to continue within this framework. The role of distal research would entail:

1. Testing deductively based theories which claim universal application
2. Testing findings of proximal research for positive universal generalizability
3. Developing and refining efficient methodologies for proximal research

Further, in shifting toward proximal inquiry strategies the educational re-searcher does not have to reject his training in statistics or research design. The inquiry methods of distal and proximal research are not qualitatively different, but differ primarily with respect to relative emphasis. Some techniques such as optimizing (Atkinson, 1972), simulating (Newell & Simon, 1972; Reitman, 1970), and cybernetic monitoring (Black, 1974; Bunderson, 1974; Merrill, 1974) are proximal inquiry methods which are being used in the context of distal law research. Stochastic modeling, statistical decision theory, and linear modeling are central to these applications as they are to conventional distal law oriented research methods of inquiry.

Other proximal law research techniques do represent a more significant departure from distal law inquiry techniques. In the applied social sciences, proximal law oriented research is illustrated by management science research including operations research and closely related industrial management and information science research. Inquiry methodology in management is charac-terized by relaxing the insistence upon experimental control, empirical observa-tion, and validity of procedures required for universal generalization. Since neither the requirement for establishing universal law nor reductive analytic isolation of effects is demanded, the research inquiry strategies tend to focus more upon operating systems and generally productive aspects of intact systems rather than upon the more *analytic* orientation of conventional distal law research. This *proximal* law orientation, well illustrated by complex simulation models which can generate simulated experimental outcomes, generally permits and even encourages a change in emphasis rather than demanding new and different inquiry methodologies.

The observation that inquiry methodologies relevant to distal and proximal law research are not qualitatively different but differ primarily with respect to relative emphasis of strategies does not imply that the development of more adequate inquiry methodology is not needed. Indeed statistical decision theory generally fits better its original agricultural applications than its social science applications (Glass, 1972).

It has been proposed that a design science is indicated (Simon, 1969). Its domain would include the inquiry methodologies associated with (*a*) establishing the information base required for design decisions and (*b*) utilizing the data base to identify the optimal design strategies. A high priority of the design scientist would be to improve existing inquiry methodologies and to develop new inquiry methodologies.

With the above discussion as background, we now turn to a brief review of different general types of inquiry methodology. Throughout this review the authors do not attempt to duplicate the information contained in books on each topic. Instead, a brief overview of the general characteristics of the inquiry methods is presented and how it fits with the above position is discussed.

DISTAL RESEARCH METHODS OF INQUIRY

Experimental Inquiry

Underlying Rationale

Experimental inquiry is the major scientific method for investigating cause–effect relationships. This method of inquiry is usually conducted in situations where at least a probabilistic relationship between the cause and effect is assumed. Experiments are conducted to assess the effect of the independent variable(s) on the dependent variable(s). The "true experiment" is usually defined as one in which the investigator can (a) manipulate at least one independent variable, (b) randomly select and assign subjects to experimental treatments, and (c) compare the treatment group(s) with one or more control groups on a least one dependent variable. The least complicated "true experiment" is the "posttest-only control group design" (Campbell & Stanley, 1963) where true randomization is possible. In this design, subjects randomly selected from the population are assigned randomly to an experimental treatment in which the independent variables is manipulated or to a control treatment in which the independent variable is not manipulated. Both groups are measured on an appropriate dependent variable. The differences observed in scores on the dependent variable are interpreted as the effects of the independent variable. More complex experimental designs (e.g., fractional factorial, split-plot, etc.) have been developed to cope with more complex research situations. The nature of the many different experimental designs will not be discussed here.

The essential nature of experimental inquiry is clear from an analysis of the simple "posttest-only control group design." Randomly selecting the subjects from a given population theoretically assures that the sample will be representative of the population. This allows the results of the experiment to be generalized to the population from which the sample was chosen. If the subjects are not randomly selected and assigned to the experimental or the control condition, the results may be biased because of systematic variance introduced by the selection or assignment procedures. If systematic bias is introduced, any significant results may be due to the initial group differences rather than the manipulated variable (experimental treatment).

If the subjects have been randomly selected and assigned to the treatment groups then by the principle of randomization the two groups are assumed to be equal on *all* variables. It is also assumed that the only differences between the experiences of the two groups during the length of the experiment are those associated with the experimental treatment (independent variable) and under the control of the experimenter. If there are differences between the two groups on the dependent variable they are assumed to be caused by the independent variable manipulated by the experimenter, since it is the only aspect of the experimental situation which is different for the two groups of subjects.

In this brief description of the basic pattern of control associated with experimental inquiry and the pattern of thinking used in explaining results, most of what has been said is more appropriate for discovering or verifying distal laws. Still, much, if not all, of this reasoning is also appropriate for selected proximal research situations. The point is, however, that distal law research in situations that do not allow the degree of control mentioned above is suspect, while proximal law research usually would not require such a high degree of control.

A brief observation about selecting treatment levels and dependent variables might shed further light on the nature of experimental inquiry and its relationship to distal and proximal law research. Statisticians commonly distinguish between two ways of selecting treatment levels. In a "fixed effect" model, inferences from the data apply only to the treatments actually examined and to no other treatments that might have been included. In a "random effects" model the treatments actually used are chosen in such a way that based on the results obtained from a sample, it is possible to make inferences about a "population" of possible treatments. Consideration of the rationale for selecting treatments is critical in determining the extent to which experimental findings can be generalized to other treatments. It may be that some distal laws (universally applicable generalizations) may be derived from or rationally fit a fixed effects model. It appears more probable that research using a random effects model will result in distal laws. A problem arises when little or no consideration has been given to the selection of the treatments relative to the degree to which findings can be generalized. Perhaps educational psychologists would be on safer ground if they did not generalize their findings beyond the treatments actually used. [The definition of the word "treatment" as used here includes the specific materials, procedures, activities, etc. used and is much more confining than the generic labels, (e.g., reinforcement, programmed instruction) we generally use. These give our experiment the appearance of greater importance and generalizability than is usually warranted.]

There has been much discussion about expected effects versus unanticipated or side effects. This points out the need to consider the set of dependent variables and outcome measures used. Is a single IQ test representative of the population if IQ tests? Does the sample of behaviors measured reflect all of the behaviors or is it only representative of the population of behaviors effected by the treatments? The answers to such questions will affect our ability to interpret and generalize our results.

We raise these concerns to emphasize that even when the method of inquiry used meets the constraints of an experimental model, the actual meaning of the data may be difficult to determine. The search for distal laws is difficult indeed! Careful consideration of all the above points is urged.

In the next two sections we will briefly discuss deterministic and probabilistic explanations of the relationships between independent and dependent variables.

Deterministic Explanation

A deterministic explanation presents a set of precise causal laws in which there is an isomorphic (one-to-one) relationship between the cause and effect. In more formal terms, the causal laws specify a set of initial conditions (cause) which are necessary and sufficient for the prediction of a precise outcome (effect).

The basic assumptions of deterministic inquiry and explanation (cf. Feigl, 1953; Nagel, 1961; Pap, 1962; Sutherland, 1973) may be specified for the existence of causal laws in a deterministic system.

1. The causal relation includes the necessary and sufficient conditions for the occurrence of the effect.
2. The cause and effect occur in close temporal and spatial proximity.
3. The cause precedes and is continuous with the effect.
4. The causal relation is asymmetrical (i.e., the cause produces the effect, but the effect does not produce the cause).

Sutherland's analysis presents four major characteristics of a deterministic system. These attributes are precise (a) observability, (b) measurability, (c) manipulability, and (d) predictability.

If the assumptions and characteristics of a deterministic system are present in an instructional situation, then precise predictions can be made of student learning or behavior in situations where the relevant variables and their interrelationships can be specified.

Probabilistic Explanation

A probabilistic explanation consists of a set of probable, though to some degree, uncertain relationships among variables. Instead of the one-to-one relationship between cause and effect found in a deterministic explanation, a probabilistic explanation involves a one-to-many relationship between the cause and effect. Thus, a given cause could result in any of several distinct effects; and a given effect could arise from several causes.

Probabilistic explanations usually assume this form: Given a set of initial conditions, a given outcome should occur on a specified proportion of trials. This proportion, the number of successful outcomes to the total number of possible alternative outcomes, is called the probability or relative frequency of the occurrence of the event. The uncertainty linked with each of these relationships arises from our inability to predict precisely whether a given event will or will not occur on a specific trial. We are only able to predict the proportion of successful trials which should occur given a random sample or a long series of trials.

Quasi-experimental Inquiry

When to Use

Campbell (1968, p. 259) states "quasi-experimental design refers to the application of an experimental mode of analysis and interpretation to bodies of data not meeting the full requirements of experimental control." In education, many of the planned interventions are so complex or occur in such complex contexts that experimental control is not possible. When the assignment of subjects to treatments or when the occurrence and/or nature of the intervention is not under the researcher's control, quasi-experimental designs can be used. "The general program of quasi-experimental analysis is to specify and examine . . . plausible rival explanations of the results that are provided by the controlled variables [Campbell, 1968, p. 259]."

External Validity

Campbell and Stanley (1963) in their discussion of quasi-experimental design describe various threats to external and/or internal validity. External validity refers to the degree to which one can generalize the results of a given study along the dimensions of populations, settings, treatment variables, and measurement variables.

Obviously, the concern for external validity implies that cause and effect relationships are being sought and that a probabilistic or deterministic nature is assumed for the phenomenon of interest. The sources of threat to external validity include (*a*) the reactive or interactive effect of testing, (*b*) the interaction effects of selection bias and the experimental variable, (*c*) the reactive effects of experimental arrangements, and (*d*) multiple treatment interference. The first threat occurs when the experiment requires the addition of tests which would not occur in the natural environment of the phenomena being studied. The other three threats occur when the number or pattern of things happening to the subjects, because they are in an experiment, differs from the natural situations to which the results will be generalized.

Internal Validity

Internal validity refers to the degree to which the basic conditions of a "true experiment" have been satisfied. The threats to internal validity (i.e., history, testing, maturation, instrumentation, statistical regression, selection, experimental mortality, and selection–maturation interaction) derive largely from not being able, in may settings, to randomly select or assign subjects to treatments. A secondary source of threat to internal validity arises from the inability to control the overall setting of the experiment; that is, other events occur in the environment besides the experimental treatment. The threats to internal validity listed earlier (for definitions see Campbell & Stanley, 1963, p. 35) actually are possible rival hypotheses to explain the results achieved. In using quasi-experimental designs the particular sources of threat to internal or external validity are determined, and judgments can be made about the plausibility of the rival hypotheses which stem from these sources. While there is some risk that these judgments will be wrong, it is generally accepted that the risk is worth taking since quasi-experimental designs allow social scientists to deal with important situations not easily treated in true experiments. Still, the quest is for distal laws and the assumption is that the phenomena studied are deterministic or probabilistic in nature. Quasi-experiments do not change the quest or the assumptions about the phenomena. Rather, they allow more situations to be studied.

Correlational Inquiry

When Should This Approach Be Used?

A second inquiry approach, used when true experiments are inappropriate, is called correlational research. Correlational research differs from the true experiment in that in correlational research "there is no manipulation of an independent variable; therefore, no distinction is drawn between an experimental and a control condition [Meyers & Grossen, 1974, p. 191]." Correlational techniques can be used in situations where the manipulation of an independent variable is not possible, while still assuming the existence of an underlying cause and effect relationship involving deterministic or probabilistic phenomena.

Why not Manipulate the Independent variable?

According to Neale and Leibert (1973, pp. 84–85) three basic reasons for not manipulating an independent variable are:

1. "A number of variables simply do not lend themselves to experimental manipulation." Some of these variables (e.g., age, sex, body size, and birth order) cannot be manipulated; some (e.g., strict control of parental child rearing methods over many years) are extremely difficult to manipulate;

and, others (e.g., death, suicide, and mourning) cannot ethically be manipulated.

2. "Direct manipulation of a relevant variable may be possible only at relatively 'weak' levels, whereas observation of natural events will involve much stronger differences in subject characteristics." For example, the experimental infliction of mild pain or discomfort might be legitimate, but the infliction of extreme pain would not be. However, since many people have experienced extreme pain, the correlational relationship between the experiences of such people and their subsequent behavior (e.g., empathy toward the injured or severely ill) might yield useful information.

3. Due to cost and time considerations, experimental manipulation may not be desirable until a correlational method indicates there is a relationship among the variables of interest. Correlational pilot studies may often suggest potential empirical relationships, which otherwise might have been overlooked or ignored, and generate fruitful hypotheses for experimental investigation [1973, pp. 84–85].

Interpretation Problems

A substantial correlation between two variables implies only that the variables are related or covary, but does not indicate the cause of the relationship. Varying one of the variables may cause the other to vary, but correlation does not indicate which of the two is the cause. For example, does better attendance result in better grades or do better grades motivate better attendance? In some cases, the relationship may not be caused by either of the two variables. Rather, some unspecified variable or process may have produced the relationship. For example, a high correlation between the number of drownings on a particular day and the amount of ice cream eaten on that day may be explained by the weather, i.e., an increase in temperature increases the likelihood of people swimming and of people eating ice cream.

PROXIMAL RESEARCH METHODS OF INQUIRY

Evaluative Inquiry

Historical Background

Evaluative methods of inquiry are developing to solve real-world problems. A major impetus for the development of evaluation came with the Elementary and Secondary Education Act (ESEA) of 1965. Under this legislation, funding was provided to develop educational programs. Several of these projects (Title I and Title III projects) were required to provide evidence of their results. Suddenly, the lawmakers wanted hard data on which to base educational decisions. The commonly used research techniques were generally seen as inappropriate, and educators turned to evaluation as a solution. However, evaluation experts were few in number and their techniques limited. Many early evaluators resorted to measurement tools that had been developed for other purposes. They underestimated the importance of "value judgments" and intuition as integral parts of evaluation, and very few of them had been trained as evaluators. As a result of these problems, educational scholars devised new models and strategies for making evaluative decisions. During the past decade, evaluation theorists have seen a need to gather and summarize information about approaches to a formal development of evaluation. Several of these scholars have developed definitions, models, guidelines, and discipline-objectives which develop this value-description science to a greater degree of sophistication.

Definitions of Evaluation

In defining evaluative inquiry, many writers point out its relationship to the more familiar basic and applied research of the well established sciences. For example, Suchman (1971, p. 45) says that evaluative research applies the scientific method "to problems which have administrative consequences," while basic research is concerned with problems of "theoretical significance." He goes on to say that evaluative and basic research use the same logic and similar tools, but evaluators attach value to the dependent variable. Their principle difference is in their purpose, not in their method. Cronbach (1974) and Glass (1972) state that evaluative inquiry provides information that is important within the decision-making context (proximal), but not for universal (distal) law generation. The evaluator seeks data from a variety of perspectives (interdisciplinary approach) under diverse and frequently adverse conditions in "the septic world of the classroom and the school." He does not reduce the variables so he can study them in "the antiseptic world of the laboratory [Stufflebeam, Foley, Gephart, Guba, Hammond, Merriman, & Provus, 1971, p. 22]." A more recent opinion states that evaluation is similar to applied scientific research, but rather than providing generalizable solutions to general problems evaluation collects specific information relevant to specific problems. It is concerned with immediately significant answers for decision making. It has an "obligation" to deal directly with personal standards and subjective judgments. Its focal point is the specific thing being evaluated (Worthen & Sanders, 1973).

All of these descriptions seem to assume that "an inquiry which is specifically directed to the solution of some practical problem is not for that reason alone to be excluded from the category of basic research" or science (Kaplan, 1964, p. 399).

Some writers distinguish between hard and soft science, claiming that description is soft, even unscientific. Such a view disregards the years of descriptive studies that were necessary to build up a knowledge base broad enough to use in discovering general physical laws. Evaluation, too, is evolving through a descriptive state into developing its own stewardship of value centered description. Many evaluators of today feel that some of the accepted methodologies of the scientific approach are applicable in their field, but they also realize the need for tools than can measure, scrutinize, and place value on intangible, practical—even intuitive—data.

As Worthen and Sanders (1973) explain, in education there are two important subsets of disciplined inquiry that apply directly to evaluation. These subsets are: (*a*) empirical inquiry, which deals with observation and experimentation to describe conditions and verify hypotheses, and (*b*) philosophical inquiry, which is based on logic, semantics, and rational analysis. The purpose of evaluation is to look for the nature, substance, function, and worth of things, not to search for cause and effect.

Some evaluators feel that evaluation is synonymous with measurement; others call it professional judgment (Scriven, 1967). Some think of it as the comparison of performance with specific objectives (Tyler, 1942, 1958) and others believe it to be a process for delineating, obtaining, and providing useful information for judging decision alternatives (Stufflebeam *et al.,* 1971). Adding to these views, Worthen and Sanders maintain that "evaluation is the determination of the worth of a thing. It includes obtaining information for use in judging the worth of a program, product, procedure, or objective, or the potential utility of alternative approaches designed to attain specified objectives [1973, p. 19]."

Future Directions

In essense then, evaluative inquiry is in its formative stage. Many descriptions are evolving that can be pooled to create methodologies and philosophies of inquiry that are unique to evaluation. What are the developments that today's evaluators see as essential for this field's future?

Two projections are presented. The first is a summary of some of the developments outlined by a Phi Delta Kappa National Study Committee on evaluation (Stufflebeam *et al.,* 1971):

1. Future evaluators will develop the "interface role" of working with the client in the most productive way.
2. Evaluators must forge their own technical tools. These tools must be more flexible, non-research oriented, and must rest more heavily on tenable assumptions than on hard data.
3. The tools need to be fit to the problems rather than continually forcing familiar but inappropriate techniques to obtain inaccurate answers.
4. Evaluators must develop new assumptions to build their investigative tools. This will probably involve the use of computers, heuristics, etc.

5. Evaluators will establish and work with a dynamic information base that can easily be reformed within its own context.
6. Unobtrusive techniques need to be developed in dealing with people since knowledge and emotions change so easily.
7. Evaluation needs a formalization of the approaches to problems that are currently attempted only intuitively.

The second summary is taken from a paper by Robert E. Stake and Terry Denny with some comments by Blaine R. Worthen and James R. Sanders (Worthen & Sanders, 1973).

1. Much more accurate representations of the goals of evaluation and the activities involved in the pursuit of those goals need to be developed. These representations will help to illustrate the disparity between these types of activities and will indicate the relative importance of the goals.
2. More accurate and informative techniques should be developed for assessing instructional materials and measuring student performance.
3. More informative diagnostic tests must be created to help in selecting from alternative instructional treatments.
4. Evaluation needs a more concrete establishment of standards and judgment of merits to measure its efforts against.
5. Formal procedures need to be developed for processing evaluation information and drawing inferences from it.
6. More accurate model evaluation projects need to appear as guidelines for similar projects.
7. More research into the critical components of evaluation is needed.
8. More people need to be trained specifically in evaluation. Many evaluators only assess the problems with their measurement tools; they need to learn to make value judgments, which is real evaluation.

Some techniques of evaluation have been developed in response to issues which evaluative inquiry has confronted. This shows that some of the suggestions made above are already bearing fruit. For example, "goal free evaluation" (Scriven, 1971) emphasizes the need to look for outcomes not specified as goals of the entities being evaluated. "Responsive evaluation" (Stake, 1972) emphasizes that evaluators should be sensitive to the needs of clients and incoming data so the evaluation design can be modified as necessary. "Transactional evaluation" (Rippey, 1973) stresses the utility of examining the types of transactions that are involved. "Adversary–advocate evaluation" (Owens, 1973) stresses the need to gather and portray both the pro and the con. "Discrepancy evaluation" (Provus, 1971) looks for discrepancies between then actual outcomes and the intended outcomes. "Formative evaluation" (Scriven, 1967; Bloom, 1971) stresses the use of evaluation to get feedback for improving products, programs, etc. during the developmental stages. "Summative evaluation" (Scriven, 1967; Bloom, 1971) emphasizes the need to determine the effect after development ceases. Other phrases which have been coined to describe techniques which reflect concern for specific issues in evaluative inquiry could be presented. Suffice it to say that techniques especially responsive to the contents and issues unique to proximally oriented evaluative inquiry are emerging.

Educational psychologists who do not know how to use some of these techniques may be hampered in dealing with important questions in proximal law research.

Operations Research

Historical Background

As operations research (OR) has evolved during the past three or four decades, its developers have inadequately attempted to pose a static definition on this "becoming" system. An accurate description emphasizes its ad hoc approach to real-life problems.

Historically, the greatest need for the expansion and application of OR came with the Industrial Revolution and the resulting societal changes. As individual roles became more and more specialized, the executive task of integrating these diverse functions to benefit the total system became an increasingly complex task. The Second World War, also *forced* the development of methodologies for integrating the many operations of automated military forces. In the industrial boom following the war, many OR technicians applied these methods to solving problems in businesses, consulting firms, educational and research institutes, and governmental agencies (Ackoff & Sasieni, 1968). The development of OR thus, resulted from the increasing complexity in man's social and industrial systems.

Characteristics

Three characteristics of OR are: (*a*) a scientific approach to practical problems, (*b*) a multidisciplinary approach, and (*c*) a total system orientation to decision making in order to obtain optimal solutions.

In dealing with practical problems, researchers using OR establish and manipulate "models" of the real system with which they are dealing, just as astronomers propose hypotheses and test them on a "model" of the universe. If one accepts the following definition of science, then this approach could be accepted as using the scientific method to interpret and explain the "phenomena of operating systems."

> Science begins with carefully disciplined observations of selected phenomena. These facts then lead the scientist to construct theories—or . . . models—that fit the facts

and constitute an intellectual description and explanation of them. These theories can then be manipulated and extended entirely within the domain of the intellect; more important, they can be made to yield predictions of what will happen under various new conditions. These consequences of the theories can then be verified by new observations of the relevant phenomena; if the consequences of one's theory check with the observed facts, his belief in its correctness is strengthened, but, if consequences and facts disagree, then he must discard the theory or modify it [Miser, 1974, pp. 904–905].

The need for a multidisciplinary approach is obvious. Since knowledge is growing at such a tremendous rate and is therefore divided into specialties, most individuals are limited in solving the major problems which confront them. OR attacks problems with a "team" consisting of specialists in various disciplines (e.g., organizational behavior, marketing, evaluation, management, computers, statistics, etc.) who can contribute significantly diversified opinions.

The essence of the total system orientation is a search for significant interactions among all the possible factors involved (Ackoff & Sasieni, 1968). Operations research seeks to view practical problems from a broad perspective rather than isolating or cutting them down to size.

Methodology

How do current OR workers implement their brand of research? Summarizing the method in six basic steps, one must:

1. Formulate the problem by a total unbiased analysis of the system. Objectives of the study, decision points, characteristics of a solution, restrictions on control, and a detailed research plan are all products of this phase (House, 1972).
2. Construct a model (usually mathematical) that accurately represents the system. These models are designed to be manipulated in order to evaluate the effects of the various decision-deciding factors (House, 1972).
3. Derive an optimal solution from the model. This solution is only applicable to the problem inasmuch as the model accurately represents the system (Hillier & Lieberman, 1967).
4. Test the model and the solution by comparing drawing board predictions and conclusions with real data and then modifying accordingly.
5. Establish controls on the model and the solution so that the solution's parameters can be modified according to the real world's changing conditions (Hillier & Lieberman, 1967).
6. Operationalize and maintain the solution through evaluations and subsequent modifications.

What methods of inquiry are used in operations research? Three common well developed theories used in OR are: (*a*) decision theory, (*b*) game theory, and (*c*) queueing theory (Plane & Kockenberger, 1972). These theories often use such mathematical techniques as (a) linear programming (Simmons, 1972; Hughes & Growoig, 1973), (b) linear and nonlinear regression (Draper & Smith, 1966), and (c) quadratic assignment (Hanan & Kurtzberg, 1972a, b; Pierce & Crowston, 1971) to analyze systems. Another tool of OR is computer simulation of systems (Gordon, 1969; Maisel & Gnugnoli, 1972). Computer simulation of real-world phenomena allows the researcher to investigate the effect of independent variables (e.g., resources, time, and cost) on dependent variables (e.g., output). The accuracy of simulation estimates is, of course, dependent on how well the theory and the mathematical techniques model real-world phenomena.

Educational Applications

OR methods could assist educational administrators make decisions which would optimize the effectiveness and efficiency of instructional systems given such constraints as time, cost, personnel, and materials. The effects of different ways to individualize instruction (e.g., using volunteers as tutors, using fifth and sixth graders as tutors for first graders, and individual study with frequent mastery tests) could be estimated with computer simulation before implementation. Such a simulation might indicate (*a*) the number of copies needed for each test and instructional unit, (*b*) the number of teachers and aids needed to supervise the system, answer questions, administer tests, keep records, diagnose learning problems, prescribe learning activities, etc., and (*c*) the number of desks, rooms, and other equipment needed, to minimize "student idle time" (e.g., waiting to take a test, get a question answered, get the next unit materials, have a test scored, or find out assignments).

The mathematical techniques of OR appear to have many benefits for educational research and evaluation. This is particularly true of quadratic assignment since many statistical indices (e.g., Kendall's tau, Spearman rank order correlation, Pearson product–moment correlation, etc.) are special cases of this more general analysis technique (Hubert & Schultz, 1976).

Other Proximal Research Methods

Simulation of Problem-Solving Behavior

The principles of computer simulation are also being used to simulate human problem-solving behavior (Newell & Simon, 1972). This allows the researcher to investigate human learning processes by comparing computer simulated behavior with actual human behavior. Attempts to simulate individual behavior have led to the application of information processing analysis to learning theory.

Cybernetic Monitoring

Cybernetic monitoring (Black, 1974; Bunderson, 1974; Merrill, 1974) was developed in the context of "learner controlled" computer assisted instruction

(CAI). Learner control means that the learner is allowed to choose what instructional component (e.g., hard or easy rule, hard or easy example, hard or easy practice, etc.) will be presented at each stage of the instruction. Cybernetic monitoring implies the monitoring of such variables as (a) the path selected by the learner, (b) learner performance at each step, and (c) response time per step. These independent variables can then be related to such dependent variables as number of errors on practice items, score on unit tests, etc. With such a detailed information base, the educational researcher can rapidly evaluate CAI materials, student learning problems, instructional sequence strategies, etc. Such research should lead to a better understanding of the instructional and learning process.

SUMMARY

The monumental number of nonsignificant differences or conflicting results commonly found in educational research may be due to the distal research methods of inquiry used. Since many of the phenomena studied in education appear to be, at least, effectively stochastic, the suitability of distal research methods is questioned. An analysis of distal and proximal research methodologies suggests that proximal research methods of inquiry may often be more appropriate than distal research methods for the real-world needs of educational psychology.

REFERENCES

Ackoff, R. L., & Sasieni, M. W. *Fundamentals of operations research.* New York: John Wiley & Sons, 1968.

Atkinson, R. C. Ingredients for a theory of instruction. *American Psychologist,* October 1972, pp. 921–931.

Bandura, A. Behavior theory and the models of man. *American Psychologist,* December 1974, pp. 859–869.

Black, H. B. *Learner control impact upon the design of TICCIT hardware, software, courseware, and implementation systems.* Paper presented at the conference of the Data Processing Institute and Canadian Information Processing Society, Ottawa, Canada, June 1974.

Bloom, B. S., Hastings, J. T., & Madaus, G. F. *Handbook on formative and summative evaluation of student learning.* New York: McGraw-Hill, 1971.

Bunderson, C. B. *The TICCIT project: Design strategy for educational innovation* (Technical Report No. 4). Institute for Computer Uses in Education, Brigham Young University, 1974.

Campbell, D. T. Quasi-experimental design. In D. L. Sills (Ed.), *International Encyclopedia of the Social Sciences* (Vol. 5). New York: Macmillan and Free Press, 1968.

Campbell, D. T., & Stanley, J. C. *Experimental and quasi-experimental designs for research.* Chicago: Rand McNally, 1963.

Cronbach, L. J. Beyond the disciplines of scientific psychology. *American Psychologist,* 1975, **30,** 116–127.

Cronbach, L. J., & Snow, R. E. *Individual differences in learning ability as a function of instructional variables.* Stanford, California: Stanford University, College of Education, 1969.

Cronbach, L. J., & Snow, R. E. *Aptitudes and instructional methods: A handbook for research on interactions.* New York: Irvington, 1975.

Draper, N., & Smith, H. *Applied regression analysis.* New York: John Wiley & Sons, 1966.

Feigl, H., & Brodbeck, M. (Eds.). *Readings in the philosophy of science.* New York: Appleton–Century–Crofts, 1953.

Glass, G. V. The wisdom of scientific inquiry on education. *Journal of Research in Science Teaching,* 1972, *9,* 3–18.

Gordon, G. *System simulation.* Englewood Cliffs, New Jersey: Prentice-Hall, 1969.

Hanan, M., & Kurtzberg, J. M. A review of the placement and quadratic assignment problems. *SIAM Review,* 1972, *14,* 324–342. (a)

Hanan, M., & Kurtzberg, J. M. Placement techniques. In M. A. Breur (Ed.), *Design automation of digital systems* (Vol. 1). Englewood Cliffs, New Jersey: Prentice-Hall, 1972. (b)

Hilgard, E. R., & Bower, C. H. *Theories of Learning.* Englewood Cliffs, New Jersey: Prentice-Hall, 1975.

Hillier, F. S., & Lieberman, F. J. *Introduction to Operations Research.* San Francisco: Holden-Day, 1967.

Holland, J. G. Research on programming variables. In R. Glaser (Ed.), *Teaching machines and programmed learning,* (Vol. II). Washington, D.C.: National Educational Association, 1965.

House, W. L. (Ed.). *Operations research—An introduction to modern applications.* Princeton, New Jersey: Auerbach, 1972.

Hubert, L., & Schultz, J. Quadratic assignment as a general data analysis strategy. *British Journal of Mathematical and Statistical Psychology,* 1976, *29*(2), 190–241.

Hughes, A., & Growoig, D. *Linear programming: An emphasis on decision making.* Menlo Park, California: Addison-Wesley, 1973.

Kaplan, A. *The conduct of inquiry.* San Francisco: Chandler, 1964.

Lumsdaine, A. A. Instruments and media of instruction. In N. L. Gage (Ed.), *Handbook of research on teaching.* Chicago: Rand McNally, 1963.

Maisel, H., & Gnugnoli, G. *Simulation of discrete stochastic systems.* Chicago–Palo Alto: Science Research Associates, 1972.

Mann, J. *Changing human behavior.* New York: Charles Scribner's Sons, 1965.

Merrill, M. D. Phase I of full strategy advisor. In *Courseware design handbook,* Institute for Computer Uses in Education Publication, Brigham Young University, 1974.

Meyers, L. S., & Grossen, N. E. *Behavioral research: Theory, procedure, and design.* San Francisco: W. H. Freeman, 1974.

Miser, H. J. What is operations research? *Operations Research,* 1974, *22*(4), 903–909.

Nagel, E. *The structure of science.* New York: Harcourt, Brace and World, 1961.

Neale, J. M., & Leibert, R. M. *Science and behavior: An introduction to methods of research.* Englewood Cliffs, New Jersey: Prentice-Hall, 1973.

Newell, A., & Simon, H. A. *Human problem solving.* Englewood Cliffs, New Jersey: Prentice-Hall, 1972.

Owens, T. R. Educational evaluations by adversary proceedings. In E. R. House (Ed.), *School evaluation: The politics and process.* Berkeley, California: McCutchan, 1973.

Pap, A. *An introduction to the philosophy of science.* New York: The Free Press of Glencoe, 1962.

Pierce, J. F., & Crowston, W. B. Tree-search algorithms for quadratic assignment problems. *Naval Research Logistics Quarterly,* 1971, *18,* 1–36.

Plane, D., & Kochenberger, G. *Operations research for managerial decisions.* Homewood, Illinois: Richard D. Irwin, 1972.

Provus, M. *Discrepancy evaluation.* Berkeley, California: McCutchan, 1971.

Reitman, W. What does it take to remember? In D. Norman (Ed.), *Models of human memory.* New York: Academic Press, 1970.

Rippey, R. M. (Ed.). *Studies in transactional evaluation.* Berkeley, California: McCutchan, 1973.

Rosenshine, B., & Furst, N. The use of direct observation to study teaching. In R. M. W. Travers (Ed.), *Second handbook of research on teaching.* Chicago: Rand McNally, 1973.

Scriven, M. The methodology of evaluation. In R. E. Stake (Ed.), *Curriculum evaluation.* American Educational Research Association monograph series on evaluation, No. 1. Chicago: Rand McNally, 1967.

Simon, H. A. *The sciences of the artificial.* Cambridge, Massachusetts: The MIT Press, 1969.

Simmons, D. M. *Linear programming for operations research.* San Francisco: Holden-Day, 1972.

Stake, R. E. *Responsive Evaluation.* Unpublished paper, December 5, 1972.

Stufflebeam, D. L., Foley, W. J., Gephart, W. J., Guba, E. G., Hammond, R. L., Merriman, H. O., & Provus, M. M. *Educational evaluation and decision-making in education.* Itasca, Illinois: Peacock, 1971.

Suchman, E. A. Evaluating educational programs. In F. G. Caro (Ed.), *Readings in evaluation research.* New York: Russell Sage Foundation, 1971.

Sutherland, J. W. *A general systems philosophy for the social and behavioral sciences.* New York: Braziller, 1973.

Tyler, R. W. General statement on evaluation. *Journal of Educational Research,* 1942, *35,* 492–501.

Tyler, R. W. The evaluation of teaching. In R. M. Cooper (Ed.), *The two ends of the log.* Minneapolis, Minnesota: University of Minnesota Press, 1958.

Worthen, B. R., & Sanders, J. R. *Educational evaluation: Theory and practice.* Belmont, California: Wadsworth, 1973.

4

Future Trends and Issues in Educational Psychology

S. J. SAMUELS
University of Minnesota

and

PAMELA TERRY
Indiana University

Educational psychology, because it is a young science, is still insufficiently organized. There does not seem to be a general agreement as to its contents as over against the delimitations of psychology in general. College and University courses in the subject are still largely the result of personal preferences on the part of the teacher in charge. Terminology is confused. One senses through the confusion of titles and terminology a wholesome movement toward a well-defined field of investigation and the possibility of eventually standardizing the concepts of educational psychology [Hall-Quest, 1915,—cited in Grinder, 1970, p. 4].

Unfortunately, the above statement made more than 60 years ago is still relevant for the field of educational psychology today. By the end of this century will it finally be proven false and become only history? What are the prospects for the field of educational psychology? Some, with an optimistic view, see a rosy future with educational psychology consisting of strong, integrated, well defined fields of study. Others, more pessimistically, fear that the field may even disappear with its functions being taken over by the many related disciplines that compose our fragmented subject area.

One of the continual problems of educational psychology is trying to define just what the area includes or excludes. As Yee (1970) noted, educational psychology courses and textbooks have long been criticized because they lack definition and fail to define parameters of the field. Because of this situation, undergraduate students with applied orientations have at times complained that portions of our courses and textbooks have lacked relevance and have been mere watered down versions of introductory psychology. One does note, however, a trend in undergraduate educational psychology toward relevance; we are extracting from psychology that which is useful and which, hopefully, will facilitate the teaching process.

Before advancing more deeply into future trends in educational psychology, the plan for this chapter should be made clear. This chapter will be divided into two parts. The first section will discuss various definitions of educational psychology and projected changes in the basic structure and orientation of the field. The relative emphasis on theory versus practice is considered. The second section will present educational controversies and issues that will affect educational psychology whatever the general orientation of the field.

DEFINITIONS OF THE FIELD

Educational psychology has had periodic identity crises as noted by Grinder (1967). These stem partly from the fact that in order to deal with the complexity of learning in real situations, the educational psychologist must strive to keep abreast of a large number of fields. The putative content of educational psychology, as seen in Table 4.1, presents a partial list of topics included in educational psychology texts, covers a wide range of subject matter and highlights the problem one faces in trying to keep up with new findings in the related fields.

Even the partial list in Table 4.1 illustrates educational psychology's tendency to overlap with several different fields, such as anthropology, biochemistry, child development, counseling and guidance, elementary education, linguistics, mathematics, measurement, psychology, statistics, secondary education, sociology, and so forth.

As a member of an interdisciplinary field, educational psychologists spend much of their time keeping up with developments in related fields that can have a bearing on educational problems. Traditionally, they have also striven to differentiate the field of educational psychology from these related areas, and the future will likely see a continuing quest for a unique identity that is separate from both education and general psychology.

A few years ago, Fredenburgh (1968) compiled definitions of educational psychology from prominent members of the field. Their views and definitions of educational psychology included "the understanding and control of instruction and teaching" (Wittrock), "the task of educational psychology is to give teachers understanding of how children learn" (Cronbach), "the technology of instruc-

TABLE 1

Topics Included in Educational Psychology Textbooks

Learning and instruction
  Behavior management
  Cognitive development
  Compensatory education
  Concept formation
  Humanistic approaches to learning
  Individualized instruction
  Instructional programming
  Learning disorders
  Learning hierarchies
  Mastery learning
  Methodology
  Motivation
  Problem solving
  Readiness
  Reasoning processes
  Research
  Task analysis
  Transfer of training
Human growth, development, and personality
  Adolescence
  Affective education
  Aptitudes
  Attitudes
  Child development
  Counseling and guidance
  Diagnosis of learning difficulties
  Emotionally disturbed development
  Genetic and environmental factors in development
  Individual differences
  Intelligence and IQ
  Interests
  Mental health
  Minority groups
  Moral and ethical development
  Personality development
  Social and emotional development
  Social interaction
  Special education for exceptional children
Measurement and evaluation
  Accountability
  Descriptive statistics
  Evaluation
  Experimental design
  Measurement
  Norm-referenced versus criterion-referenced testing
  Psychometrics
  Research methodology
  Statistics
  Test interpretation

tion and learning" (Anderson), "the usefulness of educational psychology as an applied science depends on how much its activities and outcomes are shared by teachers and psychologists alike" (Lindgren), and "A hodgepodge of *ad hoc* atheoretical investigations, in fact, general psychology applied to human behavior in a social setting" (Warburton). Ausubel (1968) considered educational psychology to be "that special branch of psychology concerned with the nature, conditions, outcomes and evaluation of school learning and retention [p. 4]." The variety of the definitions is obvious.

Educational psychology has, at least traditionally, applied psychological theories and techniques to educational concerns and problems. As Grinder (1970) has mentioned, though, "there is always the possibility that subject-matter specialists will incorporate psychological principles into their teaching, thus dispensing, once and for all, with the need for professors of educational psychology [p. 4]."

There has also been disagreement about whether educational psychology has a unique content with problems and methodologies of its own or whether it merely applies knowledge from pure science to practical problems of pedagogy. One of the important future functions of educational psychology is to serve as a clearinghouse and transmitter of basic psychological theory—translating it into lay terms, and matching the theory up with specific educational concerns. In addition to serving as a link between psychological theorists and educators, however, educational psychologists should test psychological theories by transforming them into new methodologies and applying them to real-life educational settings. There is a substantial need for educational psychologists to synthesize complex ideas and relate them to the specific problems of the classroom teacher, particularly those new problems that will be faced by the classroom teacher in the next few decades.

Among the responsibilities of educational psychologists are the following: (*a*) to introduce students to basic psychological and sociological theories underlying educational practices, (*b*) to teach educational psychology courses, (*c*) to train teachers, (*d*) to investigate educational problems through research, (*e*) to train skilled researchers, (*f*) to analyze educational problems and to develop solutions to such problems, (*g*) to evaluate present educational practices, (*h*) to verify new educational practices, (*i*) to disseminate basic research with relevance for educational problems, and (*j*) to serve as a resource for local school systems.

Knowledge versus Application

One continuing controversy that must be contended with by educational psychologists in the years ahead is the relative emphasis on theory and knowledge as opposed to practical application. Both are certainly important and a balance must be achieved. This basic issue involves the essence of what differentiates a professional from a mere technician.

The goal of having students take courses in educational psychology is not just to train them to teach, but to give them background in psychological theory that can be applied in their teaching and in their daily lives. As Terwilliger (1975) has stated, if educational psychology abandons theory and moves to "practical" foundations courses, teacher education will be equated with teacher training. What differentiates a teacher from a teacher-aide or other paraprofessional? Both may have had years of practical experience, but the professional—the teacher—is expected to have additional reserves of knowledge to call on when confronted with new or unexpected situations. Knowing the theory behind practices and rules gives the professional the freedom to depart from them and to formulate new ones when necessary.

There is, however, a growing body of opinion that there is currently too much emphasis on abstract theory. Courses with a strong emphasis on theory are branded as "too irrelevant" by students. As Yee (1970) has pointed out, educational psychology courses have often been viewed by students as a place where one learns about theories and principles of learning, development, measurement, etc., but not as a place where one learns how to apply these principles. Feldhusen (1970) has said students want and need topics of functional value in educational psychology courses. Jackson (1968) has raised the more fundamental concern that there may be little or no carry-over of the principles that teachers learn in their educational psychology courses to their teaching practice. As Klausmeier (1970) has stated, "Knowledge of theory and principles does not automatically produce better instruction." Therefore, one major future task facing educational psychologists will be to devise ways to bridge the gap between theoretical background and practical applications. Students must understand how to relate theory to real-life educational situations, and the teacher must be in an environment that recognizes and rewards effective teaching.

One of the current trends in teacher education is toward an increase in the amount of field-based experience. In many instances, this is probably motivated by the desire to put students in situations where they can gain experience in applying theory to practice. Additional field-based experience does not, by any means, imply the rejection of theory. Rather, the recognition that there is such a thing as educational theory is the one thread that is common to nearly all definitions of educational psychology described above, and the field-based experience merely provides the student with a setting for the possible melding of practice and theory. It should be pointed out, however, that simply putting the student in the field provides no magic transfer from knowledge to application. Educational psychologists have yet to develop tested field-based experiences which help students transfer what they have learned to actual teaching situations. Despite this shortcoming, however, students perceive their field-based experience as being relevant and as a useful link between theory and practice.

Another trend away from theory and toward more practical application, however, may pose a subtle but more substantial threat to the existence of educational psychology in the teacher preparation field. The threat, delineated by Samuels (1976) lies in the rapid growth of performance- or competency-based teacher education (PBTE or CBTE) programs. [In distinguishing between the terms competency and performance, competency refers to inferred knowledge, whereas performance refers to directly observable behaviors. However, as Terwilliger (1975) has noted, most educators use the terms interchangeably.]

The three main characteristics of PBTE programs are publicly stated competencies, stated criteria for evaluation, and the modularization of program. The competencies or behavioral objectives are usually extrapolated from observation of the various teacher roles and responsibilities which are found in the classroom. These competencies are behavioral in nature and make possible the easy evaluation of the prospective teacher's performance. In assessing the prospective teacher's competencies and performance, the assessment criteria that are used are derived from the extrapolated objectives. These criteria are stated in such a way that the expected levels of mastery are specified. It is important to note that both the stated objectives and the criteria needed for mastery are made public and are announced in advance in the course. The course content in PBTE programs is often provided through modules, and the teacher-in-training proceeds through the program at his or her own pace.

In practice, PBTE has been used in various ways. In some colleges the teaching methods classes are performance based but other classes such as educational psychology are not. On the other hand, there are programs where the entire teacher education program is in the form of PBTE, including all educational psychology courses. Where the latter situation exists, there are, in essence, no true educational psychology courses, for educational psychology's theoretical component has been eliminated and replaced with teaching skill mastery. Considering that one of the important characteristics of a professional is that she or he has mastered a body of theoretical knowledge which can be used in decision making, one may question the professional stature of a graduate of a teacher training institute where the entire program was performance-based teacher education.

Where the teacher certification programs are entirely in the form of PBTE, what has generally happened is that methods teachers have not only stipulated what goals they wish to achieve, but have also specified the means to attain these goals. The rationale is to start with a discrete behavioral observable goal and to develop a module which will help the student perform in the expected manner. Thus, the modules cut across many disciplines; instead of taking a separate course labeled educational psychology, the student would study modules, the contents of which might include educational psychology. If the advocates of PBTE have their way students will study discrete modules, and educational psychology as a course will not be in the curriculum.

The general tone of this section has been one of caution regarding the use of

PBTE in teacher education. This cautionary note should be qualified slightly. For some courses where the emphasis is on the development of skills, PBTE programs are excellent. However, there are other types of courses in which the goals not only embrace the development of skills, but include the acquisition of theories and concepts as well. Where knowledge of theories, concepts, and principles is a goal of the program as well as skills, the PBTE program should be modified. Competency-based teacher education programs tend to deemphasize knowledge. Many important goals of educational psychology are, however, in the knowledge domain; for example, educational psychology courses are concerned with the nature of intelligence, the role of reinforcement, punishment and extinction on performance, and other factors that tend to influence learning and retention.

One hallmark of a profession is the acquisition of a body of theoretical knowledge that is useful in aiding clients who come to the professional for help. The deemphasis of knowledge in a teacher education program reduces the teacher's status from that of a professional to that of a technician. Technicians have skills but little theoretical understanding of what it is they are doing. They may be able to perform the skill well, but they lack the insight to know how to purposively modify their performance to fit any changed circumstances.

We are all aware of the forces of stability and change in education. Many "innovative" changes do take place before there is any empirical evidence that the modification will lead to a desired outcome. But, we need to proceed cautiously and scientifically with PBTE; we need to evaluate the effects of this method. Heath and Nielson (1974) in a review article on competency-based teacher education concluded that an empirical basis for PBTE does not exist.

Are educational psychologists blameless for the possible deemphasis of educational psychology in some teacher education programs? Not at all. As a rule, we have been unwilling to specify a priori what knowledge, skills, and theories our students will master. Also, we have not been willing to specify a priori what criteria of performance will constitute satisfactory levels of learning. In addition, whatever the objectives and criteria might have been, these have not been made public and have not been disclosed to the student. Educational psychology programs that lack objectives and performance criteria have little accountability built into them. We give lip service to competency, but our students and colleagues know full well that we often fail to meet even the minimal criteria of competency. If we propose mastery of nonbehavioral "knowledge" we must specify how we "know it when we see it . . . . "

What can be done by educational psychologists to overcome these problems? We should recognize that the essential characteristics of PBTE are specification of goals and specification of criteria for evaluating these goals. These specifications must be made public. The means for accomplishing these goals are numerous. Modules are not the only way to achieve these goals. We should resist efforts to eliminate educational psychology courses, under the guise that modules will tangentially cover materials similar to what we cover in our courses. We must be willing to be accountable to students and colleagues. In fact, we do need to make our own educational psychology courses more competency based. We need to more clearly specify our objectives in terms of knowledge and skill competencies. In addition, we need to specify criteria for acceptable student performance. Since we are primarily concerned here with teacher certification programs, there is a need to stress that which is relevant and applicable. These may be difficult goals to attain, but we must make a start. Wherever possible, we must try to make our courses not only knowledge based, but performance based as well. Whenever possible, students should be involved in observation and participation programs in schools in addition to attending lectures. Ideally, we will learn to design experiences for our students so that they will be able to apply their knowledge, and so that we will be able to measure their ability to apply that knowledge. We should be willing to work cooperatively with faculty in our own departments as well as in other departments regarding goals and criteria. But the means to these goals should be maintained free from encroachment of other departments. While we will share responsibility for goals and criteria, the decision as to how best we can meet these goals should remain the responsibility of the educational psychologists.

If we show the departments we service how educational psychology aids education and if we help our students master the educational psychology goals we set up in the areas of knowledge and application, we will be making a significant advance in the training of competent teachers. As a discipline, educational psychology will also then be better able to deal with several foreseeable controversies in education in the years to come.

Educational Accountability

Change in educational psychology can be expected as a result of the growing societal demands for educational accountability. The movement toward accountability is concerned with the consequences of instructional actions and issues of general educational responsibility. The central question of the accountability movement is "What is learned?" Teachers will need to learn to verify the quality of their instruction in terms of what is learned by their students, rather than by how innovative their instructional procedures may appear.

The concept of accountability is quickly gaining favor with the public. A recent article by Samuels and Edwall (1975) pointed out increased public demand for results-oriented systems of accountability that will inform the community at large about the educational achievements realized from the expenditure of public monies and resources. Both taxpayers and educators are recognizing that the school should be accountable in some sense for the products of the educational system, just as businesses are held accountable for the quality of the products they produce.

There is evidence of an increasing trend toward legal as well as moral accountability. Test cases are already being brought to see if schools can be held negligent and responsible for punitive damages for graduating students who were, for example, never taught to read fluently (see reference "Suit for poor reader . . . "). California state law now requires that teachers be evaluated in terms of their ability to produce results in children's learning. Under the provisions of the Stull Bill, teachers must demonstrate that students have made progress in achieving the formulated objectives for each subject area.

There is confusion at present over different approaches to accountability. Combs (1973) has argued for educational accountability from a "humanistic perspective" that is, achieved through the assessment of process rather than ends. He points out that since many humanistic objectives—like values, feelings, beliefs, attitudes and personal meanings—are internal, they are difficult to measure precisely and effectively. Combs considers the goal of education to be that of changing underlying perceptions rather than external behavioral expressions and, such being the case, feels teachers should be judged in terms of their success or failure in establishing effective processes. This focus on the process of teaching is felt to lead to greater innovation and change.

There are strong objections to the idea that there can be "expressive" objectives that are statements of process rather than of ends. Popham (1972) has noted that "expressive" objectives add little clarity to an instructional plan. Instead, he feels attention should be focused on the consequences rather than on the processes of instruction. According to Popham, "We are at the brink of a new era regarding explication of instructional goals, an era which promises to yield fantastic improvements in the quality of instruction [1969, p. 3]."

If schools are to be held accountable for their job of educating, teacher education must be adequate and appropriate for the job demands. As Samuels and Edwall (1975) have pointed out, three of the most important "tools" for making responsible educational evaluation decisions are: (a) clearly specified objectives, (b) adequate measures for assessing those objectives, and (c) the creation of good communication channels between school districts and educational resource centers such as regional laboratories, research and development centers and university colleges of education to aid in upgrading the quality of education.

The problem of student assessment is of paramount importance in the demand for accountability. In order to assess whether the educational system has met its goals, there must be impartial evaluation of the students' learning. In December 1975 a program was begun in California allowing 16- and 17-year-olds who are able to pass a high school proficiency exam guaranteeing their literacy to quit school with a certificate of proficiency in place of a high school diploma. The 4-hour tests developed by the Educational Testing Service are comprised of 200 questions covering basic skills in reading, writing, and computation. Other states are closely watching the results of this California innovation.

A major contemporary issue in assessment concerns the ubiquitous use of norm-referenced tests. The historical purpose of norm-referenced testing was to classify individuals according to whether they would be likely to benefit from the established educational system. The information obtained from norm-referenced tests is comparative, providing an ordered ranking of those tested. Where the purpose of testing is to separate individuals for placement purposes, as in the military and business field, norm-referenced tests perform their job admirably. However, norm-referenced tests are not good instruments for determining if students have achieved the objectives established by the school. When used in the classroom, tests provide little useful information about what has been learned. Norm-referenced tests do not provide teachers with useful diagnostic information about their students' areas of strength or weakness and, consequently, are of little use in guiding instructional decision making.

With future societal demands for an emphasis on accountability, there should be a resultant increase in the use of criterion-referenced tests. Criterion-referenced tests are concerned with measuring what students have learned. These tests assess mastery of a topic in relationship to an established criterion of successful performance rather than providing an indication of students' relative standings. Models of mastery learning are based on the conviction that nearly all children can learn the content of instruction and that, therefore, testing should concentrate on measuring the educational progress toward mastery of a skill or knowledge criterion. Test results provide information specifically related to students' competencies and reveal those areas that need additional work.

In order to satisfy the demand for accountability, schools will need help from educational psychologists as well as input from concerned citizens in specifying the objectives for which accountability will be demanded, in selecting and designing adequate evaluation instruments, in interpreting test result data, and in improving instructional methodology.

Performance Contracting

One currently popular method of increasing accountability for student learning is through the use of performance contracting. The three main aspects of performance contracting include: (*a*) an agreement signed by the contractor to improve students' performance in basic skills by a set amount, (*b*) freedom for the contractor, within guidelines set by the school board, to use any educational technique considered effective, and (*c*) payment to the contractor that is contingent upon the students' performance—if students surpass expectations the contractor makes a profit; if students fail to achieve the goals set for them, the contractor is not paid.

Several researchers in recent years have examined performance contracting. Page (1972) has delineated the disastrous experiment in performance contracting sponsored by the Office of Economic Opportunity that led to most contracting companies' losing money and getting out of the business. A Right-to-Read performance contracting situation in Bristol, Virginia seems to be having much better results. Under this plan, the teachers and students receive bonuses for reading achievement gains made by the students instead of having a private company receive the profit. Accountability is expressed in terms of behavioral objectives that are used to guide the students, but incentive payments are given to teachers based on student performance on both standardized and criterion-referenced tests. Payments to teachers have been averaging around $1000 apiece. According to Quarios, Johnson, and Murray (1974), the Bristol project has demonstrated that student achievement can be significantly improved by the use of teacher incentive bonuses.

Currently, the only reward most teachers receive for doing an especially good job of teaching is personal satisfaction. Performance contracting that is combined with merit pay to teachers based on how well they perform their teaching responsibilities, and with student learning validly measured, may form a potent vehicle for achieving greater educational success and productivity. There is obviously a place for educational psychologists in designing successful performance contract educational systems.

In addition to future demands for greater accountability by the schools and educational systems, there will also be increasing pressure for commercial publishing companies to become accountable for their products by verifying the quality of their instructional materials in terms of their impact on learners. A few states, including California, are already beginning to restrict textbook and instructional materials that are allowed in the schools to those that have been previously validated.

There is currently a small but important trend toward having regional laboratories and R & D centers develop high quality materials with governmental support and then turn them over to commercial publishers that produce and distribute them. An example of how such procedures can work is supplied by the Southwest Regional Laboratory for Educational Research and Development (SWRL) in Los Angeles which has developed a reading program that is currently being produced by Ginn and Company. Another example is the Language and Thinking Program produced at Central Midwest Regional Laboratory with the aid of a team of consultants highly trained in educational psychology. This program is now being disseminated by a commercial publisher.

With increasing future demands for proven educational impact of new instructional materials, educational psychologists will be very much in demand for consultation, research, and development of effective educational materials, procedures, and evaluation instruments.

Cradle-to-Grave Education

One of the most certain stimuli for change in the field of educational psychology is the extension of systematic education to populations outside the narrow 5- to 21-year age scale that has been standard in American education for decades. Several factors contribute to the current move toward cradle-to-grave education.

First, the post-World War II baby boom is over, and enrollments in elementary schools, secondary schools, and even colleges are dropping or remaining static rather than increasing. One major factor for the recruitment of mid-life adults into what up until how has been the province of college youth is the prospect of declining enrollments. Already the declining birth rate has led to 600,000 fewer first graders. Whereas the current supply of college age youth between the ages of 18 and 21 numbers 17 million, by 1985 the supply will sag to 13.5 million. Faced with the dilemma of rising costs and falling enrollments, the prospect of a new cadre of student to fill the gap brings joy to the hearts of college administrators. However, whereas the adult cadre offers a potential clientele of enormous promise, we should be cognizant of the fact that these adults are not automatically ours to educate. Adults who may be paying for their courses—or companies which are footing the bill—will examine carefully how effectively their money is being spent.

The influence of the Zero Population Growth movement (ZPG) and other groups concerned with overpopulation and inadequate food supplies is likely to perpetuate the static state. The ZPG has successfully promoted the social responsibility of "nonparenthood" and has already liberalized social acceptance of families without children. General social concern with the world population crisis and the economic crunch are influencing more young couples to delay having children and to have fewer children in their families than was common in the past.

The present trend of decreasing school enrollments combined with student overenrollment in teacher education courses in the past has resulted in a situation where the number of teachers currently far outruns the number of available teaching positions. National Education Association figures released recently show that 178,300 teachers were out of work in the fall of 1974 (Maeroff, 1975).

This great pool of unemployed trained teachers can and already is exerting its political influence. In the face of threatened loss of existing jobs and additional duties and responsibilities—including larger classes as school districts seek to economize—teachers' unions are growing in strength. Strikes are more frequent than ever before. With some of the same economic pressures now beginning to hit higher education, there is growing pressure to establish strong unions to represent university and college professors as well. One obvious way to put these unemployed teachers to work is to systematically educate groups of individuals that have not been the objects of systematic instruction before.

Education for Younger Children

A natural way to increase the number of teaching positions at both elementary and college levels is to extend the range of students traditionally taught. At the 1975 annual convention of the American Federation of Teachers, delegates proposed an extension of the regular school curriculum into the early-childhood age range. The resolution, unanimously adopted, called for the establishment of a national program of universal early-childhood education starting at age three. The resolution was part of a "Educare" package designed to ensure the availability of cradle-to-grave education. Both the American Federation of Teachers and the National Education Association are exerting pressure for federal legislation to reverse the effects of declining enrollments on teachers by expanding the age range of those subject to formal education. One example of such legislation, the Child and Family Services Act of 1975 introduced in the Senate by Senator Mondale and in the House by Representative Bademas, would include 2 million dollars worth of model educational projects for young children.

Reducing the age for starting school would provide tens of thousands of new teaching jobs, and such plans are consequently emerging as a top priority among U. S. schoolteachers. In addition to the teachers' self-interest, fortunately the voluntary education of children from 3- to 5-years of age is also a contribution to society. Growth of the women's liberation movement is resulting in more mothers continuing their careers and relying on some form of day-care service for their children. Economic realities are necessitating the return to work of many more mothers of young children.

One of every three mothers with preschool children now works, compared with only one out of every eight mothers with preschool children 25 years ago. There are currently 6 million preschool children whose mothers work, but the United States has child-care facilities to handle fewer than 1 million children. Opening schools to children at earlier ages fulfills the growing need of families for child-care services. Educational psychologists, however, must grapple with the pros and cons of such issues as custodial versus educational day-care facilities for very young children, the age at which formal schooling should begin, and once begun, questions of what should be taught—and how.

Desegregation and economic pressures are clearly problems facing child-care services. There is the possibility that government financial subsidies providing day-care funds for children from lower socioeconomic levels may result in day-care "ghettos" when parents of unsubsidized middle-class children are unable to afford the cost of such centers. The higher costs proposed for the government subsidized centers are attributable to teacher salaries to pay for higher teacher–student ratios and, thus, more individualized attention for the young children. Cost versus quality education is just one conflict of many that are sure to become problems facing educational psychologists in the years ahead.

The establishment of new educational programs for vast numbers of young children can be expected to lead to increased educational research into topics related to early childhood education. There is increasing evidence that a substantial portion of intelligence may be permanently shaped before a child enters kindergarten. Thus, lowering the entry age for early education might have the potential for more powerful influences on the later intellectual development of children. Educational psychologists will be expected to supply answers to questions concerning such issues as the best modes and methods to use when teaching very young children, social and emotional development of children, competencies of preschoolers, sex-role development (more preschool teachers are likely to be male than at present), how soon reading instruction should begin, and many others.

Education of Adults

In addition to a trend toward teaching younger children, there is sure to be a future expansion of general educational services to adults beyond "normal" college age as well. Continuing education throughout a person's life span will be one of the principle objectives of the educational system in the future. The movement away from the lock-step progression through elementary, middle, high school, and college with only one's age-mates is becoming clear. Educational flexibility should become the rule rather than the exception.

There is still need for basic literacy training for the more than 23 million adults, one out of every five Americans, who cannot read, write, or compute well enough to function effectively in modern society. Such basic skills as addressing an envelope well enough so that the post office can deliver it or reading a simple paragraph and answering literal comprehension questions seem to be beyond the capabilities of many adults. Traditional methods and materials used to teach literacy skills to the elementary age student are inappropriate for the adult illiterate population, and research by educational psychologists on the specialized needs and curriculum needed for this adult group is sorely needed.

The decades ahead will certainly see a surge in the number of women continuing and returning to be educated. One effect of women's consciousness-raising groups has been the conviction among women that they can achieve career goals for themselves, but this often involves obtaining some additional education. Other women wish to finish schooling that was interrupted by marriage or by having children. More women will continue on to graduate schools and others will turn to vocational schools seeking training in jobs formerly monopolized by men. Both men and women desiring advancement in their jobs will return to schools periodically to take additional courses. This voluntary influx of mature students to schools and colleges should help counteract the dropping enrollments forecast for younger students and may also help integrate people of different ages, experience levels, and backgrounds.

Mandatory Continuing Education

In addition to voluntary courses available for adults, there may also likely be an increase in the number of mandatory continuing-education courses required of professionals. In keeping with the trend toward greater accountability, more professions are likely to require continuing proof of competency in the form of periodic recertification programs. Some health professions presently encourage their practitioners to attend "brush-up" sessions or courses presenting the newest techniques, methods, and findings in the field, but there is rarely any follow-up on who attended the sessions. The present practice of expecting professionals to voluntarily stay competent and current in their area of expertise may be overturned by the sheer numbers of new professionals in the field and consequent growing bureaucratic demands for proof of continuing competency in the form of some measure of mastery.

There is admittedly disagreement with and resistance to the idea of mandatory continuing education for adults. Mandatory education is criticized for (a) destroying the will to learn, (b) not influencing actual practice, (c) generating feelings of inadequacy, (d) creating a loathing for the teacher, the subject, and the school, and (e) creating hostility and resistance to learning, etc. (The same criticisms are often made of mandatory education for children as well.) Those opposing mandatory adult education insist there should be "continued self-education, not continued instruction [Libby, Weinswig, & Kirk, 1975, p. 799]." Attacks on required adult education courses are, however, often attacks on the teaching practices and procedures used or attacks by professionals upon the imposition of evaluation standards by bureaucrats from outside their field. If educational psychologists discover how to help people learn painlessly and even enjoyably and are able to disseminate such information to teachers, resistance to continued education would decrease.

Education of Senior Citizens

Another group of potential students likely to instigate changes in the field of educational psychology is the steadily growing pool of senior citizens. With many of them in good health, but forced into mandatory retirement by arbitrary age-cutoff points, educational planners should prepare to meet the demand for courses catering to the special needs of this population. Organizations such as the American Association of Retired Persons (AARP) are helping older citizens to achieve their goals and are concurrently helping to focus public attention on the needs, desires, and capabilities of older people.

With a larger percentage of the population surviving into old age there should be increasing interest in studying the processes of aging, particularly as it affects the learning process. In the past, research and the study of human development have tended to stop with adolescence. In future years, educational psychologists will show renewed interest in studying and teaching about both physical and psychological growth and adjustment of people throughout the entire life cycle. There is likely to be more concern and attention paid to such topics as the psychological impact of retirement, instruction in the use and management of leisure time, studies of learning and memory capabilities in old age, etc.

Educational psychologists must closely reexamine the multiple purposes of education for different subgroups of the population. Young adults may wish to take a course in order to learn some specific job-related information or skills necessary for their future careers, while senior citizens may wish to take a course just to keep their minds occupied or to satisfy curiosity about a topic. Should courses be taught the same way and cover the same content for such different groups? It is certainly possible to tailor a course for one's intended audience, emphasizing different aspects of the subject matter for different groups. Will this lead, however, to one version of the course being discounted as more superficial and less rigorous than the other? At many universities there already tends to be a mild stigma attached to taking a course through the extension division in the evening as opposed to taking the same course in the regular daily session. This is partly because many night school courses are taught by graduate students rather than by full professors and other senior faculty. Efforts will have to be made by educational psychologists to upgrade the quality and reputation of continuing education courses for adults. They will also have to deal with sociological issues such as whether age segregation should be allowed when dealing with retired persons. There may have to be some de facto age segregation if the system becomes flexible enough to offer courses to residents of retirement homes, nursing homes, and hospitals.

If large numbers of adults show enough interest in continuing education, the financial importance to the educational facilities of these adults who may have varied interests, objectives, and time constraints will provide an additional impetus for more flexibility in educational formats in the future. Some colleges and departments of educational psychology are already experimenting with varied and flexible course formats. Stanford University has held summer mini-courses lasting for 1 or 2 weeks that alumni and spouses can attend during vacations in order to keep themselves knowledgeable in a particular area of interest. The courses are taught by the top professors in the field. Other universities have experimented with weekend seminars which even busy adults can manage to attend. Some universities, such as the University of Wisconsin and Arizona State, have experimented with concentrated 5-week modules in a particular area of interest rather than a semester-long course covering several different topics. This allows students more flexibility in choosing and sequencing courses. Of course, alternatives to traditional classroom formats must also be explored. These include such issues as the role of media in meeting the educational needs of new segments of the population and the development of effective educational techniques in the use of media and technology with these populations.

There is still much room for additional experimentation and exploration of flexible scheduling that could enhance the probability of more adults actually participating in lifelong educational experiences.

Mainstreaming

Another major trend in education that has substantial implications for educational psychology is the increased integration, or mainstreaming, of handicapped children into regular classes. Education of *all* children, regardless of handicap, is becoming a right instead of a privilege and is being solidly supported by the force of law. This will tend to add more children to the pool of young requiring education, increase the number of teachers and teacher—trainers required, and increase the number of researchers involved in investigating educational problems relating to special educational needs of particular handicaps.

The variability and heterogeneity in classrooms, attributable to the inclusion of handicapped and gifted children in the same room and the diversity in maturation and development rates found in young children, should result in a trend toward increased individualization of instruction. Educational psychologists will be expected to research, develop, test and evaluate new programs dealing with individualized instruction and alternative modes of education.

An additional factor leading to increased educational research on ways of maximizing educational benefits for subjects of varying backgrounds is the growing number of highly educated parents who are demanding flexibility and increased choice in the type of education offered their children. For several years, Minneapolis has allowed parents to choose the type of education they desire for their children from among a range of different teaching styles. The Minneapolis Southeast Alternatives program includes schools ranging from traditional and continuous progress to open and free schools and has received enthusiastic parental approval.

The integration of children from widely separated school districts will tend to mix together not only black, white, Chicano, Oriental, Indian, and other minorities and subgroups of the population, but also lower-class as well as middle-class children. Educational psychologists will be able to use examples of educational diversity, such as the Minneapolis Southeast Alternatives program, to compare the effects of different learning environments on different children and may be able to offer parents better guidelines on which type of learning environment may be most advantageous for their child.

In the next few years, the schools will be handling substantial numbers of Vietnamese and Cambodian children with initial cultural and language difficulties. This, in addition to larger enrollments of Spanish-speaking students in some parts of the country, is already leading to an increased interest in developing and disseminating information on how best to teach English as a second language.

A controversial trend, yet one likely to persist and grow in the years ahead, involves educational prescreening of children for potential learning and behavioral problems. Several cities already have programs of screening and "preventive remediation," although there is currently little empirical evidence that the intervention works. One of the largest programs, in Muncie, Indiana, has screened nearly all 4000 elementary, middle, and high school students in an "Insight Unlimited" program supported by funds under Title III of the Elementary and Secondary School Act. According to Fred Clancy, Jr., the project director, all children except those with extreme handicaps are mainstreamed into regular classes where individualized programs are developed for them. This is a new area that educational psychologists will have to investigate and take a stand on.

Political Influence

In a field such as educational psychology, political influence is a fact of life. With federal money contributing directly and indirectly to the support of many educational psychologists, governmental influence will, no doubt, have important effects on the future of the field. The government acts as an employer for many in the field and will probably increase its role in this capacity in the future.

There is always the worry that governmental funding cutbacks will wipe out much educational support. For example, President Ford vetoed the 1975 Education Bill, but because this veto would have adversely affected every school district in the country, the veto was overridden by Congress in record time. We are entering an era in which money for educational funding is tighter than in past decades and it may be necessary in the future for those interested in educational progress to devote more time and attention to publicizing educational needs and benefits, indeed to lobbying.

There is always distrust of power when governmental agencies are able to control large amounts of funds. The power of the government to rank-order research areas according to set priorities and to decree what topics or areas of research will be funded and consequently studied worries some, but despite opposition, such power is likely to increase in years ahead as government, too, is monitored by the people for accountability. Educational psychologists may have to spend more of their time informing governmental agencies and public representatives of the need for and usefulness of their particular areas of study, including the importance of continued support for basic research.

One change already being implemented which intimately concerns educational psychologists is increasing control over experimentation with human subjects. Some research designs must change to accommodate such requirements as prior informed consent of subjects. The need for more stringent protection of experimental subjects is evident to the public after recent disclosures that Army experimentation involved giving LSD and other unidentified drugs to uninformed subjects and that in other research syphilis patients were not treated for their disease in order to serve as experimental controls, etc. These horrifying examples of experimental misuse by scientists devoid of ethical judgment received a great deal of publicity and seem to have encouraged a broad distrust of scientists and experimental research. In the future there is likely to be closer attention paid to the worth of proposed research in terms of cost–benefit payoffs to society, and more concern than in the past about research ethics or possible adverse consequences.

The field of educational psychology is also likely to be influenced in coming years by increased governmental protection of children's rights. Those dealing with the field of education may have to become more cognizant of the legal restrictions imposed on their activities with, for, and on behalf of children. Increased political control with important repercussions for educational psychologists is also inherent in the growing concern for rights of privacy (Federal Privacy Act, 1975). Legal restrictions on access to private records are likely to make it increasingly difficult for even bona fide researchers to gain access to children's school records and test results. Educational psychologists must explain to politicians the need for access to such records, and must use such access responsibly.

Future decades are also likely to spawn more laws and restrictions concerning the topics, materials, and procedures that will be allowed in school systems. Some issues are already centers of controversy and can be expected to continue as issues that will have to be dealt with. These include: (*a*) whether forced busing of schoolchildren between districts to achieve racial balance should continue; (*b*) whether sex education courses and materials should be allowed in schools; (*c*) whether schoolchildren should be given instruction in moral development and ethical behavior; (*d*) whether humanistic philosophy (classified by some as a religion) should be discussed in schools and teacher training courses; (*e*) whether children should be exposed to the ills of society through textbooks; (*f*) general issues of censorship—whether textbooks should be allowed in the schools that contain material offensive or unacceptable to some parents; and (g) whether texts classified as racist or sexist will be banned from the classroom.

The rioting and violence that have accompanied the forced busing issue guarantee that it will be an area of considerable significance to educational psychologists for years to come. Whether desegregation via interdistrict busing continues or not, educational psychologists will be called upon to study and evaluate the results of either action on children's learning, racial attitudes, interpersonal relations, tolerance, etc.

Controversy over textbook content, such as has occurred most violently in West Virginia, raises the issue of locus of control over acceptable content. How is authority over educational topics, materials, and techniques to be apportioned among students, parents, teachers, the school board, publishers, and the government? Under congressional pressure resulting from parental objections, the National Science Foundation recently agreed to terminate funding for a social science curriculum ("Man: A Course of Study," developed by Harvard professors Jerome Bruner and Irven DeVore, and Asen Balikci of the University of Montreal) pending a review of its merit. Some members of Congress were outraged at such "knuckling under to censorship demands." As a result of such controversies, however, educational psychologists will have to contend with longer and more thorough reviews of proposed curricula and innovative programs and must be prepared to more fully defend their educational theories, techniques, and instruments.

Some texts have been accused of being "primers for prejudice" (Britton, 1975) and states are beginning to draw up stricter guidelines for instructional materials. The California State Board of Education set out guidelines in September of 1974 governing the type of acceptable nonsexist, nonracist, nondiscriminatory language and portrayals allowed in school materials. With more restrictions governing content of educational materials, educational psychologists may be expected to help monitor texts and screen out offensive materials, to advise publishers on things to be included or avoided in their publications, to train teachers in the use of "neutral" i.e., nonsexist, language, to study and evaluate changes in children's attitudes toward various types of discrimination after using revised materials, etc.

CONCLUSION

In the future, educational psychology will face increased diversity of both students and problems. To cope with such diversity, greater flexibility will be required. The field will also face increased demands for accountability as well as increased governmental supervision and regulation. The existence of these trends, tensions, and changes points to the need for continued consideration and attention to the historical problems of definition of the content of educational psychology. We must make an effort to solve the theory versus practice dilemma in a way that does not throw away the theoretical component as some PBTE programs tend to do. Theory is essential to cope with change, and change in American education is a certainty of the future. Although we have no choice but to react to unforeseen changes that will occur in the years ahead, we can, with foresight, anticipate changes that would be detrimental to the future well-being of society and can take steps now to eliminate or stave off their occurrence. Educational psychology with a solid theoretical base can provide the tools for coping with educational problems of the future.

REFERENCES

Ausubel, D. P. Is there a discipline of educational psychology? *Educational Psychologist, 5*(3), June 1968, 1, 4, 9:

Britton, G. Primers for prejudice. *The Reading Letter, 1*(4), 1975, 5–8.

Combs, A. W. Educational accountability from a humanistic perspective. *Educational Researcher,* 1973, *2*(9), 19–21.

Feldhusen, J. F. Student views of the ideal educational psychology course. *Educational Psychologist, 8*(1), 1970, 7–9.

Fredenburgh, F. A. Educational psychology: A theoretical hodgepodge or applied science. *Educational Psychologist, 5*(3), 1968, 2, 11.

Grinder, R. E. The growth of educational psychology as reflected in the history of Division 15, (APA), part II. *Educational Psychologist, 14*(3), 1967, 27–34.

Grinder, R. E. Crisis of content in educational psychology courses. *Educational Psychologist, 8*(1), 1970, 4.

Heath, R. W., & Nielson, M. A. The research basis for performance based teacher education. *Review of Educational Research,* 1974, *44,* 463–484.

Instructional Objectives: An ER dialogue with researcher, supervisor and teacher, *Educational Researcher,* 1972, *1,* 9, p. 8–12.

Jackson, P. W. *Life in classrooms.* New York: Holt, Rinehart & Winston, 1968.

Klausmeier, H. J. The education in educational psychology. *Educational Psychologist, 8*(1), 1970, 1, 3.

Libby, G. N., Weinswig, M. H., & Kirk, K. W. Help stamp out mandatory continuing education! *Journal of the American Medical Association, 233,* 1975, 797–799.

Maeroff, G. I. Teachers push plan to start school at age 3. *Minneapolis Tribune,* July 14, 1975, p. 3B.

New York Times News Service. Muncie kindergarten program explores children's capabilities. Bloomington, Indiana *Herald Telephone,* August 3, 1975, p. 24.

Page, E. G. How we all failed in performance contracting. *Educational Psychologist, 9*(3), May 1972, 40–42.

Popham, J. W., Eisner, E. W., Sullivan, H. W., & Tyler, L. L. *Instructional objectives.* Number 3, AERA Monograph Series on Curriculum Evaluation, Chicago: Rand McNally, 1969.

Popham, J. W. Instructional objectives: An ER dialogue with researcher, supervisor and teacher. *Educational Researcher,* 1972, *1*(9), 8–12.

Quarios, R. W., Johnson, K. D., & Murray, E. M. *Increasing student achievement by teacher incentive payments—Year III.* Paper presented at the Annual Convention of the American Educational Research Association, Chicago 1974.

"Researcher: Poor reading ability can be found early." *Minneapolis Tribune,* November 16, 1972.

Samuels, S. J. *"The enemy within: Threats to educational psychology from within and outside the field."* Unpublished paper, 1976.

Samuels, S. J., & Edwall, G. E. Measuring reading achievement: A case for criterion-referenced testing and accountability. National Council on Measurement in Education Report. *Measurement in Education,* Spring 1975, *6*(2), 1—7.

Sattler, H., Woehlke, P., & Grinder, R. An empirical assessment of preference for the modular program in educational psychology. *Educational Psychologist, 9*(3), 1972, 38—40.

Social studies courts meets surprise attack in Congress. *Minnesota Daily,* March 7, 1975, pp. 19, 20.

"Suit for poor reader stirs many questions in schools." *Minneapolis Tribune,* July 23, 1973, p. 6B.

Terwilliger, J. *An Analysis of the Role of SPPFE in Undergraduate Teacher Educational Programs.* Unpublished manuscript, University of Minnesota, Minneapolis, 1975.

Yee, A. H. Educational psychology as seen through its textbooks. *Educational Psychologist,* 1970, *8*(1), 4—6.

Part II

GENERAL CONCEPTUAL
AND THEORETICAL MODELS

5

An Applied Behavior Analysis
Approach to Educational Psychology

HERBERT J. RIETH, JR.

Indiana University

and

RODNEY E. COPELAND

Southwestern Missouri
State University

WHAT CONSTITUTES AN APPLIED BEHAVIOR ANALYSIS APPROACH?

Skinnerian Approach

B. F. Skinner in his book *Science and Human Behavior* (1953) presented an environmental rationale for studying and predicting human behavior. As a result of rather extensive laboratory work, Skinner (1938) identified a set of phenomena referred to as the principles of operant conditioning, which according to Skinner, revealed the causes of behavior.

It is a matter of documented history that the principles of operant conditioning have, in fact, proved to be verifiable phenomena which correlate directly with the occurrence of human activity.

A branch of psychology referred to as applied behavior analysis (Horowitz, 1975) has evolved as a result of Skinner's work with operant conditioning, and since the 1950s has generated a body of research in education and psychology (Baer, Wolf, & Risley, 1968).

There are several distinctive features of the applied behavior analysis approach. First, the research designs and methodologies allow single subjects or single groups to be investigated and to serve as their own controls (Baer et al., 1968). Second, Skinnerians undertake to predict and control behavior by discovering the external conditions of which behavior is a function, and third, applied behavior analysts generally deal only with behaviors that are observable and measurable.

The tenets of applied behavior analysis specified by Baer et al. (1968) indicate the qualifications for an applied behavior analysis research study are that the study be applied, behavioral, and analytic. The applied dimension requires that the behavior being studied be relevant to society and its needs. The behavioral criterion requires the precise and reliable measurement of the target behavior. The analysis component involves the scientific verification of the effects of the treatment program under the auspices of single subject or single group research designs.

Throughout the remainder of this chapter the development of the applied behavior analysis approach will be traced, a clear description of operant psychology as it relates to education will be presented, and current issues in applied behavior analysis in education will be discussed.

Historical Review

Following Skinner's operant research with animals in the 1940s and 1950s, reports of experimental programs carried out in institutions and laboratory settings with extremely deviant children began appearing in the literature (Wolf, Risley, & Mees, 1964; Lovaas, Schaeffer, & Simmons, 1963; and Ayllon & Michael, 1959). These studies were followed by studies with normal preschool children in laboratory schools (Harris, Wolf, & Baer, 1964; Allen, Hart, Buell, Harris, & Wolf, 1964; Harris, Johnston, Kelley, & Wolf, 1964; and Hart, Allen, Buell, Harris, & Wolf, 1964; Bushell & Jacobson, 1968), and finally, by studies carried out in the public schools, first in special classes, (Carlson, Arnold, Becker, & Madsen, 1968; Quay, Sprague, Werry, & McQueen, 1967; Knowles, Prutsman, & Raduege, 1968; Rabb & Hewett, 1967; Patterson, 1965; Zimmerman, Zimmerman, & Russell, 1969; Birnbrauer, Wolf, Kidder, & Tague, 1965) and by the late 1960s in regular classes with normal children (Hall, Lund, & Jackson, 1968; Madsen, Becker, & Thomas, 1968; Becker, Madsen, Arnold, & Thomas, 1967; Schmidt & Ulrich, 1969; and Ward & Baker, 1968). Thus, in a very short time, basic research findings had moved out of the laboratory and into the regular classroom.

In the early institutional studies the primary emphasis was placed on eliminating deviant or deficient behavior. The behaviors targeted were often severely dehabilitating to the child and prevented the occurrence of normal interactions.

While the target behaviors were not necessarily school-oriented, they provoked the interest of educators. This is understandable because, regardless of the philosophy of an educational approach, the objective of education is to develop behavior patterns with a minimum of deviant or disruptive behavior (such as tantrums) and a maximum of appropriate behavior (such as reading).

Other distinctive features of this approach that have been responsible for the increased acceptance and utilization by educators and psychologists have included: (a) the emphasis on developing rewarding environments rather than punitive ones; (b) the single subject (rather than group) orientation of the research methodology which enhances the possibility of discovering additional effective procedures; and (c) the procedures which constitute the technology are readily acquired by practitioners.

The initial studies carried out in educational settings generally involved children in special education classrooms (Hanley, 1971). The target behaviors selected were analagous to those selected in the early institutional research since frequently they were deviant social behaviors that prevented children from surviving and achieving in regular classroom settings.

Despite this emphasis, however, some research was conducted that analyzed academic functioning. Most of this research investigated the effectiveness of token reinforcement systems in changing academic performance. The effect of token reinforcement procedures was assessed on the rate of assignment completion and the rate of correct responses on assignments by Birnbrauer and Lawler (1964); Birnbrauer et al. (1965); Cohen, Filipczak, & Bis (1968), and Tyler & Brown (1968). Tyler (1967) found that improved grades occurred in conjunction with the implementation of a token system. Wolf, Giles, and Hall (1968) and Martin, Burkholder, Rosenthal, Tharp, and Thorne (1968) reported that when students were systematically reinforced for academic work, correlated increases in achievement test scores occurred.

From that time until the present, the body of educational research has multiplied markedly. In the area of reading, for example, Nolen, Kunzelman, and Haring (1967); Haring and Hauck (1969); McKenzie, Clark, Wolf, Kothera, and Benson (1968); Axelrod (1971); Ayllon, Layman, and Burke (1972); Gray, Baker, and Stancyk, (1969); Corey and Shamow (1972); and Lahey and Drabman (1974) used token reinforcement to increase variously defined reading responses. Eisenstein (1975) utilized contingent guitar lessons with a group of third graders in an inner-city school to increase appropriate reading. Fox and Hall (1972) and Fox (1973) used free time to increase reading responses. Procedures for teaching and changing reading behavior have been explored by Lovitt and Hurlbut (1974); McNaughton (1974); Clay (1972); Lovitt (1976); Burdett and Fox (1973); Semb and Semb (1975, pp. 233–243); Glynn and McNaughton (1975); Delquadri (1976); and Tawney (1972).

Attending to task was studied by Hall, Lund, and Jackson (1968); Broden,

Bruce, Mitchell, Carter, and Hall (1970); Walker and Buckley (1968); and Cossairt, Hall, and Hopkins (1973). In the area of math, Lovitt and Curtiss (1968); Chadwick and Day (1971); Kirby and Shields (1972); Hamblin, Hathaway, and Wodarski (1974, pp. 333–340); Lovitt and Esveldt (1970); Copeland, Brown, and Hall (1974); and Hasazi and Hasazi (1972) have researched procedures for increasing math performance. Rieth, Axelrod, Anderson, Hathaway, Wood, and Fitzgerald (1974) and Lovitt, Guppy, and Blattner (1969) were successful in increasing scores attained by students on weekly spelling tests. Hopkins, Schutte, and Garton (1971) were able to accelerate the rate and quality of students' writing performance in first and second grade students. Creative writing responses have been increased by Maloney and Hopkins (1973) and Maloney, Jacobson, and Hopkins (1975, pp. 244–260).

As a result of this research in education and psychology there has been an increase in the number of systems developed to organize, disseminate, and train other personnel to systematically utilize and implement applied behavior analysis procedures in classroom environments. All of these systems include research, training, and demonstration. Examples of such systems include the Applied Behavior Analysis Follow Through Program (Bushell & Ramp, 1974), Center at Oregon for Research in the Behavioral Education of the Handicapped (CORBEH) directed by Hill Walker, The Consulting Teacher Program of the State of Vermont (McKenzie, 1972, pp. 103–124), Engleman–Becker Follow Through Program (Becker, 1972), and the Responsive Teaching Program (Hall & Copeland, 1972) to name a few.

These programs have several features in common that identify them as applied behavior analysis approaches. First, they deal with applied behaviors and include procedures that define or pinpoint target behaviors. The behavioral definitions of target behaviors are in clear observerable terms. Second, the programs stress and require the repeated measurement of the target behavior. The systems employed by the programs entail the application of clear-cut consequences for the occurrence or nonoccurrence of the specific target behaviors. Finally the programs employ applied behavior analysis research designs to determine if causal relationships exist between the behavior and the treatment or the consequences.

PRINCIPLES AND PROCEDURES INCLUDED IN THE APPLIED BEHAVIOR ANALYSIS APPROACH

This portion of the chapter will focus on the applicability of this approach to the discipline of educational psychology. The specific content concentrates on learning and the principles of applied behavior analysis and how they relate to learning. This approach closely examines the behavior emitted by the student or groups of students. Behavior has been defined by Sulzer and Mayer (1972) as any observable external act of an organism. Consequently the utilization of the approach would initially entail the selection of a behavior within the educational environment. Once selected, the behavior is defined in terms that are observable and measurable. Some behaviors are easily defined, such as correct reading responses, correct mathematics responses, handwriting responses, and correct spelling responses.

There are other behaviors, however, that are more complex to define, for example, attending behavior or attention to task that was defined by Rieth (1971) as looking at the appropriate assignment sheet or work materials. In addition, any contact with the teacher, such as raising a hand for help or discussion of the assignment, would constitute attending. In group work, attending was described as orientation toward work materials, to a reciting fellow student, to the teacher, or if responding orally, to a lesson. Creative writing responses were defined by Maloney, Jacobson, and Hopkins (1975, pp. 244–260) as the number of "different" words within the certain compositional variables. Different sentence beginnings were counted for all sentences that began with a word different from that of any previous sentence in the same story. The numbers of different nouns, adjectives, adverbs, prepositions, and action verbs were also scored for each paper. A "different" word was defined as a word used for the first time in a given category in a given five sentence story. Once a word was scored in a given category for a given paper, repetitions of that word could not be scored again as "different."

The test of the accuracy of a behavioral definition is contained in a reliability check. A reliability check involves simultaneous independent measurements recorded by two or more independent observers. Hall (1971) indicated that reliability checks are used to provide added confidence that it is indeed the behavior and not the observer's recording of the behavior that changes between various treatment conditions. Reliability is usually expressed as a percentage of agreement and can be calculated by dividing the number of agreements between the two observers by the number of observations and multiplying the quotient by 100. Hall (1971) had indicated that while there are no absolute standards, generally 80% or better has been deemed acceptable reliability for many behaviors.

Measurement of Target Behavior

Once the target behavior has been selected and defined, the next step involves the measurement of that behavior. Frequently in educational circles when one mentions measurement, people ask whether it is necessary and or feasible to measure behavior. The answers to both questions is yes since it is necessary to determine whether teaching procedures or a treatment program is working effectively. Under the applied behavior analysis approach this is accomplished by using repeated measures of selected samples of academic and social behaviors. The measurement can be used to serve as a source of feedback to the teacher, parent, and or child. The feasibility and efficiency of involving the teacher in the collection of such data are illustrated by the fact that educators typically grade papers, and the scores attained on these papers if systematically recorded would provide an accurate and sensitive measure of the students' academic performance. Further documenting evidence is presented in the *Journal of Applied Behavior Analysis* and by Hall (1971). Feasibility in many cases is related to the type of measurement that is employed. Hall (1971) has listed three major categories of measurement techniques: automatic, direct, and observational. Automatic is probably the least frequently used in applied environments because of the lack of availability of machinery to measure the behaviors due to the complexity of some of the behaviors as well as the prohibitive cost of machinery where it is available.

Direct measurement of permanent products is frequently employed to record written academic responses. For example, Rieth *et al.* (1974) recorded the scores students attained on weekly spelling tests; they recorded the frequency and percentages of written spelling responses. Smith and Lovitt (1975, pp. 283–308) recorded the percentage of correct written math responses.

Cooper (1974) reported that teachers usually translate permanent products into three categories of numerical terms. These include: (*a*) the frequency of correct academic responses, and (*b*) the percentage of correct academic responses or the rate of correct academic responses. Frequency measures are most typically used when the same number of responses is assigned or required during the data collection sessions. Percentage would be used when there are unequal numbers of responses assigned during the data collection sessions. Rate of responses is defined as the frequency of academic responses during a unit of time. Cooper (1974) indicated "that the relationship between correct and error rate generates the same type of information as is obtained with the frequency and percentage measures." He added that rate measures are sensitive to the proficiency of student performances since they are sensitive to the effects of teaching tactics on student responses because they will show very small increments of behavior change.

Within the category of observational measurement, continuous, event, duration, interval, time sample, and Planned Activity Check (placheck) recordings are included.

Continuous measurement entails making a continuous recording of every behavior. This type of recording requires a sophisticated observer and thus is of limited utility. Its usefulness can be enhanced however through the increased accessibility of such media as videotape or 8 mm cameras to facilitate the recording of the diverse and numerous behaviors emitted.

Event recording consists of making a record of the frequency of discrete events as they occur. This would include events such as correctly identified sight vocabulary words, correct oral spelling responses, and myriad social behaviors, such as talking out, pushing, hitting, etc. Burdett and Fox (1973) used event recording to measure the frequency of reading vocabulary words correctly identified. Strain, Shores, and Kerr (1976) measured the frequency of positive and negative social behavior.

Duration recording involves measuring how long the target subject engages in the target behavior during the observation interval. In certain cases this type of measurement may be more reflective of the intensity of a behavior than is event recording. This would be exemplified by a student who does not leave his seat very often; but when he does, remains out for an extended period of time. This type of measurement can be used to record the amount of time a student spends on task or the amount of time a student spends emitting academic responses during an instructional period.

Interval recording can be effectively utilized by observers other than the person responsible for managing the environment. This type of recording involves dividing the observation period into equal intervals. The intervals are usually of 10 to 20 seconds in duration. During the interval the observer notes whether or not the target behavior has occurred. This type of measurement is frequently used to record the percentage of time a student pays attention during an observation period.

Time sampling is similar to interval recording since the observation period is divided into equal intervals. Typically, however, the intervals are of longer duration, and the observer looks at the target student or students only at the end of the given interval and records whether or not the behavior is occurring only at that moment. This type of measurement can feasibly be used by a classroom teacher in recording attending behavior. For example, one might choose to observe attending behavior for a 30-minute period with the target behavior being recorded every 3 minutes. This would consist of having the teacher record whether or not the behavior was occurring at that moment.

Placheck, which was developed by Risley (1972), is frequently employed in day-care and preschool settings to record the frequency of use of various materials; activities, or areas of the classroom. The teacher utilizing this type of measurement divides the observation period into equal intervals then at the end of each interval records the number of students engaging in the target activity, materials, or classroom area. This number is divided by the total number of students in the class and multiplied by 100 to provide the percentage of participation. This would be done for each interval, and a mean would be presented to represent the score for the entire interval.

The next step in the utilization of the applied behavior analysis approach involves the selection of a design to determine if a causal relationship exists between the effects of the research or the treatment or intervention program and the change in the target behavior. Two basic designs were suggested by Baer, Wolf, and Risley (1968), including the reversal and multiple baseline designs. The reversal design involves recording repeated measures of the target behavior until the behavior attains a steady state (Sidman, 1960) which allows one to predict accurately what the level of the behavior would be in the future. The treatment or experimental procedure is introduced, and then the level of behavior occurring during the experimental period is compared with the projected baseline level of behavior. Next, to dispel criticisms that the change in behavior, be it the acquisition of reading responses or the decrease of an inappropriate classroom behavior, occurred due to maturation or some other historical variable the treatment is removed to determine if the behavior returns to the projected baseline level. If the behavior returns to this level then one has demonstrated causality.

The other design is the multiple baseline (Baer *et al.*, 1968) which is used either in the event a reversal is not feasible because (*a*) learning has taken place, for example, multiplication tables have been learned; or (*b*) the behavior has come under the effects of natural reinforcers, for example, with an increase in language a greater number of interactions occur so more attention is focused on the subject thus maintaining the level of the behavior; or (*c*) the behavior is detrimental or harmful to the subject, for example, head banging behavior. This design involves first selecting two or more independent behaviors or subjects. After that, several baselines are established simultaneously and when they attain a steady state, treatment is applied to one of the behaviors while the others remain in baseline condition. Once the procedural effect is demonstrated upon the first behavior or subject the procedure is replicated upon the second, and so forth. The use of the three types of multiple baselines is illustrated in Hall, Cristler, Cranston, and Tucker (1970). The three include procedural replication across situations, e.g., morning and noon recess; or across individuals, e.g., Tom and Mary; or across behaviors, for example, the number of talk outs and the number of out-of-seats emitted by a student. The intent as with the reversal is to establish a causal relationship between implementation of the treatment procedure and the change in behavior.

Procedures used in the applied behavior analysis paradigm fall into two categories: consequent and antecedent events. Consequent events are events following the behavior that serve to increase, decrease, or maintain the strength of the behavior. Antecedent events include events which precede the response. This latter category includes instructional procedures used to increase the probability that the response is emitted.

Consequent Events

Consequent events can be broken down into reinforcement and punishment and other response decreasing procedures. Reinforcement is defined as the procedure of following a behavior with an event which increases the frequency of that behavior (Skinner, 1938). This procedure is ubiquitous in its application in the school environment to facilitate learning. Teacher attention, for example, was used by Hall *et al.* (1968) to produce increases in the amount of time students paid attention, while teacher attention was manipulated by Thomas, Becker, and Armstrong (1968) to decrease inappropriate behavior in the classroom. Praise was used by peer tutors (Willis, Crowder, & Morris, 1972, pp. 211–221) to increase the reading achievement of remedial students.

Free time was used by Lovitt and Esveldt (1970) and access to preferred materials was used by Lovitt *et al.* (1969) to increase spelling performance of students on weekly tests, while Hopkins *et al.* (1971) used the same procedure to increase the accuracy and decrease the time it took first and second grade students to complete a writing task. Brown (1975) used an afterschool lotto game conducted by the school principal to produce marked increases in the knowledge of basic multiplication facts by fourth through sixth grade students in an inner-city elementary school.

Reinforcement has been demonstrated to be effective in increasing reading responses (Staats, Staats, Schutz, & Wolf, 1962); with reading responses ranging from letter–sound associations (Staats, Finley, Minke, & Wolf, 1964), through oral reading rates (Lovitt, Eaton, Kirkwood, & Pelander, 1970, pp. 54–71) to comprehension responses (Sulzer, Hunt, Ashby, Konarski, & Krans, 1971, pp. 455–465). The procedure has been demonstrated to be effective with preschoolers (Staats *et al.,* 1962), fourth graders with reading problems (Haring & Hauck, 1969), and 10- to 13-year-olds (McKenzie *et al.,* 1968). In mathematics, praise and teacher attention were used to modify digit reversals in addition problems (Hasazi & Hasazi, 1972) and to correct response rates (Lovitt & Esveldt, 1970; Kirby & Shields, 1972). Peer reinforcement was used by Johnson and Bailey (1974) to increase the rate of acquisition of basic arithmetic skills and lead to high rates of correct responses (Harris & Sherman, 1973).

Frequently, the development of a new academic or social behavior cannot be achieved by reinforcing the response when it occurs (Kazdin, 1975). In many cases, the response may never occur or, as in the case with many academic subject-matter areas, the desired behavior may be so complex that the elements which make up the response are not in the repetoire of the individual. For example, developing reading skills requires the use of form discrimination, sound discriminations, and their combinations. In these situations shaping may be an appropriate procedure to employ. Sulzer and Mayer (1972) defined shaping as the systematic reinforcement of successive approximations toward the behavioral goal. Responses are reinforced that either resemble the final response or that include components of that response. Shaping was used effectively by Staats *et al.* (1962) to increase the acquisition of 26 single words by six 4-year-olds and by Tawney (1972) to increase discriminative responding to critical features of a stimulus in efforts to improve performance on a letter discrimination task. Gray *et al.* (1969) used shaping to facilitate word acquisition by a group of second grade students.

Punishment has been defined by Azrin and Holz (1966) "as a reduction of the future probability of a specific response as a result of the immediate delivery of a stimulus for that response." If one applies a consequence to a behavior and as a result of the application the behavior decreases in frequency that is labeled punishment. Typically, punishment is applied to diminish the frequency of inappropriate social behaviors which are incompatible with academic achievement. Hall (1971) has indicated that punishment is the fastest way to decrease the frequency or duration of a behavior. Thus the applicability in an educational setting is to quickly diminish inappropriate behavior to allow optimum opportunities for academic learning to occur. The procedure can also be used as a means of enabling students to learn appropriate social behaviors. For best results, however, it is usually recommended that punishment be combined with reinforcement for the appropriate behavior. Thus a student would be punished for engaging in the inappropriate behavior, i.e., leaving one's seat and reinforced for engaging in the appropriate behavior, i.e., sitting in one's seat and working on an assigned task or attending to a teacher or presentation. For best results it is usually recommended that punishment be applied immediately after the behavior and that it be applied each time the behavior occurs.

Response cost (Weiner, 1962) is a response reduction procedure which involves removing a privilege, token, or reinforcer contingent upon the student's engaging in inappropriate behavior. This can be exemplified by reducing a student's free time or recess by a minute for each occurrence of an inappropriate behavior. Response costs in the form of token loss have been built into many token reinforcement systems to enhance the effectiveness of the system in decreasing inappropriate and increasing appropriate social and academic behaviors.

Time out from positive reinforcement is another response reduction procedure which has been used widely. This entails removing the student from a reinforcing environment to an isolated area. The movement of a student's desk out of the classroom into the hallway is frequently considered to be time out. Frequently, however, this procedure is ineffective because the hallway is as reinforcing an environment as the classroom. The length of time spent in time out has been found to influence the effectiveness of time out. White, Nielsen, and Johnson (1972) found while comparing the effectiveness of 1, 15, and 30 minute intervals that the 15 and 30 minute periods significantly decreased behavior. The 1 minute interval varied in effectiveness depending upon whether it preceded or followed longer durations of time out. The authors reported that when a 1 minute time out period preceded longer durations of time out the frequency of the inappropriate behavior was effectively reduced. When, however, it was used after a longer duration it was less effective in reducing the frequency of the target behavior. This finding tends to be significant since teachers and parents often arbitrarily designate long intervals of time out which diminish the efficacy of the procedures.

Antecedent Events

Heretofore the content of this chapter has addressed the effects of consequent events upon behavior. Recently, however, researchers have begun to focus on antecedent events—events which occur before the response or behavior is emitted. Thus, antecedent events would include all events which occur before the response is emitted and would consequently include instructions, instructional procedures, sequence of instructional materials, opportunities to respond, and seating arrangements.

Instructions, according to Rieth and Hall (1974), play a very important role in the classroom. Teachers use instructions to enable students to acquire academic and social skills, and they serve as the basis for initiating academic activity. Thus, clear-cut instructions are essential to enable students to initiate and correctly complete assignments.

Antecedent events *can* be used to increase the probability that students will emit appropriate behavior and thus facilitate the use of reinforcement for the emittance of the correct response. For example, Lovitt and Curtiss (1969) found that they could increase the rate of correct math computational responses emitted by an 11-year-old boy by having him verbalize the problem before writing the answer. Rieth *et al.* (1974) found that students attained higher scores on weekly spelling tests when they were given daily quizzes over a portion of the weekly word list prior to taking the weekly test.

Modeling is an antecedent event which entails demonstrating the terminal target behavior to the subject and requesting the subject or student to imitate the response or behavior. Burdett and Fox (1973) developed a reading program that contained the principles of modeling and imitation and found that the program produced substantial increases in the rate of acquisition of reading responses by target subjects. The authors divided reading into three major components: vocabulary, contextual reading, and comprehension. The modeling—imitation procedure was primarily used in conjunction with the acquisition of new vocabulary contained in the reading series. The author presented 10 new vocabulary words per session. The words were presented to the student and if the student did not correctly identify the word within 3 seconds the teacher pronounced the word for the student and requested the pupil to repeat the word. A correct pronounciation was praised. The 10 words were presented three times during the learning session. If all the words were learned then a passage containing the words was read by the student. A continuous record was made. Data presented across many students have indicated that the procedure produces significant increases in acquisition rates. The procedure has been replicated by LaForge et al. (1975, pp. 261–268) and Graves et al. (1976). Martin (1975) has analyzed the components of the procedure, finding that a standard rotation presentation of the words enabled target students to exceed the acquisition rate of students receiving a modified rotation format that entailed repeated consecutive presentations of words that were incorrectly identified. The modeling–imitation format was also successfully employed by Smith and Lovitt (1975, pp. 283–308) to increase math acquisition and productivity.

Another very important aspect is the sequence of academic materials used to develop academic skills. This involves selecting materials that are consonant with the students' academic repertoire. The proper selection and presentation should facilitate an increase in the probability of the student's emitting correct academic responses. Thus, the opportunity to obtain reinforcement for appropriate behavior is greatly enhanced.

An issue which is currently being investigated is the opportunity to make academic responses in the classroom. Preliminary observations made in inner-city classrooms with a high incidence of high risk pupils indicate that the time pupils spend making oral reading, reading comprehension, and mathematic responses is limited. For example, pupils in the first grade were found to receive an average of less than 30 seconds of individual reading per day (Fox & Hall, 1972). The amount of time spent practicing basic arithmetic facts seems to be similarly limited. Currently investigations are underway to develop environmental arrangements to optimize the efficiency of the classroom environment.

Axelrod,. Hall, and Tams (1972) found that seating arrangements had an effect upon pupil's study rates. The authors found that students had higher study rates when they sat in row arrangements as compared with table formations. This finding may not be ubiquitous but it does illustrate the fact that seating arrangements do exert an impact upon the events which occur in the classroom.

TRAINING

As the technology associated with applied behavior analysis has evolved through research and experimentation, practitioners have been quick to implement behavioral techniques in their work with children. Just as rapidly, behavioral training programs have developed primarily through university and college settings to disseminate new technology to psychologists, physicians, nurses, social workers, businessmen, paraprofessionals, and parents.

One would be hard pressed to find graduate training programs in psychology or education today that did not devote at least a portion of the curriculum to operant psychology and applied behavior analysis research, while considerable numbers of graduate programs exist that devote a majority of the curriculum to applied behavior analysis.

From the beginning it was apparent that the techniques used in carrying out behavioral treatment programs were readily teachable to persons who were nonsophisticated in operant psychology. Ayllon and Michael (1959) trained aides and psychiatric nurses to systematically deliver or withhold reinforcement contingent on specific behaviors of patients in a hospital for the mentally ill. The results of their study were quite significant in that ward personnel were successful in bringing about significant changes in the patients' behavior. Further work by Ayllon and Azrin (1968) demonstrated quite clearly that mental institution personnel were capable of carrying out the procedures involved in token systems.

Additional early evidence that operant techniques can be taught was presented by Wolf et al. (1964). In that study the authors reported that ward attendants in a children's mental hospital successfully carried out the behavioral analysis techniques regarding treatment procedures for the tantruming and self-destructive behaviors of the 3½-year-old subject. Furthermore, the parents of the child were also successful in using the behavior management techniques suggested to them by the researchers.

Following these initial demonstrations, numerous accounts have appeared in the literature indicating that persons dealing with children have been trained to carry out behavior management procedures (Harris et al., 1964; Homme, de Baca, Devine, Steinhorst, & Pickert, 1963; Jacobson, Bushell, & Risley, 1968; Birnbrauer et al., 1965; Osborne, 1969; O'Leary & Becker, 1967; McKenzie et al., 1968; Wolf et al., 1968; Hall et al., 1968; Hall et al., 1970; and Phillips, Phillips, Fixen, & Wolf, 1971).

Various training strategies have been described in the literature as educators and psychologists have attempted to develop methods to teach practitioners how to use operant psychology in applied settings. Teachers have been the focal point of a number of training projects. As mentioned previously, in the Vermont Consulting Teacher Program (McKenzie, 1972) experienced teachers become consultants who then train regular classroom teachers in how to effectively manage the education of children normally labeled retarded, disturbed, or learning disabled.

Project Follow Through (Bushell, 1974) has developed a series of teacher training workshops and considerable in-class training for inner-city teachers. Follow Through also trains parents to become teacher aides.

Center at Oregon for Research in the Behavioral Education of the Handicapped (CORBEH) (Hops, Walker, & Hutton, 1973) has developed a training program which teaches public school instructors at the lower grade levels how to manage children with behavior disorders. Trainers respond to referrals in the public schools regarding children with deviant behaviors. The trainer then goes to the classroom and works in close conjunction with the classroom teacher.

The trainer observes the target child's behavior on a 30 second interval basis, and the child earns points contingent on appropriate study behavior. The points are exchangeable for a variety of back-up reinforcers and may include the child's earning activities for the entire class. The trainer shows the teacher how to attend to appropriate behavior and ignore inappropriate behavior and then coaches and cues the teacher in doing the same.

Initially the trainer does the measuring and distributing of points. After control is established the teacher takes over the procedures. The time intervals for delivering points are gradually lengthened from 30 seconds to 10 minutes, and the teacher becomes involved only when the intervals have been lengthened to 4 minutes.

Each trainer maintains a caseload of 4 to 7 children and attempts to complete training procedures in 20 school days. The overall goal of the CORBEH training program is to devise training techniques for school counselors and psychologists to use in their consultive work with teachers.

While the three training programs just described are procedural and process oriented, a majority of the applied behavior analysis training that occurs in university and college settings is more didactic in nature; participants are lectured regarding the principles of operant psychology and expected to use their new knowledge in their applied work with children.

Unfortunately this training method is probably not very effective in changing practitioner behavior. The Responsive Teaching approach (Hall & Copeland, 1972) offers a blend of the procedures, method, and lecture approach.

In Responsive Teaching, participants hear a series of lectures on measurement technology and operant psychology. Many of the lecture sessions however contain role playing episodes, and other exercises intended to give the student an opportunity to practice using operant techniques in their interactions with children and adults.

The critical element of Responsive Teaching that results in trainees using applied behavior analysis techniques is the carrying out of an applied project.

Each student must select a behavior or skill he or she wishes to change or teach in a subject (generally a child they see in the classroom, clinic, or home) and then carry out systematic operant procedures in an attempt to modify the behavior. Measurement skills are emphasized as well as applied behavior analysis research designs.

The goal of the Responsive Teaching model is that each participant become a skilled technician who can apply operant technology in a variety of settings.

Very little research has been published that demonstrates the efficiency of the various training approaches in existence in applied behavior analysis. Educational psychology as a field perhaps has the potential to research the effectiveness of various applied behavior analysis training models. Most importantly, comparisons should be made regarding applied behavior analysis trainees and trainees from other educational and/or psychological approaches to gain answers as to which group is more effective in meeting public school educational goals with children.

SUMMARY AND IMPLICATIONS

This chapter has presented an overview of the applied behavior analysis approach to educational psychology. As the content illustrates, this approach has generated a vast body of research within a relatively brief period of time. Many of these findings have had a major impact not only upon research but also upon applied technology. From all indications this approach will continue to affect the field of educational psychology.

The applied behavior analysis approach could have a meaningful impact upon the field of educational psychology by conducting programmatic analyses, using large groups of subjects, to investigate further the single subject or small group design findings. Another very important future direction is the use of applied behavior analysis strategies to analyze and collect normative data on learning environments and learning variables. Finally, the incorporation of the procedures into training programs should expand the familiarity of educational psychologists with the applied behavior analysis technology and allow greater dissemination, application, and research.

The applied behavior analysis approach is not presented as a panacea but as a set of principles which has been demonstrated to be effective and thus meritorious of consideration as a tool within the educational psychologist's repertoire.

REFERENCES

Allen, E., Hart, B., Buell, J., Harris, R., & Wolf, M. Effects of social reinforcement on isolate behavior of a nursery school child. *Child Development,* 1964, *35,* 511–518.

Axelrod, S. Token reinforcement programs in special classes. *Exceptional Children,* 1971, *37,* 371–379.

Axelrod, S., Hall, R. V., & Tams, A. A. *A comparison of two common seating arrangements in classroom settings.* Paper presented at the Third Annual meeting of the Kansas Symposium on Behavior Analysis in Education, Lawrence, Kansas, 1972.

Ayllon, T., & Azrin, N. A motivational system for therapy and rehabilitation. In *A token economy.* New York: Appleton-Century-Crofts, 1968.

Ayllon, T., Layman, D., & Burke, S. Disruptive behavior and reinforcement of academic performance. *Psychological Record,* 1972, *22,* 315–323.

Ayllon, T., & Michael, J. The psychiatric nurse as a behavioral engineer. *Journal of the Experimental Analysis of Behavior,* 1959, *2,* 323–334.

Azrin, N. H., & Holz, W. C. Punishment. In W. K. Henig (Ed.), *Operant behavior: Areas of research and application.* New York: Appleton-Century-Crofts, 1966.

Baer, D., Wolf, M., & Risley, T. Some current dimensions of applied behavior analysis. *Journal of Applied Behavior Analysis,* 1968, *1,* 91–97.

Becker, W. C. Some effects of direct instruction methods in teaching disadvantaged children in Project Follow Through. In *Proceedings of the International Symposium on Behavior Therapy,* Minneapolis, Minnesota, 1972.

Becker, W., Madsen, C., Arnold, C., & Thomas, D. The contingent use of teacher attention and praise in reducing classroom behavior problems. *Journal of Special Education,* 1967, *1,* 287–307.

Birnbrauer, J., & Lawler, J. Token reinforcement for learning. *Mental Retardation,* 1964, *2,* 275–279.

Birnbrauer, J., Wolf, M., Kidder, J., & Tague, C. Classroom behavior of retarded pupils with token reinforcement. *Journal of Experimental Child Psychology,* 1965, *2,* 219–235.

Broden, M., Bruce, C., Mitchell, M. A., Carter, V., & Hall, R. V. Effects of teacher attention on attending behavior of two boys at adjacent desks. *Journal of Applied Behavior Analysis,* 1970, *3,* 199–203.

Brown, R. E. *Effects of an elementary school principal systematically reinforcing students for learning multiplication facts.* Unpublished doctoral dissertaion, University of Kansas, 1975.

Burdett, C. S., & Fox, W. L. *Measurement and evaluation of reading behavior word recognition, oral reading and comprehension.* Austin, Texas: Austin Writers Group, 1973.

Bushell, D., Jr. *Classroom behavior: A little book for teachers.* Englewood Cliffs, New York: Prentice-Hall, 1973.

Bushell, D., Jr., & Jacobson, J. *The simultaneous rehabilitation of mothers and their children.* Paper presented at the meeting of the American Psychological Association, San Francisco, September 1968.

Bushell, D., Jr., & Ramp, E. A. *The behavior analysis classroom.* Lawrence, Kansas, University of Kansas Behavior Analysis Follow Through Project, 1974.

Carlson, C., Arnold, C., Becker, W., & Madsen, B. The elimination of tantrum behavior of a child in an elementary classroom. *Behaviour Research and Therapy,* 1968, *6,* 117–119.

Chadwick, B., & Day, R. Systematic reinforcement: Academic performance of underachieving students. *Journal of Applied Behavior Analysis,* 1971, *4,* 311–319.

Clay, M. M. *Reading, the patterning of complex behavior.* Auckland, New Zealand: Heineman Educational Books, 1972, 111–127.

Cohen, J., Filipczak, J., & Bis, J. Case project: Contingencies applicable to special education. In J. Shlien (Ed.), *Research in psychotherapy.* Washington, D. C.: American Psychological Association, 1968.

Cooper, J. O. *Measurement and analysis of behavioral techniques*. Columbus, Ohio: Charles E. Merrill, 1974.

Copeland, R. E., Brown, R., & Hall, R. V. The effects of principal implemented techniques on the behavior of pupils. *Journal of Applied Behavior Analysis*, 1974, *7*, 77–86.

Corey, J. R., & Shamow, J. C. The effects of fading on the acquisition and retention of oral reading. *Journal of Applied Behavior Analysis*, 1972, *5*, 311–315.

Cossairt, A., Hall, R. V., & Hopkins, B. L. The effects of experimenters instructions, feedback and praise on teacher praise and student attending behavior. *Journal of Applied Behavior Analysis*, 1973, *6*, 89–100.

Delquadri, J. *The effects of various error correction procedures on reading acquisition*. Unpublished manuscript, University of Kansas, 1976.

Eisenstein, S. R. The effect of contingent guitar lessons on reading behavior. *Journal of Music Therapy*, 1975, *2*, 138–146.

Fox, R. G. *The effects of peer tutoring on the oral reading behavior of underachieving fourth grade pupils*. Unpublished doctoral dissertation, University of Kansas, 1973.

Fox, R., & Hall, R. V. *Altering pupil reading performance by differentially reinforcing tutoring behavior*. Paper presented at the meeting of the International Council for Exceptional Children, Washington, D. C., 1972.

Glynn, E. L., & McNaughton, S. S. Trust your own observations: Criterion referenced assessment of reading progress. *The Slow Learning Child*, 1975, *22*, 91–108.

Graves, M., Rieth, J. J., & Smith, J. *An evaluation of a minimal objective system for the evaluation of reading instruction*. Unpublished manuscript, University of Kansas, 1976.

Gray, B. B., Baker, R. D., & Stancyk, S. E. Performance determined instruction for training in remedial reading. *Journal of Applied Behavior Analysis*, 1969, *2*, 255–263.

Hall, R. V. *Managing Behavior*. Vols. I–III. Lawrence, Kansas: H & H Enterprises, 1971.

Hall, R. V., & Copeland, R. The responsive teaching model: A first step in shaping school personnel as behavior modification specialists. In R. W. Clark, D. R. Evans, & L. A. Hamerlynck (Eds.), *Implementing behavioral programs for schools and clinics*, Champaign, Illinois: Research Press, 1972.

Hall, R. V., Cristler, C., Cranston, S. S., & Tucker, B. Teachers and parents as researchers using multiple baseline designs. *Journal of Applied Behavior Analysis*, 1970, *3*, 247–255.

Hall, R. V., Lund, D., & Jackson, D. Effects of teacher attention on study behavior. *Journal of Applied Behavior Analysis*, 1968, *1*, 1–12.

Hamblin, R., Hathaway, C., & Wodarski, J. Group contingencies, peer tutoring and accelerating academic achievement. In R. Ulrich, T. Slachnick, & J. Mabry (Eds.), *Control of human behavior*. Glenview, Illinois: Scott, Foresman, 1974.

Hanley, E. M. Review of research involving applied behavior analysis in the classroom. *Review of Educational Research*, 1971, *40*, 597–625.

Haring, N. G., & Hauck, M. A. Improved learning conditions in the establishment of reading skills with disabled readers. *Exceptional Children*, 1969, *35*, 341–352.

Harris, F. R., Johnston, M., Kelley, C., & Wolf, M. Effects of social reinforcement on regressed crawling of a nursery school child. *Journal of Educational Psychology*, 1964, *55*, 35–41.

Harris, F., Wolf, M., & Baer, D. Effects of adult social reinforcement on child behavior. *Young Children*, 1964, *20*(1), 8–17.

Harris, J. W., & Sherman, J. A. Use and analysis of the "good behavior game" to reduce disruptive classroom behavior. *Journal of Applied Behavior Analysis*, 1973, *6*, 405–418.

Hart, B., Allen, E., Buell, J., Harris, F., & Wolf, M. Effects of social reinforcement on operant crying. *Journal of Experimental Child Psychology*, 1964, *1*, 145–153.

Hasazi, J., & Hasazi, S. Effects of teacher attention on digit-reversal behavior in an elementary school child. *Journal of Applied Behavior Analysis*, 1972, *5*, 157–162.

Homme, L. E., de Baca, P. C., Devine, J. V., Steinhorst, R., & Pickert, E. J. Use of the premack principle in controlling the behavior of nursery school children. *Journal of Experimental Analysis of Behavior*, 1963, *6*, 544.

Hopkins, B. L., Schutte, R. C., & Gorton, K. L. The effects of access to a playroom on the rate and quality of printing and writing of first and second-grade students. *Journal of Applied Behavior Analysis*, 1971, *4*, 77–88.

Hops, H., Walker, H. M., & Hutton, S. B. *Contingencies for learning academic and social skills*. Eugene, Oregon: Center at Oregon for Research in the Behavioral Education of the Handicapped, 1973.

Horowitz, F. D. Living among the ABAS—retrospect and prospect. In E. A. Ramp & G. Semb (Eds.), *Behavior analysis: Areas of research and application*. Englewood Cliffs, New Jersey: Prentice-Hall, 1975.

Jacobson, J., Bushell, D., & Risley, T. Switching requirements in a head-start classroom. *Journal of Applied Behavior Analysis*, 1968, *2*, 43–47.

Johnson, M., & Bailey, J. Cross age tutoring: Fifth graders as arithmetic tutors for kindergarten children. *Journal of Applied Behavior Analysis*, 1974, *7*, 223–232.

Kazdin, A. E. *Behavior modification in applied settings*. Homewood, Illinois: Dorsey Press, 1975.

Kirby, F., & Shields, F. Modification of arithmetic response rate and attending behavior in a seventh grade student. *Journal of Applied Behavior Analysis*, 1972, *5*, 79–84.

Knowles, P., Prutsman, T., & Raduege, V. Behavior modification of simple hyperkinetic behavior and letter discrimination in a hyperactive child. *Journal of School Psychology*, 1968, *6*, 157–160.

LaForge, J., Pree, M., & Hasazi, S. The use of minimum objectives as an ongoing monitoring system to evaluate student progress. In E. A. Ramp & G. Senb (Eds.), *Behavior analysis: Areas of research and application*. Englewood Cliffs, New Jersey, 1975.

Lahey, B. B., & Drabman, R. S. Facilitation of the acquisition and retention of sight word vocabulary through token reinforcement. *Journal of Applied Behavior Analysis*, 1974, *7*, 307–312.

Lovaas, O. L., Schaeffer, B., & Simmons, J. Q. Building social behavior in autistic children by use of electric shocks. *Journal of Experimental Research and Personality*, 1955, *1*, 99–109.

Lovitt, T. C. Applied behavior analysis techniques and curriculum research: Implications for instructions. In N. Haring & R. Schiefelbusch, *Teaching special children*. New York: McGraw-Hill, 1976.

Lovitt, T. C., & Curtiss, K. A. Effects of manipulating an antecedent event on mathematics response rate. *Journal of Applied Behavior Analysis*, 1968, *3*, 49–53.

Lovitt, T. C., Eaton, M., Kirkwood, M. E., & Pelander, J. Effects of various reinforcement contingencies on oral reading rate. In E. A. Ramp & B. L. Hopkins (Eds.), *A new direction for education: Behavior analysis*. Lawrence, Kansas: University of Kansas Press, 1971.

Lovitt, T. C., & Esveldt, K. The relative effects on math performance of single versus multiple ratio schedules: A case study. *Journal of Applied Behavior Analysis*, 1970, *3*, 261–270.

Lovitt, T. C., Guppy, T., & Blattner, J. The use of a freetime contingency with fourth graders to increase spelling accuracy. *Behaviour Research and Therapy,* 1969, *7,* 151–156.

Lovitt, T. C., & Hurlbut, M. Using behavioral analysis techniques to assess the relationship between phonics instruction and oral reading. *Journal of Special Education,* 1974, *8,* 57–72.

Madsen, C., Becker, W., & Thomas, D. Rules, praise and ignoring: Elements of elementary classroom control. *Journal of Applied Behavior Analysis,* 1968, *1,* 139–150.

Maloney, K. B., & Hopkins, B. L. The modification of sentence structure and its relationship to subjective judgments of creativity in writing. *Journal of Applied Behavior Analysis,* 1973, *6,* 425–433.

Maloney, K. B., Jacobson, C. R., & Hopkins, B. L. An analysis of the effects of lectures, requests, teacher praise, and free time on the creative writing behaviors of third-grade children. In E. A. Ramp & G. Semb (Eds.), *Behavior analysis: Areas of research and application.* Englewood Cliffs, New Jersey: Prentice-Hall, 1975.

Martin, J. *Word acquisition rates of first graders as a function of two stimulus sequencing procedures.* Unpublished masters thesis, Kansas University, 1975.

Martin, M., Burkholder, R., Rosenthal, T., Tharp, R., & Thorne, G. Programming behavior change and reintegration into school milieux of extreme adolescent deviates. *Behaviour Research and Therapy,* 1968, 371–383.

McKenzie, H. S. Special education and consulting teachers. In F. W. Clark, D. R. Evans, & L. A. Hamerlynck (Eds.), *Implementing behavioral programs for schools and clinics.* Champaign, Illinois: Research Press, 1971.

McKenzie, H. S., Clark, M., Wolf, M. M., Kothera, R., & Benson, C. Behavior modification of children with learning disabilities using grades as tokens and allowances as back-up reinforcers. *Exceptional Children,* 1968, *34,* 745–753.

McNaughton, S. S. *Behavior modification and reading in a special class.* Unpublished masters thesis, University of Auckland, 1974.

Nolen, P. A., Kunzelman, H. P., & Haring, N. G. Behavioral modification in a junior high school learning disability classroom. *Exceptional Children,* 1967, *34,* 163–168.

O'Leary, K., & Becker, W. Behavior modification of an adjustment class: A token reinforcement program. *Exceptional Children,* 1967, *37,* 637–642.

Osborne, J. G. Free-time as a reinforcer in the management of classroom behavior. *Journal of Applied Behavior Analysis,* 1969, *2,* 113–118.

Patterson, G. An application of conditioning techniques to the control of a hyperactive child. In L. Ullmann & L. Kranser (Eds.), *Case studies in behavior modification,* New York: Holt, Rinehart & Winston, 1965.

Phillips, E. L., Phillips, E. A., Fixsen, D. L., and Wolf, M. M. Achievement place: Modification of the behaviors of predelinquent boys in a token economy. *Journal of Applied Behavior Analysis,* 1971, *4,* 45–49.

Quay, H., Sprague, R., Werry, J., & McQueen, M. Conditioning visual orientation of conduct problem children in the classroom. *Journal of Experimental Child Psychology,* 1967, *5,* 512–517.

Rabb, E., & Hewett, F. Developing appropriate classroom behaviors in a severely disturbed group of institutionalized kindergarten–primary children utilizing a behavior modification model. *American Journal of Orthopsychiatry,* 1967, *1,* 275–285.

Rieth, H. J. *Experimental analysis of procedures used to modify the academic and attending behavior of students alternately placed in regular and special education.* Unpublished doctoral dissertation, University of Kansas, 1971.

Rieth, H. J., Axelrod, S., Anderson, R., Hathaway, F., Wood, K., & Fitzgerald, C. Influence of distributed practice and daily testing on weekly spelling tests. *Journal of Educational Research*, 1974, *68*, 73–77.

Rieth, H. J., & Hall, R. V. *Progressive teaching model readings for applied behavior analysis.* Lawrence, Kansas: H. & H. Enterprises, 1974.

Risley, T. R. Spontaneous language in the preschool environment. In J. Stanley (Ed.), *Preschool programs for the disadvantaged.* Baltimore, Maryland: Johns Hopkins Press, 1972.

Schmidt, G. W., & Ulrich, R. E. Effects of group contingent events upon classroom noise. *Journal of Applied Behavior Analysis*, 1969, *2*, 171–179.

Semb, G., & Semb, S. A comparison of fixed page and fixed-time reading assignments in elementary school children. In E. Ramp & G. Semb (Eds.), *Behavior analysis: Areas of research and application.* Englewood Cliffs, New Jersey: Prentice-Hall, 1975.

Sidman, M. *Tactics of scientific research.* New York: Basic Books, 1960.

Skinner, B. *The behavior of organisms.* New York: Appleton-Century-Crofts, 1938.

Skinner, B. *Science and human behavior.* New York: Wiley, 1953.

Smith, D. D., & Lovitt, T. C. The use of modeling techniques to influence the acquisition of computational arithmetic skills in learning-disabled children. In E. Ramp & G. Semb (Eds.), *Behavior analysis: Areas of research and application.* Englewood Cliffs, New Jersey: Prentice-Hall, 1975.

Staats, A. W., Finely, J., Minke, K., & Wolf, M. Reinforcement variables in the control of unit reading response. *Journal of Experimental Analysis of Behavior*, 1964, *7*, 139–149.

Staats, A. W., Staats, C. K., Schutz, E. R., & Wolf, M. M. The conditioning of textual responses using "extrinsic" reinforcers. *Journal of the Experimental Analysis of Behavior.* 1962, *5*, 33–40.

Strain, P. S., Shores, R. E., & Kerr, M. M. An experimental analysis of spillover effects on the social interaction of behaviorally handicapped preschoolers. *Journal of Applied Behavior Analysis*, 1976, *9*, 31–40.

Sulzer, B., Hunt, S., Ashby, C. L., Konearski, C., & Krans, M. Increasing rate and percentage correct in reading and spelling in a fifth grade of slow readers by means of a token system. E. A. Ramp & B. L. Hopkins (Eds.), *A new direction for education: Behavior analysis.* Lawrence, Kansas: University of Kansas Press, 1971.

Sulzer, B., & Mayer, G. R. *Behavior modification procedures for school personnel.* Hinsdale, Illinois: Dryden Press, 1972.

Tawney, J. W. Training letter discrimination in four year old children. *Journal of Applied Behavior Analysis*, 1972, *5*, 455–465.

Thomas, D., Becker, W., & Armstrong, M. Production and elimination of disruptive classroom behavior by systematically varying teacher's behavior. *Journal of Applied Behavior Analysis*, 1968, *1*, 35–45.

Tyler, V. Application of operant token reinforcement to academic performance of an institutionalized delinquent. *Psychological Reports*, 1967, *21*, 249–260.

Tyler, V., & Brown, G. Token reinforcement of academic performance with institutionalized delinquent boys. *Journal of Educational Psychology*, 1968, *59*, 164–168.

Walker, H. M., & Buckley, N. The use of positive reinforcement in conditioning attending behavior. *Journal of Applied Behavior Analysis*, 1968, *1*, 245–252.

Walker, H. M., & Hops, H. Increasing academic achievement by reinforcing direct academic performance and/or facilitative non-academic responses. *Journal of Educational Psychology*, in press.

Ward, M. H., & Baker, B. L. Reinforcement therapy in the classroom. *Journal of Applied Behavior Analysis*, 1968, *1*, 323–328.

Weiner, H. Some effects of response cost upon human operant behavior. *Journal of the Experimental Analysis of Behavior,* 1962, *5,* 201–208.

White, G. D., Nielsen, G., & Johnson, S. M. Timeout duration and the suppression of deviant behavior in children. *Journal of Applied Behavior Analysis,* 1972, *5,* 111–120.

Willis, J., Crowder, J., & Morris, B. A behavioral approach to remedial reading using students as behavioral engineers. In G. Semb, *Behavior Analysis and Education.* Lawrence, Kansas: University of Kansas, 1972.

Wolf, M., Giles, D., & Hall, R. Experiments with token reinforcement in a remedial classroom. *Behaviour Research and Therapy,* 1968, *6,* 51–64.

Wolf, M. M., Risley, T. R., & Mees, H. L. Application of operant conditioning procedures to the behavior problems of an autistic child. *Behaviour Research and Therapy,* 1964, *1,* 305–312.

Zimmerman, E. H., Zimmerman, J., & Russell, C. D. Differential effects of token reinforcement on instruction-following behavior in retarded students instructed as a group. *Journal of Applied Behavior Analysis,* 1969, *2,* 101–112.

6

The Cognitive Point of View

S. FARNHAM-DIGGORY

University of Delaware

This chapter is concerned with the problem of teaching teachers about cognitive psychology. The chapter is written for two kinds of readers: the cognitive psychologist trying a hand at teaching educational psychology, and the educational psychologist trying a hand at teaching cognitive psychology. In both cases, some degree of professional expertise is assumed, as is some degree of inexperience. This could mean that some readers will be provided with more details than they need, while others will be simultaneously provided with fewer details than they need. But since the balance should shift from topic to topic, it is hoped that everyone will find enough substance to make the chapter worthwhile.

A SPECIAL NOTE TO THE COGNITIVE PSYCHOLOGIST

Probably the most important fact about teachers is that they are not especially interested in how the human mind works although they believe they are going to be. They view teaching initially as a profession concerned with uplifting the human mind. But experienced teachers know, and student teachers soon learn, that public schooling is largely concerned with crowd control, classroom rituals, and plain survival in a system only haphazardly related to human mental development and instructional needs. That a concern for teaching survives at all is a real tribute to teachers.

The archaic institutional structure of a public school is a fact of life. Teachers must orient toward instruction that will help them get through a classroom day with as few disasters as possible. Since many of these potential disasters are concerned with learning and thinking, cognitive psychology has a legitimate place in teacher training. But one of Piaget's basic principles operates very forcefully in this situation: Teachers can assimilate only what already fits their mental structures. For the most part, that means only what they perceive to be immediately relevant to the classroom day.

This puts an extra burden on college instructors. We must be willing to go find out about that classroom day, and to select from the broad domain of cognitive psychology what will be useful to teachers. Most important: Instructors must be willing to explain exactly how the information is useful. We cannot expect teachers to do that for themselves, any more than we can expect medical students to instruct themselves in the application of surgical principles. The problem is acute when teachers are trying to combine practice teaching with classwork.

The burden is especially onerous to college instructors with expertise in cognitive areas. A second Piagetian principle is relevant here: Formal operational development produces an egocentrism of its own. A college instructor who has forged an intricate personal intellectual structure may not even *recognize* that students do not share similar interests. If forced to recognize this fact, the instructor is likely to conclude that the students are no longer worth teaching. This can be especially acute in so-called "teacher-education" courses, where students may not be quite as bright, on the average, as majors in the instructor's own discipline.

It is tempting under these conditions to pass the buck to another instructor. But we do well to remind ourselves of this: Do we really want to leave the education of our own children to adults whom we consider to be unworthy of our personal instruction? This is no time to hand over the keys to someone else. Good psychologists must strengthen their connections with public education in order to upgrade it. That means we must be willing (a) to learn what goes on in public education; (b) to figure out how cognitive psychology is relevant; and (c) to show teachers how to apply it. Granted, this may not be the same kind of intellectual stimulation found in an esoteric graduate seminar on one's own research, but it does provide some keen intellectual stimulation—nay, even drama—of its own.

A SPECIAL NOTE TO THE EDUCATIONAL PSYCHOLOGIST

Educational psychologists are usually interested in children, development, instructional design, and other warm, dynamic matters. We tend to be less interested in cold formalism and fine-grained laboratory procedures. It can be disenchanting to discover how much formalism and analytical detail has crept into cognitive psychology.

But this is an unavoidable aspect of the subject matter. Cognitive psychologists are concerned with the way an individual picks up information from the environment, represents it mentally, stores it, attaches it to other information, and reassembles it in new, pertinent, and creative ways. They are concerned with the dynamics of human learning and thinking. They are examining *processes*— the process of solving a problem, the process of recalling a name, the process of formulating an idea.

Because these are complicated issues, they require complicated theories. Simple habit chains will not do. To represent and predict complex mental activity, some cognitive psychologists have resorted to computer simulations. The idea here is a simple one: If you can make a computer draw out the implications of your theory by working through its complex steps then you have actualized a theory of thinking. Your theory is no longer fuzzy and general; it is highly specific. You can point to it. It is the program running the computer.

Not all computer simulations are actually running on machines. Cognitive psychologists will tell you such running is not especially important. The important part is understanding human behavior.

Suppose you wanted to teach an overhead projector to read. It has an "eye," an input device. Assume you have the engineering magic to put any type of reading machinery inside the projector. What do you want that machinery to do? Well, first, you say, it will have to look at a word. What is a word? How do you explain to the projector what a word is? How will the machine know it is looking at a word and not at a spider? How does a child know?

What about direction—do you want the machine to read like an English-speaking child does, from left to right? If so, how does it know where left is? How does a child know?

What about meaning? Where is meaning? Somewhere inside the machine. What form is it in? Lists? Networks of associations? How are you going to put it in there? How does it get into a child? How does it grow?

Dealing with people, we can avoid 99% of these issues. People have very conveniently programmed themselves, from birth, in ways we are only beginning to understand. When we do a psychological experiment—or design a lesson—we capitalize on what is already in the person. We do not confront our own ignorance of how it got there, or of how it might interact with the experiment and the lesson. Dealing with a simulation problem, we cannot avoid such confrontations.

Very few cognitive psychologists are actively concerned with computer simulation, but they are all concerned with the problem of modeling the mind in some way. They may be hypothesizing about stages in a comparison process

(Clark & Chase, 1972), or about the speed of a mental classification (Loftus & Loftus, 1974), or about the number of feature-testing operations in a judgment (Farnham-Diggory & Gregg, 1975). The important commonality among cognitive psychologists is their concern for processing details. No longer can we present a stimulus, measure a response, and ignore what happens in between.

Cognitive psychologists have given educational psychologists new tools for examining the processes of learning and thinking. Of course the job is difficult and often discouraging. But there is no real alternative. We cannot give up on physiology or anatomy or blood chemistry because they are hard. If we do, we will never have a proper science of medicine. We cannot give up on learning and thinking because they are hard. If we do, we will never have a proper science of education.

THE OBJECTIVES OF A COGNITIVE–EDUCATIONAL PSYCHOLOGY

What goes on in public classrooms is information processing of a highly complex order. Scanning a classroom, one sees everything that happens in cognitive laboratories happening all at once: image formation, divided attention, concept attainment, problem solving, verbal rehearsal, coding, free recall, and so forth. None of it is happening systematically, which is to say—none of it is happening in ways that are immediately relevant to the outcome of any particular experiment.

One tends at this point to give way to panic or frustration and to think again about handing over the keys. But the *real* key is one that cognitive psychologists already hold: *techniques for analyzing information processing behavior.* Cognitive psychologists know how to break a task down into stages of processing. Teachers need to learn that skill. Your instructional objective will be to show teachers how to become information-processing task analysts in their own classrooms.

A good way to begin is to have the class throw tasks at you—something remembered from high school or elementary school or kindergarten. This will usually be of a global variety ("I used to hate algebra") giving you the opportunity to make an important point: To talk scientifically, we must be specific. We will need a particular algebra problem, and some description of exactly how a student behaves while attempting to solve it. Go get a protocol, your own or someone else's. Administer a single school task to one person and record every detail of what happens.

That exercise will have a strong impact on most students. For the first time they will confront the enormity of their own ignorance. Here they are planning to be teachers without knowing the first thing about how anybody actually learns *anything,* or about what an individual's problem-solving behavior actually signifies.

If your class is too large, or if you prefer more controlled stimuli, show a film of classroom segments. The University of Indiana has made four useful films: *Keith: A Second Grader, Dick: A Fifth Grader, Greg: An Eighth Grader,* and *Alice: A High School Junior.* These are unnarrated samples of typical classroom days and provide excellent fodder for class discussions.

A third technique is to make your own TV tapes. There are many obvious advantages here: You can arrange a graded series of classroom tasks, get close-ups of eye movements or hand movements, etc., depending upon the issues you want your class to address.

Any method that works will do. The important thing is to get the class involved, with you, in the active process of trying to figure out what a student is actually doing, and how a teacher can help.

CHOICE OF A TASK ANALYSIS STRATEGY

The particular analytical technique that you choose should depend upon your own preference and background. Newell and Simon (1972) have pioneered the whole area of cognitive task analysis, and this latest book of theirs provides both historical overview and detailed examples. Four shorter articles are easier to assimilate: Hunt and Poltrock (1974) provide an analysis of general cognitive methodology, as well as a short course in Newell and Simon; Klahr (1975) explains the rationale behind simulation techniques and summarizes several important programs, including his own; Greeno (1976) has addressed education specifically, showing how three different analytical techniques can be applied to an arithmetic problem, a geometry problem, and a problem in psychophysics, respectively, and Broadbent (1975) has summarized the area for teachers.

In selecting an analytical technique that is most comfortable for your work with your own class, you will need to be concerned with level of detail. You are not going to be interested in units as small as neural impulses, for example. Consider how a teacher views a working student. The student can be observed tc *look at something,* to *copy something,* to *pick up a book,* and so forth. Those are actually very large units as cognitive psychology goes, which is to say that they cannot be understood as precisely as smaller units can be. Nevertheless, large units are the only ones that teachers will find intuitively meaningful.

Your own teaching style will determine whether you present your analytical system didactically, or lead students into it inductively. I prefer an inductive method, as illustrated below. The illustration also shows the simple step-by-step analytical technique that I have found most useful at the introductory level. It is one that teachers can readily adopt.

Instructor: Here we have a simple task, probably intended to stimulate creativity in a young child. The teacher draws a circle on the blackboard, and then says to a child, "Betty, what could you add to that, to make something? Here's the chalk. You come up here and add anything you want, and then tell us what you made." Betty rushes up, draws a little circle at the top of the big one, and then draws inside the little circle a curved line (mouth), and two circles (eyes) and says happily, "I made Frosty the Snowman!" What has happened here? What did Betty have to do, inside her head, to produce that sequence of behavior?

Student: Well, she had to remember about Frosty.

Instructor: Was that the first thing she did?

Student: No, I guess the first thing was holding the chalk.

Instructor: What had to happen even before that? What was the very first thing that had to happen?

Student: . . . Look at the blackboard?

Instructor: OK—what had to be perceived first?

Student: The circle.

Instructor: What else had to be perceived?

Student: The chalk, the blackboard.

Instructor: That information all came in through the eyes. Anything through the ears?

Student: The instructions—what the teacher said.

Instructor: So let's start with that. (Writes on blackboard:)

      Step 1. See the blackboard, circle, chalk.

      Step 2. Hear the instructions.

      Then what happens?

Student: Well, then there's the problem of understanding what the teacher wants you to do.

Instructor: OK, let's think about the instruction. What could you add to that, to make something? Here's the chalk . . . .

Student: The kid has to understand she's supposed to add something by drawing it, not by sticking it on the blackboard with scotch tape.

Instructor: So Step 3 might be:

      Step 3. Plan to draw on blackboard.

      How does that plan get put together? What goes into it?

Student: That's where remembering Frosty comes in.

Instructor: Do you think she thought of Frosty immediately? Did the circle make you think of Frosty the Snowman?

Student: No, I thought of a lamp.

Instructor: What do you suppose made Betty think of Frosty?

Student: It might have been near Christmas, or maybe it was snowing.

Instructor: So, maybe there's something like a search subroutine: What's around in my world that a circle reminds me of? Maybe you think of something right away, maybe you don't. We could represent that in this way:

    Step 4. Does the circle remind me of something?

        If not, keep thinking.

        If it does, use that to guide a plan.

    What else has to go into the plan?

Student: All those details, what Frosty looks like.

Instructor: So Step 5 is: Recall visual details.

    What else? What about motor skills?

Student: She has to remember how to draw things.

Instructor: Step 6: Recall drawing subroutines.

    Do we have everything? The last step would then be:

    Step 7. Activate plan.

Once the little program is on the blackboard (see Table 6.1) two issues can be discussed: (*a*) individual differences; and (*b*) preteaching.

Individual Differences

In the case of this particular exercise, how might boys differ from girls? The class will bring up differences in experiences, which can lead the instructor to suggest that Step 4 could be an individual difference repository. Circles may remind little boys (and big boys) of things that girls seldom think of. Age differences could also affect Step 4. There are also individual differences in visual imagery (Step 5) and in motor skills (Step 6). More broadly, there are differences in the speed at which ideas can be retrieved from memory (Hunt, Frost, & Lunneborg, 1973), in the efficiency of formulating plans (Miller, Galanter, & Pribram, 1960), and in willingness to perform publicly (Zajonc,

TABLE 6.1

Informal Simulation of a Drawing Task

Step 1	See the blackboard, circle, chalk
Step 2	Hear the instructions
Step 3	Plan to draw on blackboard
Step 4	Does the circle remind me of something?
	If not, keep thinking
	If it does, use that to guide a plan
Step 5	Recall visual details
Step 6	Recall drawing subroutines
Step 7	Activate plan

1965). At this point, particulars do not matter. The objective is to show the class that differences among children are not vague and global, but have specific sources and mechanisms which a teacher can understand and anticipate systematically.

Preteaching Particular Steps

A so-called "creativity" task is a good lead into this issue: What should a child be taught in advance? Should he be taught to draw on a blackboard? There can be little doubt about that. What about practice in recalling visual details? A child who has had art training might appear to be more creative because of his special training. Is it advisable to give all children such training? The class will probably decide yes, and will be troubled to realize that training in general cognitive skills—visualizing, recalling, and the like—is almost totally omitted from public schooling. I like to make the point here that art classes are not frills from this standpoint, but should comprise a large segment (at least 25% in my judgment) of every child's required schooling.

FORMULATING A GENERAL MODEL

After your system of task analysis has been applied to four or five different tasks, students begin to pick up commonalities. Something must always be perceived. Some language is always involved. Some motor skills or functional concepts are always involved. The person performing the task must always assemble perceptions, words, and actions into an organized sequence of activities—which we can represent in the form of little programs like the one in Table 6.1. A program may include subroutines—like the subroutine of holding a piece of chalk. It may also be influenced by strategies and rules of various kinds, including, for example, the rules of reading from left to right, or the rules of English syntax. And there are many common operations: classification, testing, recalling, noticing, keeping track, and so forth.

Having reached this point, it can be useful to provide your class with some kind of schematization. The one I use is shown in Figure 6.1.

This is a good time to launch into some lectures on basic material. Students are now aware of how much they need to know, and how the information is relevant.

CHOICE OF CONTENT

The field of cognitive psychology is large and diverse. Almost every experimental psychologist is now studying some form of information processing in

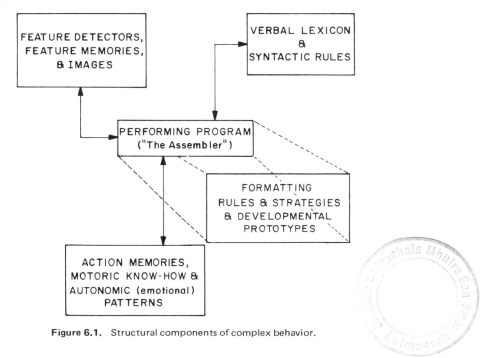

Figure 6.1. Structural components of complex behavior.

animals or humans. Of course you will not be able to transmit more than a small portion of the cognitive field to your students. Which portions you choose will depend upon the needs of your class, as well as upon your own preferences. For example, if most of your students are going into elementary teaching, you will want to emphasize the developmental cognitive literature. If your class can be subdivided into history teachers, English teachers, mathematics teachers, etc., you may want to give different assignments to each group. I like my class to be sufficiently conversant with modern research to appreciate new reports which appear in the popular media—on, for example, the cognitive consequences of malnutrition. In preparing my lectures I have drawn on the following sources, among others.

Perception and Perceptual Development

This field has changed considerably since Vernon's *Psychology of Perception,* which is still in print (Vernon, 1966) and is still a good introduction to traditional perceptual psychology. Nowadays, however, the emphasis is upon the intake of information, the active seeking out of important features in the environment. The book *The Senses Considered as Perceptual Systems* by J. J. Gibson (1966) is a provocative survey of active, searching perceivers of many species. This book does much to get us out of the impoverished environment of perceptual laboratories, and will awaken you and your students to the perceptual riches of the classroom world.

Eleanor Gibson's (1969) *Principles of Perceptual Learning and Development* provides expert coverage of laboratory research and elucidates her own theory of perceptual growth. Fortunately for educators, her theory includes extensive study of the reading process. She and her colleagues at Cornell have drawn many prominent cognitive psychologists into the study of reading (Gibson, 1965, 1972). The books by Neisser (1967) and by Reed (1973) also provide extensive coverage of modern perceptual research and theorizing from the cognitive point of view. From a more physiological viewpoint, good basic coverage can be found in the portions of the Lindsay and Norman (1977) text that are devoted to sensation and perception, Haber and Hershenson (1973), and Forgus and Melamed (1976).

Functional Knowledge

Superficially, the development of motor skills and functional knowledge may not appear to have much to do with cognition. But cognition must begin where the infant begins, with the ability to perceive things and to do things, but without the ability to talk. We must represent much of our world enactively, to use Bruner's (1964, 1966) term. All students of mental development (e.g., Piaget & Inhelder, 1969; Werner, 1961) have emphasized the motoric basis of intellectual growth. Hence, we must provide students with some information about bodily growth, the development of skills, and what it can all mean cognitively.

There is still not much systematic work in this area, compared to the areas of perception and language. We do know a lot about physical development, and Tanner is by all odds the best source. His small book *Education and Physical Growth* (1970) was written for teachers and should be read and owned by all of them, in my opinion. If that is not possible in your class, lecture from it as extensively as you can, and show the figures on transparencies. Two other good Tanner sources, for your own information, are *Growth at Adolescence* (Tanner, 1961) and an article called "Human Growth and Constitution" (Tanner, 1964). Tanner's own awareness of the relationship between physical growth and cognitive growth is indicated by the fact that he has edited four volumes with Inhelder on child development (Tanner & Inhelder, 1956–1960).

The field of motor skill development, popular in the early days of psychology, is now coming back into fashion. The best introduction to the current state of the art can be found in Pew's tutorial (Pew, 1974). Generally, as Schmidt put it, "Motor behaviorists have begun to ask questions about the kinds of processes occurring as the individual performs and learns the motor response. The tasks used have tended to shift from those that could only be scored with global measures to those that enabled the isolation of various processes and strategies and provided information about contributions of various subsystems (Schmidt, 1975, p. 225)." An article by Posner and Keele (1972), "Skill Learning" was written especially for teachers, and is a good one to assign your class. Legge (1970) has put together a useful collection of the older literature, and Bilodeau's (1966) collection is also still a good one. Keeping up with current literature is expedited by the *Journal of Motor Behavior*, a new journal that contains many articles of interest to (and written by) cognitive psychologists.

An extremely valuable set of papers and discussions on motor skill development has been edited by Connolly (1970), *Mechanisms of Motor Skill Development*. A paper of his own which illustrates the fine detail now characterizing modern studies is called "The Evolution and Ontogeny of Hand Function" (Connolly & Elliott, 1972). But there is great need for more work on motor development in children.

Language and Meaning

This field is changing rapidly, and the most up-to-date general text is the one by Herbert and Eve Clark (1977). Paperbacks by Slobin (1971) and Dale (1972) provide briefer summaries of concepts governing current psycholinguistic research. Educators have welcomed the new admission by psycholinguists that language does not exist in a syntactical vacuum. Now the question is being asked: What is the real-world context of child language? (A scant 10 years ago, that question was never considered.) Several monographs have attempted to answer the question. The seminal one is by Bloom (1970). She added context to her notes on the language development of a child and showed how the underlying grammar of two identical phrases could thereby differ. A monograph by Clark (1973) on how children generalize the meaning of words is also valuable, as is one by Nelson (1973) on the first 50-word vocabularies of 18 children. These three monographs, plus an article by Macnamara (1972), should bring you up to where developmental psycholinguistics is today.

Factors affecting language comprehension in adults are being studied with great precision. A review of their own work, and its implications for education, by Carpenter and Just (1976), illustrates current research methods and findings. A broader review is included in the Clarks' new text (Clark & Clark, 1977). Whereas early theorizing about language comprehension focused on sentences, current work is focusing on paragraphs and even entire stories. A collation of reports from pacesetters in the area can be found in the 1976 Carnegie-Mellon symposium, published under the title *Cognitive Processes in Comprehension,* and edited by Carpenter and Just (1977). This work has extensive implications for the study of reading, as well as for the study of language and language development.

You should be aware also of the new work in semantic networks. This has grown out of efforts to build computerized systems of comprehension. How can we teach a computer to understand questions the way people do? This is not a simple matter of typing information into a computer and then having the machine search the information for key words. That is trivial. People make delicate and extensive contextual adjustments which are not well understood. Norman (1973) provides an excellent summary of the problem, and a new set of papers from his laboratory shows the kind of work that is being done on it (Norman & Rumelhart, 1975). Another useful article is one by Collins and Quillian (1972), and you should also know about the contributions of Schank (1975), Winograd (1973), and Kintsch (1974).

Mental Organization

This heading refers to the middle portions of Figure 6.1, the working memory or "assembler," backed up by its kit of strategies, rules, and prototypes. Here, one gets into traditional cognitive areas of study: problem solving, concept learning, classification, attention, and memory. But nowadays, one must keep in mind that all these functions are thought about as interrelated. Hunt's (1971) article "What Kind of a Computer Is Man?" helps provide a general framework. Cotton (1975) reflects a similar point of view in an analysis of college teaching.

For general background, you should be familiar with three or four basic texts in the area, such as Lindsay and Norman (1977), Posner (1973), Massaro (1975), and Farnham-Diggory (1972). There are also several collections that should be included in your library: Gregg (1974), Chase (1973), Klahr (1976), Resnick (1976), and Kantowitz (1975). These books will provide a basic framework. To provide the framework with current information, you should regularly peruse such journals as *Cognitive Psychology, Memory & Cognition, Perception & Psychophysics,* and relevant sections of the *Journal of Experimental Psychology.*

From the developmental standpoint, your first obligation will be to get a firm grip on Piaget. *The Psychology of the Child* (Piaget & Inhelder, 1969) provides the best introduction in the originators' own words. I am not partial to any of the volumes by other authors that purport to make Piaget easy for the general reader, or for teachers. They all contain confusions and distortions of one sort or another. Piaget himself is not that hard to read once you get adjusted to his philosophical style and make allowances for some stultified translations. *The Child and Reality* (Piaget, 1973), and *Six Psychological Studies* (Piaget, 1967) provide helpful redundancy and amplification. You should be sufficiently familiar with the range of Piagetian books to be able to recommend them selectively. For example, students who plan to teach physics would enjoy *The Child's Conception of Movement and Speed* (1971).

To my knowledge, the only general textbook devoted to developmental cognition is the forthcoming one edited by Hamilton and Vernon (1977), *The Development of Cognitive Processes.* This multiply authored book should prove invaluable. Helpful symposia in this area include three classics published by the Society for Research in Child Development: *Thought in the Young Child* (Kessen & Kuhlman, 1962); *Basic Cognitive Processes in Children* (Wright & Kagan, 1963); and *European Research in Cognitive Development* (Mussen, 1965). Some of this material is dated, but it nevertheless forms an important historical link with present-day research. More recent symposia include those edited by Farnham-Diggory (1972) and Falmagne (1976). There are several specialized monographs that provide background on children's cognition: The one by Olson (1970) on the child's acquisition of the concept of diagonality is broader in scope than it sounds. So is Bryant's (1974) short book on perception and understanding in children. A difficult but important information-processing treatment of cognitive development has been authored by Klahr and Wallace (1976).

Developmental work in cognitive areas appears most often in the journals *Child Development, Journal of Experimental Child Psychology,* and *Developmental Psychology.* But developmental research appears in the "adult" journals as well, since many cognitive psychologists have become concerned with the origin and growth of the mental functions they have been studying in adults.

Reading and Mathematical Thinking

A few comments should be made here about the entry of cognitive researchers into these areas. The symposium *Language by Ear and by Eye* (Kavanagh & Mattingly, 1972) provides useful summaries of the nature and extent of this new type of educational research. It is very different from the type of research summarized by Chall (1967), so different, in fact, that the National Institute of Education has given top priority to the problem of disseminating basic research. Many educational researchers simply do not know about the new cognitive research—and do not have the background to understand it in any case. Preparing researchers and teachers to understand cognitive research on reading and mathematical thinking is therefore a vital responsibility of cognitive—educational psychology. The preparation can most conveniently follow lectures on attention and memory, since reading and calculating are special cases of those more general phenomena.

The Kavanagh and Mattingly (1972) collection just mentioned is the place to begin your study of current work on reading. Short books by Smith (1971, 1975) and Sticht (1974) are also important. Both these authors provide summaries of relevant research and theory, as well as presenting their own points of view. All four volumes contain ample bibliographies. From then on, you will need to use the current literature as a resource. Articles that illustrate current research trends are those by Farnham-Diggory and Gregg (1975), Farnham-Diggory and Simon (1975), LaBerge and Samuels (1974), Loftus and Loftus (1974), and Kintsch and Keenan (1973). By far the most comprehensive collation of new reading research will be published in three volumes, under the editorship of Lauren Resnick (forthcoming). It is tentatively entitled *Theory and Practice of Reading Instruction,* and should be available early in 1978, from Erlbaum Associates.

Modern cognitive research on reading is concerned with high-speed mental processing (decoding), and with slower-speed comprehension processes that occur in language generally. It is now felt that understanding reading is almost as complex as understanding the whole of the human mind. A comprehensive theory of reading must specify exactly how perception works during the reading process, exactly what language operations are involved, exactly what sort of functional knowledge is relevant, how memory is activated, what strategies govern the reading program, and how all this changes as a function of the type of reading task under investigation (Gregg & Farnham-Diggory, 1978). Most traditional reading research (Chall, 1967) refers to such processes only vaguely. The tools of cognitive psychology are making exact specification possible. This means we can move toward the diagnosis and treatment of reading disability as if it were an engineering problem—just as astigmatism is an engineering problem. The new cognitive research on reading is giving us the precise numbers necessary for the invention of instructional "corrective lenses." These inventions will be very different from current methods of reading instruction and will make arguments over "whole word," "phonic," and "language-experience" methods obsolete. Those are types of arguments that arise, almost superstitiously, in the absence of hard knowledge. The trouble with hard knowledge, of course, is that it is difficult to understand. It may not be easy for some teachers to understand the new cognitive research on reading, but it is extremely important for them to try.

Mathematical thinking involves imagery to a greater extent than reading does. *Mental Imagery in the Child* (Piaget & Inhelder, 1971) is important background here, along with *The Child's Conception of . . . Geometry* (Piaget, Inhelder, & Szeminska, 1964) . . . *Space* (Piaget & Inhelder, 1967) and . . . *Number* (Piaget, 1952). Two studies of adults are also especially instructive: a paper by Cooper and Shepard (1973) on the rotation of mental images, and the one by Hayes (1973) in the same volume entitled, "On the Function of Visual Imagery in Elementary Mathematics."

Other important papers on quantitative development are Gelman's (1972b) review (and you should pay special attention to her research—e.g., Gelman, 1972a; Gelman & Tucker, 1975); a theoretical analysis by Schaeffer, Eggleston, and Scott (1974); a historically important early monograph (Morrisett & Vinsonhaler, 1965); and a paper by Klahr and Wallace (1973).

As in the case of reading research, the new cognitive research on mathematical reasoning is concerned with high-speed mental processing, and with lawful stages in acquisition and performance (Groen & Parkman, 1972). New pedagogy will doubtless emerge, but it is not yet clear what form it will take or how it may differ from traditional pedagogy. One important consideration here involves the incorporation of computers and calculators into mathematics instruction. This may bring the technology of cognitive research directly into the classroom.

Teacher-Application of Basic Cognitive Content

Once you have completed some basic lectures, your teachers should begin relating the information to their own experience and classroom problems. How you arrange this will depend primarily on class size and student level. Small graduate classes should develop a piece of curriculum, justify it theoretically (including extensive task analysis), try it out, and report back on what happens. Throughout, you will need to help your students find the connections between what they are doing and the basic lecture or text material. Teachers tend to switch into seat-of-the-pants mode as soon as they are released from academic mode. They must practice using the principles they have learned, and this is largely a matter of being helped to recognize the real-world form of the principles.

If you are dealing with large undergraduate classes, some kind of workbook or project specifications should move students through a set of experiences that do not need your immediate supervision. Again, however, there must be monitoring (through brief, written assignments, for example) of the requirement that students integrate academic material with real-world experience.

SOME GENERAL ISSUES

In the remainder of this chapter, we will consider some of the issues that educational psychology has traditionally addressed: learning theory, individual differences, and classroom research. Cognitive psychology will be markedly transforming these traditional areas over the next decade. The following discussion is intended to help prepare you for the transformation.

Cognitive Psychology versus Traditional Learning Theory

By traditional learning theory I mean the theories of Hull, Spence, Guthrie, Pavlov, Skinner, and their descendants. These theories were based on the general assumption that a stimulus goes in, a response comes out, and what happens in between is summarized by a hyphen. For several decades, American psychological research reflected this theoretical philosophy. The result, as might be predicted, was a proliferation of methodological techniques for controlling stimuli and for measuring responses, but no new information about the hyphen. It is important to understand that all this resulted in little new theoretical information about human cognition.

The whole point about the nature of a response and the precision of its measurement is what it tells us—not about the nature of the stimulus and the precision of *its* measurements—but about the processes in between: the activities in the head of the behaving organism. With the emergence of cognitive psychology in the 1960s, S—R technology was finally applied to the problem of understanding the hyphen. Now, instead of a hyphen, we have mental structures and processes that are gradually being integrated theoretically into a general model of the mind.

Here is a recent example of how S—R technology is being used to reveal mental structures. Trabasso and his colleagues have been studying seriation processes (Trabasso, 1975; Trabasso, Riley, & Wilson, 1975). As children pick up information about relative length, for example, do they interrelate that information mentally? If they do, Trabasso reasoned, then their knowledge of the middle parts of the series should be acquired more slowly than their knowledge of end points. That outcome could be predicted on the basis of the serial position effect, one of those technological phenomena that S—R psychology has learned so much about.

Trabasso taught children a length series, using sticks. The children learned through paired-comparisons, two sticks at a time, until the entire series had been mastered. To test their knowledge, Trabasso asked the children transitivity questions. If Stick B was known to be longer than Stick A, and Stick C was known to be longer than Stick B, then was Stick C longer than Stick A? Trabasso found that children answered questions about the very shortest sticks and about the very longest sticks quite accurately, but they had difficulty with sticks in the middle of the series. They had originally learned those individual comparisons to a higher criterion, two-by-two. But once they had constructed a mental representation of the series as a whole, knowledge of the middle sticks showed a vagueness characteristic of the middle elements of any series. Children were not sure if Stick M was longer than Stick K or not. This result revealed that children had put their paired-associates together into a single structure and were responding to transitivity questions by accessing that structure, not by recalling each pair as a separately learned unit.

Mental structuring is what educators need to know about. It is of far less importance to know that given a list of spelling words, the ones in the middle may be learned less well than the ones on either end. The technology of traditional learning theory is only trivially applicable to education. The way Trabasso taught his young subjects about the length of sticks is not important educationally; any experienced teacher could probably have done it more efficiently; nor is the way Trabasso framed his transitivity questions important educationally. What is important educationally is the fact that children construct organized representations of material they have learned piecemeal.

The attempts of educators to use S–R learning technology as a prescription for teaching has reduced education to small, trivial, pseudoscientific pursuits. One summary of that sad fact may be found in a report from the Office of Economic Opportunity (OEO).[1] This is a summary of a national evaluation of instructional subcontracting. For a while, it seemed as if agencies, such the Westinghouse Learning Corporation, could do a better job of teaching reading than schools could—for a variety of reasons, including the fact that their livelihoods could be made to depend upon it. A subcontractor earned, say, $800 per pupil, *provided* that the pupil showed reading improvement. Five subcontractors labored for many months, and the overall result was unequivocal: Their pupils ended up further behind than ever. Class after class, city after city, subcontractor after subcontractor, no pupil learned how to read any better than students in ordinary classrooms, and in many cases not as well.

Although this OEO report was considered an indictment of subcontracting, it is more properly an indictment of the reading methods chosen. Most were Skinnerian in tone, because that type of step-by-step drill is technologically precise. But, again, it is trivial to apply the technology of traditional learning theory to education. Results will probably be worse than the results of old-fashioned teaching. Why should this be so? Traditional learning technology depends upon the systematic impoverishment of natural learning environments. A Skinnerian environment is essentially a deprived environment. The human organism has been evolved to cope with a rich diversity of stimuli. We have the capacity to sample from a stimulus flux, and to put those bits of information together purposefully. We *make something of* the welter of information that surrounds us. It is our ability to organize diversity that needs to be educated.

Cognitive Psychology versus Mental Testing

Consistent with S–R behaviorism is the assessment philosophy that "Intelligence is what intelligence tests measure." An empirically based IQ test can be

[1] OEO Pamphlet 3400-5, published in February, 1972. See also the Research report published by Battelle Memorial Institute, Columbus Laboratories, entitled "Interim Report on the Office of Economic Opportunity Experiment in Educational Performance Contracting." For information, write to: National Technical Information Service, U. S. Department of Commerce, Springfield, Virginia 22152.

composed of any items that separate smart people from not-so-smart people on some other measure. It has not been necessary to have a theory of intelligence for the tests themselves to have practical utility. But with the emergence of cognitive psychology, more theoretical sophistication can be anticipated (Resnick, 1976).

A forerunner in certain respects has been the Illinois Test of Psycholinguistic Abilities, but the theory behind it is a conglomeration of S–R notions that bears little direct relationship to test items. Modern cognitive theorizing is reflected in a study by Earl Hunt and his collaborators (Hunt, Lunneborg, & Lewis, 1975) entitled "What Does It Mean to Be High Verbal?"

Hunt took as his starting point a model similar to the schematization shown in Figure 6.1. Information is picked up by some kind of perceiving system and makes contact with long-term memory (verbal and functional stores) by means of a working memory that organizes all mental activity. Material in working memory must be ordered, make contact speedily with long-term stores, be rapidly manipulated, and efficiently integrated. Hunt and his colleagues conducted tests of these basic information processing abilities by utilizing well-known paradigms—including those of Posner, Boies, Eichelman, and Taylor (1969); Wickens (1970); Peterson and Peterson (1959); Sperling (1960); Sternberg (1966); Clark and Chase (1972); and Trabasso, Rollins, and Shaughnessey (1971)—plus some variants of their own. These tests were administered to college students who had been previously given a standard psychometric test of verbal ability. Hunt found that information processing skills were strong related, positively, to verbal ability. The processes involved in answering verbal test questions were apparently the same basic processes measured in Hunt's laboratory.

In another study, Hunt (1974) addressed the question of the strategies that an individual might use in answering a test question. In this case, the test was Raven's Matrices. Hunt demonstrated that two algorithms could solve the Matrices. One, a *Gestalt algorithm*, applied physically defined transformations to a figure (a whole). The other, an *analytic algorithm*, did not begin with a holistic figure, but with an ordered set of features. The Gestalt algorithm tested a matrix by asking, for example, if the pattern could be continued visually by the insertion of a particular answer item. There were other tests, and they all operated on something like a visual image, or iconic representation, of the matrix as a whole.

As noted earlier, the analytic algorithm operated on sets of features. The algorithm first noticed features of a matrix, represented them as an ordered collection, and then applied transformation rules to that collection. This algorithm included tests for the presence of an element in a row, and operations for the production of symmetries and complementarities.

The Matrices can be solved by either type of strategy, a fact which does not fit comfortably into the psychometric literature. As Hunt pointed out: "Nothing in the psychometric literature leads one to believe that identical general factor scores should be associated with qualitatively different styles of cognition . . . . What we require are diagnostic tests which tell us a person's cognitive style in intellectual operations, rather than an index of the person's location in a static Euclidean model of mental power [Hunt, 1974, pp. 154–155]." The title of his paper, it might be noted, is "Quote the Raven? Nevermore!"

This line of research is leading the student of individual differences away from reliance upon test outcomes, and toward the analysis of mental dynamics. What are the processes involved in answering a test question? Are the same processes involved in school learning? Surely the answer is yes. Assessment of cognitive skills will make possible not just the prediction of potential success or failure in some gross' sense, but a diagnosis of what is wrong, and what kinds of school tasks will be affected. As an analogy: If you know an individual has an allergy to butter, you will be able to predict his reaction to a wide variety of foods, and to prescribe effective substitutes—*before* he has an attack.

Cognitive Psychology versus Traditional Educational Research

The first two articles in the December issue of the *Journal of Educational Psychology* (Vol. 67, No. 6, 1975) illustrate the current state of transition from traditional to cognitive–educational research. The first report, by Cronbach and Webb (1975) is a reanalysis of an early study by Anderson (1941) on the effects of two kinds of instruction upon arithmetic achievement. One type of instruction emphasized drill, while the other emphasized comprehension of basic principles—a so-called meaning method. The instructional modes were determined by asking teachers to fill out questionnaires. About 350 fourth graders were given achievement tests of various kinds. On the basis of his statistical analysis, Anderson concluded that the drill method was more successful with low-ability students, while the meaning method was preferable for high-ability students, an illustration of the elusive Aptitude X Treatment interaction (Cronbach & Snow, 1969; Bracht, 1970).

The Cronbach and Webb paper is largely concerned with the application of more sophisticated statistical logic and techniques to Anderson's data. Additional cases were salvaged, the original sample size was increased to 430, and on the basis of the reanalysis Anderson's interaction effect disappeared. It turned out to be an artifact.

Immediately following the Cronbach and Webb report is a paper by Mayer (1975), on methods of instructing adults in computer programming. Mayer contrasted a system of instruction which drew upon familiar concepts from the wider world (e.g., "scoreboards," "ticket windows," "shopping lists," etc.) with a system which was restricted to the world of programming. Students studied a carefully constructed set of booklets which reflected these instructional differences. Achievement was closely differentiated. Students were tested on their ability to write programs, and to read (interpret) programs, at three levels of complexity. Mayer performed three experiments testing the effects of such variables as feedback and practice on both immediate acquisition and transfer. His conclusions were that instruction emphasizing real-world analogies will produce students who are good at interpreting new material, while instruction emphasizing technical rules will produce students who are good at generating new programs. There was a marginal Aptitude × Treatment interaction: Real-world analogies were somewhat more useful to low-ability students than to high-ability students—possibly, Mayer thought, because the high-ability students were capable of constructing analogies of their own. (That notion should, of course, be tested.) Mayer's major theoretical point was that students acquire mental structures in the course of learning, not merely information (Greeno, 1976; Mayer & Greeno, 1972).

The two papers—Cronbach and Webb on the one hand, and Mayer on the other—can be contrasted on several issues. Mayer used 176 subjects; Anderson used well over 400. Mayer performed a series of small experiments, chipping away at a problem; Anderson performed one giant experiment that left him with largely uninterpretable data. Cronbach and Webb imply that an even larger study would have been interpretable, but how could that be, when no one really knew what the independent variables were, nor what processes were involved in responding to the achievement tests? Mayer had control of both independent and dependent variables, and was fleshing out a model of cognitive structures. Anderson attempted to substitute statistical complexity for experimental control, and had no model of the contrasting mental states that drill pedagogy or meaning pedagogy would have been likely to produce.

The differences between these two studies illustrate what is happening to educational research. Now that experimental psychology has evolved from mindless behaviorism to cognitive science, it is capable of tackling educational issues (Farnham-Diggory, 1976). Large, statistically cumbersome classroom comparisons are no longer the only available mode for the study of schooling. We now have an experimental psychology of instruction which is largely cognitive in nature. It is a psychology predicated upon models of the human mind and factors that favor its development (Glaser & Resnick, 1972; Klahr, 1976).

ACKNOWLEDGMENTS

I am very grateful to John Cotton, James Greeno, and David Klahr for critical commentary and for suggested references.

REFERENCES

Anderson, G. L. *A comparison of the outcomes of instruction under two theories of learning.* Unpublished doctoral dissertation, University of Minnesota, 1941.

Bilodeau, E. A. (Ed.). *Principles of skill acquisition.* New York: Academic Press, 1966.

Bloom, L. M. *Language development: Form and function in emerging grammars.* Cambridge: M.I.T. Press, 1970.

Bracht, G. H. Experimental factors related to aptitude–treatment interactions. *Review of Educational Research,* 1970, *40,* 627–645.

Broadbent, D. E. Cognitive psychology and education. *British Journal of Educational Psychology,* 1975, *45,* 162–176.

Bruner, J. S. The course of cognitive growth. *American Psychologist,* 1964, *19,* 1–16.

Bruner, J. S. On cognitive growth. In J. S. Bruner, R. Olver, & P. Greenfield (Eds.), *Studies in cognitive growth.* New York: Wiley, 1966.

Bruner, J. S. Organization of early skilled action. *Child Development,* 1973, *44,* 1–11.

Bryant, P. *Perception and understanding in young children: An experimental approach.* New York: Basic Books, 1974.

Carpenter, P., & Just, M. Verbal comprehension in instructional situations. In D. Klahr (Ed.), *Cognition and instruction.* Hillsdale, New Jersey: Erlbaum, 1976.

Carpenter, P., & Just, M. *Cognitive processes in comprehension.* Hillsdale, New Jersey: Erlbaum, 1977.

Chall, J. S. *Learning to read: The great debate.* New York: McGraw-Hill, 1967.

Chase, W. G. (Ed.). *Visual information processing.* New York: Academic Press, 1973.

Clark, E. V. What's in a word? On the child's acquisition of semantics in his first language. In T. E. Moore (Ed.), *Cognitive development and the acquisition of language.* New York: Academic Press, 1973.

Clark, H. H., & Chase, W. G. On the process of comparing sentences against pictures. *Cognitive Psychology,* 1972, *3,* 472–517.

Clark, H. H., & Clark, E. V. *Psychology and language: An introduction to psycholinguistics.* New York: Harcourt Brace Jovanovich, 1977.

Collins, A. M., & Quillian, M. R. Experiments on semantic memory and language comprehension. In L. W. Gregg (Ed.), *Cognition in learning and memory.* New York: Wiley, 1972.

Connolly, K. (Ed.). *Mechanisms of motor skill development.* London: Academic Press, 1970.

Connolly, K., & Elliott, J. The evolution and ontogeny of hand function. In N. Blurton Jones (Ed.), *Ethological studies of child behavior.* Cambridge University Press, 1972.

Cooper, L. A., & Shepard, R. N. Chronometric studies of the rotation of mental images. In W. G. Chase (Ed.), *Visual information processing.* New York: Academic Press, 1973.

Cotton, J. W. Theoretical perspectives for research on college teaching: A cognitive viewpoint. *Instructional Science,* 1975, *4,* 59–98.

Cronbach, L. J., & Snow, R. E. Individual differences in learning ability as a function of instructional variables. Final Report, School of Education, Stanford University Contract No. OEC 4-6-061269-1217, U. S. Office of Education, 1969.

Cronbach, L. J., & Webb, N. Between-class and within-class effects in a reported aptitude X treatment interaction: Reanalysis of a study by G. L. Anderson. *Journal of Educational Psychology,* 1975, *67,* 717–724.

Dale, P. S. *Language development: Structure and function.* Hinsdale, Illinois: Dryden Press, 1972.

Falmagne, R. (Ed.) *Reasoning: Representation and process.* Hillsdale, New Jersey: Erlbaum, 1975.

Farnham-Diggory, S. *Cognitive processes in education.* New York: Harper & Row, 1972.

Farnham-Diggory, S., & Gregg, L. W. Color, form, and function as dimensions of natural classification: developmental changes in eye movements, reaction time, and response strategies. *Child Development,* 1975, *46,* 101–114.

Farnham-Diggory, S. Toward a theory of instructional growth. In D. Klahr (Ed.), *Cognition and instruction.* Hillsdale, New Jersey: Erlbaum, 1976.

Farnham-Diggory, S., & Gregg, L. W. Short term memory function in young readers. *Journal of Experimental Child Psychology,* 1975, *19,* 279–298.

Farnham-Diggory, S., & Simon, H. A. Retention of visually presented information in children's spelling. *Memory & Cognition,* 1975, *3,* 599–608.

Forgus, R. II., & Melamed, L. E. *Perception: A cognitive stage approach.* New York: McGraw-Hill, 1976.

Gelman, R. Logical capacity of very young children. *Child Development,* 1972, *43,* 75–90. (a)

Gelman, R. The nature and development of early number concepts. In H. W. Reese (Ed.), *Advances in child development and behavior,* Vol. 7. New York: Academic Press, 1972. (b)

Gelman, R., & Tucker, M. F. Further investigations of the young child's conception of number. *Child Development,* 1975, *46,* 167–175.

Gibson, E. Learning to read. *Science,* 1965, *148,* 1066–1072.

Gibson, E. *Principles of perceptual learning and development.* New York: Appleton-Century-Crofts, 1969.

Gibson, E. Reading for some purpose. In J. F. Kavanagh & I. G. Mattingly (Eds.), *Language by ear and by eye.* Cambridge, Massachusetts: M.I.T. Press, 1972.

Gibson, J. J. *The senses considered as perceptual systems.* Boston: Houghton Mifflin, 1966.

Glaser, R., & Resnick, L. B. Instructional psychology. In P. H. Mussen & M. R. Rosenzweig (Eds.), *Annual Review of Psychology,* Vol. 23. Palo Alto: Annual Reviews, 1972.

Gregg, L. W. (Ed.). *Knowledge and cognition.* Hillsdale: Erlbaum, 1974.

Gregg, L. W., & Farnham-Diggory, S. How to study reading: an information processing analysis. In L. Resnick (Ed.), *Theory and practice of reading instruction.* Hillsdale, New Jersey: Erlbaum, forthcoming.

Greeno, J. Cognitive objectives of instruction: Theory of knowledge for solving problems and answering questions. In D. Klahr (Ed.), *Cognition and instruction.* Hillsdale, New Jersey: Erlbaum, 1976.

Groen, G. J., & Parkman, J. M. A chronometric analysis of simple addition. *Psychological Review,* 1972, *79,* 329–343.

Haber, R. N., & Hershenson, M. *The psychology of visual perception.* New York: Holt, Rinehart & Winston, 1973.

Hamilton, V., & Vernon, M. D. (Eds.). *The development of cognitive processes.* London: Academic Press, 1977.

Hayes, J. R. On the function of visual imagery in elementary mathematics. In W. G. Chase (Ed.), *Visual information processing.* New York: Academic Press, 1973.

Hunt, E. What kind of computer is man? *Cognitive Psychology,* 1971, *2,* 57–98.

Hunt, E. Quote the Raven? Nevermore! In L. Gregg (Ed.), *Knowledge and cognition.* Hillsdale, New Jersey: Erlbaum, 1974.

Hunt, E., Frost, N., & Lunneborg, C. Individual differences in cognition. In G. Bower (Ed.), *Advances in learning and motivation,* Vol. 7. New York: Academic Press, 1973.

Hunt, E., Lunneborg, C., & Lewis, J. What does it mean to be high verbal? *Cognitive Psychology,* 1975, *7,* 194–227.

Hunt, E., & Poltrock, S. The mechanics of thought. In B. Kantowitz (Ed.), *Human information processing: Tutorials in performance in cognition.* Hillsdale, New Jersey: Erlbaum, 1975.

Kantowitz, B. H. (Ed.). *Human information processing: Tutorials in performance and cognition.* Hillsdale, New Jersey: Erlbaum, 1975.

Kavanagh, J. F., & Mattingly, I. G. (Eds.) *Language by ear and by eye.* Cambridge: M.I.T. Press, 1972.

Kessen, W., & Kuhlman, C. (Eds.). Thought in the young child. *Monographs of the Society for Research in Child Development,* Serial No. 83, 1962.

Kintsch, W. *The representation of meaning in memory.* Hillsdale, New Jersey: Erlbaum, 1974.

Kintsch, W., & Keenan, J. Reading rate and retention as a function of the number of propositions in the base structure of sentences. *Cognitive Psychology,* 1973, *5,* 257–274.

Klahr, D. Steps toward the simulation of intellectual development. In L. B. Resnick (Ed.), *The nature of intelligence.* Hillsdale, New Jersey: Erlbaum, 1976.

Klahr, D. (Ed.). *Cognition and instruction.* Hillldale: Erlbaum, 1976.

Klahr, D., & Wallace, J. G. The role of quantification operators in the development of conservation of quantity. *Cognitive Psychology,* 1973, 301–327.

Klahr, D., & Wallace, J. G. *Cognitive development in children: An information-processing view.* Hillsdale, New Jersey: Erlbaum, 1976.

LaBerge, D., & Samuels, S. J. Toward a theory of automatic information processing in reading. *Cognitive Psychology,* 1974, *6,* 293–323.

Legge, D. (Ed.). *Skills.* Baltimore: Penguin Books, 1970.

Lindsay, P., & Norman, D. A. *Human information processing* (2nd ed.), New York: Academic Press, 1977.

Loftus, E. F., & Loftus, G. R. Changes in memory structure and retrieval over the course of instruction. *Journal of Educational Psychology,* 1974, *66,* 315–318.

Macnamara, J. Cognitive basis of language learning in infants. *Psychological Review,* 1972, *79,* 1–13.

Massaro, D. W. *Experimental psychology and information processing.* Chicago: Rand McNally, 1975.

Mayer, R. E. Different problems-solving competencies established in learning computer programming with and without meaningful models. *Journal of Educational Psychology,* 1975, *67,* 725–734.

Mayer, R. E., & Greeno, J. Structural differences between learning outcomes produced by different instructional methods. *Journal of Educational Psychology,* 1972, *67,* 725–734.

Miller, G. A., Galanter, E., & Pribram, K. *Plans and the structure of behavior.* New York: Holt, Rinehart & Winston, 1960.

Morrisett, L. N., & Vinsonhaler, J. (Eds.). Mathematical thinking. *Monographs of the Society for Research in Child Development,* Serial No. 99, 1965.

Mussen, P. (Ed.). European research in cognitive development. *Monographs of The Society for Research in Child Development,* Serial No. 100, 1965.

Neiser, U. *Cognitive psychology.* New York: Appleton, 1967.

Nelson, K. Structure and strategy in learning to talk. *Monographs of the Society for Research in Child Development,* Serial No. 149, 1973.

Newell, A., & Simon, H. A. *Human problem solving.* Englewood Cliffs: Prentice-Hall, 1972.

Norman, D. A. Memory, knowledge, and the answering of questions. In R. L. Solso, (Ed.), *Contemporary issues in cognitive psychology: The Loyola symposium.* New York: Wiley, 1973.

Norman, D. A. & Rumelhart, D. E. *Explorations in cognition.* San Francisco: Freeman, 1975.

Olson, D. *Cognitive development: The child's acquisition of diagonality.* New York: Academic Press, 1970.

Peterson, L. & Peterson, M. J. Short term retention of individual verbal items. *Journal of Experimental Psychology,* 1959, *58,* 193–198.

Pew, R. W. Human perceptual motor performance. In B. H. Kantowitz (Ed.), *Human information processing: tutorials in performance and cognition.* Hillsdale, New Jersey: Erlbaum, 1974.

Piaget, J. *The child's conception of number.* New York: Norton, 1952.

Piaget, J. *Six psychological studies.* New York: Random House, 1967.

Piaget, J. *Science of education and the psychology of the child.* New York: Orion Press, 1970.

Piaget, J. *The child's conception of movement and speed.* New York: Ballantine Books, 1971.

Piaget, J. *The child and reality.* New York: Grossman Publishers, 1973.

Piaget, J., & Inhelder, B. *The child's conception of space.* London: Routledge & Kegan Paul, 1967.

Piaget, J., & Inhelder, B. *The psychology of the child.* New York: Basic Books, 1969.

Piaget, J., & Inhelder, B. *Mental imagery in the child.* New York: Basic Books, 1971.

Piaget, J., Inhelder, B., & Szeminska, A. *The child's conception of geometry.* New York: Harper & Row, 1964.

Posner, M. *Cognition: An introduction.* Glenview: Scott, Foresman, 1973.

Posner, M. I., & Keele, S. W. Skill learning. In R. M. W. Travers (Ed.), *Handbook of research on teaching.* Washington, D. C.: American Educational Research Association, 1972.

Posner, M., Boies, S., Eichelman, W., & Taylor, R. Retention of visual and name codes of single letters. *Journal of Experimental Psychology Monographs,* 1969, *79*(1), Part 2.

Reed, S. *Psychological processes in pattern recognition.* New York: Academic Press, 1973.

Resnick, L. B. *The nature of intelligence.* Hillsdale, New Jersey: Erlbaum, 1976.

Resnick, L. B. *Theory and practice of reading instruction.* Hillsdale, N. J.: Erlbaum, forthcoming.

Schaeffer, B., Eggelston, V. H., & Scott, J. Number development in young children. *Cognitive Psychology,* 1974, *6,* 357–379.

Schank, R. C. The structure of episodes in memory. In D. G. Bobrow & A. Collins (Eds.), *Representation and understanding: Studies in cognitive science.* New York: Academic Press, 1975.

Schmidt, R. A. A schema theory of discrete motor skill learning. *Psychological Review,* 1975, *82,* 225–260.

Slobin, D. *Psycholinguistics.* Glenview: Scott, Foresman, 1971.

Smith, F. *Understanding reading.* New York: Holt, Rinehart & Winston, 1971.

Smith, F. *Comprehension and learning.* New York: Holt, Rinehart & Winston, 1975.

Sperling, G. The information available in brief visual perceptions. *Psychological Monographs,* 1960, *74,* No. 11.

Sternberg, S. High-speed scanning in human memory. *Science,* 1966, *153,* 653–654.

Sticht, T. G. *Auding & reading: A developmental model.* Human Resources Research

Organization, 1974. (Order directly, 300 North Washington St., Alexandria, Virginia 22314.)

Tanner, J. M. *Growth at adolescence.* Oxford: Blackwell, 1961.

Tanner, J. M. Human growth and constitution. In G. A. Harrison *et al.* (Eds.), *Human biology: An introduction to human evolution, variation, and growth.* New York: Oxford University Press, 1964.

Tanner, J. M. *Education and physical growth.* New York: International Universities Press, 1970.

Tanner, J. M., & Inhelder, B. (Eds.), *Discussions on child development,* Vols. I–IV. London: Tavistock, 1956–1960.

Trabasso, T. Representation, memory, and reasoning: How do we make transitive inferences, In A. D. Pick (Ed.), *Minnesota symposia on child psychology,* Vol. 9. Minneapolis: University of Minnesota Press, 1975.

Trabasso, T., Riley, C. A., & Wilson, E. G. The representation of linear order and spatial strategies in reasoning: A developmental study. In R. Falmagne (Ed.), *Reasoning: Representation and process.* Hillsdale, New Jersey: Erlbaum, 1975.

Trabasso, T., Rollins, H., & Shaughnessy, E. Storage and verification stages in processing concepts. *Cognitive Psychology,* 1971, *2,* 239–289.

Vernon, M. D. *The psychology of perception.* Baltimore: Penguin Books, 1966.

Werner, H. *Comparative psychology of mental development.* New York: Science Editions, 1961.

Wickens, D. Encoding categories of words: An emprical approach to meaning. *Psychological Review,* 1970, *77,* 1–15.

Winograd, T. *Understanding natural language.* New York: Academic Press, 1973.

Wright, J. C., & Kagan, J. (Eds.). Basic cognitive processes in children. *Monographs of the Society for Research in Child Development,* Serial No. 86, 1963.

Zajonc, R. B. Social facilitation. *Science,* 1965, *149,* 269–274.

7

Humanistic Psychology: Theoretical-Philosophical Framework and Implications for Teaching

DON E. HAMACHEK

Michigan State University

PROLOGUE

The two major objectives of this chapter are to explore the meaning and intent of humanistic prochology and its implications for enhancing teaching and learning. Enroute, we will take a look at the philosophy and theory upon which this psychological position is built. In addition, we will sample the views of some of the major contributors associated with this stance in order to better understand the theoretical blueprint that has guided the construction of the basic tenets of contemporary humanistic psychology.

It may be useful for you to know at the outset that I do not see myself as being rigidly humanistic, however you may define that term. I have no illusions about humanistic psychology offering all the answers or being the best position for all persons engaged in educational and/or psychological work. I suppose another way of saying this is to tell you that I am by no means a dedicated disciple of humanistic points of view. It would be more accurate to say that my own personal learnings tend in the *direction* of being clinical and humanistic as opposed to being experimental and behavioristic.

I see humanistic psychology as having a great deal to offer, but it is more than a dressed-up version of the phenomenological—existential movement that has had a long history in Europe and in Western thought. It is more than saying to a student, "Be free, grow, expand, follow your feelings, do what you want, be yourself." And it is more than a poetic accounting of a person's dreams, feelings, and experiences. Which leads us to ask an important first question.

WHAT IS HUMANISTIC PSYCHOLOGY?

Before we can answer this question, we need first of all to acknowledge the fact that there is no single position that is identifiable as *the* humanistic psychology approach. Although different theorists may give it different emphases, I think it would be fair to say that humanistically inclined persons generally perceive each individual as an integrated whole, rather than fragmented into different "selves" unrelated to each other.

Humanistic psychology can also be characterized by its efforts to develop a body of scientific knowledge about human behavior that is guided primarily by a conception of how a person views him/or herself rather than through the study of lower animal forms. The idea of deriving principles of behavior and learning from experimental studies with rats, pigeons, monkeys, and even chickens, was uncongenial to a significant number who felt that the way to understand human behavior was to study, of all things, human behavior. And in the broadest sense of the word, this is what humanistic psychology is all about. It enables us to focus on the *human* meanings, *human* understandings, and *human* experiences involved in growth, teaching, and learning.

The view of human behavior that grows out of a humanistic framework is one which focuses on how persons, in a social context, are influenced and guided by the personal meanings they attach to their experiences. It is a psychological stance that focuses not so much on persons' biological drives, but on their goals; not so much on stimuli impinging on them, but on their desires to be or to do something; not so much on their past experiences, but on their current circumstances; not so much on "life conditions" per se, but on their perceptions of those conditions. Hence, the emphasis is on the subjective qualities of human experience, the personal meaning of an experience to persons, rather than on their objective, observable responses.

Humanistic psychology, then, is composed of all those currents of psychological thought in which human behavior is viewed somewhat as each individual views him—or herself—that is, as a person rather than as an animal or a machine.

BASIC HUMANISTIC CONCEPTS

James F. T. Bugental, the first president of the American Association for Humanistic Psychology when it was formed in 1962, identified the goal of humanistic psychology as "The preparation of a complete description of what it means to be alive as a human being [1967, p. 7]." In another source, Bugental (1965, pp. 11–12) has suggested five basic postulates for a humanistic perspective of human behavior, which may help give additional meaning to this point of view.

1. *Man, as man, supersedes the sum of his parts.* I suppose you could say that this is something like concluding that Bernstein's score for *West Side Story* is more than the summation of the number of musical notes that went into composing it.

2. *Man has his being in a human context.* The unique nature of man is expressed through his relationships with other people, and in this sense humanistic psychology is concerned with a person's potential in an interpersonal context.

3. *Man is aware.* This suggests that, whatever the degree of consciousness, man is aware of himself and his existence. That is, how persons behave in the present is related to what happened in their past and is connected by their hopes for the future.

4. *Man has choice.* This is an important outgrowth of the influence of existential thought. It simply means that awareness leads to choice, and when persons choose they become not bystanders, but active participants in experience.

5. *Man is intentional.* A person's "intent" is reflected in his choices. That is, a person "intends" through having purpose, through valuing, and through seeking meaning in his life. It is through this "conscious deliberateness," as it might be called, that a person structures his identity and distinguishes himself from other species.

Three key terms commonly associated with humanistic positions are "self-actualization," "self-fulfillment," and "self-realization." Although there are many different opinions within the humanistic movement, there are certain important common features that can be identified—for example, Charlotte Buhler (1971), a prominent spokesperson for humanistic psychology, has stated that "humanistic psychologists see the goal of life as using your life to accomplish something you believe in, be it self-development or other values. From this they expect a fulfillment towards which people determine themselves [p. 381]." Thus, the idea of self-understanding in order to make better choices about how one can better go about the business of living a creative and fulfilling life are central concepts in the humanistic psychology position. Indeed, the whole construct of self is an important one, an idea we turn to next.

Role of the Self in a Humanistic Framework

With the emphasis on how persons perceive themselves, on personal meanings, values, choices, and perceptions, it seems only natural that the idea of self, or self-concept, occupies a prominent place in humanistic psychology. Although the use of self-concept was first introduced by William James (1890) in his landmark book, *Principles of Psychology,* the idea of the self all but dropped out of sight during the first 30 years or so of this century. Behavioristic psychologists pretty much held the fort in those days and thought it too "internal" and hence too unobservable to be of much value.

Over time, however, the idea of self-concept has emerged as a kind of unifying principle of personality for psychologists and educators with a humanistic bent. The self is internal; it is that part of each person of which he is *conscious*—I think Jersild (1952) has described it as well as anyone:

> The self is the individual known to the individual. It is that to which we refer when we say I. It is the custodian of awareness; it is the thing about a person which has awareness and alertness, which notices what goes on and notices what goes on in its own field [pp. 9–10].

All in all, the self occupies a central seat of importance in humanistic psychology because it emphasizes the individual as he sees himself and, even more, it underscores the role of consciousness in human behavior. It offers a way for taking into account the subjective experience of each individual and for trying to understand the meaning of that experience from that person's point of view.

Contributions of Phenomenology and Existential Psychology

Since humanistic psychology, phenomenology, and existential psychology are frequently used in the same breath by persons discussing humanistic viewpoints, it may help us to be clearer about the theoretical structure and philosophical roots of humanistic psychology by briefly examining the meaning of each of these terms and their relationships to each other.

Let us begin with existentialism. This is basically a twentieth-century philosophy that stresses each person's responsibility for determining his or her own fate. It is an introspective philosophy that expresses each individual's awareness of personal contingency and freedom to choose among alternatives for behaving. Indeed, the existential outlook maintains that a person's essence (being, behavior, personality, "self") is *created* by his or her choices. As Jean-Paul Sartre succinctly put it: "I am my choices." Within this framework, each individual is seen as having absolute freedom. In fact, even refusing to choose represents personal choice. Thus, the criteria for behavior are within the individual, which, in effect, makes each person the architect of his or her own life. The major pillars of the existential position have been stated in the form of three propositions (Morris, 1966, p. 138):

1. I am a *choosing* agent, unable to avoid choosing my way through life.
2. I am a *free* agent, absolutely free to set the goals of my life.
3. I am a *responsible* agent, personally accountable for my free choices as they are revealed in how I live my life.

A chief tenet of existentialism is the idea that humans struggle to transcend themselves—to reach beyond themselves—always oriented to their possibilities. In this sense, the idea of transcendence boils down to what Morris (1954) has called man's capacity for "dynamic self-consciousness." Another way of saying it is that not only can a person think but he or she can also think about (criticize and correct) his or her thinking. Not only can a person feel, but he can have feelings about his feelings. We are not only *conscious,* but we are *self*-conscious.

Phenomenology is a related philosophical position within the humanistic framework and represents a view which asserts that reality lies not in the event, but in the phenomenon, that is, an individual's *perception* of the event. It is interesting to note that in its original usage, a phenomenon is "that which is known through the senses and immediate experience rather than through deductions."

Combs and Snygg (1959), two psychologists who have been very influential in developing the phenomenological position, have written that:

> This approach seeks to understand the behavior of the individual from his point of view. It attempts to observe people, not as they seem to outsiders, but as they seem to themselves. People do not behave solely because of external forces to which they are exposed. People behave as they do in consequence of how things seem to them [p. 11].

From a phenomenological point of view the idea is that each person behaves in a manner consistent with his or her "perceptual field," which is a more or less fluid organization of personal meanings existing for every individual at any given instant in time. The idea of perceptual field is variously called one's private or personal world, one's psychological field or life space, or one's phenomenal field. Rogers (1951), for example, notes that "The organism reacts to the field as it is experienced to perceived. This perceptual field is, for the individual, 'reality' [p. 483]." In other words, a person responds not to an "objective" environment, but to the environment as he or she perceives and understands it. For the person in question, it is reality no matter how much he or she may distort and personalize it. The idea of how one's perception of "reality can influence behavior is nicely illustrated in the following example cited by Combs and Snygg (1959):

> Several years ago a friend of mine was driving in a car at dusk along a Western road. A globular mass, about two feet in diameter, suddenly appeared directly in the path of the car. A passenger screamed and grasped the wheel attempting to steer the car around the object. The driver, however, tightened his grip on the wheel and drove directly into the object. The behavior of both the driver and the passenger was determined by his own (perceptions). The passenger, an Easterner, saw the object in the highway as a boulder and fought desperately to steer the car around it. The driver, a native Westerner, saw it as a tumbleweed and devoted his efforts to keeping his passenger from overturning the car [p. 20].

Phenomenology is difficult to define with precision. It is an old term, now stewing in its own metaphysical juices, that allows for so much individuality that there could be almost as many phenomenologies as there are phenomenologists. Why? Because the essential concern is with *meaning,* and meanings can vary extensively.

In sum, we could say that the emphasis of existential psychology is on personal choice, freedom, and responsibility, while the phenomenological emphasis is our perceptions, personal meanings, and subjective experiences. Since humanistic psychology is an orientation that focuses on human interests and values, a person's ability to make conscious choices, and man's perceptions of him- or herself, we can readily see how the incorporation of existential and phenomenological ideas into this system is really a natural blending of overlapping concerns and views regarding human behavior.

MAJOR CONTRIBUTORS TO HUMANISTIC PSYCHOLOGY

As humanistic psychology has emerged as a theoretical discipline to stand as a legitimate "third force" next to psychoanalytic and behavioristic psychology, certain key persons have been instrumental in helping it develop from its philosophical origins. The input of Charlotte Buhler and James Bugental has already been mentioned. The contributions of Abraham Maslow have been high among those who have pointed consistently to the "human" aspects of behavior, to the positive aspects of humankind, to a person's inner-directed and conscious motivations, and to an individual's self-selected goals. Maslow was ever concerned with what was possible for man and as a consequence he devoted his attention more to what a person could *become* than to what a person had been. As Maslow (1962) expressed it:

> From Freud we learned that the past exists now in the person. Now we must learn . . . that the future also exists *now* in the form of ideals, hopes, goals, unrealized potentials, mission fate, destiny etc. One for whom no future exists is reduced to

the concrete, to hopelessness, to emptiness. . . . Striving, the usual organizer of most activity, when lost, leaves the person unorganized and unintegrated [p. 48].

Gordon Allport (1955) was another strong advocate of a humanistic psychology because as he saw it:

Some [views of man] are based largely upon the behavior of sick and anxious people or upon the antics of captive and desperate rats. Fewer theories have derived from the study of healthy human beings, those who strive not so much to preserve life as to make it worth living. Thus we find many studies of criminals, few of law-abiders; many of fear, few of courage; more on hostility than affiliation; much in the blindness of man, but little on his vision; much on his past, little on his outreaching into the future [p. 18].

Carl Rogers has been another important contributor to the humanistic position and probably more than any other person has influenced teachers' ideas about the importance of a student's "freedom to learn." Indeed, a book by Rogers (1969) with that very title outlined his ideas for enhancing teaching and learning—ideas that had been spawned and nurtured by over 40 years of experience with persons in a psychotherapeutic context. Rogers' ideas have been important ones because they have emphasized the human *relationship* aspects of education, that tenuous, elusive connection between student and teacher, the content of which renders learning exciting and meaningful or dull and impersonal. In Rogers' judgment, "Learning which takes place 'from the neck up' [and which] does not involve feelings or personal meanings [has] no relevance for the whole person [p. 4]." Unfortunately, Rogers' views can be easily misinterpreted, an idea we will get into more when we discuss the role of the teacher operating within a humanistic context.

The citation of the five contributors I have mentioned up to this point is by no means exhaustive. Other names (and basic references associated with each) that could be added include: Adler (1956), Combs and Snygg (1959), Fromm (1947, 1964), Goldstein (1939), Horney (1945), May (1953), Moustakes (1966), Murphy (1947), and Murray (1938). I have limited this list to the earlier contributors because it is from their writings that contemporary humanistic psychology has taken its substance and shaped its form. More contemporary contributors will be noted later in this chapter.

Common Criticisms Leveled at Humanistic Positions

Most of us, I suspect, share the inclination to want to overlook the shortcomings of either persons or ideational systems whose point of view tends to reflect our own biases or preferences. Just as those of us with a humanistic slant can more objectively spot the "flaws" in the purely cognitive and behavioristic approaches to teaching and learning, so, too, can those aligned with other positions see more clearly the shortcomings of humanistic approaches. We may or may not agree with the criticisms, but our attention to them may help us to re-examine what we might otherwise take for granted as "truth."

A major criticism of humanistic psychology is that it seems like too much common sense and too little like science. A related criticism is that it is based upon a naïve type of phenomenology. Essentially this criticism means that there is more to understanding human behavior than a study of conscious processes may allow us to observe. One psychologist, for example, notes that "such a psychology of consciousness has an element of common-sense appeal. . . . It does make sense to the layman; it accords with what he is ready and able to recognize in himself. . . . Because it overstates its claims, however, it may tend to promote the state of affairs away from which we have been striving—every man his own psychologist [Smith, 1950]." I suppose we might quarrel with whether it is such a bad idea to work in the direction of helping persons to be their own psychologists—I see virtue in that, not evil—but the fact remains it is a criticism worth considering for its moderating effect. As for its being too little science, Maslow (1968a) himself has vigorously asserted: "Only science can progress." Indeed, he went on to say that "Science is the only way we have of shoving truth down the reluctant throat [p. v]."

Child (1973, pp. 19–22) has discussed four of what he calls "defects" in the humanistic positions. They are, I think, fairly representative of the criticisms most frequently leveled at this position by proponents of other psychological systems. Let us examine them briefly.

One of the criticisms is that humanistic psychology is too vague, in the sense that the concepts used are ambiguous and subject to individual interpretation. *Authenticity,* a favorite concept among humanistically inclined psychologist and educators, is a good example. Critics wonder how it is possible to recognize an "authentic" person or an "authentic" act. A person described as a "fully functioning" individual or a student engaged in a "real and meaningful learning experience" would be examples of other "vague" concepts.

A second criticism has to do with the difficulty in verifying conceptual conclusions. "How," ask the critics, "can we verify or confirm the existence of an authentic person or a fully functioning individual or a real and meaningful learning experience? How can we go beyond the subjectivity involved in deciding what, for example, is 'authentic'?"

A third criticism is related to the idea that it is difficult to accumulate objectively verified knowledge. Say the critics, "How can we objectify 'real' learning when what is 'real' is so subjectively determined? That is, what is real for one student may be unreal to another. How do we know whom to believe?"

Still a fourth criticism leveled at the humanistic position is what Child calls a "trend toward sentimentality." From the critics' point of view, this means that there is more to understanding human behavior than that which is embodied in simple religious optimism or in emphasizing the power of positive thinking or stressing the infinite capacity of the human will to achieve good.

All in all, critics of humanistic psychology view it as being too "soft," not rigorous enough to encourage the sort of tough, objective scientific investigations necessary to render it more than a "common-sense" psychology. Now we may agree that humanistic psychology is neither theoretically nor philosophically inclined to be "tough" and coldly "objective" in the usual sense, but that does not excuse us from being as rigorous as possible in defining humanistic psychology as a psychological system and operationalizing its applications.

Just as we can be critical of humanistic psychology for its possible shortcomings, we can also applaud it for its strengths, an accounting to which we turn next.

SOME STRENGTHS AND VIRTUES TO CONSIDER

Humanistic psychology, first and foremost, has the virtue of reflecting what seems to be an enduring and universal human value—at least among the free countries of the world—and that is a regard for individual choice and responsibility. Indeed, even in authoritarian systems individuals are expected to be responsible for whatever limited aspects of their lives remain within their choice. The respect for individual initiative and freedom is best illustrated by the quest of modern American youth for more personally satisfying ways of life. Their loud protests against mechanization are due not just to the specific frustrations of feeling dehumanized, but also to the more general sense that extreme mechanization is incompatible with each person's importance and value as a unique center of awareness and freedom.

I think another way of saying this is that humanistic psychology considers people in terms of what it means to feel and live and think and behave as human beings. It lends itself easily and readily to general discussions or probing analyses of personal ideals, of fulfillment, of self-actualization, and of authenticity and what it means to be real. Child (1973) suggests that perhaps the most persuasive virtue of humanistic psychology is the "intuitive rightness" of the model. By this he does not mean absolute correctness, but rather that the humanistic model is one that "agrees with most people's intuitive impression of what it is like to be a human being, and that this agreement is one important item of positive evidence for the scientific value of the model [p. 18]."

Your experience may have shown you, as mine has, that when people seek self-understanding or insight into their feeling worlds or search for solutions to emotional hauntings, they usually do not choose books that explain behavior only in terms of stimulus conditions and response possibilities. Rather, what they do is to choose books and articles that allow them to explore the inner person, the hidden self in more personal, affective ways. Humanistic psychology encourages this latter kind of learning, which is why, I suspect, it has a strong natural appeal to many.

Another strength of the humanistic position is that it offers a flexible framework within which to observe and study behavior. It is an open rather than a closed system. Humanistic psychology used properly is not a psychology that says feelings are more important than thinking or personal perceptions are more crucial than observable behavior. It is, or at least should be, a psychology which considers the total person in a total environment of interpersonal relationships and intrapersonal feelings. A humanistic position (a distorted one, in my view) we frequently hear about is one which says, in effect: "Your feelings and personal values are more important than anything else and so long as I can accept you for where you are and where you want to go then I will have done my best for you as a teacher (or friend, spouse, parent, or what have you)." Humanistic psychologists and educators who promote this latter position are as inflexibly myopic in denying the importance of external conditions as are extreme behaviorists who berate the significance of internal feelings. A balanced humanistic psychology starts with a simple, but profound assumption: Both the inner person and the outer world are important in influencing the final form in which behavior is expressed and feelings are felt.

Up to this point we have looked at the theoretical and philosophical framework of humanistic psychology along with an examination of strengths and weaknesses commonly associated with this position. Let us turn our attention now to how this framework can be translated into strategies and practices which may enhance teaching and learning.

IMPLICATIONS OF HUMANISTIC PSYCHOLOGY FOR EDUCATIONAL PROCESSES

From a humanistic slant, the major goals of education are to help develop the individuality of persons to assist individuals in recognizing themselves as unique human beings, and to help students actualize their potentialities. These are broad goals and probably no more or no less than what any teacher would want regardless of his view of human behavior. Actually, the difference lies not so much in the goals, but in the means for achieving them. I think Maslow (1968b) stated the difference most clearly when he wrote:

> We are now being confronted with a choice between two extremely different almost mutually exclusive conceptions of learning [One] is what I want to call for the sake of contrast and confrontation, extrinsic learning i.e., learning of the outside learning of the impersonal, of arbitrary associations of arbitrary conditioning that is

of arbitrary meanings and responses. In this kind of learning most often it is not the person himself who decides, but rather a teacher or an experimenter who says, 'I will use a buzzer," "I will use a bell, ' ' I will use a red light, ' and most important, 'I will reinforce this or that. ' In this sense, learning is extrinsic to the learner, extrinsic to the personality and is extrinsic also in the sense of collecting associations, condition ings, habits or modes of action. It is as if these were possessions which the learner accumulates in the same way that he accumulates keys or coins and puts them in his pocket. They have little or nothing to do with the actualization or growth of the peculiar, idiosyncratic kind of person he is [p. 691].

This does not mean that extrinsic learning and the conditions which promote it are unimportant. It means, rather, that the emphasis is on intrinsic learning and those conditions which foster it.

A major implication for educational processes growing from this point of view is the emphasis on helping students decide for themselves who they are and what they want to be. The further implications are that students can decide for themselves, they have conscious minds that enable them to make choices, and that through their capacity to make choices they can at least have a chance at developing the sense of self necessary for productive, actualizing lives. (You may recognize the influence of existential psychology here.) In other words, a meaningful educational experience (external) can assist a student toward finding out *what is already in him or her* (internal) that can be refined and developed further.

Another major implication growing from humanistic approaches to education is the idea that in order to enhance teaching effectiveness we must try to understand students from their point of view. As mentioned earlier, this is quite consistent with a little truism growing out of perceptual psychology that asserts that people behave in terms of what is believed to be true about reality as it is *perceived.* Combs and Snygg (1959) have discussed this idea more fully. If we hope to be as effective as we can be as teachers, then the suggestion is that we attempt to see the world as the student sees it, accept it as truth for him, and not attempt to force him into changing. This does not mean that we should not challenge what students believe or avoid presenting them with alternatives, it only suggests that to maximize our effectiveness *we need to start where the student's perceptions are and not where our own happen to be at the moment.*

Humanistic education starts with the idea that students are different, and it strives to help students become more like themselves and less like each other. Another significant implication emerging from this point of view is that good teaching is best done through a process of helping students explore and understand the personal meanings that are inherent in all their experiences. Indeed, humanistic psychology stresses the idea that adequate persons are, among other factors, the products of strong personal values. Recent efforts to include "value clarification" exercises in teacher preparation programs and public education reflect the growing response to the importance of recognizing how personal values influence human behavior (Simon, Howe, & Kirschenbaum, 1972; Stewart, 1974).

Sometimes students get the idea that how they feel and what they think is not very important compared to scientific and objective facts. From a humanistic psychology point of view, *over*emphasizing narrowly scientific and impersonally objective learning tends to inhibit the development of personal meanings. Indeed, an overemphasis of that which is either purely subjective or purely objective violates the basic concern humanistic psychology has for the education of the *total* person. Both Brown (1971) and Bower (1967, pp. 76–87) have presented strong, forceful positions outlining the need for the integration or flowing together of the affective and cognitive elements in humanistic education. I think the implication here has been nicely stated by Combs (1962):

> Many students perceive school as a place where one is forced to do things which have little pertinence to life as he experiences it. Education must be concerned with the values, beliefs, convictions and doubts of students. These realities as perceived by an individual are just as important, if not more so, as the so-called objective facts. This does not mean that factual materials are not useful in making sound value judgments or in formulating constructive social policies, but rather that an overemphasis on the scientific and the objective impedes self-fulfillment. Facts have no value in themselves alone. It is only as facts find there way into human organization of convictions, beliefs, frames of reference and attitudes that they come to fruition in intelligent behavior [pp. 68–69].

The question remains, how can we translate the theory and philosophy within a humanistic framework into meaningful principles for teaching and learning experiences? Let us turn our attention to this important question.

INSTRUCTIONAL PRINCIPLES DERIVED FROM A HUMANISTIC FRAMEWORK

Humanistic psychology does not offer a formalized theory of instruction. It tends to take a holistic rather than atomistic approach to the study and understanding of teaching and learning. More specifically, it is a psychology that seeks to understand behavior—inside the classroom and out—within an everyday living context of preceptions, personal meanings, and relationship variables rather than within the more laboratory-oriented paradigm of operant conditioning, reinforcement schedules, S–R bonds, and the like. This does not mean that operant conditioning does not go on or that reinforcement schedules never occur, or that S–R bonds do not exist. These things do go on and do exist as classroom realities. The reason we do not hear much about these phenomena when teaching and learning are discussed within a humanistic framework is that they are primarily ways to make things happen and to explain how they happen from an outsider's point of view. I think that most sensible (i.e., the most nonfanatic) humanistic psychologists and educators would probably agree that many of the behavioristic principles (reinforcement contingencies, operant conditioning, and so on) which are applied to classroom settings do work and can be beneficial. Recent books by Glavin (1974), Klein, Hapkiewicz, and Roden (1973), O'Leary and O'Leary (1973), and Poteet (1973), to name a few, have marshalled together a substantial body of evidence to demonstrate that classroom behavior and learning can indeed be modified through the use of behavioristic techniques. The issue is not whether approaches of this sort work—they do—but rather, where teachers choose to put their emphasis. Teachers can choose to emphasize (underscore, lean in the direction of) those events and experiences that are external to students or to emphasize those things which are more internal. What does this mean in practice? Well, as a general rule, humanistically-inclined teachers are more concerned with understanding students than they are with manipulating them; they are more involved with the discovery of subjective, personal meanings to explore further than they are with looking for objective, observable behaviors to reinforce; they are more concerned with the question of what is a good relationship than they are with the question of what is a good reward.

I do not see the emphasis a person chooses as being an either—or issue. That is, I don't think that as teachers or psychologists we are either subjective *or* objective, manipulative *or* understanding, cognitively forused *or* feeling oriented. Emphasis of one approach does not mean (necessarily) exclusion of the other(s). What it does mean, however, is that instruction will very likely be done in a somewhat different manner, with somewhat different goals, and will be described in somewhat different ways depending on where the emphasis is placed. We may understand these differences more clearly by looking at two variables which stand out as crucial factors in humanistic approaches to teaching and learning: (1) relationship variables and (2) climate variables.

Relationship Variables Are Important

For humanistically inclined teachers, good teaching begins with a relationship between student and teacher. How that relationship is perceived and interpreted, and the feeling tone associated with it can, for better or for worse, affect the teacher's teaching and the learner's learning. There is an excellent chapter in Rogers' book, *Freedom to Learn* (1969, pp. 103–127), which discusses the importance of interpersonal relationships in facilitating learning, along with summarizing research findings to support this as an important component to effective teaching. Of course the quite legitimate question that always gets asked is: "Does attention to relationship variables actually help students *learn* more?" The evidence does not allow us to say that students always learn more in classrooms where teachers pay attention to the quality of interpersonal relationships, feelings, and personal perceptions, but it does allow us to say that students learn at least as much and, in addition, usually *feel* better not only about what they have learned, but about themselves. Rogers (1969), for instance, summarized his review of research by noting: "we may say, with a certain degree of assurance, that for attitudes I have endeavored to describe [Rogers is talking about attitudes which bear on and reflect the nature of a teacher's relationship to students] are not only effective in facilitating a deeper learning and understanding of self in a relationship such as psycho-therapy, but that these attitudes characterize teachers who are regarded as effective teachers, and that the students of these teachers *learn more* [italics mine], even of a convenional curriculum, than do students of teachers who are lacking in these areas [p. 119]."

There is no magic in this, no Eastern mysticism. Being sensitive to relationship variables does not mean that one gives up thinking in favor of feeling or that academic standards are lowered. It does, however, suggest that we strive for a more reasonable balance between emotional processes and academic products so that we do not end up overstressing production and performance (externals) to the exclusion of attitudes and feelings (internals).

An excellent book by Brophy and Good, *Teacher–Student Relationships: Causes and Consequences* (1974), consolidates much of the recent research that has been done in this area. We have always known that the nature of a teacher's relationship to students can influence—for better or for worse—students' behavior, but new research is showing us that teacher–student relationships are more clearly two-way streets than we may have thought. For example, Brophy and Good make the point that "students influence teacher behavior at the same time that their own behavior is being influenced by the teacher [p. viii]." Apparently, teacher–student relationships are reciprocal and mutually reinforcing. Individual differences in students make differential impressions upon teachers, which, in turn, trigger a cyclical process of differential teacher behaviors and attitudes that begin to affect teacher–student interaction patterns and student learning. Attention to relationship variables can help us understand these phenomena more clearly. Humanistically oriented teachers are inclined to do this and, in that way, keep touch with interpersonal emotional processes while keeping academic goals squarely in sight.

Climate Variables Make a Difference

In a very real sense, every classroom—whether in first grade or graduate school—is a miniature, transient society with its own members, rules, organizational structure, social order, and hierarchy of authority. Just as each person develops unique characteristics, so, too, does each classroom. Indeed, it would not be going too far to say that each class develops its own "personality," which, for better or for worse, is the collective blend of the individual personalities within it. I've noted, for instance, in classes of my own that one class can be somewhat quiet and withdrawn, while a second is outgoing and assertive; still another can be cold and detached, while a fourth is warm and receptive. The kind of personality a class develops is not a chance happening. It is, rather, the outgrowth of student–student and teacher–student relationships that, together, give a classroom's evolving personality both form and substance.

Every class has, as it were, a social–emotional–intellectual climate that can make a crucial difference in how students perform academically and how they feel about themselves personally. Research shows that not only do these "climate" factors influence how much is learned, but also how long the learning lasts (Anderson, 1968, 1970; Johnson, 1970).

How a class functions and the kind of "personality" it reflects depend to a very large extent on the teacher and the sort of personal style that is projected in his or her everyday behavior. However we look at it, the teacher occupies a central position as leader of the class. How a class behaves as a group or feels about itself depends to a large extent on how the teacher handles his or her role. The now classic White and Lippitt (1968) studies of the effects of different social climates on group behavior demonstrate well how behavior is affected by "climate" variables. In earlier research, H. H. Anderson and his co-workers (1946a,b) found that classroom climates were very much influenced by certain teacher behaviors. For instance, where teachers relied largely on dominating techniques, there were more signs of interpersonal conflict. Tension was a major climate variable. On the other hand, where more cooperative working methods were used, spontaneity and social contributions were more frequent. Cooperativeness was a major climate variable. Moreover, it was noted that the longer a class was with a teacher, the greater was the effort. In addition, it was noted that when a class changed teachers, the conditions disappeared, only to be replaced by those in classes where the new teacher had been before.

For humanistically oriented teachers, relationship and climate variables make a difference. They are among those very "human" factors that either enhance a total learning experience or interfere with it. The qualities of a positive or negative relationship cannot be seen, but the consequences of it can be. A tense or cooperative climate is not directly observable, but it is something that is felt and sensed. All in all, climate variables and relationship variables are outgrowths of the quite human transactions that constitute the phenomenological reality of every classroom at every level of education.

WHAT HUMANISTIC APPLICATIONS TO EDUCATION DO NOT MEAN

Inasmuch as humanistic application to classroom settings include ideas such as the importance of personal choice, relationship variables, individual meanings, private perceptions, the value of an emotionally healthy classroom atmosphere, and the like, it seems all too easy to conclude that, to be an effective humanistic teacher, one needs simply to be a warm, freedom-granting nice person who is willing to let students do pretty much as they please. An example of how this simplistic view is promulgated is found in a recent book by Kolesnik entitled, *Humanism and/or Behaviorism in Education* (1975), which is allegedly designed to enlighten readers to the various slants commonly linked to each of these two major psychological positions. Discussing humanistic teachers, the author states that this is the kind who "is first and foremost a warm, friendly, sympathetic, understanding, sensitive human being who loves her students and has a genuine desire to help them [p. 146]." The behavioristic teacher, so claims Kolesnik, says that: "It is not enough for a teacher to be a 'warm, friendly person.' She must also be a skilled technician, a behavioral engineer (p. 83)." In addition, the behavioristic teacher "believes that learning involves a certain amount of hard work and discipline. She expects her students to work hard and she works hard herself [p. 111]."

These statements are exactly the sort of overstated and unsupported generalizations that encourage the erroneous, misleading, and all too ubiquitous idea which suggests that humanistic teachers have only to "love" their students and that this will be the antidotal potion that cures motivational ills and innoculates against that dreaded disease known as "not learning." It is surely not true that "all" a humanistic teacher has to do is to be warm, friendly, and loving within an essentially permissive classroom climate in order to enhance learning and self-actualization. Were it only that easy. Nowhere have I found A. H. Maslow or Carl Rogers, or Arthur Combs or Gordon Allport declaring: "Expecting your students to work hard is not all that important, because the thing that really matters is being a warm and friendly person."

Unfortunately, I have seen too many alleged "humanistic" teachers use this distortion of the humanistic position as a convenient way of avoiding the hard work and organized preparations that may otherwise go into gearing up for their classes. For others, a "humanistic" approach is sometimes used as a front to mask their private fears of being rejected or disliked if they "expect" too much or "work" their students too hard.

Humanistic applications to educational settings do not mean that we set no standards or that we let students, willy-nilly, do as they please. There are some valuable lessons we can learn from Summerhill (A. S. Neill's totally "free" school in Suffolk, England) in this regard. On the basis of in-depth interviews with 50 former Summerhill students, Bernstein (1967, 1968) found that attending a school with an atmosphere of total freedom (students take what they want, come to class when they want) was not so inspiring as it may seem. One student, for instance, who had attended Summerhill for 10 years, confessed that classes were rather "humdrum" and that it was rather easy to be led astray by new students who did little or no studying. In fact, he went on to state that procrastination was an attitude one could easily pick up at Summerhill. The disenchantment with the lack of academic emphasis was further evidenced in the fact that only 3 of 11 parents—all former Summerhill students—sent their own children to Summerhill! The 3 parents who did send their children to Summerhill took them out before age 13, almost wholly because of their convictions that not enough emphasis was placed upon the academic side of learning.

Somewhere between too much freedom and too much control there is a fulcrum point that allows us to balance and weigh the advantages of student choice and teacher guidance. The bulk of learning research, not to mention good old common sense, suggests that the best way to encourage motivation and learning is to blend a student's choices, interests, whims even, with a teacher's guidance, direction and experience. There is little question but that the Summerhill philosophy is appealing. It does, after all, seem to make good sense to allow students to study only those subjects and topics that have intrinsic value because then the problem of extrinsic motivation is eliminated altogether. However, it is the rare and fortunate student who is able and willing to put together fragmented bits of information if left entirely to his own cunning and devices. There is a fine line between allowing students to have choices and *abandoning* them to those choices. Rational, sensible humanistic teachers will not take the easy route and leave students with unstructured choices, but they will present them with *guided alternatives.*

An important footnote we might add to this is that when a person does pretty much what he wants to do, then he may seldom be stretched beyond the safety of his own choices. I say "safety" of his own choices because there is evidence to indicate that when one does only what he chooses to do, he feels less successful and competent, even if he succeeds at what he chooses to do, than one who accomplishes a task that he did not choose and that represents another person's expectations. Luginbuhl (1972) has noted, for example, that if a person succeeds at a problem that he chose from a number of problems, his feelings of success may be blunted by the knowledge that he influenced the situation to make the success more possible. This suggests that it may not be wise for a teacher to permit students to have their own way (e.g., choose the number or kind of books to read or the kind of paper to write, etc.) *all of the time.* Living up to a teacher's expectations (e.g., writing a report on an assigned topic, getting it done and in on time) can be another way students can feel successful and thereby add to their feelings of competence and self-esteem.

WHAT HUMANISTIC APPROACHES TO EDUCATION DO MEAN

I am sure you may think of others, but I would like to share with you some ideas related to what humanistic approaches to education mean—at least to me.

1. Humanistic approaches to teaching and learning keep in mind that students bring their total selves to class. They bring heads that think and feel. They bring values that help them to selectively filter what they see and hear, and they bring attitudinal sets and learning styles that render each student unique and different from all the rest. Humanistic teachers do not only *start out* with the idea that students are different, but they recognize that students may still be different at the *end* of an academic experience. Indeed, they may even applaud that fact. They recognize that because students may have the same learning experience—in terms of exposure to similar ideas and content—that this is no guarantee that they will use, interpret, or feel in similar ways about the experience.

2. Humanistic approaches to education recognize that not only must teachers thoroughly understand their subject matter and make wise use of research-demonstrated principles of motivation and learning, but they must understand themselves and make wise use of the self as an important teaching aid. Effective teachers recognize that it is not only *what* they say that is important, but *how* it is said, both of which influence and are influenced by relationship and climate variables. I have discussed this idea of teacher self-understanding at greater length elsewhere (Hamachek, 1975, pp. 331–371).

3. Humanistic approaches to teaching and learning emphasize the here and now. This is simply a way to help students be tuned into current reality and contemporary experiences. For example, in an educational psychology class, rather than talking about individual differences that may exist "out there" in a hypothetical classroom with hypothetical students, how about discussing the individual differences in *this* classroom, with *these* students? Rather than lecturing on the differential consequences of different group climates, how about examining and discussing the group climate of *this* classroom at *this* time? Rather than merely discussing ways to evaluate and grade students "you may teach someday," how about discussing the grading and evaluation that is going on in *this* and other classes at *this* time during *this* term or semester? This leads us naturally to a fourth idea.

4. Humanistic approaches strive to create experiences that involve thinking *and* feelings. One good way to avoid feeling and encourage just thinking is to stay in discussions that are primarily there-and-then oriented. It is easy enough involve students in abstract discussions about the group dynamics of a White—Lippitt study or even of a hypothetical class, but it might be more meaningful in a more personal way to blend thinking and feeling in a here-and-now experience. Let me show an example of what I mean. Take the group dynamics topic. A way to approach this is actually to create different "climates" by role playing different leadership styles. One way to do this is to bring a series of questions to class (the sorts of questions that easily arouse opinions—e.g., "Should class attendance be mandatory?" "Should grading be abolished?" and so forth) and then to passively, nondirectively wonder if anyone would like to

discuss them. Usually, there is a good bit of searching for leadership that goes on and lots of rambling discussion. And then, after 10 or 15 minutes—depending on the time you have—you can move subtly into a more democratically run classroom by asking for suggestions for what to discuss, giving feedback, synthesizing responses and, in general, create a "we" feeling. From this you gradually move into a more dictatorial and authoritarian mode by asserting more and more of your own views in forceful, even put-down ways. Depending on how skillfully you are able to role play the laissez-faire, democratic, and authoritarian styles, your students will experience for themselves the feelings associated with differential classroom climates. Now students have not only something to think about, but a feeling framework within which a more cognitive structure can fit. They can see for themselves that different students respond in different ways to different classroom climates and leadership styles. The ways to "enact" ideas in order to combine thinking and feeling are practically endless.

5. Humanistic approaches to teaching and learning *do* mean that teachers work at being involved, creative persons who are actively caught up in the total educational process. Teachers who walk into their classes wondering. "What shall we talk about today?" or "What would you like to do today?" are not necessarily humanistic teachers.

6. Humanistic approaches to education strive to personalize teaching and learning so as to encourage a here-and-now involvement with thinking and feelings in a human process of people-to-people transactions. In my own classes, I like to encourage students to speak their views in the more personal first-person pronoun "I." It is interesting to note what happens. Students begin to listen to each other because they soon sense that other persons are talking *to* them and not *for* them. Encouraging students to speak for themselves rather than for others is one of those little things a teacher can do to help create a learning climate that is a dynamic blend of cognition and affect. For example, I would not passively stand back and listen to a student say something like: "I think that when you study about teacher self-understanding it makes you aware of aspects in yourself that you might improve. Rather, I would more actively encourage him or her to "own" the statement in a more personal but risky way such as: "I think that my study of teacher self-understanding made me aware of aspects in myself that I might improve."

7. Humanistic approaches to teaching and learning do mean being flexible. By far, the single most repeated adjective in research literature describing good, or effective teachers is "flexibility (Hamachek, 1969)." Alleged "humanistic" teachers who believe that all they have to do is be warm, open individuals who allow students to do whatever they want may not have rigid or authoritarian attitudes, but they are no less dogmatic than those who believe that the traffic flow of learning experiences and activities is best determined entirely by the teacher.

In other words, a true "humanistic" teacher does not seem to be overwhelmed by a single point of view to the extreme of being afflicted by a kind of intellectual myopia. Good humanistic teachers are, in a sense, "total" teachers. That is, they are able to do what they have to do to meet the demands of the moment. A total humanistic teacher can be firm and evaluative when necessary (say "No!" or "You can do better than that" and mean it) or accepting and permissive (say "I really like what you've done" or "Do it your way" and mean that, too) when appropriate. It depends on many things, and teachers who take into account the inner moods and external conditions of classroom life seem best able to move with the tides of shifting classroom circumstances.

IN RETROSPECT

This chapter has endeavored to tour you through some of the basic philosophical and theoretical groundings of humanistic psychology. Essentially, it is a third force position which stresses the importance of perceptions, individual choice, personal meaning, and individual responsibility. It is a psychology that provides a framework and a language for understanding the inner person and for teaching in such a way as to enhance the integration of cognitive processes and affective outcomes. I've tried to delineate areas of weaknesses and strengths, along with pointing to some its implications for teaching and learning.

REFERENCES

Adler, A. *Practice and Theory of Individual Psychology,* New York: Harcourt, Brace and World, 1927.

Allport G. W. *Becoming: Basic considerations for a psychology of personality.* New Haven: Yale University Press, 1955.

Anderson, G. J., & Walberg, H. J. Classroom climate & group learning. *International Journal of Educational Sciences,* 1968(2), 175–180.

Anderson, G. J., & Walberg H. J. Classroom climate & group learning *International Journal of Educational Sciences,* 1968(2), 175–180.

Anderson, H. H., & Brewer, J. E. Studies of Teachers Classroom Personalities, II. *Applied Psychology Monographs,* 1964, (8). (a)

Anderson, H. H., Brewer, J. E., & Reed, M. R. Studies of teachers' classroom personalities, III. *Applied Psychology Monographs,* 1946, (46). (b)

Ansbacher, H. L., & Ansbacher, R. R. (Eds.). *The individual psychology of Alfred Adler: A systematic presentation in selections of his writings.* New York: Basic Books, 1956.

Bernstein, E. Summerhill After 50 years, the first follow-up. *The New Era,* 1967, *48.*

Bernstein, E. Summerhill: A follow-up study of its students. *Journal of Humanistic Psychology,* Fall, 1968, 123–136.

Bower, E. M. The development of cognitive–affective processes through education. In E. M. Bower & W. G. Hollister (Eds.), *Behavioral Science Frontiers in Education.* New York: Wiley, 1967.

Brophy, J. E., & Good, T. L. *Teacher–student relationships: Causes and consequences.* New York: Holt, Rinehart & Winston, 1974.

Brown, G. I. *Human teaching for human learning: An introduction to confluent education.* New York: The Viking Press, 1971.

Bugental, J. F. T. *The Search for Authenticity.* New York: Holt, Rinehart & Winston, 1965.

Bugental, J. F. T. *Challenges of Humanistic Psychology.* New York: McGraw-Hill, 1967.

Buhler, C. Basic theoretical concepts of humanistic psychology. *American Psychologist,* 1971, *26,* 378–386.

Child, I. L. *Humanistic psychology and the research traditions: Their several virtues.* New York: Wiley, 1973.

Combs, A. W. Perceiving and becoming. In *Perceiving, behaving, becoming.* Association for Supervision & Curriculum Development Yearbook, Washington, D.C.: National Education Association, 1962, 65–82.

Combs, A. W., & Snygg, D. *Individual behavior.* (Rev. ed.). New York: Harper & Row 1959.

Fromm, E. *Man for himself.* New York: Holt, Rinehart & Winston, 1947.

Fromm, E. *The heart of man.* New York: Harper & Row, 1964.

Glavin, J. P. *Behavioral strategies for classroom management.* Columbus, Ohio: Merrill, 1974.

Goldstein, K. *The organism.* New York: American Book, 1939.

Hamachek, D. E. Characteristics of good teachers and implications for teacher education. *Phi Delta Kappan,* February, 1969, 341–345.

Hamachek, D. E. *Behavior dynamics in teaching learning, and growth.* Boston, Massachusetts: Allyn & Bacon, 1975.

Horney, K. *Our inner conflicts.* New York: Norton, 1945.

James, W. *Principles of psychology* (2 vols.). New York: Holt, 1890.

Jersild, A. T. *In search of self.* New York: Bureau of Publications, Columbia University, 1952.

Johnson, D. W. *The social psychology of education.* New York: Holt, Rinehart & Winston 1970. 238–240.

Klein, R. D., Hapkiewicz, W. G., & Roden, A. H., (Eds.). *Behavior modification in educational settings.* Springfield, Illinois: Thomas, 1973.

Kolesnik, W. B. *Humanism and/or behaviorism in education.* Boston, Massachusetts: Allyn & Bacon, 1975.

Luginbuhl, J. E. R. Role of Choice and Outcome of Feelings of Success and Estimates of Ability, *Journal of Personality and Social Psychology,* 1972, *22,* 121–127.

Maslow, A. H. Some basic propositions of a growth & self-actualization psychology. In A. W. Combs (Ed.), *Perceiving, behavior, becoming.* Association for Supervision & Curriculum Development Yearbook, 1962.

Maslow, A. H. *Toward a psychology of being* (2nd ed.). Princeton, New Jersey: D. Van Nostrand, 1968. (a)

Maslow, A. H. Some educational implications of humanistic psychologies. *Harvard Educational Review,* Fall, 1968, *38,* 685–696. (b)

Maslow, A. H. *Motivation and Personality* (2nd ed.). New York: Harper & Row, 1970.

May, R. *Man's search for himself.* New York: Norton, 1953.

Morris, V. C. *Existentialism and education,*

Morris, V. C. Existentialism and education, *Educational Theory.* 1954, *4,* 252–253.

Morris, V. C. *Existentialism in education.* New York: Harper & Row, 1966.

Moustakes, C. *The authentic teacher.* Cambridge, Massachusetts: H. A. Doyle, 1966.

Murphy, G. *Personality: A biosocial approach to origins and structure.* New York: Harper & Row, 1947.

Murray, H. A. *Explorations in personality.* New York: Oxford, 1938.

O'Leary, K. D., & O'Leary, S. G. *Classroom management: Behavior modification techniques.* Elmsford, New York: Pergamon Press, 1973.

Poteet, J. A. *Behavior modification: A practical guide for teachers.* Minneapolis, Minnesota: Burgess, 1973.

Rogers, C. *Client-centered therapy.* Boston, Massachusetts: Houghton-Mifflin, 1951.

Rogers, C. R. *Freedom to learn.* Columbus, Ohio: Charles E. Merrill, 1969.

Simon, S. B., Howe, L. W., & Kirschenbaum, H. *Values clarification.* New York: Hart, 1972.

Smith, M. B. The phenomenological approach to personality theory: Some critical remarks. *The Journal of Abnormal & Social Psychology,* 1950, *45,* 516–522.

Stewart, J. S. *Toward a theory for values development education.* Unpublished doctoral dissertation, Michigan State University, 1974.

White, R., & Lippitt, R. Leader behavior and member reaction in three social climates. In D. Cartwright & A. Zander (Eds.) *Group dynamics* (3rd ed.), New York: Harper & Row, 1968. 318–335.

Part III

SPECIFIC INSTRUCTIONAL
APPROACHES

8

Mastery Learning

LORIN W. ANDERSON
University of South Carolina
and
JAMES H. BLOCK
University of California, Santa Barbara

Mastery learning is both a philosophy of school learning and an associated set of specific instructional practices. Consequently, this chapter is organized around a discussion of this philosophy and these related practices. It consists of two sections. We begin with a discussion of the philosophy underlying teaching for mastery. In this section we examine the concept of "mastery" in learning and some of the assumptions that the acceptance of this concept seems to make with respect to the nature of instruction, and the nature of the teacher.

In the second section we outline our approach to teaching for mastery. Based on the underlying assumptions stated in the first section, our mastery strategy (and most other mastery approaches) begins with the notion that most students can achieve a high level of learning if instruction is approached systematically—if help is provided for students when and where they have difficulties, if students are given an adequate amount of time to learn, and if teachers establish some clear criterion of mastery performance. In the second section we indicate the ways by which these ideas can be put into practice in the classroom. We also briefly mention alternative implementation procedures which are used by other approaches to teaching for mastery. We would suggest that the reader compare our suggestions for implementation with those mentioned in the present chapter as well as with those presented in the succeeding chapters of this volume.

Before we begin with our discussion, let us briefly address ourselves to one important question: What value does an understanding of mastery learning have for teachers of educational psychology?

Since the publication of Jerome Bruner's book in 1966 entitled *Toward a Theory of Instruction* (if not much earlier), educational psychologists have attempted to bridge the gap between theories of learning (which Bruner describes as "descriptive" theories) and theories of instruction (which he describes as "prescriptive" theories). We believe that mastery learning (or, perhaps more appropriately, teaching for mastery) is a prescriptive theory; one more closely resembling a theory of instruction. In addition, however, this theory is consistent with many of the principles of theories of learning identified by Hilgard and Bower (1975, pp. 608–609). These principles, derived from both behavioral and cognitive theories of learning, deal with the importance of "learning by doing," reinforcement, highlighting the relevant perceptual features of the learning task, meaningful organization of knowledge from simplified wholes to more complex wholes, learning at higher taxonomic levels, cognitive feedback that can be used to correct faulty learning, and the like. In summary, then, we believe that mastery learning is a systematic, organized approach to classroom teaching which is based upon sound principles of learning.

As a consequence, we believe that mastery learning is a set of instructional procedures and ideas about classroom instruction which teachers of educational psychology can adopt for virtually any course in the educational psychology curriculum. In addition, it is a set of procedures that can be taught to students in courses concerned with classroom instruction so that these students can adopt these procedures in the teaching of their own particular content areas in public and private schools. With this brief justification in mind, we now turn to our discussion of the concept of mastery and teaching for mastery.

THE CONCEPT OF MASTERY

The basic premise of mastery learning is that virtually all students, rather than a few, can master most of what is now being taught in school. What do we mean by the term "mastery" in learning? We would define mastery in a manner similar to Morrison (1931). Mastery refers to "the actual acquisition of learning products by the learner [p. 63]." Thus mastery implies the designation of both the desired learning outcome and the level of performance which will be accepted as an indication of the acquisition of the learning outcome.

The definition implies, of course, that a learner either masters or fails to master a desired learning outcome. There are no degrees in the attainment of mastery. As Morrison (1931) rather strongly states "To speak of degrees in the attainment [of mastery] is as absurd as to speak of degrees of the attainment of the second floor level of a building or of degrees in which the learner has attained the other side of the stream, or indeed of degrees of completeness of any sort whatever [p. 36]."

The concept of mastery is often used interchangeably with two separate, but related, concepts: competency and proficiency. While mastery is a part of competency and of proficiency, mastery, as we use it, is not the same as either. Competency, as we see it, is a two-dimensional construct (cf. R. W. White, 1959). The first dimension is, in fact, mastery. In other words, mastery can be thought of as the intellectual component of competency. A competent learner has acquired a variety of learning products. However, competency also consists of the attainment of self-confidence or the sense of being able to cope. This attainment of self-confidence is the emotional or affective component of competency. While mastery may provide the foundation for the development of learner self-confidence, and hence competency, mastery and competency are related concepts, not synonymous.

Proficiency refers to the efficiency with which the individual makes use of the acquired learning products. While mastery refers to the *effectiveness* of the learning process in producing the desired learning product, proficiency refers to the *efficiency* of the use of the learning product once it has been acquired. Consider, for example, the student of educational psychology who is being taught to apply certain principles of motivation to the design of instructional strategies. At first, his application is hesitant, cautious, and rather slow. However, his finished product indicates that he was able to apply the principles correctly. Over a period of time and with fairly consistent use the individual begins to apply the principles with greater ease and efficiency. He has become proficient with respect to that learning outcome.

We believe that proficiency follows mastery, that is, an individual must master something before he can become proficient. One speculation is that learners become proficient through practice of a previously mastered learning outcome. Thus, in one respect, proficiency resembles what some psychologists have termed "overlearning"; while mastery represents what we may call "original learning."

In essence, then, we see the relationship among mastery, competency, and proficiency as follows. Mastery is a precondition for both competency *and* proficiency. The positive affective consequences that usually accompany mastery help to produce a competent individual. Finally, through practice and continued use of a particular learning, competent individuals become proficient.

We feel it is necessary to make one further distinction at this point: the distinction between *mastery* and *teaching for mastery*. The term mastery refers to the outcome of the teaching–learning process. Thus a definition of mastery would seem to be crucial for all teachers who are concerned with certifying students on the basis of their terminal learning or performance with respect to a certain body of knowledge, skills, and abilities, *whether or not they believe virtually all students can attain mastery or whether or not they are desirous of teaching so that a great number of students will attain mastery.* Teaching for mastery, on the other hand, is a process by which most students in a class are helped to attain the specified learning outcomes. Our discussion in this chapter, therefore, focuses on the question of whether or not teachers wish to increase the number of students who actually achieve mastery. In order to decide whether or not to teach for mastery, the teacher must be aware of certain propositions and assumptions which underlie our teaching for mastery strategy. We now turn to a discussion of these propositions and assumptions.

PROPOSITIONS AND ASSUMPTIONS CONCERNING THE NATURE OF SCHOOLING

We view schooling as basically a purposeful activity. That is, there is some reason, or set of reasons, for individuals to enroll in school, in general, and in certain courses, in particular. In addition, we believe that whether or not these purposes are accomplished has important implications for the psychological well-being of the individual as well as for the survival and betterment of society. Teaching for mastery presumes that these purposes can be identified. Once identified, we see schools as being responsible for helping students to realize these purposes.

What are these purposes? While the particulars given for students to attend school may vary considerably from one place to another, from one school level to another, and from one subject matter to another, lying behind all these particulars is, we believe, a basic view that the major purpose of schooling is to help the learner interact effectively with his environment by being able to attain and perform effectively in three sets of sociocultural roles "those which one's society will normally assign one, those in the repertoire of one's social system one may appropriately aspire to, and those which one might reasonably elaborate for oneself [Inkeles, 1966, p. 265] ." We believe that the preparation of the learner for both self-chosen and socially-imposed roles implies that the individual must be provided with a broad base of skills and abilities. In fact, the broader the base, the more opportunities the individual will have to move in the various directions that he might choose. In addition, we believe that these skills need to be not only intrapersonal but also interpersonal and extrapersonal, that is, not only cognitive, affective, and psychomotor, but also social and ecological.

Further, the preparation of individuals for future as well as present roles implies that this base be composed of at least two distinct sets of skills and abilities. One set will enable the individual to function effectively in *currently assigned or self-elaborated roles.* A second set will enable the individual to acquire additional skills and abilities that he might need to handle a variety of new roles that might emerge in the future. In other words, schools should help prepare the student for both the present and the future. The student should possess not only learning products which he can apply in a given present situations but also so-called "learning to learn" processes which will enable him to handle future situations and problems, whatever they might be. Examples of this latter set would include cognitive strategies (see Gagné, 1974) and a desire for future learning.

At the present time most schooling is geared to preparing individuals with the skills and abilities needed to perform in societally imposed roles. Little thought has been given to the kinds of skills and abilities that an individual might need in the future for his continued personal development.

PROPOSITIONS AND ASSUMPTIONS CONCERNING THE NATURE OF THE LEARNER

Perhaps the basic belief which underlies teaching for mastery is that virtually all learners who enroll in a particular course can acquire the desired learning outcomes of that course. Underlying this belief is an antecedent belief that individuals do not differ in their capacity for learning; rather, individuals may differ in their capacities to *benefit from a particular instructional mode or form.* This is to say that individuals do not have a single capacity to learn. They, instead, have a variety of capabilities; some adaptive to certain instructional forms, others adaptive to other instructional forms (Thorndike, 1926; Thurstone, 1938). Thus, individuals require differential and appropriate instruction that gears *what* they are taught and *how* they are taught to the background they bring to the teaching–learning process. This, of course, requires some kind of individualized instruction. Throughout this chapter, however, we will attempt to make and defend the point the individualized instruction *does not* need to take place in an individual- or self-paced learning situation.

These assumptions concerning the nature of the learner are not new. It may be informative to the reader to trace the history of these ideas in educational thinking. The basic belief that all can learn can be traced directly back to John Locke in the late seventeenth century in his treatise "Some Thoughts Concerning Education." Locke believed that man was capable of almost anything. He further believed that if the course of study was set out in a sequential manner, and if the learner persevered long enough, he would master the objectives of a course of study (Cronbach, 1972). Much the same line of thought can be found in the early writings of Comenious, Pestalozzi, and Herbart (Bloom, 1974).

It was not until the early part of the twentieth century that this philosophy was put into practice in the United States. Carleton Washburne (1922) implemented the philosophy in the Winnetka, Illinois public schools, using an *individualized, self-paced* instructional procedure. At approximately the same time, Henry Morrison (1926) at the University of Chicago suggested implementing the philosophy using an *individualized, group- or teacher-paced* instructional procedure. However, the technology for sustaining these systems was sorely lacking and they were rather short-lived.

The seminal paper of John Carroll (1963) renewed interest in the idea of teaching for mastery. Carroll suggested that a student's capacity to learn could be subdivided into a series of aptitudes for particular subject matters. Further, according to Carroll, a student's aptitude for a particular subject matter could predict either the level to which he could learn the subject in a given time or the time he would require to learn the subject to a given level.

Carroll chose to opt for the latter interpretation. He defined aptitude in terms of the amount of time the student would need to learn to a given level under ideal conditions. Students with high aptitudes for a given subject would learn it quickly, while students with low aptitudes would learn more slowly.

With this alternative view of individual differences in mind, Bloom (1968) and Keller (1968) proposed instructional procedures designed to foster learning for mastery. Bloom's strategy resembled Morrison's in that it was a group-paced, yet individualized, set of instructional procedures. The notion of group-paced, individualized instructional procedures added an important dimension to the assumptions concerning the nature of the learner. Not only could virtually all students learn, but they could learn in ways that were similar to one another.

Keller's strategy, on the other hand, resembled Washburne's in that it was both self-paced and individualized. The teaching for mastery strategy that will be presented in the next section is more aligned to Bloom's ideas than to Keller's, although alternative interpretations such as Keller's will be mentioned as we see necessary and appropriate.

PROPOSITIONS AND ASSUMPTIONS CONCERNING THE NATURE OF CLASSROOM INSTRUCTION AND TEACHING

Closely aligned to the belief that virtually all learners can learn is the belief that we can teach so that all who *can* learn, *do* learn. This belief has implications concerning the nature of classroom instruction. Our basic assumption concerning the nature of classroom instruction is simple and straightforward: Instruction is the *bridge* that links the learner to the desired learning outcomes. The "bridge" analogy is useful for two reasons. First, it implies that instruction must begin where the learner *is* and help him to move to where he *should be*. Second, it points out the mutual responsibility of the teacher and the learner. The teacher must build an appropriate "bridge"; however, the learner must cross that "bridge." The teacher, then, has a limited, albeit important, responsibility with respect to student learning. He cannot actually cause the student to learn.

The teacher's major responsibility centers on providing a quality of classroom instruction that is adaptive to the entering characteristics and that, at the same time, facilitates the attainment of the desired learning outcomes. As we have indicated earlier in this chapter, the amount of time to learn is one of the crucial variables in mastery learning. We believe that the time it takes a student to learn a particular skill or ability depends almost entirely on two major factors: the learner's entering competency and the quality of the instruction vis-à-vis this competency.

The first factor is concerned with the academic history of the learner which he brings to the learning situations. This general factor can be broken down into its cognitive and affective components. The cognitive components consist of the learner's *previous* learning products which are related to, and required for, the *present* learning products. The affective component consists of the learner's interest in achieving the desired product and his confidence in his ability to achieve it.

In regard to the second factor we believe that classroom instruction that is of high quality is designed to overcome four major instructional problems. The first problem is how to get students to attend to the source or sources of the instructional stimuli in the first place. We would call this the *attentional* problem. The second is how to get students to attend to the important stimuli presented by this source or these sources. This might be termed the *presentational* problem. A third problem is how to get students to interact mentally with the instructional stimuli. We would label this the *involvement* problem. The fourth problem is how to encourage students to continue to mentally interact with the stimuli until the desired learning product has been acquired. This might be called the *encouragement* problem.

The general solution to these problems has been to make teaching a proactive rather than a reactive process; one which is concerned with the management of *learning* rather than *learners*. In other words, the teacher is asked to steer the teaching–learning process rather than be steered by it. This emphasis on proactive teaching has several implications for the teacher. We will discuss these implications briefly in the next section and in some detail in the last half of this chapter.

PROPOSITIONS AND ASSUMPTIONS CONCERNING THE NATURE OF THE TEACHER

Within the framework of the nature of classroom instruction, what is the role of the teacher? We see the teacher as being a *craftsman* who is concerned with the management of individual learning within a group context. The teacher is a craftsman in the sense that teaching reflects elements of both a *science* and an *art*. Like a scientist, a craftsman produces basically the same result time after time. But like an artist, a craftsman can use his or her own personal touches in producing these results. We believe that the teacher as a craftsman assumes the role of a proactive teacher. In this role, the teacher must become accustomed to *explicit valuing, planning, managing, evaluating,* and *revising*. Let us consider each of these briefly.

Explicit Valuing

As educators we all have values concerning what "ought to be": what the important learning outcomes are, what level of performance constitutes "mastery" in a particular course, and how we should teach for these important learning outcomes. The first implication for teachers who intend to teach for mastery is that they take the time to think through their values and to make these values *explicit*. That is, they must make public exactly what their values are with respect to these important educational issues. It is often difficult to open up one's values to public scrutiny. As Block (1973) writes "To value something in the abstract or in private may be relatively easy; to make one's values concrete and public is much more difficult, because this opens one up to possible criticism by those who disagree with one's values [p. 35]."

Since criticism will often follow a statement of one's values, teachers must stand ready to defend the choices and decisions they have made. Why were certain content elements included and others excluded? Why was 80% set as the mastery performance standard? These questions require answers based on a sound, well thought out rationale.

Planning

Teachers desiring to teach for mastery must also make several decisions which we would include under the category of planning. The teacher should develop a careful and systematic plan for managing student learning over the entire course before the course actually begins. The planning function is actually a series of subfunctions. First, the teacher needs to "chunk" the desired learning outcomes into manageable units and to order the identified learning units. Second, he or she needs to decide on ways in which the attainment of the desired learning outcomes can be facilitated. Third, he or she needs to develop or select procedures for gathering information concerning the extent to which the desired learning outcomes of each unit and the entire course have been attained by the students. These procedures provide feedback to the students concerning the quality of their learning and to the teacher concerning the quality of the instruction. Fourth, the teacher needs to develop corrective instruction. In the next major section of this chapter we will present our views on planning in greater detail within the context of our suggested mastery teaching strategy.

Managing

The teacher wishing to teach for mastery must also become accustomed to managing. Once the planning has been accomplished the teacher must manage the learning situation to see that the plan is implemented correctly and that the students are learning as expected. Thus, should a particular learner encounter a common learning problem, the teacher can react to the problem quickly and easily. He need not manufacture a solution on the spot. This frees the teacher to concentrate classroom time and energy on any uncommon learning problems that may arise.

The essence of managing seems to focus on the teacher's ability to communicate with the students and to make effective decisions based on obtained information. One aspect of teacher–student communication is the necessity of systematically *orienting* the students to *what* they are going to learn, to *how* they are going to learn, and to what *standard* they are expected to learn at both the *course* and *learning unit* level.

Evaluating

The teacher must also become accustomed to evaluating. The evaluation procedures must be based on the course objectives and the explicit performance standard. This implies, first, that all of the instruments used to assess learning must be carefully constructed so as to be highly content valid, that is, they must test what was actually taught. Second, this implies that the most appropriate grading procedure is a mastery/nonmastery grading procedure. Either the student has mastered or has failed to master the entirety of course objectives.

Revising

The teacher employing a mastery learning approach must become accustomed to revising both the design and the implementation of the instructional plan. One of the central ideas behind mastery learning concerns the need to improve student learning through a systematic procedure involving original instruction/ feedback/corrective instruction.

We believe that a similar line of thinking applies to the improvement of instruction in a mastery learning program. The teacher designs and implements an "original" mastery system. Feedback is provided through the use of the various information gathering techniques. Subsequent revisions of the design and/or implementation of the program (i.e., "corrective procedures") must be made on the basis of the information gathered.

OUR APPROACH TO MASTERY LEARNING

In this section we will set out our teaching for mastery strategy. In order to relate this section to the previous sections, we shall discuss our strategy within the framework of the five implications for teachers that were presented in the prior section. When possible we will point out alternative interpretations and applications which might be useful for teachers of educational psychology to consider.

Explicit Valuing

As we have said, the teacher must begin by selecting his desired instructional objectives and the standard of performance which will be taken as indicative of mastery. Both of these tasks are extremely difficult.

Given the entire *course of study* that constitutes educational psychology, the teacher is first confronted with the need to select from this virtually infinite body a finite amount of desired learning outcomes that will compose his particular *course*. When there is an attempt to make the infinite finite there is a need to select portions for inclusion at the expense of other portions.

We have found that some teachers already possess objectives while others do not. Whether or not teachers possess instructional objectives we strongly urge them to form a course *table of specifications*. A table of specifications is essentially a graphic way of expressing basically cognitive instructional objectives. The rows of the table designate the major content areas that students are expected to master. The columns designate the possible intellectual operations students may be expected to exhibit with the content areas of interest. In order to categorize or classify the possible intellectual operations we have found it useful to use a modification of Bloom's (1956) taxonomic levels, that is, does the teacher expect the student to know, comprehend, apply, analyze, synthesize, and/or evaluate?

If the teachers already possess course objectives the construction of a table of specifications requires that they separate the objective into its *verb* and its *object*. The *object* is the *content* portion of the objective and should appear as one of the rows of the table. The *verb* is the *intellectual operations* portion of the objective and should be matched with one of the column designations. The objective itself is preserved by placing an X in the cell which corresponds with the appropriate row and column.

If teachers do not possess course objectives we would suggest that they examine their existing course materials (e.g., textbooks, journal articles, manu-scripts) and pull out the major content areas of interest. They then write each designated content area .in one of the rows of the table. Next, for each designated content area they ask themselves the following question: "What intellectual operations do I want the students to be able to perform on or with this area of content?" Instructional objectives are then indicated by placing an X in the appropriate cell of the table. For those teachers who do not already possess instructional objectives, but who are interested in writing objectives before constructing the tables of specifications, we would recommend the text by Kryspin and Feldhusen (1974) for an excellent treatment of the topic.

We have urged teachers to move away from the notion of coverage of material to an increased emphasis on the student's ability to "operate" on or with the relevant content. We believe that for students in educational psychology the "ability to operate" on or with the relevant content is equally as important as, or perhaps more important than, being exposed to the vocabulary, factual knowledge, and principles of educational psychology. These abilities to operate will more likely enable the students of educational psychology to *think in the manner of an educational psychologist,* rather than to learn *about* educational psychology. The reader will note that this thinking is in line with our view of the purpose of schooling presented earlier in this chapter.

While we have emphasized the use of a course table of specifications, several approaches to mastery learning have focused to a greater extent on unit by unit objectives (e.g., Keller, 1968; Born, 1971; Corey and McMichael, 1970; Hap-kiewicz, 1971a, 1971b; Chandler, 1973; and Littlejohn, 1973) than on objec-tives over the entire course. This difference in emphasis indicates a difference in the interpretation of mastery in the various approaches. These alternative approaches believe that mastery of all of the units in the course is equivalent to mastery of the entire course. We believe, on the other hand, that mastery of all of the units is not equivalent to mastery of the entire course. Rather, mastery over the course must be established on the basis of the learner's performance vis-à-vis the *course* objectives.

Once the teacher has delineated the course objectives, he must set mastery performance standards. Our approach to teaching for mastery makes use of at least two systematic evidence gathering devices: final, comprehensive examina-tions and diagnostic–progress tests. The final examination is administered at the completion of the course and the results are used to certify the students as "masters" or "nonmasters" with respect to the course objectives. The diagnostic–progress tests are administered periodically throughout the course to check on the effectiveness of the instructional plan, and to provide students and teachers with information concerning specific areas of strengths and weaknesses. It is necessary to set performance standards for both types of instruments.

It is imperative that these performance standards are *meaningful,* not *arbi-*

trary. Without meaningful standards we are in no better a position to certify student learning than we are when we choose to certify student learning vis-à-vis the performance of other students in the class (that is, norm-referenced interpretation of test results). We believe that standards become increasingly meaningful as they approximate Block's (1972) characteristics of an ideal performance standard. Such standards:

1. would be derived from the same values that guide the choice of the instructional objectives, that is, they would not be value-free standards;
2. would be derived in such a manner as to allow the teacher to *logically* or *empirically* defend the superiority of the standards vis-à-vis other possible standards;
3. would be absolute standards in three senses: They would divide students into those who are masters and those who are not; they would evaluate student learning only on the basis of his learning and not in relation to the learning of others in the class; and, they would be the sole standards used to judge a student's learning;
4. would be attainable given reasonable amounts of resources—both human and nonhuman resources as well as time;
5. would be standards which are representative of *mastery* and not *proficiency*.

As a first approximation to the setting of mastery standards we would offer the following suggestions. For final examinations we would suggest that teachers use the standard which characterized "A" work in the past. This suggestion would at least partially conform to criteria 1, 3, and 4 (above). For diagnostic–progress tests we would suggest that teachers set as a standard a certain percentage correct on the test. In general we would suggest 85 to 90% as an initially appropriate standard. This level of performance is quite frequently used (e.g., Hapkiewicz, 1971a, 1971b; Chandler, 1973; Littlejohn, 1973) and has at least a modicum of research support (Block, 1970). The reader should be aware, however, that other approaches to mastery teaching (e.g., Keller, 1968; Corey & McMichael, 1970; Born, 1971) set a mastery standard of 100% correct. Suffice it to say that careful consideration should be given to the setting of mastery standards.

Planning

As we alluded to in our earlier discussion, there are several teaching functions which can be subsumed under the category of planning. First, the teacher must construct a final, comprehensive examination. Of course teachers who already possess a final examination that they believe "taps" their course objectives need not consider this planning function.

We would suggest that the final examination meet two criteria. First, it should be summative in that it "sums up" student learning over the entire course. Second, it should be criterion- and domain—referenced in that it "sums up" student learning with respect to *what* he was expected to learn, rather than how well he has learned relative to his peers. With respect to these two criteria we would refer interested teachers to the excellent source books by Bloom, Hastings, and Madaus, 1971; Gronlund, 1973; and E. L. Thorndike, 1971 (see especially Chaps. 4, 6, and 7).

Once the teacher has constructed the final examination, he or she next divides the course into a series of teaching—learning units. Rather than look at the course in its entirety, we have found it useful to break the course down into a number of teaching—learning units. Each of the units will contain only a particular subset of the course objectives. The units can then be taught so that mastery of each unit's objectives will culminate in mastery of the overall course objectives.

There are at least two ways of identifying teaching—learning units. One way is to return to the course table of specificiations and parse the table into small subsets of related objectives. Each subset of objectives constitutes a teaching—learning unit. We have found that useful teaching—learning units cover about 2 to 3 weeks of objectives. In actual practice, the length of time spent on learning units has ranged from 4 days (e.g., Keller, 1968) to $2\frac{1}{2}$ weeks (e.g., Chandler, 1973).

If the course is largely textbook oriented we have suggested a second way of identifying teaching—learning units. Teaching—learning units can roughly correspond to the chapters of the textbook. It is not necessary for a single chapter to constitute a learning unit. Several related chapters may be combined into one unit, or a chapter may be broken down into one or more units depending on the length of time desired for each learning unit.

Once the teaching—learning units have been identified, the teacher must decide on the order in which the units will be taught. Some approaches to mastery teaching (e.g., Hapkiewicz, 1971a, 1971b) order the units virtually by default. The units correspond with the chapters of a textbook and are taken in the order in which they appear in the text. Little or no consideration is given to the relationship of one unit to the other units in the course.

We would suggest that the teacher attempt to arrange the units in some sequential manner, either hierarchically or nonhierarchically. Hierarchical sequencing requires a careful task analysis and a subsequent examination of the required prerequisite skills and abilities necessary to master each successive unit (cf. Gagné, 1968; White, 1973). The teacher attempting to design hierarchical units must answer the question "What does the learner have to be able to do before he can master the present unit?" Thus hierarchical sequencing focuses mainly on the relationship among the *intellectual operations* required by each of the succeeding units.

Nonhierarchical sequencing (e.g., Chandler, 1973) focuses on a careful examination of the *content* to be learned. This type of sequencing is often done for pedagogical reasons. For example, an instructor may feel that a student should consider behavioral approaches to motivation before cognitive approaches to motivation. The reasons for placing the behaviorist approach before the cognitivist approach might include the desire to provide the student with a historical perspective or the desire to develop the cognitivist perspective on the basis of disagreements with the behaviorists' approach.

Once the teacher has the teaching–learning units identified and arranged in some order, he or she proceeds to draw up a table of specifications for each unit. To a great extent this entails the breaking down of the general *content areas* into sets of *content elements*. We have found the following types of content elements to be useful in drawing up unit tables of specifications: terms (or new vocabulary), facts (or verbal information), concepts, principles, and procedures (Block & Anderson, 1975). Thus rather than the rows of the table consisting of general content areas, they consist of the specific content elements that are parts or portions of the general content areas. The columns of the unit tables are the same as those for the course table in that they contain the possible intellectual operations that the students might be expected to perform on or with the content elements.

The teacher now possesses instructional objectives, performance standards, a final examination, and a number of teaching–learning units, complete with tables of specifications, arranged in some order. He or she next turns to the development of the instructional plan for each unit.

Let it be clear that we are proposing a group-based approach to individualized instruction in which students are able to learn cooperatively with their classmates. By group-based, here, we are referring to the fact that instruction is provided for all the students in a class and the entire class moves from unit to unit as a group. The teacher has the responsibility of setting the date for the completion of each learning unit. We believe it is this emphasis on the group-based plan that most clearly differentiates our approach to teaching for mastery from other approaches which the reader will encounter in this volume. Most approaches to mastery learning employ learner-paced instruction (e.g., Keller, 1968; Corey & McMichael, 1970; Born, 1971; Hapkiewicz, 1971a, 1971b; Chandler, 1973).

The group-based instructional plan should focus on four major factors. In the design of the plan the teacher must include materials and/or activities which serve (*a*) to attract the students' attention, (*b*) to present the students with information concerning *what* they are to learn and *how* they are to learn it, (*c*) to help the students to become involved in the learning process, and (*d*) to encourage the students when necessary to keep them actively involved in the learning process for a period of time sufficient for learning to occur. Let us consider each of these in turn.

The major purpose of attracting the students' attention is so that they are "with the teacher" when information about the unit's learning is being presented. The teacher's ideas and thoughts concerning solutions to the attention problem should be built into the instructional plan.

Once the teacher has designed attention-getting activities, he or she next designs methods of presenting the class with specific information concerning *what* they are to learn in the unit. There are several methods of presentation which can be used. The students can be given the unit table of specifications which will provide an overview of the entire unit. For particular portions of the units (that is, particular class periods or particular assignments) the students can be given study or adjunct questions (cf. Frase, 1970; Rothkopf, 1970), or they can be provided with a set of "advance organizers" (Ausubel, 1968).

Next, the teacher has to design whole-class activities which will lead to the attainment of the desired unit objectives. These activities may include lectures, discussions, audiovisual presentations, worksheets, and laboratory activities. Once these are designed into the plan, the teacher must also plan to inform the students of the basic activity or activities that will be used in teaching each unit for mastery.

Now, the teacher must design ways of getting the students actively engaged in the process of learning. Generally, this involves the use of some type of incentive for learning. The incentives may be built in as either internal or external incentives. If the teacher wishes to build in internal incentives we encourage him or her to use materials and/or activities which play on the students' background (that is, their prior experiences, interests, concerns) and on their desire to seek out, rather than to avoid, stimulation and excitement. If the teacher wishes to build in external incentives we encourage him to use *material incentives* (e.g., grades), *social incentives* (e.g., praise) and/or *learner-preferred activities* (that is, activities in which the student would be likely to engage were he free to choose) (Premack, 1965).

In addition, the teacher can help the students to become actively involved in learning by asking them to perform various learning strategies while they are in the presence of the learning activity. For example, if the major type of learning activity is a teacher lecture, the teacher may ask the student to:

1. take notes in some systematic manner
2. take notes only on those ideas with which the student disagrees
3. be able to summarize in 100 words the "meat" of the lecture.

Various types of learning strategies can be designed for each of the classroom activities to be employed by the teacher.

Next, the teacher must design ways of maintaining the students' involvement once it initially has begun. This most frequently takes the form of some type of encouragement by the teacher, either oral or written.

Once the teacher has designed the group-based instructional plan he must design the unit diagnostic–progress tests. The function of these tests is to provide feedback to both the teacher and the students concerning the extent to which the unit objectives have been achieved as a result of the original instruction. We would suggest that information be provided to the students on an objective by objective basis. Some approaches to teaching for mastery (e.g., Keller, 1968; Corey & McMichael, 1970; Born, 1971; Hapkiewicz, 1971a, 1971b) provide information on the students' performance over all of the objectives in the unit. We believe that the objective by objective approach provides more specific information concerning the learner's misunderstandings. The total score approach only provides information concerning whether or not the learner has mastered the unit.

We would suggest that teachers write at least two forms of the diagnostic–progress test. The first form can be used to assess the effects of the original instruction. The second form (which we call a *review test*) can be used to assess the effects of the corrective instructional procedures.

Finally, the teacher must develop the corrective instructional procedures for the unit to be used by those students who failed to attain the mastery standard on the unit diagnostic–progress test after the original instruction. The combination of the feedback provided to the students via the diagnostic–progress tests and the procedures for allowing the students to correct their errors and misunderstandings seems to be one of the keys to the success of mastery learning programs. We have one cardinal rule for the development or selection of correctives in our mastery learning approach. They must teach for the same objectives as does the group-based plan, but they must do so in ways that differ from this plan. This is to say that different types of activities should be used to facilitate learning and that, if necessary, different incentives be used to foster student involvement. For example, if the original instructional activity requires the student to read a textbook, the corrective activity may require the student to listen to a lecture, view a slide–tape presentation, or become involved in a discussion of the items on the diagnostic–progress test. We have suggested the use of the following general types of correctives: alternative textbooks, workbooks, audiovisual materials, academic games, programmed instruction materials, tutoring, and small group study sessions. Some approaches to mastery teaching, however, provide correctives which are quite similar in nature to the activities provided in the original instruction (Keller, 1968; Corey & McMichael, 1970; Born, 1971; Chandler, 1973). For example, if the major activity in original instruction was reading the textbook, the corrective activity may be rereading portions of the textbook or reading parts of an alternative textbook.

We would further suggest that the teacher provide specific corrective activities for each of the items, or clusters of items, on the diagnostic—progress tests. In this way, the learner engages in activities which are the most relevant to his particular misunderstandings. Some mastery approaches (e.g., Keller, 1968; Chandler, 1973) provide a general set of activities for the entire set of items on the feedback device.

In order to communicate to the learner the particular activities that are tied to particular test items, we would recommend the use of a "corrective sheet" which can be given to students after the diagnostic—progress test results are in. This sheet would simply indicate the number of each item on the test and the objective tested by each item. Beneath each objective it would then list the particular corrective activity or activities that the student might use to review and/or restudy the material in the unit relevant to the particular objective.

Managing

Once the teaching plan has been carefully designed, the teacher must manage the classroom situation to see that the plan is implemented correctly and student learning is progressing as expected.

The teacher's managing function begins with an orientation session for all students in the course. It is imperative that the students be oriented to the "game plan." Specifically, the teacher must carefully delineate the responsibilities that he will assume and those that he expects the students to assume. The teacher needs to communicate to the students the instructional objectives, the grading procedure, the use of the diagnostic—progress tests, and the use of the corrective activities. If used, he should also explain the use of adjunct questions, tables of specifications and the like.

The typical implementation of the mastery teaching plan would follow this skeletal outline.

1. Present the students with information concerning *what* they are going to learn in each unit.
2. Present the students with information concerning the activity or activities for each unit.
3. Announce the date of the diagnostic—progress test and the mastery standards on the test.
4. On a day by day basis, present the student with information concerning *what* and *how* he is to learn. Use incentives and suggest learning strategies to help the students become involved in learning.
5. Administer the diagnostic—progress test at the designated time.
6. Have students correct their own tests.
7. Meet with nonmasters on the unit. In this meeting:
    a. Hand out the "corrective sheet."

    b. If necessary, set up times at which students can make use of the necessary corrective activities.

    c. Give the students the *review* diagnostic–progress test and tell them to do only those items which correspond to the incorrect items on the diagnostic–progress test. Further, tell them to write their answers to the review test only after they have completed the corrective activity or activities.

8. After all of the learning units have been completed, administer the final summative test.

Evaluation

In our mastery strategy, evaluation takes on three forms. First, the teacher must grade the students. As we have already indicated, the grading procedure should be based on the course objectives and the performance standard or standards. We have encourated teachers to assign only grades of mastery/non-mastery or the equivalent (e.g., "A/F") on the basis of student performance on the final, comprehensive examination. This approach seems to be compatible with the definition of mastery presented earlier in this chapter. For a great variety of reasons, most approaches to teaching for mastery (e.g., Keller, 1968; Hapkiewicz, 1971a, 1971b; Chandler, 1973; Littlejohn, 1973) have assigned grades ranging from A through F.

In addition, some approaches (Littlejohn, 1973) grade on the basis of a mid-term examination, final examination and course projects. Other approaches (Hapkiewicz, 1971a, 1971b) grade on the basis of the cumulative results on the unit tests, or some combination of the unit tests and the final examination. Still other approaches (Keller, 1968) grade on the basis of the *number of units* successfully mastered.

We realize that our suggested grading procedure, even though it is most compatible with our definition of mastery, presents several potential problems for the teacher. One potential problem concerns the amount of student anxiety created by this type of evaluation. We believe that an appropriate, well-planned orientation procedure can help to alleviate this anxiety to some extent. In addition it seems useful to provide additional information to the students throughout the course and especially on the eve of the final examination.

In this regard, we have found it useful for teachers to reemphasize their dual roles as *teacher* and *certifier*. In the role of teacher, teachers attempt to the best of their ability to help all students learn, that is, their responsibility in this role is to the students. In the role of certifier, however, teachers have to make a judgment as to whether or not a student is, in fact, a qualified individual with respect to the course objectives, that is, their responsibility is to their profession since that profession has given them the responsibility of certifying students. We have found this realistic approach to the problem to be quite effective, although other approaches to this problem need to be devised and implemented.

In addition to grading students, the teacher must communicate to the students the meaning of the grades received. We would suggest that each student be given a modified version of the course table of specifications. In this modified table, the teacher places an "M" in each cell which represents an objective mastered by the student and an "NM" in each cell which represents an objective the student has failed to master. The student can see at a glance which course objectives he or she mastered and which he or she did not. The student can also use the the table to see how the grade mirrors his or her performance over the desired course objectives.

Lastly, with respect to the evaluation responsibility of the teacher, the teacher should check on the overall effectiveness of the present mastery learning program. Clearly if the mastery learning program has produced no greater student learning than the customary group-based methods, then the teacher may wish to stop teaching for mastery. But if the program has produced notably greater student learning, the teacher may want to continue teaching for mastery and to upgrade the program so that it produces even better results.

If the teacher has previously taught the course by nonmastery methods, the effectiveness of the mastery program can be seen by comparing the number of students who received an "A" in the mastery program with the number receiving an "A" in the nonmastery program. This comparison is facilitated, of course, if the same final examination is used in both courses.

If the teacher has not previously taught the course we would offer the following information which might help the teacher in checking on the program's effectivness. Commonly, we find the most successful mastery learning strategies help about 30 to 50% of their students to earn "A's" the first time they are used. Thus, the teacher might expect somewhere from 30 to 50% of their students to receive mastery (or "A") grades the first time the program is implemented.

Revision

As we have pointed out earlier, the revision of the mastery learning programs roughly corresponds to the "corrective" portion of the actual teaching for mastery strategy. We believe that the teacher should revise his initial attempt at teaching for mastery with the help of the information gathered throughout the implementation of the mastery program.

The information available comes from the diagnostic—progress tests, review tests, and the final, summative test. From the diagnostic—progress tests the teacher obtains information concerning the quality of the original instruction in particular units. Low mean scores on the unit diagnostic—progress tests usually indicate that there are problems with the original instruction on that unit. From the review tests the teacher obtains information concerning the quality of the corrective instruction. Low mean scores on the unit review tests indicate that there are problems with the corrective activities. Finally, a comparison of the results of the diagnostic–progress tests with particular relevant sections of the final summative test gives teachers information with respect to particular units in relation to the entire course. This information provides the teacher with a start toward improving the existing mastery learning program.

One caution must be pointed out in this regard, however. In order to revise the actual *design* of the mastery learning plan, the teacher must be quite certain that the plan was *implemented* properly. Too often when a problem is seen in the attainment of the desired learning outcomes in a particular unit, immediate attempts are begun to revise the design of the plan. Little or no attention is paid to the extent to which the plan was correctly implemented. A check on the effectiveness of the implementation of the plan requires some type of systematic observation of the learners and/or questionnaries presented to the learners asking them to what extent they made use of various instructional activities, corrective activities, and review tests. If several students did not actually participate in the mastery learning strategy we would suggest that they be differentiated from those who participated fully. Only the results pertaining to students who participated fully in the mastery program should be used to evaluated and revise the *design of the instructional plan.*

SUMMARY

In this chapter we have described the philosophical basis underlying teaching for mastery and one approach to teaching for mastery that we believe follows from this philosophical basis. We would like to close with the following comments.

First, it is obvious that the planning stage requires considerable work over a period of time to develop properly. We would suggest, therefore, that you develop your mastery learning program over some period of time. A skeletal program might include the delineation and statement of instructional objectives, the designation of the mastery performance standard(s), the delineation of learning units, the construction of the summative test and diagnostic–progress tests for each unit, the use of the same original instruction as is currently being used, and the selection of an all purpose corrective activity (such as small group discussion or peer tutoring). As time permits, additional elements can be included.

Second, in return for your time and effort you may get called to task by your colleagues and/or administration. The administration may be concerned over "too many 'A's." Their first reaction to the appearance of so many "A's" is that your standards have slipped and are simply too low. Colleagues, on the other hand, may be concerned about their failure to produce similar results. They may even begin to treat you as union members traditionally have treated "rate busters." They may attempt to downgrade your efforts by saying that your program "spoils" students, that is, that you are spoon-feeding students.

Earlier we mentioned the necessity of defending one's values. We believe that it is with respect to the above stated issues that you will need to do a great deal of defending. We hope that our initial discussion of our conception of mastery and the basic assumptions underlying teaching for mastery may provide you with some ammunition for this defense. In the long run, however, you, as a teacher of educational psychology, must decide whether the additional time and effort required, and the potential barbs of your administrators and colleagues, are worth the opportunity to have a consistent and positive impact on most of the students who enroll in a course or a program.

In conclusion, we would contend that the elements and functions involved in a mastery learning program are simply those elements and functions that are components of good teaching. Unfortunately, the label of "mastery learning" (or any other label for that matter) might tend to "turn people off," and they unfortunately avoid any and all elements of a program with that given label. We believe the reader will find that many of the elements and functions presented in this chapter are central to the strategies for teaching educational psychology presented in the following chapters of this volume. We would hope that the reader will pick out these elements as they are encountered. Our hope is that the ideas of mastery teaching are adopted and implemented in the teaching of educational psychology. We are less concerned that our particular approach to teaching for mastery is adopted. We are even less concerned that the label of "mastery learning" be attached to the program once it is designed and implemented.

REFERENCES

Ausubel, D. P. *Educational psychology: A cognitive view.* New York: Holt, Rinehart & Winston, 1968.

Block, J. H. *The effects of various levels of performance on selected cognitive, affective, and time variables.* Unpublished doctoral dissertation, University of Chicago, 1970.

Block, J. H. Student learning and the setting of mastery performance standards. *Educational Horizons,* 1972, *50,* 183–191.

Block, J. H. Teachers, teaching and mastery learning. *Today's Education,* 1973, *63,* 30–36.

Block, J. H., & Anderson, L. W. *Mastery learning in classroom instruction.* New York: Macmillan, 1975.

Bloom, B. S. (Ed.). *Taxonomy of educational objectives: Handbook I, cognitive domain.* New York: David McKay Company, 1956.

Bloom, B. S. Learning for mastery.*Evaluation Comment,* 1968, *1*(2).

Bloom, B. S. An introduction to mastery learning theory. In Block, J. H. (Ed.), *Schools, society and mastery learning.* New York: Holt, Rinehart & Winston, 1974.

Bloom, B. S., Hastings, J. T., and Madaus, G. F. *Handbook on formative and summative evaluation of student learning.* New York: McGraw-Hill, 1971.

Born, D. G. *Instructional manual for the development of a personalized instruction course.* Center to Improve Learning and Instruction, University of Utah, 1971.

Bruner, J. S. *Toward a theory of instruction.* Cambridge: Harvard University Press, 1966.

Carroll, J. B. A model of school learning. *Teachers College Record,* 1963, *64,* 723–733.

Chandler, T. A. *Utilization of a contract approach in a graduate educational psychology course.* Paper presented at the American Educational Research Association Annual Meeting, New Orleans, 1973.

Corey, J. R., & McMichael, J. S. *Using personalized instruction in college courses.* New York: Meredith Corporation, 1970.

Cronbach, L. J. Book review of *Mastery learning: theory and practice.* In *International Review of Education,* 1972, *18,* 250–252.

Frase, L. T. Boundary conditions for mathemagenic behaviors. *Review of Educational Research,* 1970, *40,* 337–347.

Gagné, R. M. Learning hierarchies. *Educational Psychologist,* 1968, *6,* 1–6.

Gagné, R. M. *Essentials of learning for instruction.* Hinsdale, Illinois: Dryden Press, 1974.

Gronlund, N.E. *Preparing criterion-referenced tests for classroom instruction.* New York: Macmillan, 1973.

Hapkiewicz, W. G. *Mastery learning options in teaching educational psychology.* Unpublished manuscript, Michigan State University, 1971. (a)

Hapkiewicz, W. G. *Mastery learning options in teaching Education 411: Educational Psychology. Final Report.* Unpublished manuscript, Michigan State University, 1971. (b)

Hilgard, E. R., & Bower, G. H. *Theories of learning (Fourth Edition).* Englewood Cliffs, New Jersey: Prentice-Hall, 1975.

Inkeles, A. Social structure and the socialization of competence. *Harvard Educational Review,* 1966, *36,* 265–283.

Keller, F. S. Goodbye, Teacher . . . . *Journal of Applied Behavioral Analysis,* 1968, *1,* 79–89.

Kryspin, W. J., & Feldhusen, J. F. *Writing behavioral objectives: A guide to planning instruction.* Minneapolis: Burgess, 1974.

Littlejohn, M. T. *A mastery approach for large classes in introductory educational psychology.* Paper presented at the American Educational Research Association Annual Meeting, New Orleans, 1973.

Morrison, H. C. *The practice of teaching in the secondary school.* Chicago: University of Chicago Press, 1926.

Morrison, H. C. *The practice of teaching in the secondary school. (2nd ed.)* Chicago: University of Chicago Press, 1931.

Premack, D. Reinforcement theory. In D. Levine (Ed.), *Nebraska symposium on motivation.* (Vol. 13.) Lincoln, Nebraska: University of Nebraska Press, 1965.

Rothkopf, E. Z. The concept of mathemagenic behaviors. *Review of Educational Research,* 1970, *40,* 337–347.

Thorndike, E. L. *The measurement of intelligence.* New York: Teachers College, Columbia University, 1926.

Thorndike, R. L. (Ed.). *Educational measurement* (2nd ed.). Washington, D.C.: American Council on Education, 1971.

Thurstone, L. L. Primary mental abilities. *Psychological Monographs,* 1938, No. 1.

Washburne, C. W. Educational measurement as a key to individualizing instruction and promotion. *Journal of Educational Research,* 1922, *5,* 195–206.

White, R. T. Research into learning hierarchies. *Review of Educational Research,* 1973, *43,* 361–375.

White, R. W. Motivation reconsidered: The concept of competence. *Psychological Review,* 1959, *66,* 297–333.

9

Competency-Based Formats in Educational Psychology

ROBERT L. HOHN

University of Kansas

The establishment and implementation of competency-based (CB) approaches to instruction, both in teacher-training programs and other educational formats have proliferated in recent years (Menges, 1975). Essentially, CB formats emphasize the demonstration of behaviors critical to the professional field by the trainee. The movement was given impetus by USOE funding of Model Elementary Teacher Education Programs in 1970 requiring some form of performance criteria to be employed in program evaluation. The American Association of Colleges for Teacher Education (AACTE) has produced a recent series of papers which examine competency or performance-based education (Andrews, 1972; Massanari, 1971; Merwin, 1973; Cooper & Weber, 1972). Recent financial support from the Fund for the Improvement of Post Secondary Education, established through the Education Amendments Act of 1972, has fostered CB approaches in other professional areas as well as teacher education. Some of the areas funded were: nursing education at Mt. Hood Community College; public and community service at the University of Massachusetts–Boston; and public safety at the University of California–Riverside (Gwaltney, 1973). While educational psychologists are becoming increasingly involved in CB applications in those fields and others, this chapter will emphasize teacher training as the best illustration of the issues and problems raised by this approach.

The CB movement has accelerated in teacher education for a myriad of theoretical, political, and practical reasons which are worthy of review. Perhaps most importantly, the notion that teaching may be viewed as a set of identifiable skills that can be practiced and improved, as in microteaching (McDonald & Allen, 1967), has led to a reconceptualization of teacher training. A related belief is that teaching behavior can be studied in its own right as a natural act rather than as a derivation of psychological theories of thinking and learning (Smith, 1971). Both views tend to reduce emphasis on traditional theoretical content and convert training programs to more functional, experience-based formats. The rationale for this transformation is not unsupported; reviews of research derived from traditional psychological theories of learning and teaching provide a pessimistic summary of the usefulness of these constructs to educational practice (Dubin & Taveggia, 1968; Rosenshine & Furst, 1971; Stephens, 1967).

Elam (1971) examined the historical context in which CB programs have arisen and described several additional factors which have encouraged the movement. The most important of those that he cited were:

1. the development of technological advancements permitting business and industry to enter the educational field, have placed emphasis on the preparation of educational "products" with marketable skills or competencies,
2. the underlying concepts of CB programs fit the desires of educational critics and recent taxpayer pressures to hold teachers "accountable" for their actions,
3. dissatisfaction with the ability of traditional programs to prepare teachers to deal with urgent needs of society, such as teaching minority group children, has also had impact (Conant, 1963),
4. the expanded voice of teachers expressed through their unions has led to greater teacher input into preparation programs and renewed examination of what specific skills teachers themselves believe they require (Fisher, 1970).

The term "competency" requires some explanation before proceeding, particularly in contrast to the word "performance" for which it is often interchanged. In adopting the descriptor "performance-based teacher education," the AACTE distinguished between performance as denoting specific teacher behavior, and competency denoting knowledge acquisition and product completion by the trainee. They chose the term performance-based, yet argued that this term is not limited to only performance criteria (Elam, 1971). It would appear that the term was ill-chosen. Strong relationships between teacher "performances" and student achievement have never been clearly demonstrated (Heath & Nielson, 1974; Rosenshine & Furst, 1971). Moreover, the predominantly behavioral association most educators and psychologists apply to the word performance, tends to restrict the meaning that was apparently intended. The inexact state of our present knowledge of what constitutes the necessary skills of an effective teacher or other professional seems to be best represented by an as yet undetermined blend of knowledge and related performances and skills. The more inclusive term "competency" may better describe the terminal goals toward which most training programs strive. As Anderson and Block state elsewhere in this book, the term competency may also imply the attainment of self-confidence or the sense of being able to cope successfully with the demands of a given task, as well as to the mastery of performances relevant to that task. If this affective component is viewed as a necessary ingredient of professional expertise as well, then the term competency may be more appropriate in describing the intent of most professional programs.

WHAT ARE COMPETENCY-BASED PROGRAMS?

For an instructional program to be classified as competency-based, the following elements are considered essential by the AACTE (Elam, 1971):

1. Competencies to be demonstrated by the student are derived from explicit conceptions of teachers' roles and are publicly stated in such a manner that students' learned behaviors are related to specific competencies.

2. Criteria to be employed in assessing competencies are explicit in stating expected levels of mastery under specified conditions.

3. Assessment of competency depends on student performance as the primary source of evidence and strives for objectivity.

4. Student's rate of progress is determined by demonstrated competency rather than time or course completion.

5. Instructional program is intended to facilitate the development of student achievement of specified competencies.

From this definition, CB approaches require explicit objectives related to teaching that are publicly provided the trainee in advance and serve as the basis for evaluation of the student's progress. It does not appear necessary that all possible outcomes of a training program be competency-related, only that there is an active, ongoing attempt at identifying critical teaching behaviors and specifying them in terms of student performance.

In addition to these essential elements, CB programs have become associated with a variety of structural and theoretical characteristics which are not necessary to the basic concept of competency-based training. These include modular instruction; interdisciplinary, field-based demonstration; trainee participation; and continual evaluation. Learning "modules" have been employed in which specific objectives are mastered within shorter periods of instruction and practice than the typical college quarter or semester (Houston, Hollis, Jones, Edwards, Pace, & White, 1972). Modules often purport to provide a variety of alternative instructional strategies and routes leading to the same objective(s). They are designed to encourage self-pacing and independence within the program and permit students to match their learning styles and preferences with available alternatives. Under these conditions, the learner accepts responsibility for being held accountable for meeting established criteria at the close of instruction. Attendance at specific lectures, reading an assignment by a certain date, and other traditional structural requirements are deemphasized (Houston & Howsam, 1972).

Most modules and courses in CB programs require applications and demonstrations of critical behaviors in field settings rather than within the campus classroom. Such an arrangement often requires an interdisciplinary approach utilizing the expertise of professionals representing the traditional domains of teacher training as well as related areas. It may also require the formal as well as informal employment of classroom teachers for purposes of field-based training and support (Shearron, 1975).

In addition, CB programs appear to encourage greater participation of trainees in planning their own program and adapting course objectives to their particular strengths and weaknesses. The apparent hope is that prospective teachers will become more effective decision makers as teachers if provided the opportunity to share responsibility at an early time. This strategy often facilitates an additional characteristic of many CB programs, that of continual feedback. By involving the trainee in the development of a personalized program, evaluation of one's emerging competence becomes formative rather than summative, and is expected to aid the individual in recognizing and judging one's potential as a teacher (AACTE, 1974).

The reader is urged to examine several programs for a more detailed description of how the CB format is implemented and conducted at various training centers. Descriptions of programs worthy of consideration are provided by Burke (1971), Dickson and Saxe (1973), Giles and Foster (1972), and Shearron and Johnson (1973). Analytic reviews of programs and their components have been prepared by Elfenbein (1972), Houston and Howsam (1972), and Schmieder (1973).

Competency-based programs tend to blur distinctions between those disciplines that have traditionally contributed to the training of teachers, such as educational psychology, philosophy, sociology, etc. The interdisciplinary, field-based approach, which characterizes many programs, tends to change training into a set of experiences wherein the usual course structure associated with teacher education is modified. An introductory course in educational psychology, for example, may not be required; rather competencies related to the psychology of education are acquired throughout the program.

The educational psychologist involved in CB programs may thus be asked to assume a new role, a role that may limit one's autonomy and alter one's professional identity to some degree. This would appear desirable to the extent that such an alteration leads to an improved program and superior products. However, the accumulated knowledge, experience, and techniques that our professional field brings to teacher preparation should be recognized and encouraged as a unique and important contribution to any program.

The remainder of this chapter will discuss those issues and problems that will be of particular concern to the educational psychologist considering teaching or research involvement in a CB program. Issues related to instruction will be examined first, specifically those related to content, pedagogical techniques and assessment procedures. Research problems and questions will be addressed in a subsequent section.

INSTRUCTIONAL ISSUES — CONTENT

The content to be taught in CB programs is dependent upon what competencies are deemed necessary to training. The process of competency identification will be considered first with a subsequent analysis of the role of theory in competency selection. Program structure and sequence will be discussed at the close of this section.

Identification of Competencies

The question of what should be learned by a prospective trainee depends on what skills one conceives of as necessary for competency. Most programs determine terminal objectives through faculty consensus, or with the collaboration of public school personnel, professional organizations and others directly affected (Elfenbein, 1972). Such attempts have generally led to lists of competencies written in behavioral terms, which then become the performance goals of the program. Some examples of competencies in one program are: "The teacher specifies goals and objectives," "The teacher evaluates learner performance," "The teacher determines the instructional needs of learners" (Shearron & Johnson, 1973). A catalog of teacher competencies synthesized from a variety of sources exemplifies this approach (Dodl, Gant, Nelson, & Jung, 1973). Drumheller (1974) has argued that such a strategy yields too many objectives, making it difficult for the learner to perceive interrelationships between them. He proposes that CB teacher education should emphasize fewer and more global behaviors to maximize efficiency and morale.

Most behaviors included on competency lists were selected on the basis of traditional models or analyses of teaching. As already suggested, there is little research evidence supporting any one particular teaching skill as necessary to efficient instruction. This does not mean that educators have no ideas about relevant competencies; rather it indicates that research methodology has not yet been applied so that the many available hypotheses about necessary skills can be adequately tested. Ongoing and future research may alter our state of knowledge, but at present it seems imperative that teacher educators take steps to identify important competencies in as valid a manner as possible. Continuous evaluation of those competencies after they have been tentatively identified seems crucial.

Brown and Okey (1973) have developed a classification system that generates groups of objectives (called "competency clusters") through a task analysis approach. Four diverse groups of educators—preservice teachers, employed teachers, principals/supervisors, and teacher educators—were asked to place the competencies among three experience levels—beginning teacher, experienced teacher, and master teacher. Although there was marked disagreement as to the best location of some clusters, high agreement was found for a majority. Clusters such as "effective lecturing," "constructing evaluation measures," and "gaining student attention" were assigned with 70% or more agreement to the beginning teacher level. This approach seems promising for purposes of program development and planning as well as competency identification.

Thomas (1973), dissatisfied with panel approaches to identification of teacher competencies, used a combined questionnaire and group discussion technique with mixed groups of 156 classroom teachers and supervisors of varying experience and background. Much agreement was noted after group discussion; for example, both groups rated human relations competencies as most important and evaluation skills as least important. Interactions were noted between ratings of different competencies and experience of teacher, grade level of teacher, school socioeconomic status, and ethnicity.

Both these studies point out the complexity involved in the identification of program competencies, when judgmental rather than empirical procedures are employed. Not only are multistage, multimeasurement procedures needed, but a careful consideration of differences among and within those groups of educators serving as judges must be made. Finally, the importance of various competencies seems to depend upon the particular role and function to be assumed by the trainee.

Theory versus Practice

Most programs tend to emphasize only that content that transfers directly to the performance of teaching skills. Although this trend is in keeping with the primary objective of CB education, one needs to examine the basic assumptions underlying this emphasis with caution. Knowledge of teaching is not considered a competency in most programs, rather it is defined as an enabling objective or facilitator of terminal competencies (Dodl, 1973). Competencies are defined in terms of behavior applicable to all teachers and are often referred to as generic (Shearron & Johnson, 1973). For example, in a course stressing reinforcement principles, written recall and description of reinforcement techniques would be an enabling objective. A subsequent objective might require the teacher–trainee to demonstrate appropriate reinforcement techniques in a real classroom setting. Competency might only be acknowledged however, when the trainee produced a desirable change in pupil behavior (an increase in achievement, reduction of disruptive behavior, or an increase in some social response) as a result of the reinforcement techniques employed. Most advocates of CB programs stress this final level of performance (described as consequence objectives, for example, by Houston & Howsam, 1972) as the level at which students are held accountable (Dodl, 1973; Schalock, 1973).

The basic goal in this sequence is to provide only that knowledge which is directly related to the consequence(s) of interest. Inevitably this leads to a deemphasis of theory for theory's sake and stresses only theoretical knowledge which is instrumental to teacher performance. Broudy (1972) has argued that such a training approach creates a learning situation in which teachers are not professional in the traditional sense, but become apprentices trained to operate as "didactical machines." He further states that if "individual teachers are to do more than operate as didactical machines, they will have to be adept in context building, i.e., in the interpretive uses of theory." His distinction between theory as rule-generating (as evidenced by operant conditioning principles) and theory as context-building (e.g., broader, contrasting positions on the nature of reinforcement is quite instructive (Broudy, 1968). Certainly, rule-generating theories instrumental in teacher performance should be emphasized in CB programs. However, the educational psychologist must continue to insist that the competent teacher should also acquire a broad reservoir of interpretive theory and knowledge to resort to when technical skills fail, as they often do when confronted with the irregularities of educational practice.

Structure and Sequence of Programs

Program development to date has followed a two-stage vertical structure. Specific knowledge components or enabling objectives precede the acquisition of generic competencies. In terms of Bloom's taxonomy of the cognitive domain (1956), final training objectives emphasize the application level. As already suggested, there may be a deemphasis or narrowing of knowledge and comprehension outcomes. Mastery of the set of competencies deemed necessary for the competent professional by the program designers terminates training.

Little consideration has yet been given to the sequence through which competencies are to be acquired. It appears to be assumed that demonstration of all necessary skills regardless or oder of acquisition is sufficient for competence. Often the flexibility allowed by such an approach is viewed as a strength in that it constitutes an individualized component useful for student growth (Elam, 1971).

There is a growing body of literature however, that suggests that organization and sequence of content may have a direct result on program effectiveness. For example, Fuller (1969) has established that teachers progress through a developmental sequence of concerns about their profession. This sequence contains a preteaching phase which is marked by nonconcern with the specifics of teaching, an early teaching phase characterized by self-evaluation (based on one's ability to control a class, to understand and explain subject matter, and to cope with a superior's evaluation), and a later teaching phase in which the well-being of pupils is considered. Although further clarifying research on this sequence is needed, it would appear that most programs meet the needs of teachers in a sequence different from the sequence in which teachers feel those needs (Fuller & Brown, 1975). Mastery of competencies which allow the reduction or removal of self-concerns should occur early in programs, following Fuller's conceptualization. This might be accomplished by the implementation of individual counseling procedures, brief, actual teaching experience prior to course work, and continual support and feedback by trainers.

Other researchers have suggested rationales for different program sequences. Scott (1974) described seven "levels of involvement" from the traditional college classroom through contrived settings to field settings that demand increasing degrees of autonomy of the trainee. Each level requires different competencies for success, and students move from a lower level to a higher one as objectives are met. Scott's system is similar to Turner's "Levels of Criteria" (1971) in which the prospective teacher moves up a hierarchy reflecting increasing correspondence to the actual teaching situation. Each level in this proposal requires different forms of evidence of mastery from cognitive outcomes at the lowest levels to short- and long-term pupil behavior change at the highest. In both rationales, sequence is relatively fixed. These views and those of others suggest that the question of appropriate program structure and sequence, rather than being resolved, is just beginning to emerge as a serious object of study.

INSTRUCTIONAL ISSUES—CURRICULAR TECHNIQUES

Competency-based programs as well as other training formats have used a variety of curricular techniques in the preparation of professional personnel. Only those of recent origin and of frequent usage will be discussed here. These will include the development of modules, microteaching, simulation techniques, field-based demonstrations, and individualization procedures.

Modularization

Most learning modules adapted for use in CB programs are designed to individualize instruction so that the learner is able to identify objectives, progress at one's own rate in one's own style, identify strengths and weaknesses, and recycle when objectives have not been achieved (Klingstedt, 1972) For the instructor, modularization may require a more thorough identification of concepts and principles that most directly lead to effective teaching practice, thus "streamlining" instructional content. Although the potential of modules is appealing, and many have advocated module use (Cooper & Weber, 1972; Houston & Howsam, 1972; Klingstedt, 1972), research has not yet established their effectiveness. In fact, modules have often been poorly constructed. Lawrence (1974) in a review of 200 modules, found that two-thirds used measurement procedures and criteria which were inconsistent with competency statements, one-half did not provide specific criteria, and almost one-half did not cover the range of outcomes implied in the competency statement. Other modules suggested activities which were judged as not likely to generate the kind of evidence needed for competency to be determined and did not require demonstration of the competency other than in single "command performance" situations.

Some research has indicated however that modular materials can be a useful tool for changing teacher behavior. Borg and Stone (1974) found that two modules on teacher language ("encouragement" and "extension") produced significant gains for five of seven specific behaviors. The module packages included reading, viewing, written practice, and audiotape recording components, and were as efficient as more expensive microteaching procedures. Merwin (1974) demonstrated that self-instructional modules designed to provide knowledge of and ability to perform higher-order questioning skills in social studies classrooms were effective and positively valued by trainees. The findings indicate that modules can be designed that are consistent with competency statements and effective in producing necessary behavior change.

Microteaching

Microteaching (Allen & Ryan, 1969; McDonald & Allen, 1967) or the use of videotape to record a trainee's teaching of specific concepts to selected students and to provide feedback, has been incorporated into many competency-based programs. Research seems to indicate that this technique is effective in improving trainees' ability to perform specific teaching skills such as questioning, providing reinforcement, prompting, etc. (see Peck & Tucker, 1973 for a review of pertinent studies). Microteaching procedures have been incorporated into mini-courses, or self-instructional packages of training materials (Borg, Kelley,

Langer, & Gall, 1970). Used in this format, 10 teacher skills were observed to change significantly from pretraining levels, and most were maintained as late as 39 months after initial assessment (Borg, 1972).

Microteaching techniques seem to be more effective when the behaviors to be learned are of the "low-inference" category, however (Rosenshine, 1970). Behaviors such as "clarifying objectives" (Emmer & Millet, 1968), "assuming responsibility" (Limbacher, 1969), and "refocusing" (Borg, 1972) that require high inference have not been significantly modified by microteaching experience. This set of findings may be attributable more to the observation systems employed than to the efficacy of microteaching as a training technique, but they do suggest a potential limitation to its generalizability. Nevertheless, microteaching remains a promising tool in the acquisition of specific competencies.

Simulation Techniques

There is a trend in CB programs, as well as in more traditional teacher education programs, for instruction to utilize simulation procedures. While microteaching is one type of simulation, other techniques have been developed which employ peer role-playing. (Twelker, 1967) gaming, or "in-basket" procedures (Shulman, 1965). Simulation does allow a prospective teacher to come into closer contact with the criterion situation for which one is being trained. For the technique to be effective, however, Fitzpatrick and Morrison (1972) contend that comprehensiveness (a broad range of different aspects of the criterion situation are present) and fidelity (the degree to which each simulated aspect approximates the criterial aspect) are necessary. However, the more closely one tries to simulate a real criterion situation, the less reliable is one's measurement of the performance in question, because control becomes more difficult. Problems in reliability may account for the dearth of well-controlled studies of simulation to date. A future task for educational psychologists and other researchers is to develop procedures which judiciously balance comprehensiveness and fidelity with measurement considerations so that the effectiveness of simulation in producing competence can be determined.

Field-Based Emphasis

With the stress placed in most programs on early placement of prospective teachers in the field, educational psychologists will more frequently be required to demonstrate educational applications of psychological principles in school classrooms. For example, Piagetian theory and its application to education might be illustrated by the instructor administering conservation tasks to 6-, 7-, and 8-year-old children in the school. Prospective teachers could practice this skill under the supervision of the instructor, receive feedback, and compare results. However, there is inherent difficulty in establishing and maintaining good university and public school relationships, required by field-based instruction. Other than time and scheduling problems, the objectives of training may be incompatible with the classroom teacher's plans for his or her class. Part of this problem can be alleviated by involving public school personnel in planning the instructional program from its onset, as recommended by the American Association of Colleges for Teacher Education (AACTE) (1974, p. 20).

Individualization

The term individualized instruction has been widely used in education. Most CB programs have incorporated this concept into their design (Elfenbein, 1972; Houston & Howsam, 1972). However, a good deal of confusion seems to exist as to what individualization means, how and when it should be employed, and what outcomes should result.

Gagné and Briggs (1974) have described individualized instruction in reference to five educational techniques: independent study, self-directed study, learner-centered programs, self-pacing, and student-determined instruction. Independent study involves teacher—student agreement as to the purpose of study in only a general way, as in preparing for doctoral examinations. Self-directed study and self-pacing both require agreed upon objectives of a specific nature, but do not restrict the means and materials necessary to learning in self-directed approaches or the rate at which learning is to occur in self-paced formats. Learner-centered programs allow all decision making as to objectives, style, materials, pacing, and evaluation to be made by the learner, while student-determined instruction provides for student judgment in any or all of the above. Obviously individualization can be instituted in a multitude of ways. Chapters elsewhere in this volume examine these techniques more extensively.

Three questions related to the use of individualization techniques in CB formats need to be answered by program designers: (1) When are individualized objectives and resultant alterations in evaluation procedures appropriate? (2) How may self-directed study and self-pacing be employed? and, (3) Which individual differences in aptitude, learning style, personality trait, or interests affect training?

The answer to the first question depends upon the amount of flexibility permitted in the training program. Combs (1972) and Nash and Agne (1971) have criticized CB teacher education programs for maintaining the status quo by ignoring the humanistic concerns and personal desires of its trainees. This does not have to be the case. CB programs can be compatible with personal objectives of trainees by providing time and recognition of individual goals to be acquired.

As long as these objectives are defined so that methods of achieving and measuring them are based on observable performance, the program remains competency-based.

Self-directed study and self-pacing have been found to improve performance and attitudes toward a variety of courses taught in higher education (Alpern, 1966; Hamilton, 1967; Himmel, 1972; Johnston & Pennpacker, 1971; Morriss & Kimbrell, 1972), but complete training programs which incorporate these principles are rare. One ongoing program which does is the Personalized Teacher Education Program at the Texas R & D Center (Butts, Carter, Colton, Gibb, Hall, & Rutherford, 1970). A 5-year analysis of the program revealed that desirable effects on a variety of teaching behaviors and attitudes were obtained which were still in existence up to 1 year after training (Fuller, Peck, Brown, Menaker, White, & Veldman, 1969). Although research examining total programs is useful, further investigation of the effects of various components of self-paced, self-directed programs is also necessary. This may be particularly true in CB programs where these techniques are considered fundamental.

Relationships between selected learner characteristics and instructional methods are frequently found and have been well documented (Goldberg, 1969; Glaser & Resnick, 1972). Teacher-training studies have also noted interactions between individual differences and performance. For example, research by Hunt and Joyce (1967) and Murphy and Brown (1970) indicates that the conceptual systems of teacher trainees correlate positively with reflective teaching and with tendencies to aid students and sanction search behaviors. Turner (1975) has questioned the utility of aptitude—treatment interaction (ATI) studies in teacher education however. He argued that sorting out the many personal characteristics and various treatments that could produce interactions is costly, and that treatment—treatment studies are more essential if teacher work success is to be optimized. Nevertheless, the strong emphasis in most CB programs on individualization suggests that program designers and evaluators should concern themselves with characteristics of those selected for training in order to improve the probability of individual success.

INSTRUCTIONAL ISSUES—ASSESSMENT TECHNIQUES

In an early report on program development, Rosner (1972) identified the development of assessment procedures as the "most significant and critical step in the design, establishment and maintenance of CB teacher education [p. 31]." Yet an AACTE committee later lamented that "assessment has been neglected or attempted in piecemeal fashion, sometimes apparently as an afterthought [AACTE, 1974, p. 18]." The need for appropriate assessment can be considered in two ways: (a) the evaluation of trainee behaviors so that acquisition of competencies during a program component can be validly determined and (b) evaluation of CB programs and program components in comparison to other systems of training or in relation to long-term teacher success. The first issue will be described here; the second will be discussed under the later section on research problems.

Selection of Criteria and Assessment Strategies

Most CB proponents have advocated the demonstration of ability to promote desirable pupil learning as the major means of assessing teacher competency (Houston & Howsam, 1972; Merwin, 1973; Shearron & Johnson, 1973). As Gage and Winne (1975) have stated however, "using student achievement as a basis for evaluating teacher effectiveness . . . is limited to the final, or summative assessment of trainees. More relevant to training is assessment of specific teacher behaviors and their patterning." Determining appropriate, smaller units of teaching behavior and assessing them validly and reliably is not easy however. Quirk (1974) argued that analyzing teacher performance into finer elements may reduce the reliability of individual measures of behavior, particularly when paper and pencil tests are used as criteria. Cox (1974) countered that this concern may not be applicable to criterion-referenced instruments which are designed to assess an individual's attainment of specific behaviors, instead of normative status within a defined population. One resolution of this issue may lie in the use of domain-referenced measurement. A domain consists of a "subset of knowledge, skills, understandings or attitudes where the essential attributes of the content which the student is expected to acquire and the behavior through which he or she is expected to demonstrate such acquisition are carefully described [Baker, 1974]." Domains should function so that a large number of test items can be generated according to given rules and randomly sampled to constitute comparable tests. Reliability of individual measures is thus improved by accurately assessing probabilities of correct performance for items within a domain. Popham (1974) maintained that domain-referenced tests will be more sensitive to the results of instruction because they need not produce high between-student score variance as do norm-referenced tests; "if most learners can master a given behavior domain as reflected by performance or a domain-referenced test, all the better [p. 36]." Obviously, specifying the domains describing teaching or other areas of professional competence is a complex task. Baker (1974) provides some guidelines helpful in specifying domains: the utilization of domain descriptions or behavioral objectives, identification of content limits, statement of criteria for constructed responses, clarification of item format, and provision of clear directions.

It seems clear, however, that assessment of competencies will depend on criteria other than performance on cognitive measures to satisfy the demands of the CB movement. Other assessment techniques, perhaps requiring multiple sets of indicators, may be necessary. Houston (1973) advocates, for example, observation of teacher behaviors, such as encouraging students to independent action, appearing confident, etc., and learner behaviors (attentiveness, activity, etc.) as necessary to completely assess the competency "the teacher creates a positive affective climate conducive to optimal learning [p. 202]." Such a multiple outcome approach may require more sophisticated observation techniques than are currently in use, since pertinent behaviors appear to necessitate a high level of inference.

Soar (1973) suggested greater reliance on observation of teacher and student behaviors for the attainment of higher level objectives, or those requiring more time to develop. The use of observation to verify competency is aided when behaviors are conceptualized as being composed of hierarchically arranged measures, allowing clearer meaning of what constitutes the desired teacher behavior. Soar (1974) describes how "gentle teacher control" could be defined through use of the Florida Climate and Control System (Soar, 1966, p. 106):

1. No more than 10% of teacher directions will be above Level 3 on a 5-point scale of coerciveness
2. At least 50% of teacher directions will be at Level 2 or below
3. No more than 10% of pupil behavior will be resistive or disobedient
4. At least 50% of pupil work should have little supervision.

Although such an observation system still requires difficult judgments as to what level of "coerciveness" or "disobedience" is attained, this procedure does represent an important step toward clarifying and organizing criteria for the assessment of complex competencies.

In arguing against reliance on student achievement as a sole criterion for assessing a teacher training technique, Gage (1974) suggested the use of "proximate criteria" or those further down the causal chain that ultimately lead to pupil outcomes. For example, do trainees have some respect and liking for the particular skill or technique they are in the process of attaining? Does the program component have the intended effect on the trainee's behavior, i.e., is the expected new skill implemented by the trainee when given the opportunity to employ it? Gage feels that if trainee attitudes and behavior are influenced as intended one is justified in regarding the training component as validated. Such an approach requires some confidence in the trainee's ability to evaluate what is being taught, as to its usefulness, interest, and so forth. Musella (1970) was optimistic in this regard; however, research already cited by Fuller (1969) indicated that teachers in the early phases of training may not be ready for such analysis. Perhaps the use of unobtrusive measures as recommended by Gage (1974) could serve as additional validation of the preliminary value of training components. If a module were selected voluntarily, how many trainees elected to complete it? What is the quality of the student's progress through the module determined by observation of study time spent, number of references used, frequency of contact with instructor, etc.? Answers to such questions might provide corroborating evidence for stated opinions by learners.

Performance tests have received attention as a strategy for assessing teacher competence. They employ pupil performance as the criterion for teacher effectiveness yet recognize and control for factors beyond the control of the teacher which may influence student behavior. The assumptions that there are diverse instructional means which may all bring about one particular outcome and that no one technique or competence invariably produces learner achievement are basic to their use (Popham, 1971). They involve providing the teacher trainee with one or more instructional objectives, material about the topic to be taught, and sample test items. The trainee is then given an opportunity to prepare a lesson designed to accomplish the objectives using whatever instructional strategy or strategies considered appropriate by the trainee. The lesson is then conducted with learners randomly selected. A posttest based on the objectives, but not known to the trainee, is administered after instruction, and pupil performance provides an estimate of teacher competence.

When first developed, performance test methodology was thought to be insensitive to differences between individual teachers (Millman, 1973; Popham, 1971). However, the approach has been found to validate the effectiveness of components within a CB program (Levine & Sharp, 1975). Ward, Morine, and Berliner (1974) have recommended the technique as a formative device for diagnosis of specific skills individual teachers may have acquired. Teacher performance is compared to norms accumulated from other trainees, performance of master teachers, and specific performance criteria. These researchers report high reliability for their tests, and stability of performance across parallel lessons is noted. The research that has been described here seems to recommend the continued development and application of performance tests to assessment of CB program components.

Levels of Competence

Related to the issue of what criteria to employ in order to assess competency acquisition during CB programs is the problem of how to distinguish among levels of competence. Most CB programs have adopted mastery/nonmastery or "go–no-go" assessment strategies in which mastery is awarded when minimal criteria are met. At best, the establishment of minimal standards is a complex task (Merwin, 1973). At worst, the decision made may be so narrow that "no-go" is attributed to performance that is completely unacceptable and "go" to any other performance that is not.

Although it is perhaps premature to conceive of distinctions between teachers who "very successfully" lead discussions, and "satisfactorily" lead discussions, it does seem that the identification of differential levels of competence within dimensions of teacher behavior warrants future attention. Reactions of students trained under pass/fail formats often reveal dissatisfaction with the lack of a challenge encountered after meeting minimal standards (Karlins, Kaplan, & Stuart, 1969; Parker, 1974). Research is needed to determine where hierarchical levels are possible, where different levels of competence make a difference in improving pupil behaviors, and where the use of differential levels of competence improves grading practices. In describing hierarchically arranged observation systems, Soar (1973) has indicated one research direction, as in the description of "gentle teacher control" referred to earlier.

Remedial Procedures

CB programs have emphasized formative assessment of trainees, hoping to provide them frequent information about the adequacy of their performance during the program. Little attention has been paid to assessment that leads to remedial procedures; that is, provides information as to what should be done differently during subsequent training. Remediation should not just be repeating the activity from which the individual did not learn initially. The provision of alternative routes to competency as advocated by most programs suggests the need for assessment strategies designed to determine not only failure or success, but the best learning pattern for individual trainees.

The emerging field of domain-referenced testing provides for remediation of cognitive objectives. In the process of domain specification, the relevant attributes of appropriate responses are not only clearly described, but possible inaccurate responses (distractors) are also identified (Baker, 1974). Determining which inaccurate response has occurred should indicate to an instructor what new practice or training is necessary for the correct response to be acquired. Development of domain-referenced specifications of teacher performance could prove useful in determining what kinds of remediation would be effective.

Student Assessment

The increased participation of trainees in planning and revising their own programs requires increased attention to problems of how to incorporate student assessment into program development. The use of student ratings of teacher effectiveness has become an accepted procedure in course and instructor evaluation in higher education (Costin, Greenough, & Menges, 1971; Trent & Cohen, 1973). However, employing student feedback to evaluate entire programs is relatively new. Parker (1974) used student evaluation of a CB program as well as faculty ratings. While there is some agreement between the two groups, he indicates that different dimensions of the program were viewed by the two groups as being most critical; for example, students emphasized the need for greater interaction with faculty and a greater variety of learning experiences, while faculty stressed the problems of reliability and validity of assessment measures. Student ratings of the program were positive in most respects. A study of student reactions to a CB program in special education also revealed high ratings for the program when compared to what students had experienced in earlier courses (Wixson, 1975). While these studies and others currently in progress reveal general student support for most components, traditional evaluation problems, such as Hawthorne effect, have not yet been resolved. Evaluating a complete program, when it is the only training program one is involved in, may be a difficult task for trainees. If program development is to rely on student assessment in the future, problems associated with the validity of student judgments and the relative weight students attach to program characteristics must be resolved.

ADDITIONAL RESEARCH ISSUES

Potential or ongoing research efforts have been identified in the preceding description of instructional issues whenever possible. However, several lines of research seem so fundamental to the implementation, evaluation, and improvement of CB programs that these need to be considered in a separate section. These issues include the relationship of teacher performance to pupil achievement, the training of affective teaching behaviors, program assessment and evaluation, and program component assessment.

Teacher Performance and Student Achievement

The relationship between teacher behavior and student achievement is crucial to the CB concept. For competencies to serve as the basis for a training program, they must be shown to be important to professional effectiveness. Student learning is ordinarily inferred as a sign of professional competence in teaching. Nevertheless, research to date reveals few strong relationships between specific teaching skills and pupil achievement (Dunkin & Biddle, 1974; Rosenshine & Furst, 1971).

Gage and Winne (1975) argue that past research on teacher effectiveness can be useful, however, if clusters of studies of given teacher behavior are examined, rather than their individual significance. They recommend a modification of an approach described by Light and Smith (1971) referred to as "vote-counting," in which studies revealing positive, negative, or no relationships between a selected teacher variable and a specific student outcome are categorized and tallied. The modal category is assumed to give an estimate of the direction of the true relationship between the variables. This approach requires a large number of reviews of selected teacher variables which hold promise of affecting student achievement. The need for further experimental research continues, however, particularly in settings where appropriate controls for confounding variables which affect the teacher–pupil relationship are possible. Merwin (1973) and Soar (1973) recount a number of methodological problems involved in implementing necessary controls.

If such research is to be conducted then some coordinated analysis of the many teacher behaviors identified in the literature seems necessary. Potter (1973) has stated that research and development efforts should be conceptually based, with a clear statement of philosophy or model of teaching preceding competency identification and research. A step in this direction might involve the development of a taxonomy of teacher behavior as suggested by McDonald (1973). He argued that traditional descriptors are not related to pupil learning and that teacher performance might be classified according to those pupil behaviors with which they are associated. A beginning categorization scheme might be in terms of task characteristics accompanying learning outcomes (interest, autonomy, etc.), characteristics of responses to be acquired (type and complexity of student product), and according to the learning paradigm followed.

Medley (1974) has made a similar suggestion in light of difficulties in determining relationships between teacher behavior and pupil learning. He suggested that research linking teacher competencies to behaviors or experiences of pupils that are known to produce learning is of high priority. In such research, pupil behavior that "mediates" achievement becomes the dependent variable, rather than pupil achievement iself. Competencies might be identified and evaluated in terms of whether they lead to these mediating activities, rather than whether they produce achievement directly. Research by Rothkopf (1970) on "mathemagenic activities" illustrates the role of mediating behaviors in learning. Research is needed that both identifies additional mediating activities and describes teacher competencies that produce them.

Affective Training Outcomes

Most CB programs have emphasized the acquisition of cognitive and performance skills as vital to professional competence. Critics contend, however, that affective objectives, such as those of human relations skills, increased achievement motivation, and higher levels of moral judgment, have been ignored (Alschuler & Ivey, 1972). From a social–psychological perspective, the teacher's influence as expressed through moral communication, sanctions, and attitudes greatly affect a student's own moral committments as well as attitudes toward subject matters and their value (Bidwell, 1973). Others argue that by insisting on acquisition of already established competencies, CB education fails to develop trainees' capacities for independent action and free choice (Nash & Ange, 1972).

Unfortunately, training research in which teacher affective behavior serves as the major dependent variable is rare, perhaps because of measurement problems or inadequate research methodologies. Little is known about the structure and sequence of programs designed to produce appropriate affective change; it may well be that traditional program designs emphasizing cognitive and performance outcomes are inadequate. The consistent finding that practice teaching causes student-teachers' attitudes to become more rigid, negative, and authoritarian toward pupils (reviewed in Khan & Weiss, 1973) may reflect the current state of affairs. It appears that research and evaluation of affective training programs, such as those ongoing at the Center for Humanistic Education at the University of Massachusetts and the Center for Development and Research in Confluent Education at the University of California, Santa Barbara, seem critical (Brown, 1975). Of particular interest in studies of affective training will be the interaction of affective behaviors (i.e., awareness of one's emotions) and skills traditionally associated with effective teaching (clarity, firmness, etc.). That is, do affective behaviors acquired by prospective teachers complement traditional performance or do they interfere with the accomplishment of other teaching skills? Is there a change in the kinds of pupil achievements observed if affective teaching behaviors are stressed? The importance of these questions points to the need for researchers in CB programs to increase their efforts in this area.

Program Assessment and Evaluation

Unresolved Problems and Needs

McDonald (1974) has argued that summative evaluation of the effectiveness of CB programs at this time is premature. He bases his argument on the following:

1. Programs are not yet sufficiently developed, with enough graduates to yield worthwhile evaluation data.
2. Criteria for evaluating program effects are niether clearly defined nor agreed upon.
3. Preparation for adequate evaluation designs which provide for comparisons of planned variations has not yet been done (pp. 19–20).

Evidence for the first point is readily apparent in the literature. For example, researchers at Western Kentucky University evaluate 40 graduates of the CB program annually, a sample so small that they fear it limits their ability to make conclusive statements about their findings (Sandefur & Adams, 1973). Other researchers indicating positive effects of CB training (Parker, 1974; Sybouts, 1973) acknowledge the tentativeness of their conclusions because of small sample sizes and the developmental nature of their efforts.

The need for clearly defined criteria for the assessment of specific competencies has already been described. Program criteria are also unsettled. Medley (1974) has proposed that program evaluation be applied to the relationship between teacher training and student teacher behavior, and the term "program validation" be used to describe relations between student teacher behavior and pupil outcomes. Programs would thus be evaluated in terms of whether the student teacher behaves in ways intended as outcomes of the program—Level Three according to Turner's criteria (1971). Aubertine and Potter (1974) make a similar recommendation arguing also that program evaluation need not await agreement as to what these particular behaviors are. Rather, formative evaluation should be conducted with evaluation of program attainments emphasized. For example, how satisfactory are the lists of competencies to be acquired? Have competencies and training procedures been validated against a student achievement criterion?

The third of McDonald's concerns is perhaps most important for those educational psychologists and others conducting program research. Systematic variations in program design as well as alternative definitions of what constitutes teaching competence are needed. Schalock (1974) in describing the kinds of studies that need to be done in closing the knowledge gap relative to CB approaches suggests that one dimension requiring variation is the level of competency required, i.e., knowledge and performance or production of pupil behavior change. These variations would be especially useful in making CB/non-CB comparisons, but could be also used to explore differences within CB programs espousing similar definitions of competency. Another source of planned variation might be the entry characteristics of trainees (Soar, 1975). Entering characteristics, such as conceptual level (Hunt & Joyce, 1967) or anxiety level (Young & Van Mondfrans, 1972), could be assessed, with trainees randomly assigned to training experiences, in order to determine ATIs. Other variations associated with program sequence, nature, and extent of field experiences and type of instructional delivery system may also be worthy of examination. The time, effort, and coordination needed for program assessment and evaluation of this type, probably requires large-scale funding and multi-institution cooperation.

External Validity

Basing program comparisons upon estimates of knowledge acquired by trainees or performance of teacher behaviors, rather than pupil achievement or other outcome variables, requires consideration of the external validity of the measures employed. If knowledge of teaching is to be compared across programs some type of external examination seems necessary. The National Teacher Examinations may be useful for this purpose as they are designed to be comparable from form to form through a statistical weighting technique. Quirk, Witten, and Weinberg (1973) reported that they appear to be moderately correlated with undergraduate courses grades, that it is assumed, relate to knowledge acquired during the course. If performance of teacher behavior is to be compared then systematic observation as described by Soar (1973) seems necessary. The vast number of observation systems available (see Simon & Boyer, 1967, 1970) indicates that review and selection of valid and reliable instruments rather than new instrument development is a major priority. These two assessment strategies are exemplary of externally valid measures of knowledge and performance which might be used in comparisons of program effectiveness.

Cost—Benefit Comparisons

In assessment of program change, there are factors of cost and time as well as resulting benefits that are associated with each program innovation. If the costs of training are equal for all strategies employed, then attention to comparative benefits only would be appropriate. If both costs and benefits are significantly different then it is essential that both be assessed and reported. As Dubin and Taveggia (1968) suggested in their review of various pedagogical methods, if little difference can be found in the benefits of instructional techniques, then costs per instructional unit should be considered in relative decision making.

Comparisons of CB programs should include cost—benefit data as well as more traditional psychometric measures if program evaluation is to be conducted. Hite (1973) estimates that initial CB budgets in teacher training will be at least two and a half times that of standard teacher-education programs. Added costs peculiar to CB programs involve (a) developing program materials and processes, (b) individualizing instruction, and (c) involving field personnel in the management and operation of programs. To this list should be added costs associated with a substantial research and evaluation component which Scriven (1974) feels is necessary for CB to be most effective. It should be pointed out that costs vary according to how competency is defined or to be demonstrated (on a knowledge basis or in terms of pupil behavior change), the size and extent of the field component, the nature and amount of remedial procedures which need to be developed, and the faculty—student ratio employed.

Most new program descriptions hide data relevant to cost. There is a beguiling tendency to lower the faculty—student ratio, or make available new equipment and materials to program innovations such as CB training. Until researchers report cost—benefit data for all conditions under investigation, however, program evaluation will be difficult. Even with such data, the relative merits of outcomes attained by virtue of the program under study, and the possible sacrifice, neglect, or distortion of other objectives must still be weighed.

Assessment of Program Components

The contribution of specific program components should also be of future research interest. Turner (1975) insists that to optimize teacher success attributable to training, procedures must clearly facilitate future learning and continued skill acquisition by trainees. Program components are optimally useful only when they interact with some subsequent treatment or experience such as student teaching. For example, Copeland (1975) found no increased use of higher-order questioning or probing questions during student teaching as a result of earlier microteaching experience. Such a finding probably illustrates the general rule that no one program component will determine later performance in more applied settings; professional competence is derived from a variety of earlier interacting program experiences.

Certain instructional techniques which have been incorporated into CB programs also require more extensive investigation. As already indicated, the use of individualized instruction generates a variety of associated problems. For example, Parker (1974) reports an "end-of-quarter crunch" upon faculty time and resources because of the self-paced feature of the Weber State program. Perhaps the provision of additional reinforcement for "early starters" in self-paced programs, as advocated by Powers and Edwards (1974), would be a practical way of dealing with such a problem. This is just one example of how instructional techniques may require adaptation to the CB format, with a resultant need for analysis of the adaptation and its effects.

CONCLUSION

This chapter has attempted to describe the composition of CB programs, related instructional issues, and research needs pertaining specifically to teacher training. The great diversity of program components, the numerous unresolved questions, and the aura of critical self-analysis accompanying most programs reveal an approach to training that is still in the process of evolution. It is hoped that developing programs remain flexible and open to modification as the many issues raised by CB applications are slowly resolved. Necessary flexibility will be maintained if programs involve educational psychologists, who by virtue of their background and training are uniquely suited to analyze, refine, and evaluate changes in training practice.

REFERENCES

Allen, D., & Ryan, K. *Microteaching*. Reading, Massachusetts: Addison-Wesley, 1969.

Alpern, D. K. In place of recitations: An experiment in teaching. *Teachers College Record,* 1966, *67,* 589–594.

Alschuler, A. S., & Ivey, A. The human side of competency-based education. *Educational Technology,* 1972, *12*(November), 53–55.

American Association of Colleges for Teacher Education, Committee on Performance-Based Teacher Education. *Achieving the potential of PBTE: Recommendations.* Washington: American Association of Colleges for Teacher Education, 1974.

Andrews, T. E. *Manchester interview: Competency-based teacher education/certification.* Washington: American Association of Colleges for Teacher Education, 1972.

Aubertine, H., & Potter, D. Task force on evaluating program effectiveness. In W. R. Houston (Ed.), *Competency assessment, research and evaluation.* Washington: American Association of Colleges for Teacher Education, 1974.

Baker, E. Beyond objectives: Domain-referenced tests for evaluation and instructional improvement. *Educational Technology,* 1974, *14*(June), 10–16.

Bidwell, C. E. The social psychology of teaching. In R. M. W. Travers (Ed.), *Second handbook of research on teaching,* Chicago: Rand McNally, 1973.

Bloom, B. (Ed.) *Taxonomy of educational objectives: Handbook I: Cognitive domain.* New York: David McKay, 1956.

Borg, W. R. The mini-course as a vehicle for changing teacher behavior: A three year follow-up. *Journal of Educational Psychology,* 1972, *63*(December), 572–579.

Borg, W. R., Kelly, M. L., Langer, P., & Gall, M. *The minicourse: A micro-teaching approach to teacher education.* Beverly Hills, California: Macmillan Educational Services, 1970.

Borg, W. R., & Stone, D. R. Protocol materials as a tool for changing teacher behavior. *Journal of Experimental Education,* 1974, *43,* 34–39.

Broudy, H. S. The role of the foundational studies in the preparation of teachers. In *Improving teacher education in the United States.* Bloomington, Indiana: *Phi Delta Kappa,* 1968, 1–35.

Broudy, H. S. *A critique of performance-based teacher education.* Washington, D.C.: American Association of Colleges for Teacher Education, 1972.

Brown, G. I. The training of teachers for affective roles, In K. Ryan (Ed.), *Teacher education: Seventy-fourth yearbook of the National Society for the Study of Education, Part II.* Chicago: University of Chicago Press, 1975.

Brown, J. L., & Okey, J. R. *Identifying and classifying competencies for performance-based teacher training.* Paper presented at the American Educational Research Association Convention, New Orleans, February, 1973.

Burke, C. *The individualized, competency-based system of teacher education at Weber State College.* Washington American Association of Colleges of Teacher Education, 1972.

Butts, D. P., Carter, H., Colton, T., Gibb, E. G., Hall, G. E., & Rutherford, W. *The block program: A personalized teacher educational professional program.* R & D Report Series No. 54. Austin, Texas: The University of Texas Research and Development Center for Teacher Education, 1970.

Combs, A. W. Some basic concepts for teacher education. *Journal of Teacher Education,* 1972, *22,* 286–290.

Conant, J. *The education of American teachers.* New York: McGraw-Hill, 1963.

Cooper, J. M., & Weber, W. A. *Competency-based teacher education: A scenario.* Washington: American Association of Colleges for Teacher Education, 1972.

Copeland, W. D. The relationship between micro-teaching and student teacher classroom performance. *Journal of Educational Research,* 1975, 289–293.

Costin, F., Greenough, W., & Menges, R. Student ratings of college teaching: Reliability, validity and usefulness. *Review of Educational Research,* 1971, *41,* 511–535.

Cox, R. C. Confusion between norm-referenced and criterion-referenced measurement. *Phi Delta Kappan,* 1974, *55,* 319.

Dodl, N. R. Selecting competency outcomes for teacher education. *Journal of Teacher Education,* 1973, *24* (Fall), 194–199.

Dodl, N., Gant, J., Nelson, P., & Jung, H. A. *Catalog of teacher competencies.* Tallahasse: Florida State University, unpublished manuscript, November, 1971.

Drumheller, S. J. Competency-based teacher education must emphasize fewer and more global behaviors to maximize efficiency and morale. *Educational Technology,* 1974, *14,* 5–11.

Dubin, R., & Taveggia, T. C. *The teaching-learning paradox: A comparative analysis of college teaching methods.* Eugene, Oregon: University of Oregon Center for the Advanced Study of Educational Administration, 1968.

Dunkin, M. J., & Biddle, B. *The study of teaching.* New York: Holt, Rinehart & Winston, 1974.

Elam, S. *Performance-based teacher education: What is the state of the art?* Washington: American Association of Colleges for Teacher Education, 1971.

Elfenbein, I. *Performance-based teacher education programs: A comparative description.* Washington: American Association of Colleges for Teacher Education, 1972.

Emmer, E. T., & Millet, G. B. *An assessment of terminal performance in a teaching laboratory. A pilot study.* Austin, Texas: The University of Texas Research and Development Center for Teacher Education, 1968.

Fisher, G. D. In *Addresses and Proceedings of the 108th Annual Meeting of the National Education Association* (Vol. 108). San Francisco: 1970.

Fitzpatrick, R., & Morrison, E. J. Performance and product evaluation. In R. L. Thorndike (Ed.), *Educational measurement* (2nd ed.). Washington: American Council on Education, 1971.

Fuller, F. F. Concerns of teachers: A developmental conceptualization. *American Educational Research Journal,* 1969, *6,* 207–226.

Fuller, F. F., & Brown, O. H. Becoming a teacher. In K. Ryan (Ed.), *Teacher education: 74th Yearbook of the National Society for the Study of Education, Part II.* Chicago: University of Chicago Press, 1975.

Fuller, F. F., Peck, R. F., Brown, O. H., Menaker, S. L., White, M. M., & Veldman, D. J. *Effects of personalized feedback during teacher preparation on teacher personablity and teaching behavior.* R & D Report Series No. 4, Austin, Texas: University of Texas Research and Development Center for Teacher Education, 1969.

Gage, N. L. Evaluating ways to help teachers to behave desirably. In W. R. Houston (Ed.), *Competency assessment, research and evaluation.* Washington: American Association of Colleges for Teacher Education, 1974.

Gage, N. L., & Winne, P. H. Performance-based teacher education. In K. Ryan (Ed.), *Teacher education: 74th Yearbook of the National Society for the Study of Education, Part II.* Chicago: University of Chicago Press, 1975.

Gagné, R. M., & Briggs, L. J. *Principles of instructional design.* New York: Holt, Rinehart & Winston, 1974.

Giles, F. T., & Foster, C. *Changing teacher education in a large urban university.* Washington: American Association of Colleges for Teacher Education, 1972.

Glaser, R., & Resnick, L. B. Instructional psychology. In P. A. Mussen & M. R. Rosenzweig (Eds.), *Annual Review of Psychology,* 1972, *23,* 207–276.

Goldberg, L. Student personality characteristics and optimal college learning conditions. *Oregon Research Institute Research Monograph, 9,* No. 1, 1969.

Gwaltney, C. (Ed.). *Chronicle of higher education.* Washington: 1973, 21–22.

Hamilton, R. H. An experiment with independent study in freshman history. *Liberal Education,* 1967, *53,* 271–278.

Heath, R. W., & Nielson, M. A. The research basis for performance-based teacher education. *Review of Educational Research,* 1974, *44,* 463–484.

Himmel, C. E. College learning with and without formal classroom instruction. A comparison. *Psychology in the Schools,* 1972, *9,* 272–277.

Hite, H. The cost of performance-based teacher education. *Journal of Teacher Education,* 1973, *24,* 221–224.

Houston, W. R. Designing competency-based instructional systems. *Journal of Teacher Education,* 1973, *24,* 200–204.

Houston, W. R., Hollis, L. Y., Jones, H. L., Edwards, D. A., Pace, A. A., & White, S. J. *Developing instructional modules.* Houston: University of Houston, College of Education, 1972.

Houston, W. R., & Howsam, R. B. (Eds.) *Competency-based teacher education: Progress, problems and prospects.* Chicago: Science Research Associates, 1972.

Hunt, D. E., & Joyce, B. R. Teacher trainee personality and initial teaching style. *American Educational Research Journal,* 1967, *4,* 253–260.

Johnston, J. M., & Pennypacker, H. S. A behavioral approach to college teaching. *American Psychologist,* 1971, *26,* 219–244.

Karlins, M., Kaplan, M., & Stuart, W. Academic attitudes and performance as a function of differential grading systems: An evaluation of Princeton's pass–fail system. *Journal of Experimental Education,* 1969, *37,* 38–50.

Khan, S. B., & Weiss, J. The teaching of affective responses. In R. M. W. Travers (Ed.), *The second handbook of research on teaching.* Chicago: Rand McNally, 1973.

Klingstedt, J. L. Learning modules for competency-based education. *Educational Technology,* 1972, *12* (November), 29– 1.

Lawrence, G. Delineating and measuring professional competencies. *Educational Leadership,* 1974, *31,* 298–302.

Levine, M. G., & Sharp, V. F. Use of teaching performance tests to validate the effectiveness of a performance-based program of teacher education. *Educational Technology,* March, 1975, 40–42.

Light, R. J., & Smith, R. V. Accumulating evidence: Procedures for resolving contradictions among different research studies. *Harvard Educational Review,* 1971, *41,* 433.

Limbacher, P. C. A study of the effects of micro-teaching experiences upon practice teaching classroom behavior. *Dissertation Abstracts International,* 1969, *30,* 189.

Massanari, K. *Performance-based teacher education: What's it all about?* Washington: American Association of Colleges for Teacher Education, 1971.

McDonald, F. J. *A taxonomy of teaching behavior.* Address to Division 15, American Psychological Association Convention, Montreal, August, 1973.

McDonald, F. J. Conceptual model of R & D for CBE. In W. R. Houston (Ed.), *Competency assessment, research and evaluation.* Washington: American Association of Colleges for Teacher Education, 1974.

McDonald, F. J., & Allen, D. W. *Training effects of feedback and modeling procedures on teaching performance.* Palo Alto, California: Stanford University Press, 1967.

Medley, D. M. *Research and assessment in PBTE.* Paper presented at the American Associa-
    tion of Colleges for Teacher Education Leadership Training Conference on
    Performance-based Teacher Education. St. Louis, April, 1974.
Menges, R. Assessing readiness for professional practice. *Review of Educational Research,*
    1975, *46*(Spring), 173–208.
Merwin, J. *Performance-based teacher education: Some measurement and decision-making
    considerations.* Washington: American Association of Colleges for Teacher Educa-
    tion, 1973.
Merwin, W. C. Competency-based modules for in-service education. *Educational Leadership,*
    January, 1974, 329–332.
Millman, J. *Psychometric characteristics of performance tests of teaching effectiveness.*
    Paper presented to the American Educational Research Association, New Orleans,
    February, 1973.
Morriss, C. J., & Kimbrell, G. M. Performance and attitudinal correlates of the Keller
    method in an introductory psychology course. *Psychological Record,* 1972, *22,*
    523–530.
Murphy, P. D., & Brown, M. M. Conceptual systems and teaching styles. *American Educa-
    tional Research Journal,* 1970, *7,* 529–540.
Musella, D. Improving teacher evaluation. *Journal of Teacher Education,* 1970, *21,* 15–21.
Nash, R. J., & Agne, R. M. Competency in teacher education: A prop for the status quo?
    Journal of Teacher Education, 1971, *22*(Summer), 147–156.
Parker, R. Weber State College evaluates PBTE after three years. *Phi Delta Kappan,* 1974,
    55(January), 320–324.
Peck, R. F., & Tucker, J. A. Research on teacher education. In R. M. W. Travers (Ed.), *The
    second handbook of research on teaching.* Chicago: Rand McNally, 1973.
Popham, W. J. Performance tests of teaching proficiency: Rationale, development and
    validation. *American Educational Research Journal,* 1971, *8,* 105–117.
Popham, W. J. Teacher evaluation and domain-referenced measurement. *Educational Tech-
    nology,* 1974, *14*(June), 35–37.
Potter, D. A. *A research strategy for performance-based education.* Paper presented to the
    American Educational Research Association Convention, New Orleans, February
    1973.
Powers, R. B., & Edwards, K. A. Performance in a self-paced course. *Journal of Experimen-
    tal Education,* 1974, *42* (Summer), 60–64.
Quirk, T. J. Some measurement issues in competency-based teacher education. *Phi Delta
    Kappan,* 1974, *55*(January), 316–319.
Quirk, T. J., Witten, B. J., & Weinberg, S. F. Review of studies of the conconcurrent and
    predictive validity of the National Teacher Examinations. *Review of Educational
    Research,* 1973, *43*(Winter), 89–114.
Rosenshine, B. Evaluation of classroom instruction. *Review of Educational Research,* 1970,
    40, 279–300.
Rosenshine, B., & Furst, N. Research in teacher performance criteria. In B. O. Smith (Ed.),
    Research in teacher education: A symposium. Englewood Cliffs, New Jersey:
    Prentice-Hall, 1971.
Rosner, B. *The power of competency-based teacher education: A report.* Boston: Allyn &
    Bacon, 1972.
Rothkopf, E. Z. The concept of mathemagenic activities. *Review of Educational Research,*
    1970, *40,* 325–336.
Sandefur, J. T., & Adams, R. D. A case study of second-year teacher education graduates.
    Journal of Teacher Education, 1973, *24*(Fall), 248–249.

Schalock, H. D. Closing the knowledge gap. In W. R. Houston (Ed.), *Competency assessment, research and evaluation.* Washington: American Association of Colleges for Teacher Education, 1974.

Schmieder, A. A. *Competency-based education: The state of the scene.* Washington, American Association of Colleges for Teacher Education, 1973.

Scott, H. V. Levels of involvement: A descriptive model for teacher education. *Educational Technology,* 1974, *14*(March), 48–51.

Scriven, M. If the program is competency-based, how come the evaluation is costing so much? In W. R. Houston (Ed.), *Competency assessment, research and evaluation.* Washington: American Association of Colleges for Teacher Education, 1974.

Shearron, G. F. Field-based support systems for research and evaluation. In G. E. Dickson (Ed.), *Educational comment 1/1975 Research and evaluation in operational competency-based teacher education programs.* Toledo, Ohio: University of Toledo, 1975.

Shearron, G. R., & Johnson, C. E. A CBTE program in action: University of Georgia. *Journal of Teacher Education,* 1973, *24*(Fall), 187–193.

Shulman, L. S. Seeking styles and individual differences in patterns of inquiry. *School Review,* 1965, *73,* 258–286.

Simon, A., & Boyer, E. G. (Eds.). *Mirrors of behavior: An anthology of classroom observation instruments.* Philadelphia: Research for Better Schools, Vols. 1–6, 1967; Vols. 7–14, summary, and supplementary Vols. A and B, 1970.

Smith, B. O. Introduction. In B. O. Smith (Ed.). *Research in teacher education.* Englewood Cliffs, New Jersey: Prentice-Hall, 1971.

Soar, R. S. *An integrative approach to classroom learning.* NIMH project Numbers 5-RIMH01096 (University of South Carolina) and 7-RIIMH02045 (Temple University), 1966.

Soar, R. S. Accountability: Assessment problems and possibilities. *Journal of Teacher Education,* 1973, *24*(Fall), 205–212.

Soar, R. S. Classroom observation. In W. R. Houston (Ed.), *Competency assessment, research and evaluation.* Washington: American Association of Colleges for Teacher Education, 1974.

Soar, R. S. The Medley–Soar–Toledo model for research in teacher education. In G. E. Dickson (Ed.), *Educational comment 1/1975 research and evaluation in operational competency-based teacher education program.* Toledo, Ohio: University of Toledo, 1975.

Stephens, J. M. *The process of schooling.* New York: Holt, Rinehart & Winston, 1967.

Sybouts, W. Performance-based teacher education: Does it make a difference? *Phi Delta Kappan,* 1973, *54*(January), 303–304.

Thomas, A. *Determining priorities among competencies: Judgments of classroom teachers and supervisors.* Paper presented at the American Educational Research Association convention, New Orleans, February 1973.

Trent, J. W., & Cohen, A. M. Research on teaching in higher education. In R. M. W. Travers (Ed.), *The second handbook of research on teaching.* Chicago: Rand McNally, 1973.

Turner, R. L. Levels of Criteria Appendix A. In Project No. 1-0475, U.S.O.E. *The power of competency-based teacher education.* Committee on national program priorities in teacher education, 1971.

Turner, R. L. An overview of research in teacher education. In K. Ryan (Ed.), *Teacher education 74th yearbook of the National Society for the Study of Education, Part II.* Chicago: University of Chicago Press, 1975.

Twelker, P. A. Classroom simulation and teacher preparation. *School Review,* 1967, *75,* 197–204.

Ward, B. A., Morine, G., & Berliner, D. C. Assessing teacher competence. In W. R. Houston (Ed.), *Competency assessment, research and evaluation.* Washington: American Association of Colleges for Teacher Education, 1974.

Wixson, S. Student's reactions to competency-based special education courses. *Exceptional Children,* 1975, *41,* 437–438.

Young, J. I., & Van Mondfrans, A. P. Psychological implications of competency-based education. *Educational Technology,* 1972, *12*(November), 15–18.

10

Instructional Systems: Development, Evaluation and Management of Learning Environments

ROBERT D. TENNYSON

University of Minnesota

Instruction is a phenomenon that involves both the planning of an environment where learning can take place and the delivery of a content to the student. How to facilitate learning in a planned environment has been a major concern of educational psychologists (Anderson, 1967; Frase, 1975; Gagné & Rowher, 1969; Glaser & Resnick, 1972; McKeachie, 1974). Edward L. Thorndike, considered America's first educational psychologist, conducted his research on learning in the setting of the conventional classroom rather than in the laboratory environment (1913a, 1913b). Since Thorndike, learning in the classroom environment has been studied increasingly because of the minimal impact of laboratory learning on "real-world" classroom learning (McKeachie, 1974) and because of the complexity of factors that influence the effectiveness and efficiency of classroom instruction. Effectiveness refers to how much of what is taught is learned by the student, while efficiency refers to the time expended by the student in learning what is taught. Factors that contribute to the divergence in student learning include student attitude and aptitude, presentation of the stimulus properties, delivery system (e.g., lecture, computer, videotape), management procedures, and evaluation methods. Although educational psychologists have long dealt with these factors, it has only been recently that they have investigated variables and conditions directly related to the planning of a total learning environment.

Instructional systems is the term applied to this planning effort; it includes the processes of development, evaluation, and management. The instructional systems concept of development uses a scientific approach to the planning and implementation of the learning environment. Growth of this approach to instructional development has been facilitated by major inputs from fields of inquiry outside educational psychology, such as computer science, management information sciences, and educational technology. Wherever possible, research and theory from these areas are applied to each phase of the instructional development process. Of these areas, computer science has had the most substantial impact with such contributions as design strategy variables, content structure, efficiency of design concepts, and alternative student control methods (Alpert & Bitzer, 1970).

INSTRUCTIONAL DEVELOPMENT MODELS

Models of instructional development which have been proposed attempt to define a set of prescriptive variables that can be used to develop instructional materials (e.g., Briggs, 1970; Gerlack & Ely, 1971; Kemp, 1971; Merrill, 1971; Popham & Baker, 1970). These models have usually included the basic concepts of Glaser's (1965, 1966) five part development model (i.e., behavioral objectives, pretest, instructional activities, posttest, and revision) and have used an algorithmic approach to the development process in which the output of one step becomes the input for the next. In reality these newer instructional development models, even with the increased complexity and decision strategies, offer the same general characteristics as Glaser's original model.

Recent models of instructional development (e.g., Davies, 1973; Gagné & Briggs, 1974) emphasize the basic principles of design rather than the conventional algorithmic steps. These principles are based primarily upon instructional research and theory and, just as importantly, upon applied development experiences. Another recent trend toward a scientific approach to instructional development is seen in the increased emphasis on the use of evaluation (R. D. Tennyson, 1976). Although evaluation has always been part of the instructional development plan, it traditionally was relegated to the last step in the process. Even the Davies (1973) model, which is one of the best of the current instructional development models, has only a minimal consideration of evaluation. The impetus for increased use of evaluation in development is part of a larger societal movement towards accountability in education (cf. Saylor & Alexander, 1974). It is necessary to expand the scope of evaluation in instructional development and make it a part of each phase of the development system (Scriven, 1975; Silvern, 1972).

The various phases of the instructional development process—assessment, design, production, and implementation (see Figure 10.1)—will be discussed in this chapter, but not in terms of the conventional instructional development model. Rather, for each phase of the process, appropriate development and evaluation activities will be reviewed and suggested. It is assumed that each developer will define his or her own specific strategy of development based upon the decisions made from an analysis of the situation. Two factors which make this model unique should be noted. First the instructional development model represented in Figure 10.1 does not have the revision cycle of conventional models of instructional development (i.e., Glaser's original mode), and second, evaluation is an integral activity of each phase, not a separate step or function.

ASSESSMENT PHASE

Instructional development begins with an assessment of the learning environment to determine if an instructional need or problem exists. This environment is assessed to provide data to answer the question, "would an instructional development effort be feasible and desirable?" This activity defines the conditions and parameters of the problem from which specifications for the instructional development project can be proposed. The procedures and findings of the assessment phase are evaluated for the purpose of determining whether to (a) adopt currently available instructional materials, or (b) modify existing instruction, or (c) develop new instructional materials. If either (b) or (c) is selected, then the instructional development would follow through the remaining phases (see Figure 10.1). Selection of the first alternative, to adopt, would require only the implementation phase. The assessment phase involves two concurrent processes: (a) the specification of the instructional problem, learner characteristics, situational variables, and objectives; and, (b) the evaluation of the assessment process and its results to determine the feasibility of adopting, modifying or developing instructional materials.

Specifications

An instructional problem is usually assessed and defined in terms of curriculum needs and goals. This relationship of instructional development to curriculum development is a fairly recent phenomenon (C. L. Tennyson, 1976). The concern for instructional and curriculum problem identification is directly related to federal support for schools. Since the implementation of Title I, Elementary and Secondary School Act of 1965, educators have had to develop

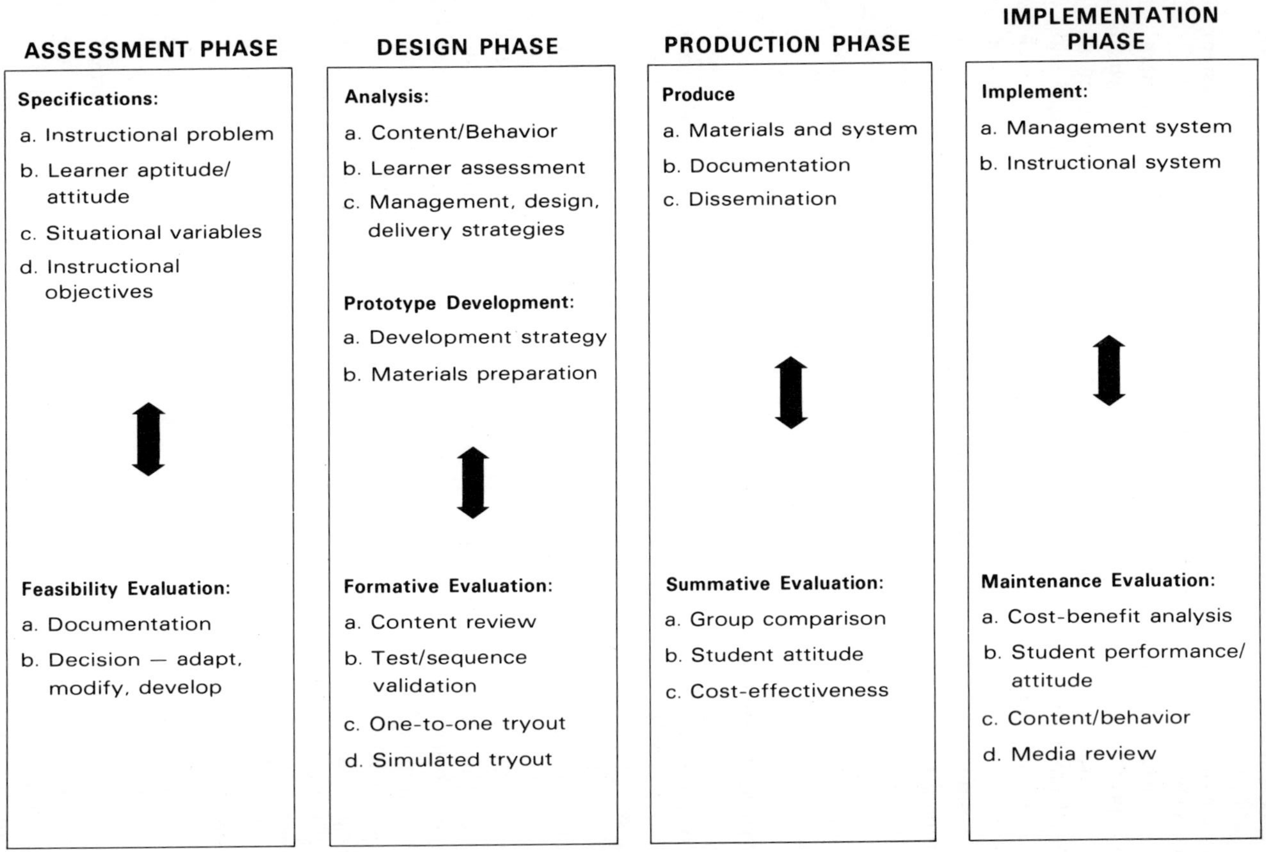

Figure 10.1. Phases in the development and evaluation of learning environments.

ASSESSMENT PHASE

Specifications:
a. Instructional problem
b. Learner aptitude/attitude
c. Situational variables
d. Instructional objectives

Feasibility Evaluation:
a. Documentation
b. Decision — adapt, modify, develop

DESIGN PHASE

Analysis:
a. Content/Behavior
b. Learner assessment
c. Management, design, delivery strategies

Prototype Development:
a. Development strategy
b. Materials preparation

Formative Evaluation:
a. Content review
b. Test/sequence validation
c. One-to-one tryout
d. Simulated tryout

PRODUCTION PHASE

Produce
a. Materials and system
b. Documentation
c. Dissemination

Summative Evaluation:
a. Group comparison
b. Student attitude
c. Cost-effectiveness

IMPLEMENTATION PHASE

Implement:
a. Management system
b. Instructional system

Maintenance Evaluation:
a. Cost-benefit analysis
b. Student performance/attitude
c. Content/behavior
d. Media review

detailed goals and objectives that were "behavioral, measurable, and representative of cognitive, affective, and psychomotor domains" in order to obtain federal funds (R. D. Tennyson, 1976). The original curriculum needs assessment procedures initiated a new emphasis in educational evaluation to accurately define the goals and objectives of education. Space does not permit a complete review of the curriculum evaluation methods, but they are well defined in these sources: Phi Delta Kappa National Study Committee on Education (1971) report, Stake (1967, 1969), Provus (1971), and Grobman (1968).

Instructional Problem

Assessment methods used in the specification of the instructional problem are still for the most part qualitative, but the trend is toward obtaining data from quantitative sources, for example, surveys, job analysis, competency analysis, and curriculum goal analysis. Such data can be acquired and interpreted by analyzing school curriculum, governmental educational policies, other governmental regulations (e.g., affirmative action), community needs, societal concerns, and educational research and theory. The instructional problem assessment process should provide information which specifies the needed content and behaviors to be learned within a given segment of the curriculum.

Learner Aptitude/Attitude

Research has demonstrated that assessing the aptitudes and attitudes of the target population should be considered when designing instructional materials (Cronbach & Snow, in press; R. D. Tennyson & Woolley, 1971; R. D. Tennyson & Boutwell, 1973; Tobias, 1975). The assumption is that learning can be facilitated if the instruction can be adapted to the aptitude of the individual learner. Likewise, learner attitude seems to be an increasingly important factor in the development of learning environments (Gagné, 1972).

Situational Variables

Before establishing instructional objectives, the resources and facilities of the learning environment need to be assessed (Davies, 1973). These include not only the instructional resources of the learning environment, but also the resource capabilities (facilities, funding, and staff) for doing the instructional development. Davies (1973) emphasizes the need to maximize the instructional resources, however, constraints inherent in those resources must also be recognized. The concept of constraints implies both the physical limitations and the capabilities of the resources for facilitating learning. The analysis of the situational variables should provide information on the characteristics of the learning environment, that is, the potential learning and instructional capabilities of the available resources and facilities, and the requirements for modification and development activities.

A review of currently available instructional materials is part of the situational assessment. A quantitative procedure for evaluating existing instruction has been developed by Merrill and Wood (1974). The Merrill and Wood assessment procedures evaluate instructional materials according to the content structure, the student behaviors (desired and obtained), and the instructional (design) strategy. At the present time this is the only research work investigating the analysis of instructional materials using quantitative measures.

Instructional Objectives

The above assessment procedures provide the information needed to specify the instructional objectives of the learning environment. Objectives defined at this point in the development process have the task of defining the desired student outcomes that are to be a result of instruction. Basically, the objectives determined in the Assessment Phase should specify the intended behaviors and content to be learned (C. L. Tennyson & R. D. Tennyson, 1975). The events and conditions of learner evaluation and criteria of performance are not specified here; those activities are associated with the Design Phase and will be discussed later in this chapter.

Information obtained during the assessment process forms a set of specifications for solving the instructional problem. This information is validated and the rationale for the solution decision is documented as part of the feasibility evaluation.

Feasibility Evaluation

The purpose of this evaluation is to document the feasibility of carrying out one of three types of instructional development (adopting, modifying, or developing) given the specifications derived from assessing the learning environment (see Scriven, 1975, for a complete review of this area).

Documentation

Feasibility evaluation focuses on documenting both the validation of the assessment procedures and the rationale of the specifications (Provus, 1971); that is, complete information should be provided on how the data were collected, from whom they were collected, and what method of validation was used. For example, if data were collected from school faculty (or other identifiable groups), were they surveyed with constructed response instruments or questioned about their opinions; if data were from societal sources, were individuals or representatives from organizations contacted; or if data were from educational policies, were the policies consistent with known research findings or desired results?

Documentation should also demonstrate how the objectives directly relate to the specifications derived from assessing the problem, the learners, and the situational variables (Saylor & Alexander, 1974). For example, if a job analysis survey in a specific profession was conducted, the findings could be reviewed by experts in that profession. Assessment procedures are evaluated and documented in terms of their proximity to standard methodology and consistency of the data interpretation.

An additional form of evaluation involves an anlysis of the likelihood that a developmental effort would result in a product which justifies the estimated expenditures in time and resources (Temkin, 1974). Currently, most cost-estimation procedures used in instructional development are designed for either summative evaluation or for continuing use of the product (Silvem, 1972; Temkin, 1974). By applying the principles of cost-effectiveness, which include direct costs and learning effectiveness and efficiency, to this front-end assessment it would be possible to establish more precise cost-evaluation data.

Decision

It is at this point that the decision can be made as to how to proceed in solving the instructional problem. One form of documenting this solution is to prepare a proposal that states the rationale for the instructional development decision and the specifications for accomplishing the stated objectives (Foley, & R. D. Tennyson, 1976).

DESIGN PHASE

The second phase of instructional development deals directly with the design of the instructional materials. Design is the area of instructional development that has received the most research efforts and the most theoretical development; yet it is probably the least used phase in instructional development. This paradox occurs because of the division of work and interest between the researcher and the developer. Instructional researchers have traditionally focused their research energies on design variables in attempts to specify those conditions that might facilitate learning. However, much of this research has been done in the conventional learning laboratory environment and on tasks that rarely approximate real-world subject matters. Since the individual studies only focus on a few variables at a time, no one study can be applied to the design of instructional materials. There are, of course, reviews of the literature which summarize investigations; but these are not written to explain how to design instructional materials—certainly a major concern of the developer. The failure to apply research findings is probably due to poor communication, not necessarily to unwillingness by developers to use research findings. That some are recognizing this problem can be seen by the publication of books and articles on applied design considerations authored by researchers; for example, Gage and Berliner (1975), *Educational Psychology;* Gagné and Briggs (1974), *Principles of Instructional Design;* Klausmeier, Ghatala, and Frayer, (1974), *Conceptual Learning and Development;* Merrill and R. D. Tennyson (1977), *Concept Teaching: An Instructional Design Guide;* and Snelbacker (1974), *Learning Theory, Instructional Theory and Psychoeducational Design.* For another example, a review of authors in the developers' journal, *Educational Technology,* would demonstrate that researchers are producing materials that explain design procedures in nontechnical terms. Frase's (1975) review of the research in instructional technology shows a shift in experimental design procedures away from the experimental psychologists' learning laboratories and research paradigms to methodologies and design strategies that can be generalized readily to real-world learning environments. The Design Phase (see Figure 10.1) consists of three major components; analysis, prototype development, and formative evaluation.

Analysis

The analysis component of instructional development functions to bridge the gap between the general guideline specifications of the Assessment Phase and the actual development of the instructional materials. The tasks associated with this activity include an analysis of the content and behaviors defined in the instructional objectives, construction of the learner evaluation materials, and selection of management, design, and delivery strategies. A portion of the formative evaluation activities (content review and test and sequence validation) are performed concurrently with the above identified tasks.

Content/Behavior

The design of instruction ultimately centers on the subject matter to be learned and the behavior required of the students in regard to that content. This component of the Design Phase refers to the analysis of the content and behavior of instruction (see Figure 10.1). Formerly, such an analysis consisted mainly of a flow-charting of tasks or activities in terms of behavior statements and content statements or combinations of both. Instructional developers, as well as researchers, have found, however, that conventional organization of subject matter is an inadequate structure for an efficient learning sequence (R. D. Tennyson, 1972). Because of the programming difficulties arising from the design of computer-based courseware, instructional developers have adapted the concepts of artificial intelligence to analysis of content (cf. Simon, 1969). For example, Bunderson (1973) proposed that when designing instruction, the content can be analyzed to determine the most efficient arrangement of that knowledge for purposes of learning not for purposes of disciplined organization (cf. Landa, 1974). Merrill and Boutwell (1973) presented a scheme in which the content and behavior can be analyzed separately and then interacted for purposes of selecting an appropriate design strategy for the instructional sequence. Gagné's (1970, 1974) approach for analyzing a task implies that a univariate analysis is all that is required. But Merrill and Boutwell are viewing the problem from a more applied viewpoint than Gagné who argues from a theoretical position. Research does not support either position directly, but the implications for designing efficient instruction would seem to favor an approach that analyzes both the content and desired behaviors.

Learner Assessment

Design of the learner assessment procedures follows immediately after the analysis of the instructional content/behavior and involves the construction of an instrument(s) to evaluate whether or not the learner has met the instructional objectives defined in the Assessment Phase. Information concerning the level of behavior in relationship to the content/behavior analysis and the parameters for the kinds of situations in which the behavior should be measured can be specified in performance objectives. The purpose of such objectives is to define what Mager (1962) refers to as the events and conditions for measurement of learning outcomes. An event describes what activity is to be learned and specifies at what level of behavior the learner is to perform that activity (Boutwell & R. D. Tennyson, 1972). The level of behavior indicates whether or not the event is to take place in a familiar or newly encountered situation. The conditions under which the event is to occur describe the form of the test. Conditions also describe the testing environment and how the test results are to be scored or evaluated. Once the performance objectives have been prepared, a test can be constructed according to the events and conditions under which the performance objectives are to be demonstrated (R. C. Anderson, 1972).

Criterion for acceptable performance on the test should be established once the test and instructional materials have been validated. Rather than allocating an arbitrary standard, for criterion performance, such as the often assigned level of 90%, performance criterion should be based on realistic expectations derived from the target population's interaction with the instructional and testing materials.

Management Strategy

A contribution to instructional design from a discipline outside of education and psychology is from management information sciences. The term "systems" itself and the concepts of general systems theory are, in part, derived from management information sciences. A concern in the design of the instructional materials is the design of the management system (see Figure 10.1). The management strategy design will depend on the size of the instructional development project. If only one course is being developed it is possible to have only one form of management strategy, while if several courses or even an entire curriculum are being developed the management strategy can include many options. Advanced management systems use computer technology extensively. The options available for the management system depend on the specifications for both the learning environment and the instructional materials. The need for management systems has been generated by educational policies and research findings that indicate the positive value of more individual instruction and evaluation. Certain computer technologies interfaced with management systems techniques provide multiple learning alternatives in the learning environment. Management systems are designed from strategies specific to individual program needs rather than from general variables of strategy. One exception to this practice was the TICCIT (Time-shared, Interactive, Computer-Controlled Information Television) project at Brigham Young University (Bunderson, 1973; Merrill, 1973). Although TICCIT combined computers and television hardware, the unique contribution of that system was the application of instructional research and theory to the design of a total learning environment. The management strategy for TICCIT involved a learner control format with a computerized advisement and counseling program. The student could progress through the instructional sequence at his or her own rate unless performance fell below a predetermined mastery level, in which case the system would advise the student on how to proceed.

Design Strategy

The design strategy to be used in sequencing the presentation of the instructional materials can be selected from the findings of the content and behavior analysis. In both Merrill and Boutwell (1973) and Gagné's (1970) schemes of analyzing content and behaviors, a specific set of design strategies is most appropriate for a given behavior. Gagné (1972) defines three basic cognitive behaviors—verbal information, intellectual skills, and cognitive strategy. Each of these three levels of behavior requires a different method for presenting the instructional materials and different types of learning behavior for the student.

Verbal information includes that behavior which demands recall of finite information. Gagné does imply not just rote recall, but also the remembering of the critical elements of a finite piece of information. A major contribution of Gagné's (1965) book on the hierarchy of learning is that experimental psychology has provided more information on the lower levels of learning than on the higher levels. A summary of research paradigms in the educational and psychology research journals dealing with instructional concerns shows an increase in work at the two higher levels of behaviors (White, 1973; White &

Gagné, 1974). For example, research on paired-associate variables will continue, but as Jenkins (1974) observed, that line of research has not been answering fundamental questions about either learning or instruction. Jenkins and others are now concentrating on the concept of contextualism, which is based upon the relationship of multiple behaviors, and, in certain other forms, the structure of the learning environment, for example, the taxonomical structure of content (Airasian & Bart, 1975). Probably the most distinguishing characteristics of verbal information instruction is the need for repetition (Gagné maintains that something is learned at this level at the first exposure) and presentation of the information in a complete contextual form. The purpose of the instruction is to provide sufficient cues to help for later recall. Paired-associate learning research has demonstrated the importance of cues (Paivio, 1975); but without the complete contextual framework, associative learning is, at best, considered short-term memory.

The most exciting work in instructional research has been in the areas of intellectual skills and cognitive strategies. Intellectual skills imply the ability to transfer from the learned stimulus to newly encountered stimuli. For example, the student learns in the instruction that certain instances represent a concept based upon defined critical attributes; and when presented new instances of that same concept, the student can identify the instances correctly because he or she can identify the critical attributes.

Intellectual skills include two types of behavior, classification and rule using. Classification behavior is defined as the ability to identify newly encountered instances (Mechner, 1965), while the definition for rule using behavior is the ability to apply the appropriate rule to solve a newly encountered problem.

The design strategy for concept instruction is well summarized in a variety of sources (e.g., R. D. Tennyson & Boutwell, 1974a, 1974b). Klausmeier *et al.* (1974) provide a review of the extensive research in conceptual learning and update Clark's (1971) earlier review of the literature. Merrill and R. D. Tennyson (1977) provide instructional development procedures along with the design strategy for concept learning. This design strategy for concept instruction has evolved over the last 5 years. The first research efforts established the basic strategy of the design; that was, that nonexamples when containing the same variable attributes (from the subordinate concepts), contribute to the effective learning of concepts (Houtz, Moore, & Davis, 1973; Klausmeier & Feldman, 1975; R. D. Tennyson, Woolley, & Merrill, 1972). Later research work has refined the design strategy in terms of the critical and variable attributes (R. D. Tennyson, 1973), analytical descriptors and prompting (R. D. Tennyson *et al.,* 1975), and number of instances (Klausmeier & Feldman, 1975).

The similarity of the design strategies for rule using and classification is seen in the work of Scandura and his colleagues (Scandura, 1970; Scandura & Durrin, 1968; Scandura & Voorhies, 1971). However, the use of nonexamples was a problem in the rule using strategy because of the false assumption that incorrect solutions were nonexamples. A recent research study by R. D. Tennyson and C. L. Tennyson (1975) showed that the design strategy should not include incorrect solutions but the presentation of coordinated rules simultaneously; rules that are structurally similar (coordinated) should be presented at the same time. The basic design strategy in this study of rule using instruction presented the rule statements, instances of the rules, and practice in solving problems.

This research in rule using and the applied work of Klausmeier and his colleagues on the taxonomical structure of concepts provides further evidence of the potential impact of the content analysis on the design of instruction. Future research efforts for both rules and concepts will be looking at the implications of subordinate, superordinate, and coordinate concepts and rules in the design of instruction (see Merrill & R. D. Tennyson, 1977). These questions are important because instruction involves more than the teaching of single concepts or rules as in a laboratory experiment. The learning environment is composed of multiple concepts and rules, and behavior requirements range from verbal information to cognitive strategies. Future research paradigms need to look at interactive design strategy variables for the learning of behaviors and content at the different levels.

The term cognitive strategy (Gagné, 1972) is a departure from the conventional terminology used in the defining of that highest level of behavior. Bloom, Englehart, Furst, Hill, and Krathwohl (1956) used evaluation and others have used synthesis, rule finding (Merrill & Boutwell, 1973), creativity (Worthen, 1968), and productive thinking (Johnson, Parrott, & Stratton, 1968). Cognitive strategy implies basically the process of determining a problem and the application of a unique solution(s) to the solving of the problem. The research and applied work of Johnson (1968; Stratton, Parrott, & Johnson, 1970) on productive thinking provide conditions that can be of potential use for instructional development. For example, the need for practice in creativity seems to be an important learning variable. Evaluation of a student's response is not a matter of it being judged good or bad, or right or wrong, rather it is an assessment on how uniquely creative the answer is in relation to the problem. The purpose of the instruction is to teach a concept of creativity based upon a set of criteria. Johnson's research shows that creativity of an answer can be controlled by manipulating the parameters and conditions of acceptability in the learning environment. Assessment is, of course, based upon how well the student's effort at creativity meets the established criteria levels. In actual practice, Johnson has developed an interval rating scheme (1 to 5 points, with 5 the highest level of creativity) and a training program for his judges. Two things are clear in Johnson's instructional program; the students need to learn the criteria for acceptable creativity, and the judges have to be well trained to recognize the various levels of creativity.

Delivery Strategy

Design strategies are selected in reference to the content and behaviors to be learned. Continuing to the next component of the design phase, the delivery strategy should be selected with regards to the design strategy, the situational variables, and the management strategy. The variables and criteria in media selection models differ widely; most are technology oriented, although a recent model by Merrill and Goodman (1972) recommends selection of media according to design, behavior, and resource capabilities. The flexibility in media selection models results from both the focus of the authors and the almost total lack of empirical data on whether students learn better from one form of media than another. An additional factor that should be considered in media selection is the concept of transmediation; a transfer from the original media to another media form. The transmediation capability is a factor to consider with individual learner variables (Foley & R. D. Tennyson, 1976).

There does appear to be a renewed research interest in educational technology. Previously, audiovisual research was typified by the cross-media comparison studies; for example, a class taught by television was contrasted with an instructor-taught class. That research paradigm focused on the hardware instead of on the instructional materials design. Current research on technology is investigating the unique application of design variables to specific media. An area of educational technology research which is only now being investigated deals with production variables. The question of what is displayed in a visual is an example of some of the work by Flemming (1970). The inherent properties or characteristics of the technology that can be manipulated by the developer are variables that need further investigation. Related to this line of questioning on production variables is learner attitude towards the technology or display mode. Intrinsic motivation factors might also be future variables to be considered in the design and development of instruction (Day, Berlyne, & Hunt, 1971; Kahoe & McFarland, 1975).

Prototype Development

The procedures for the development of a prototype of the instructional materials comprise the second element of the Design Phase. The assumptions and conditions associated with development have gone through a series of changes as the result of applied development work rather than of research findings. Original product development methods were nothing more than elaborated teaching methods. Basic changes in development techniques were precipitated by the introduction of technology into education. Skinner's (1954) application of the principles of behaviorism to instructional development were enhanced by technology that could efficiently display the stimuli in small units (Skinner, 1958). Audiovisual systems seemed to be the panacea for developing effective instruction (Finn & Allen, 1962). Even such nonhardware areas as programmed instruction were heavily influenced by technology-based development. However, the trial and error method of development has added a level of sensibility to the process. Technology is now viewed as a component, a variable to be considered in instructional development, not as the controlling factor. As the research on production variables advances, a more scientific approach to the actual development part of the instructional development process will develop. Because of the lack of empirical knowledge on this topic the evaluation procedures become important. Current understanding of the development process comes from clinical, case work projects rather than true experimental situations, and as the development cases increase certain variables and conditions will obtain a quasi-scientific value.

Another important element of efficient development is formulating a plan for administering the development process. The tasks to be accomplished to actualize the various instructional strategies into a prototype should be outlined, personnel assigned to each, and a schedule of completion dates set.

Each strategy dictates certain development decisions. To operationalize the management strategy, each segment of the instruction should be specified as either teacher- or design-dependent, or under direct learner control, and provisions should be made for branching, remediation, etc. Details of the design strategy as to how the content will be presented (e.g., kinds and arrangement of examples, etc.) must be determined in the context of the chosen delivery system. Tasks particular to that delivery system(s) should be outlined (e.g., procuring graphics, storyboards, etc.) and the content narrative written in a form amenable to the delivery system (it may be a script, text, computer storybook, etc.). Additional elements to be considered are message design (Flemming, 1970) and transmediation (Foley & R. D. Tennyson, 1976). These variables relate to the various ways in which a learner could perceive and interpret a message due to its presentation by a delivery system. Care must be taken to avoid misrepresentation. Once content is coded into a message on a delivery system, one-to-one and simulated tryouts can be instrumental in detecting any perceptual errors on behalf of the learner.

Formative Evaluation

In general, the purpose of formative evaluation is to obtain data necessary for making revisions and refinements of the instructional materials during the design (see Figure 10.1). Refinement refers to adjustments within single elements of the instructional design (i.e., content/behavior analysis, performance objectives, tests, and management, design, and delivery strategies) that do not affect the other elements; while revisions, on the other hand, refer to alternations in one element such that it produces changes in one or more of the other elements.

Data used for making revisions and refinements are derived concurrently with each element of the Design Phase processes. Formative evaluation includes such activities as review of the content/behavior analysis by subject matter experts (SMEs), validation of the test and instructional sequence, a one-to-one tryout of the prototype materials, and finally a tryout of the materials in a simulated learning environment.

Content Review

Formative evaluation in the Design Phase can begin with a review and critique of the content structure by subject matter experts. The scope and sequence of the subject matter for instruction (content structure) is typically determined by a consensus of opinion from the scholars in that discipline. If the analysis of the content and behavior during the Design Phase has resulted in the alteration of the conventional content structures review by subject matter experts will help to ensure the integrity of that content. This review process can be particularly useful in making refinements of the content structure, since learners are usually too naïve to offer criticism. The techniques for conducting a content review are presented in several curriculum development sources (e.g., Saylor & Alexander, 1974).

Test and Sequence Validation

The learner evaluation instrument should be validated prior to the development of the prototype instructional materials for two basic reasons. First, the instrument should be designed to evaluate student learning of the defined content/behavior area not just an assessment of student learning of the specific instructional materials. Thus, the test should be developed in direct relation of the performance objectives (cf. R. C. Anderson, 1972). Second, a validated test can be used for evaluating the structure (sequence) of the instructional content/behavior.

Instructional sequences can be classified into one of three general types—hierarchical, algorithmic, and random (R. D. Tennyson, 1972). For hierarchical sequences, lower order content/behaviors need to be learned before efficient learning of higher order behaviors can take place (Gagné, 1970). In algorithmic (information processing) sequences, the output of one unit of the content/behavior becomes the input for the next. In random sequences, the content and behavior can be learned in any order, although certain "logical" orders might be more efficient.

In certain learning environments, the sequence of the content might be a critical factor which requires further empirical study. For example, if a hierarchical sequence is assumed, then the lower order behaviors must be learned prior to the higher order, but such a sequence may result in additional on-task learning time in contrast to a possibly more efficient sequence without a hierarchical structure. In such situations, an evaluation of the instructional sequence is in order. Even though instructional theorists maintain the assumption that hierarchy of content is possible, the research evidence does not seem to support it (Gagné & Paradise, 1961; Merrill, 1965; White, 1973). Most instructional sequence research has focused on logical order versus random order, usually showing no significant differences. Where logical orders were found to be more effective, the logical order was usually an algorithmic sequence (R. D. Tennyson, 1972).

One-to-One Tryout

The procedure for a one-to-one evaluation of the instructional materials prototype involves the developer observing and taking notes as the learner works through the instructional materials (Eiss, 1972; Bloom, Hastings, & Madous, 1971; Wittrock & Wiley, 1970; Cronbach, 1963). Purposes of the one-to-one tryout are to identify any unclear directions or formats, to identify editorial problems, to identify any misunderstandings in the content, and, for technology components, to identify either hardware or software problems. A one-to-one tryout usually takes place in a laboratory setting outside the learning environment; therefore, performance scores are usually not reliable measures for evaluating whether or not the materials meet the performance objectives of the instruction. In fact, it is appropriate for the developer to work with the learner to help clarify segments of the instruction which are not clear. When the one-to-one tryout is completed, the data (observations, student comments, student performance behavior) should be studied for possible revisions of the instructional materials. Depending on the amount and severity of the revisions, a second one-to-one tryout might be necessary. All major revisions of the instructional materials should be completed before beginning the simulated tryout.

Simulated Tryout

The purpose of the simulated tryout is twofold. First, information is obtained for making refinements of the materials prior to full production. Variables to be considered include pretest/posttest scoring patterns, confidence ratings, and learner time spent on the instruction materials. Second, posttest scores from the simulated tryout can be used to establish criterion for student performance. That is, the criterion for a test is founded upon normative data if it is to reflect a reasonable expectation for a given population of learners. Learning from instructional materials can be inferred if a significant gain in student performance occurs between the pretest and the posttest. More extensive data interpretation beyond observation of score differences, will result from using multiple forms of data (e.g., pretest/posttest scores, confidence ratings and learning time).

By using pretest/posttest scoring patterns it is possible to identify instructional areas that might need refinements. There are four possible response patterns for diagnosing potential problems in the instructional materials. A response pattern of pretest–missed/posttest–passed implies learning; therefore, no refinements would seem necessary. In the cases where the posttest items were missed, learning cannot be inferred. In either case (missed/missed or passed/missed) the instructional materials probably require further refinement, and for the passed/missed pattern revisions might even be considered. In a situation where the student passes both items, it could be that the student already knew the content/behavior. The instruction could then be designed for bypassing (branching) instruction passed on the pretest.

A second source of data comes from the students' rating of their confidence in responding to each test question. (For a review of the confidence testing literature see Echternacht, 1972). One method of confidence rating is to ask the learner to rate his or her chances of a correct answer, that is, very sure (better than a 50:50 chance of a correct answer), fairly sure (about a 50:50 chance) or guess (less than a 50:50 chance of a correct answer). The purpose for using confidence rating data is to estimate retention of the content and behaviors learned. Research data indicate that if a student has a good score and a high confidence rating then it is likely that he or she will remember the content; but, a good score with a low confidence rating indicates that the student probably understood the content for the posttest but will not likely retain it over time. This type of rating pattern could also demonstrate inadequate instruction.

A third source of data, which is only now being studied thoroughly in relationship to instructional development, is time expended by the student in learning (L. W. Anderson, 1976; Rothkopf, 1968). Time data collected on both the amount of time spent by the students using the instruction directly and the amount of time spent studying with outside sources can be used in assessing the efficiency of the instruction. Also, student time expended in learning can influence motivation for continued learning. That is, if the student perceives that he or se is actually learning something in a reasonable amount of time then the motivation can be maintained for additional instruction, but if learning is not perceived as progressing, motivation for learning decreases. Time data can be collected on overall learning time and for individual units of instruction, practice time, tests, or any other segment of the learning environment.

PRODUCTION PHASE

The purpose of this third phase of instructional development is to produce the instructional prototype for use in the learning environment. Packaging the instructional materials usually implies that someone other than the original developer will be using the product. In most instructional development projects the assumption is that the product will be design-dependent rather than teacher-dependent. The design dependent concept increases the potential market of users. The need for packaging and disseminating instructional materials to reduce duplication of effort has resulted in the establishment of several clearinghouses for instructional products dissemination. These organizations have been operating only for a short time, so it is not possible to comment on their impact. Each of the clearinghouses has begun establishing minimal standards for both documenting the instructional development procedures and dissemination procedures. Without doubt, in time, the instructional product clearinghouse system will become more sophisticated and serve a larger clientele.

Documentation of instructional materials in a systematic procedure started with the guidelines for programmed instruction issued by the National Education Association (1969). Those guidelines dealt with providing information on the rationale for decisions made in the design and included results of formative and summative evaluations. The original list still covers the main points for documentation of instructional development. Missing from those guidelines are the data and conclusion of the Assessment Phase, several components of the Design Phase, much of the information in the summative evaluation to be presented in this chapter, and all of the Implementation Phase (see Figure 10.1). Documentation standards now follow those established for research reporting and test construction.

Summative Evaluation

Concurrent with the production of the instructional materials is the evaluation of those materials in the learning environment where the materials are to be used. The purpose of this summative evaluation is to document the degree to which the instructional materials meet the objectives of the instructional development effort. This evaluation centers on the degree that students learn the defined content and behaviors (R. D. Tennyson, 1976). Evaluation data for the documentation should include student performance reported in gain scores and compared with a control group(s), student learning time, learner attitudes, and costs. These data should be collected by presenting the instruction in the conventional learning environment; that is, as much as possible, the students should view the instructional materials as part of their normal learning experiences. The purpose here is to minimize the experimental effect that is present in the formative evaluation procedures.

Group Comparison

Summative evaluation provides documentation that the developed instructional materials actually teach the content and behaviors defined in the instructional objectives. Gain scores as discussed in the formative evaluation section can be used here, but a more powerful method would be some type of multiple group comparison study in which the performance of students who receive the instruction is compared with the performance of students who receive some alternative instruction. There are variations of this control group design and many sources which illustrate them (e.g., Merrill & R. D. Tennyson, 1977). The basic format is a two group design, one group with the instructional materials and a second without. Each group receives the pretest and posttest(s). In practice this design has been thoroughly abused by the so-called cross-media comparison studies used in the early audiovisual experiment which tried to compare the "conventional" form of instruction with the mediated instruction (R. D. Tennyson & Boutwell, 1971). These studies were criticized, in part, because they failed to clearly identify any basic conditions of the conventional group, and in those studies that demonstrated statistical differences (in favor of the mediated instruction) the audiovisual presentation was usually better designed and developed than the conventional. This control group design can be useful in a summative evaluation if basic descriptive information on the control group is given in the documentation.

A second important purpose of summative evaluation is determining the efficiency of the instruction. Only recently have developers actually attempted to collect these type of data, but most instructional development sources (e.g., Gagné & Briggs, 1974; Davies, 1973) do not provide information on why or how to collect time data. Efficient instruction can decrease the amount of time required for learning, thus making time available for additional learning, saving money where productivity is a goal, and usually improving motivation. Time data can be collected simultaneously with effectiveness data. Basic time data would indicate (*a*) time necessary for directions, (*b*) time required for the different instructional units, (*c*) time required for outside study, and (*d*) total time required for learning the objectives.

Student Attitude

Learner attitude toward the instruction seems to be gaining as much value in evaluating instruction as efficiency and effectiveness (Doyle & Whitely, 1974). The immediate problem is how to measure student attitudes in terms of conventional instructional methods. The most reliable form of student evaluation has been the single question, "How do you rate this instructor's overall teaching ability?" (Doyle & Whitely, 1974). This question is not comforting or suitable when attempting to evaluate an instructional product. Attitudinal responses should be specific to the definable characteristics and/or variables of the instruction. Composite scores are rarely useful in assessing quality of the instructional product, so wherever possible, attitudinal data should be collected from instruments and methods designed specifically to evaluate the instruction under development.

Cost-Effectiveness

Calculating the costs of development and the estimated operation costs is usually the final component of summative evaluation. The purpose of this evaluation is to determine the "cost–effectiveness" of the product (Coffarella, 1975). The real costs of the instructional development are derived from not only the direct expenses of development but also from the expected life of the product and the level of student learning (Wilkinson, 1972). For example, an instructional product that may be considered expensive to develop might result in better learner performance than a less expensive product. The formulas available to calculate cost–effectiveness have become increasingly sophisticated as most institutions have had to justify the high costs of initial development (Roid, 1974). Documentation of costs should be provided in as much detail as possible, the same as for the other data collected in the summative evaluation. This would make it possible for a potential user to examine the costs and interpret them according to his or her own perspective, just as he or she would interpret the learning effectiveness data. Amortization of costs should always be a factor in cost-evaluation. Initially high instructional development costs can be absorbed over the expected shelf life of the product or if sold commercially, by the number of units sold.

At the conclusion of the production phase, the instructional materials can be put into standard use in the learning environment, either in the classroom by the teacher or through commercial production by the developer. The final effort in this phase is dissemination. It is at this point that the fourth phase of instructional development and evaluation should begin (see Figure 10.1).

IMPLEMENTATION PHASE

Recall that the decision for acquisition of new instructional materials for the learning environment is made in the Assessment Phase. The three possible decisions to be made for acquiring the instructional materials were (a) adopting currently developed materials (systems), or (b) modifying currently available materials by applying the appropriate phases of instructional development, or (c) developing new materials according to the design, and production phases. This final phase of instructional development is the implementation of these materials in the learning environment, regardless of how they were obtained. The two parts of this phase involve implementing the instructional materials and then managing an evaluation system which maintains the materials in relationship to the total learning environment.

Implementation

If a new management system for the learning environment was developed in conjunction with the development of new instructional materials, then the management system should be installed prior to the introduction of the new materials. The conditions of the management system need to be operational first to ensure that the various instructional materials components can function to their full capabilities (R. D. Tennyson, 1976). Too often new instructional materials lose their potential when the management system is not ready. Even though implementation is considered a major phase here, it has only been recently that procedures for implementing new instruction have been discussed in the instructional development literature (e.g., Gagné & Briggs, 1974). However, these procedures are for the most part on the "how-to-do-it" level. Obviously this is another area of instructional development that needs research and theoretical work.

Maintenance Evaluation

Evaluation of the learning environment after implementation of new instructional materials can influence the actual useful life of the materials. Maintaining the materials at or near the original level of effectivenss is the purpose of this final phase of evaluation.

Cost–Benefit Analysis

One of the first considerations in this area deals with the question: "Are the instructional materials still worth using?" In other words, do the benefits derived from the product justify the costs? Some of the benefits identified by Silvern (1972) include such factors as learning performance, positive learner attitudes, and efficiency of the materials and the management system. Efficiency of the management system refers, in part, to the ability of the system to adjust to innovation and updates in the learning environment. An efficient management system should signal change that is required to maintain or even improve the learning environment.

Student Performance and Attitude Review

Performance of the students during and after participation in the learning environment is probably the most important source of data for the maintenance evaluation. Student performance while in the environment provides immediate information on the degree to which instructional materials enable students to meet the objectives of the instruction. There are, however, two additional sources of data which can be used in this evaluation. They come from curriculum evaluation models and are usually referenced in connection with needs assessment procedures (Saylor & Alexander, 1974; Provus, 1971). The first is student performance in the succeeding instructional materials. Is the student acquiring the appropriate behaviors necessary for entrance into the succeeding instruction? The second is student performance after transferring into a noninstructional environment. In other words, is the instruction meeting those long-term goals of the learning environment?

Student attitudes toward the instruction may fluctuate because of either changes in the student population itself or changes imposed by the instructional materials. It is also probable that student imposed changes may occur from shifts in student characteristics in terms of prerequisite skills and backgrounds, thus necessitating changes in the instructional materials. Student attitudes are also affected by the instructional materials, and some of the factors which might initiate negative attitudes are out-of-date visuals, poor photographic displays (including inadequate film and film strips), missing resource materials, or any other components of the system which do not meet the technical standards of the original product (Davies, 1973).

Content/Behavior and Media Review

Another form of maintenance evaluation involves updating the content to keep the instructional materials current. Certain disciplines or subject matter areas are more susceptible to changes (or revisions) than others; however, the user should establish and follow procedures to review the content for any possible changes. It is good evaluation practice to assume that changes will occur and that periodic changes in the developed instructional materials will be necessary. Likewise, the behaviors required in relation to the content should be reviewed for possible updating.

With the increased use of technology in learning environments, the technology, as well as the courseware and software, must be evaluated and maintained. Wherever possible, new media resources should be incorporated into the system. This can be considered as either prolonging the life of developed materials or adding to the management or delivery systems. For example, computerizing tests could introduce a new media form which adds years to the usage of the instructional materials. Integrating new media into existing materials systems could definitely improve the efficiency of the instruction and even the effectiveness of the learning.

SUMMARY

Instructional systems refers to the development, evaluation, and management of learning environments according to scientific procedures. This chapter has focused on that process of instructional systems dealing with the development and evaluation of instructional materials (defined as instructional development) while briefly commenting on management in reference to a system for administering the instructional materials in a learning environment. Management is, of course, a much broader concept that includes the administration of the learning environment itself. The concept of learning environment as used here was not restricted to either an educational classroom or a media resource center situation. Learning environments imply any setting where learning is anticipated and/or encouraged. The purpose of the instructional systems approach is to provide an environment where learning effectivenss and efficiency are facilitated. The concepts and principles of instructional systems are certainly applicable to less goal-oriented learning environments, for example, a museum of natural history.

The process of instructional development was represented here as four phases which include both development and evaluation components. This organization by phases was based upon a review of the literature dealing with theoretical models of instructional development and, also, the applied work of instructional developers. The need for an instructional development model showing decision strategies and processes for the various phases and components is necessary, but the actual model structure should be determined as part of the decision making process in the Assessment Phase. The conditions and situations of each instructional development project are uniquely different, even when approached by the same organization, requiring an individually derived strategy for the development. The revision loop of the conventional instructional development model becomes impractical when appropriate evaluation methods are employed throughout the development process.

Recent research trends have been toward variables and conditions associated with design of the instructional materials. Methods of design involve such factors as strategies for presenting the stimulus properties, management strategies for selecting appropriate stimulus materials (e.g., adaptive models and aptitude treatment interaction models), relationships of content structures to design strategies, methods for transmediation, and technological strategies. The scope of the research is large, but many areas of the instructional development process have not been adequately studied. However, given the present direction in educational psychology toward research in instructional systems, there will be a continuing impact on the development, evaluation, and management of learning environments.

REFERENCES

Airasian, P. W., & Bart, W. M. Validating a priori instructional hierarchies. *Journal of Educational Measurement*, 1975, *12*, 163–173.

Alpert, D., & Bitzer, D. L. Advances in computer-based education. *Science*, 1970, *167*, 1582–1590.

Anderson, L. W. An empirical investigation of individual differences in time to learn. *Journal of Educational Psychology,* 1976, *68*(2), 226–233.

Anderson, R. C. Educational psychology. *Annual Review of Psychology,* 1967, *18,* 129–164.

Anderson, R. C. How to construct achievement tests to assess comprehension. *Review of Educational Research,* 1972, *42,* 145–170.

Bloom, B. S., Englehart, M. D., Furst, E. J., Hill, W. H., & Krathwohl, D. R. *A taxonomy of educational objectives: Handbook I, the cognitive domain.* New York: Longmans, Green, 1956.

Bloom, B. S., Hastings, J. T., & Madaus, G. F. *Handbook on formative and summative evaluation of student learning.* New York: McGraw-Hill, 1971.

Boutwell, R. C., & Tennyson, R. D. Instructional objectives: Different by design. *NSPI Journal,* 1972, *10*(7), 7–10.

Briggs, L. J. *Handbook of procedures for the design of instruction.* Pittsburgh, Pennsylvania: American Institute for Research, 1970.

Bunderson, C. V. *The TICCIT Project: Design Strategy for Educational Innovation* (Technical Report No. 4). Provo, Utah: Brigham Young University, Institute for Computer Uses in Education, September, 1973.

Clark, D. C. Teaching concepts in the classroom: A set of teaching prescriptions derived from experimental research. *Journal of Educational Psychology, Monographs,* 1971, *62,* 253–278.

Coffarella, E. P. How little do we know about the cost–effectiveness of instructional technology? *Educational Technology,* 1975, *15,* 56–58.

Cronbach, L. J. Course improvement through evaluation. *Teachers College Record,* 1963, *64,* 672–685.

Cronbach, L. J., & Snow, R. E. *Aptitudes and instructional methods: A handbook for research on interactions.* New York: Irvington Press, in press.

Davies, I. K. *Competency based learning: Technology, management, and design.* New York: McGraw-Hill, 1973.

Day, H. I., Berlyne, D. E., & Hunt, D. E. *Intrinsic motivation: A new direction in education.* Montreal, Canada: Holt, Rinehart & Winston, 1971.

Doyle, K. O., Jr., & Whitley, S. E. Student ratings as criteria for effective teaching. *American Educational Research Journal,* 1974, *11,* 259–274.

Echternacht, G. J. The use of confidence testing in objective tests. *Review of Educational Research,* 1972, *42,* 217–236.

Eiss, A. F. *Evaluation of instructional systems.* New York: Gordon & Breach, 1972.

Finn, J. D., & Allen, W. H. (Eds.). Instructional materials: Educational media and technology. *Review of Educational Research,* 1962.

Flemming, M. J. Perceptual principles for the design of instructional materials. *Viewpoints,* 1970, *46*(4).

Foley, L. M., & R. D. Tennyson. *A Systems Approach to the Design of Instruction.* Minneapolis, Minnesota: University of Minnesota, Instructional Systems Laboratory, June, 1976.

Frase, L. T. Advances in research and theory in instructional technology. In F. N. Kerlinger (Ed.), *Review of research in education* (Vol. 3). Itasca, Illinois: Peacock, 1975.

Gage, N. L., & Berliner, D. C. *Educational psychology,* Chicago: Rand McNally, 1975.

Gagné, R. M. *The conditions of learning.* New York: Holt, Rinehart & Winston, 1965.

Gagné, R. M. *The conditions of learning (2nd ed.).* New York: Holt, Rinehart & Winston, 1970.

Gagné, R. M. Domains of learning. *Interchange,* 1972, *3,* 1–8.

Gagné, R. M. Task analysis–its relation to content analysis. *Educational Psychologist,* 1974, *11*(1), 11–18.

Gagné, R. M., & Briggs, L. J. *Principles of instructional design.* New York: Holt, Rinehart & Winston, 1974.

Gagné, R. M., & Paradise, N. E. Abilities and learning sets in knowledge acquisition. *Psychological Monographs,* 1961, *75,* 14 (whole number 518).

Gagné, R. M., & Rohwer, W. D., Jr. Instructional psychology. *Annual Review of Psychology,* 1969, *20,* 381–418.

Gerlack, V. S., & Ely, D. D. *Teaching and media: A systematic approach.* Englewood Cliffs, New Jersey: Prentice-Hall, 1971.

Glaser, R. The design of instruction. In J. I. Goodlad (Ed.), *The changing American school,* 65th Yearbook of the National Society for the Study of Education. Chicago: University of Chicago Press, 1966.

Glaser, R. Toward a behavioral science base for instructional design. In R. Glaser (Ed.), *Teaching machines and programmed learning,* II. Washington, D. C.: National Educational Association, 1965.

Glaser, R., & Resnick, L. B. Instructional psychology. *Annual Review of Psychology,* 1972, *23,* 207–276.

Grobman, H. *Evaluation activities of curriculum projects: A starting point,* AERA Monograph Series on Curriculum Evaluation, R. E. Stake (Ed.). Chicago: Rand McNally, 1968.

Houtz, J. C., Moore, J. W., & Davis, J. K. Effects of different types of positive and negative instances in learning "nondimensioned" concepts. *Journal of Educational Psychology,* 1973, *64,* 206–211.

Jenkins, J. J. Remember that old theory of memory? Well, forget it! *American Psychologist,* 1974, *29,* 785–795.

Johnson, D. M. *Improvement of problem solving processes* (Final Report Project No. 5-0705). Washington, D. C.: United States Office of Education, Bureau of Research, 1968.

Johnson, D. M., Parrott, G. L., & Stratton, R. P. Production and judgment of solutions to five problems. *Journal of Educational Psychology Monograph Supplement,* 1968, *59*(6, pt. 2).

Kahoe, R. D., & McFarland, R. E. Interactions of task challenge and intrinsic and extrinsic motivations in college achievement. *Journal of Educational Psychology,* 1975, *67,* 432–438.

Kemp, J. E. *Instructional design: A plan for unit and course development.* Belmont, California: Fearon, 1971.

Klausmeier, H. J., & Feldman, K. V. Effects of a definition and a varying number of examples and nonexamples on concept attainment. *Journal of Educational Psychology,* 1975, *67,* 174–178.

Klausmeier, H. J., Ghatala, E. S., & Frayer, D. A. *Conceptual learning and development, a cognitive view.* New York: Academic Press, 1974.

Kulhavy, R. W., Yekovick, F. R., & Dyer, J. W. Feedback and response confidence. *Journal of Educational Psychology,* 1976, *68,* 522–528.

Landa, L. *Algorithmization of instruction.* Englewood Cliffs, New Jersey: Educational Technology, 1974.

Mager, R. F. *Preparing instructional objectives.* Palo Alto, California: Fearon, 1962.

McKeachie, W. J. Instructional psychology. *Annual Review of Psychology,* 1974, *25,* 161–193.

Mechner, F. Science education and behavioral technology. In R. Glaser (Ed.), *Teaching machines and programmed learning. II: Data and directions.* Washington, D. C.: National Education Association, 1965.

Merrill, M. D. Correction and review on successive parts in learning in hierarchical task. *Journal of Educational Psychology,* 1965, *56,* 225–234.

Merrill, M. D. *Instructional design: Readings.* Englewood Cliffs, New Jersey: Prentice-Hall, 1971.

Merrill, M. D. *Premises, propositions, and research underlying the design of a learner controlled computer-assisted instruction system: A summary for the TICCIT system* (Working Paper 44). Provo, Utah: Brigham Young University, Division of Instructional Services, June 1973.

Merrill, M. D., & Boutwell, R. C. Instructional development: Methodology and research. In F. N. Kerlinger (Ed.), *Review of research in education* (Vol. 1). Itasca, Illinois: Peacock, 1973.

Merrill, M. D., & Goodman, R. I. Selecting instructional strategies and media: A place to begin. In J. Edling (Ed.), *Instructional Development Institues.* San Diego, California: United States International University, 1972.

Merrill, M. D., & Tennyson, R. D. *Concept teaching: An instructional design guide.* Englewood Cliffs, New Jersey: Educational Technology, 1977.

Merrill, M. D., & Wood, N. D. *Instructional strategies: A preliminary taxonomy.* Invited address presented to the Special Interest Group for Research in Mathematics Education at the meeting of the American Educational Research Association, Chicago, Illinois, April 1974.

National Education Association. *Recommendations for reporting the effectiveness of programmed instruction materials. Supplement I–general manual. Supplement II–technical manual.* Washington, D. C.: Joint Committee of Program Instruction and Teaching Machines, Division of Audiovisual Instruction, 1969.

Paivio, A. Coding distinctions and repetition effects in memory. In G. H. Bower (Ed.), *The psychology of learning and motivation.* New York: Academic Press, 1975.

Phi Delta Kappa National Study Committee on Evaluation, D. Stufflebeam, (Chairman). *Educational evaluation and decision making.* Itasca, Illinois: Peacock, 1971.

Popham, W. J., & Baker, E. L. *Systematic instruction.* Englewood Cliffs, New Jersey: Prentice-Hall, 1970.

Provus, M. *Discrepancy evaluation for educational program improvement and assessment.* Berkeley, California: McCutcheon, 1971.

Roid, G. H. Issues in judging the cost-effectiveness of self-instructional programs: A case study in programmed dental instruction. *Improving Human Performance,* 1974, *3,* 49–63.

Rothkopf, E. Z. Two scientific approaches to the management of instruction. In R. M. Gagné & W. R. Gephart (Ed.), *Learning research and school subjects.* Itasca, Illinois: Peacock, 1968.

Saylor, J. G., & Alexander, W. M. *Planning curriculum for schools.* New York: Holt, Rinehart & Winston, 1974.

Scandura, J. Role of rules in behavior: Toward an operational definition of what (rule) is learned. *Psychological Review,* 1970, *77,* 516–533.

Scandura, J. M., & Durnin, J. Extrascope transfer in learning mathematical rules. *Journal of Educational Psychology,* 1968, *54,* 350–354.

Scandura, J. M., & Voorhies, D. J. Effects of irrelevant attributes and irrelevant operations on rule learning. *Journal of Educational Psychology,* 1971, *62,* 352–356.

Scriven, M. Evaluation prospectus and procedures. In W. J. Popham (Ed.), *Evaluation in education: Current applications.* Berkeley, California: McCutchan, 1975.

Scriven, M. The methodology of evaluation. *Perspectives of curricular evaluation.* AERA Monograph Series. Chicago: Rand McNally, 1967.

Silvern, L. C. *Systems engineering applied to training.* Houston, Texas: Gulf Pub., 1972.

Simon, H. A. *The sciences of the artificial.* Cambridge, Massachusetts: MIT Press, 1969.

Skinner, B. F. Science of learning and the art of teaching. *Harvard Educational Review,* 1954, *24,* 86–97.

Skinner, B. F. Teaching machines. *Science,* 1958, *128,* 269–977.

Snelbecker, G. E. *Learning theory, instructional theory and psycho-educational design.* New York: McGraw-Hill, 1974.

Stake, R. E. (Ed.). *Perspectives of curriculum evaluation,* AERA Monograph Series on Curriculum Evaluation. Chicago: Rand McNally, 1967.

Stake, R. E. Language, rationality, and assessment. In W. H. Beatty (Ed.), *Improving educational assessment and an inventory of measures of affective behavior.* Washington, D. C.: Association for Supervision and Curriculum Development, 1969.

Stratton, R. P., Parrott, G. L., & Johnson, D. M. Transfer of judgment training to production and judgment of solution on a verbal problem. *Journal of Educational Psychology,* 1970, *61,* 16–23.

Temkin, S. Making sense of benefit–cost analysis and cost effectiveness analysis. *Improving Human Performance,* 1974, *3,* 39–48.

Tennyson, C. L. *Elements of Curriculum Development.* Minneapolis, Minnesota: University of Minnesota, Instructional Systems Laboratory, May, 1976.

Tennyson, C. L., & Tennyson, R. D. Instructional objectives—who needs them??!! *Improving Human Performance,* 1975, *4*(1), 12–16.

Tennyson, R. D. A review of experimental methodology in instructional task sequencing. *AV Communications Review,* 1972, *20,* 147–159.

Tennyson, R. D. Effect of negative instances in concept acquisition using a verbal learning task. *Journal of Educational Psychology,* 1973, *64,* 247–260.

Tennyson, R. D. The role of evaluation in instructional development. *Educational Technology,* 1976, *16,* 17–24.

Tennyson, R. D., & Boutwell, R. C. A quality control design for validating hierarchical sequencing of programmed instruction. *NSPI Journal,* 1971, *10,* 5–10.

Tennyson, R. D., & Boutwell, R. C. Methodology for defining instance difficulty in concept teaching. *Educational Technology,* 1974, *14*(2), 19–24. (a)

Tennyson, R. D., & Boutwell, R. C. Methodology for the sequencing of instances in classroom concept teaching. *Educational Technology,* 1974, *14*(9), 45–49. (b)

Tennyson, R. D., & Boutwell, R. C. Pretask versus within-task anxiety measures in predicting performance on a concept acquisition task. *Journal of Educational Psychology,* 1973, *65,* 88–92.

Tennyson, R. D., Steve, M. W., & Boutwell, R. C. Instance sequence and analysis of instance attribute representation in concept acquisition. *Journal of Educational Psychology,* 1975, *67,* 821–827.

Tennyson, R. D., & Tennyson, C. L. Rule acquisition design strategy variables: Degree of instance divergence, sequence, and instance analysis. *Journal of Educational Psychology,* 1975, *67,* 852–859.

Tennyson, R. D., & Woolley, F. R. Interaction of anxiety with performance on two levels of task difficulty. *Journal of Educational Psychology,* 1971, *62,* 463–468.

Tennyson, R. D., Woolley, F. R., & Merrill, M. D. Exemplar and non-exemplar variables which produce correct concept classification behavior and specified classification errors. *Journal of Educational Psychology,* 1972, *63,* 144–152.

Thorndike, E. L. *The original nature of man. Educational psychology, I.* New York: Teachers College, 1913. (a)

Thorndike, E. L. *The psychology of learning. Educational psychology, II.* New York: Teachers College, 1913. (b)

Tiemann, P. W., & Markle, S. M. An elaborated hierarchy of types of learning. *Educational Psychologist,* 1973, *10,* 147–158.

Tobias, S., & Ingber, T. *Achievement treatment interactions.* Paper presented at the meeting of the American Psychological Association, Chicago, August 1975.

U. S. Office of Education, *State plan administrator's manual, ESEA, Title III.* Washington, D. C. The Office, 1971.

White, R. T. Research into learning hierarchies. *Review of Educational Research,* 1973, *43,* 361–375.

White, R. T., & Gagné, R. M. Past and future research on learning hierarchies. *Educational Psychologist,* 1974, *11*(1), 19–28.

Wilkinson, G. L. Needed: Information for cost analysis. *Educational Technology,* 1972, *12,* 33–38.

Wittrock, M. C., & Wiley, D. E. *The evaluation of instruction.* New York: Holt, Rinehart & Winston, 1970.

Worthen, B. R. Discovery and expository task presentation in elementary mathematics. *Journal of Educational Psychology Monograph,* 1968, *59,* 1–3.

11

The Personalized System
of Instruction—A New Idea
in Higher Education

ROBERT E. SPENCER and GEORGE SEMB

University of Kansas

HISTORY—WHAT'S SO NEW ABOUT THE PERSONALIZED
SYSTEM OF INSTRUCTION?

The personalized system of instruction (PSI) represents a radical departure from traditional teaching methods. While many conventional approaches to higher education endorse (*a*) norm-referenced grading, (*b*) instructor-scheduled pacing, (*c*) use of textbooks to dispense course content, (*d*) a single course instructor, and (*e*) the use of the lecture to deliver information rather than to motivate, PSI typically consists of five contrasting features: (*a*) mastery learning, (*b*) student-pacing, (*c*) reliance on textbooks accompanied by structured study materials, (*d*) student proctors, and (*e*) the utilization of lectures as vehicles for motivation (Keller, 1968). Before describing each of the components in detail, it might be useful to trace the development of PSI. Several innovators isolated parts of the system, but it was not until Keller and his associates integrated all the ingredients that PSI adopted its present form.

Early Innovations of PSI

Several seemingly independent teaching innovations have occurred at different times in the twentieth century. In the early 1930s Byron Taylor developed a course for high school students in industrial arts (the "integrative procedure") which encompassed all the basic components of PSI except the use of student proctors (Taylor, 1935). In 1963, Olgierd Celenski taught a self-paced course in electrical engineering at the University of Ottawa (Celenski, 1974). "Correspondence instruction," used by universities for many years, is also similar to PSI except for an extended lag between testing and grading and the omission of student proctors. Although these examples have excluded student proctors, the concept of students as teachers is not a new one.

As early as the sixteenth century, students taught other students in the classroom. Jesuit teachers used student "decurions," each of whom was responsible for the instruction of 10 students and who functioned in much the same manner as student proctors today. Decurions served as tutors, maintained student records, listened to recitations, and carried on other instructor-related duties (Cole, 1950, 319–320, 607–609). In the early nineteenth century, Andrew Bell and Joseph Lancaster developed systems called "mutual-tuition" and "monitorial," in which students assumed much the same role as the Jesuit decurions (Cole, 1950).

No single aspect of present-day PSI is really new. Furthermore, the system itself has several close relatives. Helen Mills (1972), for example, developed such a system to teach English composition at American River College. Military training centers, as Keller (1968) points out, have used such a system for years. The early innovation that most closely resembled PSI, however, was developed by Mary Ward (Washburne & Marland, 1963). Ms. Ward taught elementary mathematics at San Francisco State Normal School in 1912. She developed instructional materials that allowed students to teach themselves and that required only the occasional assistance of a student teacher. Thus, students were taught on an individualized basis and were allowed to progress at their own rate, two important features of current PSI practice. An equally important contribution of Ms. Ward's work, however, was to encourage her fellow teachers to adopt and extend her program to a schoolwide system of self-paced curriculum materials.

Keller and His Associates

Higher education is typically the last branch of education to endorse change and innovation (Ruskin, 1974). Its resistance to innovation becomes evident when compared to the changes in preschool and elementary school education that have occurred during the past several decades. It is interesting to note that personalized instruction is flourishing in higher education; only recently has it begun to have an impact on secondary and elementary education.

The Personalized System of Instruction was initiated by Fred Keller, Gil Sherman, Rodolpho Azzi, and Carolina Martuscelli Bori, four psychologists well schooled in basic reinforcement theory. Their discontent with inefficient methods of teaching in higher education, together with the advent of programmed instruction, teaching machines, and the publication of Skinner's paper, "The Science of Learning and Art of Teaching" (1954), created a receptive climate for change. Perhaps a chronological account of their first attempts at PSI will illustrate how the system developed and expanded.

In March, 1963, Sherman, Bori, and Azzi concluded a trip designed to gather information for the development of a psychology department at the University of Brasília. Their final stop was at the home of Fred Keller, who was also to participate in the formulation of the new department. Keller remained at Columbia University to fulfill his teaching responsibilities, while the other three return to Brazil to make final arrangements for the new psychology department. Meanwhile, in August 1963, at the American Psychological Association, Keller presented the blueprints of PSI (Keller, 1966, pp. 91—93). Two months prior to joining his colleagues in Brazil, Keller taught three students in a mini-lab course using PSI; the students reacted favorably. After arriving in Brazil, however, Keller was unable to implement the plan because Brazil was undergoing a change in government. Sherman and Keller returned to the United States; Azzi and Bori remained at Brasília and initiated the project a few months later. In the fall of 1965, however, PSI came to a halt at Brasília due to the political interruption of all university functions. Meanwhile, Sherman and Keller continued to use PSI, and their work began to arouse interest and discussion (Keller, 1974; Sherman, 1974a). It was not until Keller published "Good-bye teacher . . ." (Keller, 1968), however, that PSI really began to attract national attention.

The recent opening of the Center of Personalized Instruction at Georgetown University is another indication of the spreading interest in PSI. The Center acts as an information clearinghouse for PSI through its workshops, conferences, and publications, such as the *Personalized System of Instruction Newsletter* and the *Journal of Personalized Instruction.* Workshops serve as training centers by providing structured settings for the development of course materials and policy. The *Newsletter* offers perhaps the best record of PSI's development during the past decade, including current research projects and a record of scheduled events. The *Journal of Personalized Instruction* is an international, user-oriented, multidisciplinary journal which publishes articles related to the analysis and improvement of personalized instruction.

THE BASIC COMPONENTS OF PSI

A common practice for sorting students in many educational endeavors is the use of the normal curve. The continued use of this grading system is remarkably predictable. Given that students enter a typical university course with *differing* aptitudes but are exposed to *equal* amounts of instruction, *identical* instructional methods, and *comparable* amounts of time in which to learn the material, it follows that the students may perform at varying levels of proficiency, i.e., "A," "B," "C," etc. Thus, such grading practices may reflect no more than initial differences between students.

The use of the normal curve for grading purposes has several undesirable side effects. First, the normal curve produces a predictable number of failures. Second, it creates a self-fulfilling prophecy. That is, teachers begin each semester with the expectation that only a certain percentage of students will thoroughly master *all* the course material. When it comes time to assign grades, the students' achievement corresponds to the teachers' original expectations. In addition, as Bloom (1968) has noted, the normal distribution is the "most appropriate to chance and random activity."

PSI approaches education from a different perspective. The goal of PSI is to have students master *all* of what is presented. Thus, ideally, there should be no differences in student performances, since all the students have mastered all of the material. The concept of mastery learning is the cornerstone of PSI. As such, it is the first component to be discussed.

Mastery Learning

In mastery learning, all students have the *opportunity* to do well. Differences in student abilities are compensated for by the amount of time allowed for learning (Carrol, 1963). That is, mastery learning allows students to progress at a rate compatible with their own ability and other demands on their time. Thus, individual differences are seen only in the *rate of acquisition,* not in the *amount* learned.

A PSI course is usually broken down into small units of material, and students are required to master one unit before proceeding to the next (the unit perfection requirement). Thus, a common feature of mastery learning in PSI is the use of frequent evaluation (testing). Frequent testing permits the continual monitoring of student progress and guarantees that the student will not progress to more difficult material before demonstrating mastery of material which preceded it.

Mastery learning is typically defined as 90–100% correct. Implicit in mastery learning is the opportunity to redo an assignment without penalty. Thus, PSI allows students to take alternative forms of the test until the specified level of mastery is achieved. When mastery learning is incorporated in a curriculum, several changes in standard classroom procedures must follow, such as student self-pacing.

Self-Pacing

Self-pacing means that students decide when they are ready to be tested over each unit of material. Thus, self-pacing allows for individual differences in the rate at which students work. Since students progress at different rates, the instructor cannot use the lecture method to disseminate course content. Thus, an alternative delivery system is necessary; PSI relies on the written word.

The Written Word

The typical PSI course is divided into a series of units. A unit usually consists of a reading assignment, a chapter in a book, and a set of instructional objectives (Mager, 1962). Instructional objectives list the important points in each unit, typically through the use of a study guide. Each unit in the study guide typically includes: an introduction, a suggested procedure for learning the material, and a set of practice exercises. Introductions are often designed to be entertaining and, therefore, presumably motivating. Procedures usually take the form of instructions to read a set of materials. Practice exercises provide the student with an opportunity to respond actively.

Student Proctors

A typical student proctor is recruited from the previous semester and receives course credit or money for proctoring. Proctors are responsible for approximately 10 students and perform several classroom duties. They are available to answer questions and clarify ambiguities in course materials prior to administering quizzes. After a student takes a quiz, they evaluate the student responses and apply both positive and directive feedback to their weaknesses. Further, they decide whether the student should progress on to the next unit or restudy the present unit. Finally, as Keller (1968) states, the use of proctors provides "a marked enhancement of the personal–social aspect of the educational process."

PSI obviously changes the nature and structure of the university classroom. For instance, self-pacing means that the same students are not always present on the same day, while the use of student proctors changes the number of "teachers" available to students. Still another change is the use of a lecture as a motivational device.

Motivational Lectures

Lectures and demonstrations in PSI typically occur several times during the semester. Frequently, a lecture or demonstration is provided for students who have passed a certain number of units. Attendance is optional, and students are not held responsible for any information presented in the lectures. Lectures are usually announced a few days in advance, and students may earn the opportunity to attend them by progressing through a required number of units. Thus, they provide an opportunity for enrichment and are so designed to serve a motivational function.

Although PSI is usually defined by the five components described previously, several instructors have modified the original plan. For example, some instructors do not use motivational lectures and others use different types of proctoring systems. These modifications will be discussed later in this chapter under the section The Future of PSI.

RESEARCH IN PSI

PSI versus Traditional Course Formats

Early research attempted to compare PSI with traditional classroom instruction. Keller (1968) reported that introductory psychology students earned higher course grades if they were taught by PSI format than if they were instructed in a traditional lecture format. In the following year, McMichael and Corey (1969) demonstrated that students taught by PSI achieved higher final exam scores and rated the course more favorably. Furthermore, Corey, McMichael, and Tremont (1970) showed that PSI students retained more than lecture students in subsequent tests 5 and 9 months after the completion of the course.

Also in 1970, Sheppard and MacDermot compared the effects of PSI and lecture procedures on students' performance and course ratings. Their results were similar to those reported in the previous studies. Finally, Born, Davis, Whelan, and Jackson (1972), and Born, Gledhill, and Davis (1972) also investigated differences in student study time. Both PSI and traditional students were required to study in a prescribed study center with materials available to them only in that center. The results revealed that PSI students spent more time studying in the center, but when class hours *plus* study hours were computed for both groups, total study time was the same. Even though both procedures required the same amount of study time, PSI students performed with greater proficiency than students in the traditional lecture/discussion class.

While the above studies were all done in the field of psychology, several researchers have compared PSI and traditional teaching methods in other disciplines. For example, Alba and Pennypacker (1972) compared pre- and posttest scores of education students enrolled in a PSI section and in a traditional section. Posttest results showed significantly greater changes in the PSI section as compared to the traditional section. The following year, Austin and Gilbert (1973) and Wei-Ming Leo (1973) reported that PSI students performed markedly higher in physics and chemistry, respectively, than students in the traditional sections. Protopapas (1974) found that general biology students performed higher on the final exam and rated the course higher, if taught by PSI as opposed to using a traditional format. Bailey (1975) demonstrated that students in a PSI French class achieved greater posttest gains on a standardized foreign language test (listening and writing) than students in the traditional class. However, students in the traditional class achieved greater gains on the reading portion of the test.

Bailey (1975) is not alone in reporting that traditional instruction sometimes produces outcomes comparable to PSI. Lloyd (unpublished) reviewed 29 studies that compared PSI to traditional classroom procedures and found PSI to be significantly superior in 17 cases, partially superior in 4, and no different in 8. None of the comparisons favored traditional methods. Kulik (1976) reviewed 31 studies that compared PSI and traditional teaching methods and found results comparable to the Lloyd (unpublished) review.

Although the evidence appears to suggest that PSI is at least comparable, if not superior, to more traditional programs, the research does not indicate that PSI is *always* better. However, when one considers a review done by Dubin and Taveggia (1968), the results of PSI research are more dramatic. After an exhaustive analysis of research on different college teaching techniques available prior to 1968, Dubin and Taveggia (1968) concluded that "no particular method of teaching is measurably preferred over another when evaluated by student examination performances." In light of the Dubin and Taveggia review (1968), the apparent superiority of PSI over other methods assumes considerably more significance. PSI appears to be the first instructional system in higher education that does, in fact, make a difference.

Component Analysis

If an experimental procedure is particularly complex or costly, it may be beneficial to analyze the *components* of the procedure. Component analysis allows one to determine which features of the experimental method contribute to its success. If such analysis indicates, for example, that a particular component contributes significantly to the effectiveness of the total package, a researcher may, at that point, analyze the *cost* of that component.

Mastery Learning

Several studies have examined the effects of grade level requirements on academic performance. Semb, Hopkins, and Hursh (1973) found that grades were an important factor in maintaining high levels of academic performance. C.

Whitehurst and G. J. Whitehurst (1975) reported that students who were forced to earn an "A," or fail, performed with superior results to students who had an option of receiving an "A," "B," "C," "D," or "F." Course evaluations from the two groups, however, did not differ significantly.

Bostow and O'Connor (1973) reported that students who were required to redo a unit test (remediation), performed better than students who were not required to remediate. Although Bostow and O'Connor (1973) did not require students to master material at a certain level, their study supports the contention that student performance is higher if students are given the opportunity to redo an assignment. Several other investigators, however, have examined the effects of different levels of mastery criterion on student performance. Johnston and O'Neill (1973) compared a 90%, 75%, 60%, and no mastery criterion, and found that the higher the mastery level, the higher the performance level achieved. They also reported that the number of quizzes that was retaken increased with increasing mastery levels. Semb (1974) compared a 100% mastery criterion to a 60% mastery criterion and found that students performed higher on major exams when they were required to perform at a 100% mastery level as opposed to a 60% level. Finally, Davis (1975) examined student performance under a 100% mastery criterion and a 50% criterion and found similar results.

Mastery of PSI is a costly component of PSI in terms of grading time, since the number of tests to be graded is increased. Nevertheless, the research seems to indicate that students should *at least* be given the opportunity to redo assignments if higher levels of performance are to be achieved. Further, if a mastery criterion is to be used, Johnston and O'Neill (1973, p. 268) suggest that "with respect to criteria the teacher should start high and go higher."

Unit Size and Review Units

Several studies have analyzed the effects of unit length on academic performance and study behavior. Oftentimes, however, these studies also involve a comparison of frequent and infrequent quizzing. Since the frequency of quizzing is directly related to unit size, these studies will be considered together.

Mawhinney, Bostow, Laws, Blumenfeld, and Hopkins (1971) examined the effects of quiz frequency on study behavior and found that frequent quizzing procedures produce remarkably consistent study behavior, as compared to study behavior generated by infrequent hour exams. Nelson and Bennett (1973) reported that students' rate of progress in a PSI course is more consistent when units are small. Semb (1974) found that students perform approximately 20% better on major exams when the material is broken into units than when it is presented as a single assignment. O'Neill, Johnston, Walters, and Rasheed (1975) reported similar results. Williams and Lawrence (1975) reported that students who are quizzed frequently over small units perform higher on later major exams when compared to students who are quizzed less frequently over larger units.

Born (1975), however, found conflicting results. He reported no difference on later major exams between students who had frequent quizzing over small units and those who had had less frequent quizzing over large units.

Another important feature that appears to increase exam performance and retention is the use of review units interspersed throughout a course. Although Semb (1975) found no differences in performance on parts of a final exam covered by a review unit, Semb, Spencer, and Phillips (1976), in a follow-up study, found that the elimination of all review units produces inferior results on a final exam as compared to the elimination of only a few of the review units. Davis (1975) found that students that were required to answer review items that appeared on unit tests scored higher on a final examination and a 3-month follow-up examination than did students who did not answer the review items.

In conclusion, frequent quizzing and the use of review units, like mastery learning, add to the expense of operating and administering a course. However, the results of research in this area generally support the notion that if student performance is to be enhanced, then instructors should incorporate a few review units into a course and quiz over small units of material as frequently as possible.

Self-Pacing

Student self-pacing, as originally outlined by Keller (1968), was designed to allow students an unlimited amount of time to complete a course. However, university constraints, such as withdrawal policies and end of the semester deadlines, often impose time contingencies on students that prevent their having unlimited time to complete a course. Thus, research on student versus instructor pacing should be interpreted in light of the constraints that universities impose.

Green (1974) concluded that student pacing may contribute to higher course ratings that are typically associated with PSI courses. Semb, Conyers, Spencer, and Sanchez-Sosa (1975) found that pacing does not seem related to academic performance. Robin and Graham (1974) also found similar results. They reported that, when students paced themselves as opposed to being paced by the instructor, there were no differences on final retention or unit examiation performance. However, student pacing was rated more favorably than instructor pacing.

Freedom of pacing frequently leads to problems, the most serious of which is procrastination. Sutterer and Holloway (1975), for example, reported that students complete very few assignments early in the semester and many late in the semester. This creates a serious problem of logistics, since most tests are administered during the last few weeks of the course. Another problem inherent in student pacing is the number of student withdrawals and/or incompletes. Several investigators (Sheppard & MacDermot, 1970; Born et al., 1972; Philippas & Sommerfeldt, 1972; Born & Whelan, 1973; Hess, 1974) have documented that a greater number of students withdraw or receive incompletes for PSI courses than for traditional courses. Thus, student pacing seems to create several problems for the PSI instructor. Research that has dealt with these problems will be discussed later in this chapter.

Written Word

Most of the research conducted on this component of PSI has concentrated on the effects of study questions on student performance. Jenkins and Neisworth (1973) reported that students answered approximately 61% of the test items correctly when objectives were provided for those items, as opposed to approximately 34% for the same test items when no objectives were provided. Miles, Kibler, and Pettigrew (1967) demonstrated that a group of students performed 15.2% better on unit examinations when they were provided study questions as compared to another group of students who were not given study questions. Semb *et al.* (1973) found that students answered study question items 20 to 30% more frequently than nonstudy question items. These results seem to support the importance of providing students with study objectives.

A similar line of research has concentrated on the use of study questions in the classroom. Semb (1975) and Spencer and Semb (1975) have investigated the use of student-answered study questions to replace unit quizzes. Semb (1975) found that handing in written answers to study questions produced performance that was no different than taking unit quizzes. Spencer and Semb (1975), in a systematic replication, however, found a 5% to 10% difference in student performance when students handed in study questions rather than take a unit quiz. The results of this study also indicated that if instructors are going to use study questions as a substitute for unit quizzes, then the grading criteria should be set high. Peters (1975, pp. 89–99) found that students who were required to have their answers to study questions checked before being allowed to take a unit quiz, performed higher on unit quizzes and also completed the course requirements faster than students who did not have their study questions monitored.

A final emphasis in this area of research deals with the effects of study questions or programmed materials on more complex educational tasks such as concept formation (Semb & Spencer, 1976). Although this research is still primitive, results seem to indicate that one can "program" concept learning (Miller & Weaver, 1975, pp. 44–57). Sanchez-Sosa, Semb, and Spencer (1975) found that students not only performed better on recall items when study questions were provided, but also on more complex, generalization tasks. In addition, Miller (1975, pp. 243–250) has reported that a text designed to teach concept formation does so better than more traditional texts.

Student Proctors

Very little research has been conducted on the effects of undergraduate proctoring on student performance. Most studies have concentrated on students' evaluations of proctors and proctors' evaluations of their own experiences. Both types of evaluations have been very positive, with no exceptions (e.g., Born & Herbert, 1971; *PSI Newsletter* No. 8, 1973).

In one experimental investigation of proctoring, Farmer, Lachter, Blaustein, and Cole (1972) investigated the effects of varying degrees of proctoring and no proctoring on student progress through a PSI course and retention of material (as measured by the final examination). They found that students who had some portion of their quizzes proctored progressed faster through the course than students who were not proctored. Furthermore, students who were proctored performed significantly higher on the final examination than students who were not proctored. However, there were no differences between the varying degrees of proctoring.

Calhoun (1975, pp. 151–157) examined the effects of various characteristics, such as sex, age, and academic background, on proctor effectiveness. The only significant result that Calhoun found was that the rate at which a student progresses through the course is correlated with the proctor's past experience of being a proctor. That is, veteran proctors apparently encouraged faster rates of student progress than individuals who were proctoring for their first semester.

The use of student proctors, who took the course the previous semester, is not always possible. In addition, various problems are related to the use of undergraduate proctors, such as selection, training, and administration.

Motivational Lectures

Lectures and demonstrations in PSI courses are frequently not well attended, particularly if they are not required (Lloyd, Garlington, Lowry, Burgess, Euler, & Knowlton, 1972; Sheldon, Sherman, Wolf, Minkin, & Minkin, 1975, pp. 225–242). Several other investigators (Ferster, 1968; Whitehurst, 1972) have reported decreases in attendance at optional lectures as the term progressed. This evidence does not necessarily eliminate the function of a lecture. However, it appears from previous research that some type of contingency will probably be required to produce high levels of attendance.

IMPLEMENTATION AND RESEARCH EFFORTS IN EDUCATIONAL PSYCHOLOGY

PSI has been utilized by several instructors of educational psychology in diverse college settings (Walter Hapiewicz, Michigan State University; Philip Young, Towson College; J. G. Sherman, Georgetown University; and Lawrence Sherman, Miami University). In addition, Samuel Dietz at Georgia State University has taught a graduate level course in educational psychology. James Shoen at North Adams State College and Ronald Gentile at SUNY, Buffalo, have also taught advanced and introductory level courses. The *Directory of Teaching*

Innovations in Psychology (Maas & Kleiber, 1975) provides additional examples of the use of PSI in educational psychology.

Besides implementing PSI procedures in the classroom, several educational psychologists have researched the effectiveness of PSI. Research in the field of educational psychology, like research in other subject areas, first compared PSI to the more traditional teaching formats. Fox (1975) reported that students in PSI outperformed traditional lecture students on a common posttest and retention test, and rated the course more favorably than students in the lecture classes. Several other investigators have found similar results (Gentile, 1971; Johnson & Sulzer-Azaroff, 1974; and Breland & Smith, 1975). In addition to comparisons of PSI and traditional teaching, several educational psychologists have analyzed the effectiveness of the various components of PSI. For example, Nelson and Bennet (1973) investigated the effects of unit size on rate of progress through the course. Fraley and Vargas (1975) investigated the effects of different pacing contingencies on rates of completion. Johnson, Maas, and Perkins (1976) evaluated the effects of oral versus written quiz procedures on student performance and preferences. In general, the results of these studies support the findings reported previously (see the section entitled Component Analysis, p. 249).

THE FUTURE OF PSI

The field of personalized instruction faces several serious problems. First, many of the studies have been less than perfect in terms of experimental rigor. It is not the purpose of the present study, however, to discuss research methodology, but rather to state that it is an important consideration, one that has been discussed at length elsewhere (Semb, 1976).

Problems and Some Possible Solutions

In addition to the various cautions that a researcher must be aware of, several articles (Hess, 1974; Gallup, 1974; Green, 1974) have pointed to the practical problems that exist in PSI. One such problem results from student pacing. Several procedures for alleviating this problem have been investigated.

Basically, these procedures involve a combination of some type of instructor and student pacing. For example, Malott and Svinicki (1969) used a "Doomsday" contingency. If students failed to complete the course by the end of the semester (Doomsday), they received an "F" in the course. Semb *et al.* (1973) used the concept of a minimum rate contingency to maintain student progress, and Miller, Weaver, and Semb (1974) reported that instructor-set target dates, backed up by a withdrawal contingency, produced higher rates of quiz-taking then no target dates and contingencies. Semb *et al.* (1975, pp. 348–368) found that bonus points for maintaining certain rates of progress decreased withdrawal rates. Lloyd and Knutzen (1969) suggested that what is needed is a contingency early in the semester, because once students begin working, they typically continue to work at a steady rate until all the material has been mastered.

Another problem in PSI is the construction of written materials. It requires a great deal of time to develop a good set of materials for a PSI course, and instructors usually do not have much time to devote to this chore. However, the increased availability of commercial materials may help alleviate the problem.

The use of undergraduate students who completed the course the previous semester (external proctors) may also create problems for the PSI instructor, particularly if a large number of student proctors is involved. Instructors must have a selection and training procedure to ensure that the proctors selected are of high caliber and that they understand the procedures to employ in the classroom. It is also necessary to monitor the proctor's grading accuracy to ensure quality control in the classroom. All of these procedures require the instructor's time. In addition, many universities will not allow instructors to award course credit for proctoring. One solution to this problem is to pay proctors. However, this also is not always possible. Therefore, several other systems have been developed to replace the student proctor.

One such technique is the use of "internal" proctors (Sherman, 1974(b)). The first 10 students who master the first unit become "internal" proctors over that unit. Students who miss the chance to become a proctor on that unit may become a proctor over the next unit, if they are one of the first 10 to master the next unit, and so on. Johnson and Sulzer-Azaroff (1975) compared external proctoring to internal proctoring and found no difference in student examination performance or preference for either system.

Another technique that has been investigated is self-grading, in which students check their own quizzes against model answers. After students report that they have mastered the quiz, the instructor orally interviews them over one or two important concepts in the unit. If the student passes the interview, he or she is eligible to progress to the next unit. Blackburn, Semb, and Hopkins (1975) found that the self-grading procedure was just as effective, as measured by four major exams, as the external proctoring system.

Another problem faced by PSI users is the unusually large number of "A's" earned by their students. Frequently, administrators voice an objection to this grading practice. To counter their objections, it is often necessary for PSI users to present administrators with student performance data to document that an "A" in their course is equivalent to an "A" in other courses.

Future Research Areas

Most research in PSI has used static group experimental designs. However, group designs have one serious disadvantage; they do not take into account the effects of a given procedure on the *individual*. This does not mean that group designs are not useful, but they are best used to answer actuarial questions, such as what proportion of students performs best under one method of instruction as compared to another (Semb, 1976). Education, and in particular PSI, however, should be more concerned with questions which ask how a procedure affects individual students. Thus, PSI research should utilize more individual, single-subject designs in its future research attempts. Such designs allow one to make statements about the relationship between a procedure and its effect on the individual student.

Single-subject designs will also allow the researcher to assess the benefits of the proctoring role. Because of the current demand for accountability among administrators and legislators, it is appropriate that PSI researchers develop measures to quantify the impact of proctoring. Perhaps, for example, future research should focus on the social interaction skills that may also be enhanced by the proctoring experience. Furthermore, there is also a need for addressing such issues as cost comparison analysis, retention effects, higher level objectives, and the effect that PSI has on study habits and other academic skills.

Currently, PSI contains two performance based systems, mastery learning and motivational lectures. Progressing from one unit to the next and attendance at optional lectures are based upon the individual's performance and progress. Perhaps, PSI needs to develop other performance based systems. One such system might deal with unit size. Students could increase the size of the unit to be quizzed over by performing well on progressively larger units of material. Another performance based system might be developed to teach students how to pace themselves. For example, a system might be designed in which the instructor sets the initial pace of the course, and students earn the opportunity to self-pace.

Also in the area of student pacing, researchers should investigate the effects of student pacing in open-ended settings, where end of term time constraints are nonexistent. The utility of PSI in nonacademic settings, such as staff training for institutions, should also be assessed. If PSI is found to be effective in other settings, then its generality will be greatly enhanced.

REFERENCES

Alba, E., & Pennypacker, H. S. A multiple change score comparison of traditional and behavioral college teaching procedures. *Journal of Applied Behavior Analysis,* 1972, *5,* 121–124.

Austin, S. M., & Gilbert, K. E. Student performance in a Keller-plan course in introductory electricity and magnetism. *American Journal of Physics,* 1973, *41,* 1.

Bailey, L. G. Contingency management in college foreign language instruction. In J. M.

Johnston (Ed.), *Behavior research and technology in higher education.* Springfield, Illinois: Charles C Thomas, 1975.

Blackburn, T., Semb, G., & Hopkins, B. L. The comparative effects of self-grading on class efficiency and student performance. In J. M. Johnston (Ed.), *Behavior research and technology in higher education.* Springfield, Illinois: Charles C Thomas, 1975.

Bloom, B. S. *Evaluation comment.* Los Angeles: Center for the Study of Evaluation of Instructional Programs, University of California, May, 1968, Vol. 1, No. 2.

Born, D. G. Exam performance and study behavior as a function of study unit size. In J. M. Johnston (Ed.), *Behavior research and technology in higher education.* Springfield, Illinois: Charles C Thomas, 1975.

Born, D. G., Davis, M., Whelan, P., & Jackson, D. College student study behavior in a personalized instruction course and in a lecture course. In G. Semb (Ed.), *Behavior analysis and education—1972.* Lawrence: Follow Through Project, 1972.

Born, D. G., Gledhill, S. M., & Davis, M. L. Examination performance in lecture discussion and personalized instruction courses. *Journal of Applied Behavior Analysis,* 1972, *5,* 33–43.

Born, D. G., & Herbert, E. A further study of personalized instruction in large university classes. *Journal of Experimental Education,* 1971, *40,* 6–11.

Born, D. G., & Whelan, P. Some descriptive characteristics of student performance in PSI and lecture courses. *Psychological Record,* 1973, *23,* 145–152.

Bostow, D. E., & O'Connor, R. J. A comparison of two college classroom testing procedures: Required redmediation versus no remediation. *Journal of Applied Behavior Analysis,* 1973, *6,* 599–607.

Breland, N. S., & Smith, M. P. *Cognitive and affective outcomes of PSI mastery programs as compared to traditional instruction.* Paper presented at the meeting of the American Educational Research Association, April, 1975.

Calhoun, J. F. Proctor characteristics and functioning in the personalized system of instruction. In J. M. Johnston (Ed.), *Research and technology in college and university teaching.* Gainesville: University of Florida, Psychology Department, 1975.

Carrol, J. A. A model of school learning. *Teacher's College Record,* 1963, *64,* 723–733.

Cole, L. *A history of education—Socrates to Montessori.* New York: Holt, Rinehart & Winston, 1950.

Celenski, O. Announced repetitive test. In J. G. Sherman (Ed.), *Personalized system of instruction: 41 germinal papers.* Menlo Park, California: W. A. Benjamin, 1974.

Corey, J. R., McMichael, J. S., & Tremont, D. T. *Long-term effects of personalized instruction in an introductory course.* Paper presented at Eastern Psychological Association, Atlantic City, April 1970.

Davis, M. L. Mastery test proficiency requirement affects mastery test performance. In J. M. Johnston (Ed.), *Behavior research and technology in higher education.* Springfield, Illinois: Charles C Thomas, 1975.

Davis, M. L. Some effects of an integrated review procedure. In J. M. Johnston (Ed.), *Research and technology in college and university teaching.* Gainesville: University of Florida, Psychology Department, 1975.

Dubin, R., & Taveggia, T. C. *The teaching–learning paradox.* Eugene: University of Oregon Press, 1968.

Farmer, J., Lachter, G., Blaustein, J. J., & Cole, B. K. The role of proctoring in personalized instruction. *Journal of Applied Behavior Analysis,* 1972, *5,* 401–404.

Ferster, C. B. Individualized instruction in a large introductory psychology course. *Psychological Record,* 1968, *18,* 521–532.

Fox, P. A. The development and use of media as an instructional tool. A Ford Foundation Venture Project, 1975.

Fraley, L. E., & Vargas, E. A. *Distributions of learning behaviors in an individualized college course under two contingency schedules.* Paper presented at the meeting of the American Psychological Association, Chicago, September 1975.

Gallup, H. F. Problems in the implementation of a course in personalized instruction. In J. G. Sherman (Ed.), *Personalized system of instruction: 41 germinal papers.* Menlo Park, California: W. A. Benjamin, 1974.

Gentile, J. R. *Educational psychology principles applied to educational psychology courses.* Paper presented at the meeting of the American Psychological Association, Washington, D.C., September 1971.

Green, B. A. Pacing: Self and otherwise. *Personalized System of Instruction Newsletter,* 1974, *3,* 2–3.

Green, B. A. Fifteen reasons not to use the Keller plan. In J. G. Sherman (Ed.), *Personalized system of instruction: 41 germinal papers.* Menlo Park, California: W. A. Benjamin, 1974.

Hess, J. H. Keller plan instruction: Implementation problems. In J. G. Sherman (Ed.), *Personalized system of instruction: 41 germinal papers.* Menlo Park, California: W. A. Benjamin, 1974.

Jenkins, J. R., & Neisworth, J. T. The facilitative influence of instructional objectives. *Journal of Educational Research,* 1973, *66,* 254–256.

Johnson, K. R., Maas, C. A., & Perkins, M. R. The effects of oral vs. written quiz procedures on student performance and preference in a personalized instruction course. In B. A. Green (Ed.), *Personalized instruction in higher education: Proceedings of the Second National Conference.* Washington, D.C.: Center for Personalized Instruction, Georgetown University, 1976.

Johnson, K. R., & Sulzer-Azaroff, B. *Personalization through peers as proctors: An evaluation of PSI for a large introductory educational psychology course at the University of Massachusetts.* Paper presented at the meeting of the American Psychological Association, New Orleans, August 1974.

Johnson, K. R., & Sulzer-Azaroff, B. The effects of different proctoring systems on student examination performance and preference. In J. M. Johnston (Ed.), *Research and technology in college and university teaching.* Gainesville: University of Florida, Psychology Department, 1975.

Johnston, J. M., & O'Neill, G. W. The analysis of performance criteria defining course grades as a determinant of college student academic performance. *Journal of Applied Behavior Analysis,* 1973, *6,* 261–268.

Keller, F. S. A personal course in psychology. In R. Ulrich, T. Stachnik, & J. Mabry (Eds.), *Control of human behavior.* Glenville, Illinois: Scott, Foresman, 1966.

Keller, F. S. "Good-bye teacher . . . " *Journal of Applied Behavior Analysis,* 1968, *1,* 78–89.

Keller, F. S. New reinforcement contingencies in the classroom. In J. G. Sherman (Ed.), *Personalized system of instruction: 41 germinal papers.* Menlo Park, California: W. A. Benjamin, 1974.

Kulick, J. A. PSI: A formative evaluation. In B. A. Green (Ed.), *Personalized instruction in higher education: Proceedings of the Second National Conference.* Washington, D.C.: Center for Personalized Instruction, Georgetown University, 1976.

Lloyd, K. E. *Behavior analysis and technology in higher education.* Unpublished, Drake University, 1975.

Lloyd, K. E., & Knutzen, J. J. A self-paced programmed undergraduate course in experimental analysis of behavior. *Journal of Applied Behavior Analysis,* 1969, *2,* 125–133.

Lloyd, K. E., Garlington, W. K., Lowry, D., Burgess, H., Euler, H. A., & Knowlton, W. R. A note of some reinforcing properties of university lectures. *Journal of Applied Behavior Analysis,* 1972, *5,* 151–156.

Maas, J. B., & Kleiber, D. A. *Directory of teaching innovations in psychology.* Washington, D.C.: American Psychological Association, 1975.

Mager, R. F. *Preparing instructional objectives.* Palo Alto, California: Fearon, 1962.

Malott, R. W., & Svinicki, J. G. Contingency management in an introductory course for one thousand students. *Psychological Record,* 1969, *19,* 545–556.

McMichael, J. S., & Corey, J. R. Contingency management in an introductory psychology course produces better learning. *Journal of Applied Behavior Analysis,* 1969, *2,* 79–83.

Mawhinney, V. T., Bostow, D. E., Laws, D. R., Blumenfeld, G. J., & Hopkins, B. L. A comparison of students studying behavior produced in daily, weekly, and three-week testing schedules. *Journal of Applied Behavior Analysis,* 1971, *4,* 257–264.

Miles, D. T., Kibler, R. J., & Pettigrew, L. E. The effects of study questions on college students' test performance. *Psychology in the Schools,* 1967, *32,* 25–26.

Miller, L. K. The effects of a behaviorally engineered textbook and two traditionally designed textbooks on concept formation in university students. In J. M. Johnston (Ed.), *Research and technology in college and university teaching.* Gainesville: University of Florida, Psychology Department, 1975.

Miller, L. K., Weaver, F. H., & Semb, G. A procedure for maintaining student progress in a personalized university course. *Journal of Applied Behavior Analysis,* 1974, *7,* 87–91.

Miller, L. K., & Weaver, F. H. The use of "concept programming" to teach behavioral concepts to university students. In J. M. Johnston (Ed.), *Behavior research and technology in higher education.* Springfield, Illinois: Charles C Thomas, 1975.

Mills, H. *Commanding communication—individualized instruction in sentence writing (Teacher's manual).* Carmichael, California: Quest, 1972.

Nelson, T. F., & Bennett, M. L. Unit size and progress rates in self-paced instruction. *Journal of College Science Teaching,* 1973, *3*(2), 130–133.

O'Neill, G. W., Johnston, J. M., Walters, W. M., & Rasheed, J. A. The effects of quantity of assigned material on college student academic performances and study behavior. In J. M. Johnston (Ed.), *Behavior research and technology in higher education.* Springfield, Illinois: Charles C Thomas, 1975.

Peters, R. DeV. Pre-quiz monitoring of study materials improve performance in two PSI courses. In J. M. Johnston (Ed.), *Research and technology in college and university teaching.* Gainesville: University of Florida, Psychology Department, 1975.

Philippas, M. A., & Sommerfeldt, R. W. Keller vs. lecture method in general physics instruction. *American Journal of Physics,* 1972, *40,* 1300–1306.

Protopapas, P. A report on the use of the Keller plan in a general biology course at Lowell State College. In J. G. Sherman (Ed.), *Personalized system of instruction: 41 germinal papers.* Menlo Park, California: W. A. Benjamin, 1974.

PSI Newsletter. Washington, D.C.: Georgetown University, Center for Personalized Instruction, 1971–1976.

Robin, A. L., & Graham, M. Q. Academic responses and attitudes engendered by teacher pacing versus student pacing in a personalized instruction course. In R. Ruskin & S. Bono (Eds.), *Personalized instruction in higher education: Proceedings of the First*

National Conference. Washington, D.C.: Center for Personalized Instruction, Georgetown University, 1974.

Ruskin, R. S. *The personalized system of instruction: An educational alternative.* ERIC/ Higher Education, Research Report No. 5, Washington, D.C., 1974.

Sanchez-Sosa, J. J., Semb, G., & Spencer, R. E. *Using study guides to promote generalization performance in university instruction.* Paper presented at American Psychological Association, Chicago, September 1975.

Semb, G. The effects of mastery criteria and assignment length on college student test performance. *Journal of Applied Behavior Analysis,* 1974, *7,* 61–70.

Semb, G. An analysis of the effects of hour exams and student-answered study questions on test performance. In J. M. Johnston (Ed.), *Behavior research and technology in higher education.* Springfield, Illinois: Charles C Thomas, 1975.

Semb, G. Building an empirical base for instruction. *Journal of Personalized Instruction,* 1976, *1,* 17–27.

Semb, G., Conyers, D., Spencer, R., & Sanchez-Sosa, J. J. An experimental comparison of four pacing contingencies. In J. M. Johnston (Ed.), *Behavior research and technology in higher education.* Springfield, Illinois: Charles C Thomas, 1975.

Semb, G., Hopkins, B. L., & Hursh, D. E. The effects of study questions and grades on student performance in a college course. *Journal of Applied Behavior Analysis,* 1973, *6,* 631–642.

Semb, G., & Spencer, R. E. Beyond the level of recall: An analysis of complex educational tasks in college and university instruction. In L. E. Fraley & E. A. Vargas (Eds.), *Behavior research and technology in higher education.* Gainesville: University of Florida, Psychology Department, 1976.

Semb, G., Spencer, R. E., & Phillips, T. W. The use of review units in a personalized university course. In B. A. Green (Ed.), *Personalized instruction in higher education: Proceedings of the Second National Conference.* Washington, D.C.: Center for Personalized Instruction, Georgetown University, 1976.

Sheldon, J., Sherman, J. A., Wolf, M. M., Minkin, B. L., & Minkin, N. "Hello, teacher . . . . " or optional lectures, discussions with instructors, and assigned proctors: Their effect on students' ratings of a PSI course and performance on generalization tests. In J. M. Johnston (Ed.), *Research and technology in college and university instruction.* Gainesville: University of Florida, Psychology Department, 1975.

Sheppard, W. C., & MacDermot, H. G. Design and evaluation of a programmed course in introductory psychology. *Journal of Applied Behavior Analysis,* 1970, *3,* 5–11.

Sherman, J. G. Application of reinforcement principles to a college course. In J. G. Sherman (Ed.), *Personalized system of instruction: 41 germinal papers.* Menlo Park, California: W. A. Benjamin, 1974. (a)

Sherman, J. G. PSI: An historical perspective. In J. G. Sherman (Ed.), *Personalized system of instruction: 41 germinal papers.* Menlo Park, California: W. A. Benjamin, 1974. (b)

Skinner, B. F. The science of learning and the art of teaching. *Harvard Educational Review,* 1954, *24,* 86–97.

Spencer, R. E., & Semb, G. *Using study questions to replace unit quizzes in university instruction.* Paper presented at American Psychological Association, Chicago, September 1975.

Sutterer, J. R., & Holloway, R. E. An analysis of student behavior with and without limiting contingencies. In J. M. Johnston (Ed.), *Behavior research and technology in higher education.* Springfield, Illinois: Charles C Thomas, 1975.

Taylor, B. M. Integration in the classroom. *California Journal of Secondary Education,* April, 1935, 283–286.

Washburne, C. W., & Marland, S. P. *Winnetka: The history and significance of an educational experiment.* Englewood Cliffs, New Jersey: Prentice-Hall, 1963.

Wei-Ming Leo, M. Chemistry teaching by the Keller plan. *Journal of Chemical Education, 50,* 1.

Whitehurst, G. J. Academic responses and attitudes engendered by a programmed course in child development. *Journal of Applied Behavior Analysis,* 1972, *5,* 283–291.

Whitehurst, C., & Whitehurst, G. J. Forced excellence versus "free choice" of grades in undergraduate instruction. In J. M. Johnston (Ed.), *Behavior research and technology in higher education.* Springfield, Illinois: Charles C Thomas, 1975.

Williams, R. L., & Lawrence, J. The effects of frequency of quizzing in a lecture course. In J. M. Johnston (Ed.), *Research and technology in college and university teaching.* Gainesville: University of Florida, Psychology Department, 1975.

12

Process Approaches to the Teaching of Educational Psychology

HENRY P. COLE and LOUISE S. MUSSER

University of Kentucky

In the past decade much has been accomplished in the area of process approaches to instruction, especially at the elementary and secondary school levels. Process education theories and definitions have influenced the design and sampling of objectives, course content, curriculum materials, and instructional methods in many major projects. But the theory of process education need not be limited to elementary and secondary schools; it is sufficiently broad to apply to instruction at any level. It is the purpose of this chapter to examine approaches to the teaching of college and university introductory level educational psychology courses from the perspective of process education theory and to describe the characteristics of ideal process approaches to teaching educational psychology.

PROCESS EDUCATION DEFINED

Process education is concerned first and foremost with fostering highly generalizable skills or strategies that allow the learner to cope effectively with a constantly changing world. Teaching particular facts, concepts, and relationships (discipline content) is secondary to teaching basic skills or strategies that can be used to solve a wide variety of problems. High order problem-solving skills of this nature cannot be learned without specific facts, concepts, relationships, and experiences that serve as the vehicle by which a wide array of process skills are learned. The generalizable skills, not the content of instruction, are the goals in process approaches. Students must acquire specific content, but only because it provides both the informational basis and the means for acquiring and applying the skills to be learned. This definition is consistent with earlier definitions which have been set forth and used in the design of instruction (Borton, 1970; Cole, 1972; Gagné, 1965, pp. 1–8; Schroder, Karlins, & Phares, 1973; Parker & Rubin, 1966; Rubin, 1969; Seferian & Cole, 1970).

Perhaps an example will help illustrate the differences between traditional and process approaches to education. In a traditional social studies curriculum, the objectives are to learn certain rules, data, and relationships. Under such an approach, great care is usually taken in selecting the specific content to be learned. Students are expected to learn about the resources, raw materials, and industrial and agricultural products of various states and regions. Thus, knowing how much cheese is produced annually by Wisconsin, how many lakes Maine has, the number of automobiles produced by Detroit, and many other facts and relationships become educational goals in themselves. Often the entire curriculum becomes a collection of "got to knows." Instructors present these facts and students store them up for tests or papers. Important goals of process education, such as the skilled use of reference materials to locate information, the construction of reasonable inferences from available data, and the clear and concise organization and communication of information, are only secondary objectives under such traditional approaches to instruction.

In a process approach to the teaching of social studies, the primary objectives are these broad skills themselves. Students are expected to learn how to find specific information when it is needed, how to use it, and for what purposes. It matters little if children acquire these skills through the study of Wisconsin or Kentucky, cheese or tobacco, or any other set of suitable data and relationships that provides a problem for analysis. In process education the teaching of social studies becomes more like the teaching of reading: Students learn basic skills useful in virtually any context. Reading teachers care much less about particular content and information than about basic literacy: the comprehension, interpretation, extrapolation, and generalization of ideas. Process education specifies similar goals for any course, be it social studies or educational psychology.

Educational psychology courses tend to be much like traditional social studies courses. Most are organized with the mastery of specific facts, concepts, and relationships as their primary goals. It is hoped that this knowledge will somehow produce competent teachers. Seldom do such courses use specific course content to develop highly general skills, probably because it is easier to identify specific content that students are to learn in a given course, but quite difficult to decide which skills are the most useful to the student's effective functioning as a future teacher.

Justifications for Process Approaches

The justification for process education is the same at any level of instruction. The specific content of any field is so massive and growing so fast it is possible for a given student to learn only a tiny fraction of what is collectively known. The only feasible approach to the problem is to assist the student to learn some of the more central, influential, and useful information in a field and to attempt to teach those skills which will enable him to apply, adapt, and continually expand that limited knowledge. In addition, although the substantive knowledge in any area can always be "looked up," as Gagné (1965, 1970) has pointed out on numerous occasions, process strategies or skills can be acquired only as the individual abstracts them from a wide variety of problem-solving situations (Cole, 1972, p. 32). The processes of reading, relating well to other persons, or effectively communicating information, ideas, and feelings cannot be looked up in the way that most questions that appear on typical educational psychology examinations can. A practicing teacher cannot look up how to manage the classroom social environment, resolve a conflict among students, or make a choice among curriculum materials for a child who has difficulty reading. Process skills are attitudes and cognitive capabilities that are generally applicable to a wide variety of problems. Because of the conditions required for their learning, and because of their universal applicability, process skills are the appropriate goals for any instruction.

Specific facts, information, and relationships also tend to be forgotten rapidly (Gage & Berliner, 1975, p. 143), whereas process skills, once learned, tend to be retained lifelong and to improve with experience. Furthermore, once skills or strategies are abstracted from specific data and learned, they can be used to direct the search for additional data, as well as to organize and interpret that new data (Bruner, 1964, 1973).

The specific facts and concepts that often are the main content of academic courses tend to be discipline bound, useful only within certain narrow contexts or situations. However, real-life problems frequently demand interdisciplinary approaches. The problems faced in teaching are no exception. Process skills are interdisciplinary; the pursuit of knowledge and problem solving in any given discipline has much in common with that pursuit in other disciplines (Roberts, 1966; Tanner, 1966). Process skills cut across the artificial boundaries between fields and disciplines and encourage adaptive and informed problem solving in various situations, including the cognitive, interpersonal, personal, social, political, and emotional.

Process skills are themselves the basis for all learning. The assimilatory and accommodative behavior which we usually call learning, the basis for comprehension of all facts and relationships, and the continuing adaptive behavior of any individual, all rest upon basic process skills. The acquisition of a wide array of these skills results in a healthy, competent, and effective person who has a "will to learn" (Bruner, 1968), a desire to "make meaning" (Postman & Wiengartner, 1969), and a compelling desire to grow in wisdom, competence, and compassion (Maslow, 1962; White, 1959).

Process and Nonprocess Approaches

Educational psychology, as the course is usually taught at an introductory level, primarily serves an audience of persons who intend to become or who already are teachers (Cohen, 1973). It also serves other persons within the helping professions such as counseling, social work, or educational administration. There are a number of different approaches to the teaching of educational psychology courses to these groups. Which of these can be considered to be process approaches within the theoretical framework of process education?

Traditional Approaches

Perhaps the most common approach to the teaching of educational psychology is the use of a textbook as the means to define the goals, content, and sequence of learning activities for a course. Students are required to read given units or chapters of textual material. They attend classroom lectures and discussions on the content of these materials, and are then tested on their knowledge of it. Learning the material is generally construed to mean being able to recognize, recall, state, and apply in some situations (usually multiple choice tests) the major information, concepts, and principles presented in the text and lectures. The focus is usually on theories and methods of educational and psychological research and inquiry. Individual students' needs and interests and their limitations in translating the complex and abstract course content into informed and competent teaching performance are ignored (Feldhusen, 1970, p. 7).

Of course, it can be argued that any concept or principle that is learned and later applied to some problem or generalized to some new situation, has become, in fact, a process skill. The line between content and process is often blurred. However, there is great variation in the generalizability and utility of different types of information. Knowing how to implement various schedules of reinforcement in general and in a wide variety of applied situations, along with knowing their probable effects upon persistence of behavior is much more useful than knowing the details of three famous experiments which illustrate different reinforcement schedules. The former content becomes a process skill, but the latter does not unless specific provision is made to teach for this transfer.

It also occasionally has been suggested that traditional approaches, because they teach about psychological processes of development, motivation, perception, attention, learning, and memory, and because the students themselves are using these processes to learn course content, are process approaches. However, if both the goals and content of such traditionally organized educational psychology courses are examined, it becomes clear that they do not represent a process approach as defined by the theory of process education.

Whether a given approach is process oriented depends upon broad objectives that underlie the course and how and for what purpose specific content is sampled for study. In order to be considered a process approach, the broad objectives must be concerned with the development of student competence in highly general skills. These skills must be justified as a worthy goal of instruction by a logical rationale that relates their mastery to effective professional performance within given task areas or process skill domains. The specific course content should be selected from the infinite array of potential content so as to best serve the development of these skills. The content selected and studied for the purpose of skill development needs not be the same for every student within a given course and would usually be different from student to student.

Traditional educational psychology courses do indeed teach *about* important processes and skills. They also depend upon the students' previously learned attentional, learning, memory, perceptual, reading, and studying skills. The content that is the focus of instruction can indeed equip students with information and concepts which may or may not be applied later in solving some problem or directing some action. For example, a teacher often needs to use appropriate theories of needs, motivation, and learning along with instructional design principles to select suitable materials and methods for a student who is displaying certain behavior patterns. However, unless the course specifically includes objectives that posit these and related process skill goals, and unless instruction is deliberately designed to provide practice in this skillful application of theory, the student cannot be expected to automatically generalize the information and theories learned nor to apply them to problems encountered in teaching. Learning in one area will not ensure learning in another area because both the conditions for learning and the final performances required are different for the two (Gagné, 1970; Gagné & Briggs, 1974, pp. 23–33). Empirical studies have confirmed that measured cognitive and attitudinal changes that result from study of information, theories, and principles in college courses are not accompanied by changes in the functional behavior of the teacher in actual teaching. Aspy (1972) found little correlation between teachers' factual knowledge of learning theory and their behavior in the classroom. The translation of course content, theory, and principles to skillful teaching behavior requires deliberate instruction of students in experiential settings (Schmuck, 1970, pp. 707–735).

PSI and Related Approaches

Much of the innovation in the teaching of educational psychology in recent years has been concerned with the application of techniques of individualization of instruction, including programmed learning, criterion-referenced testing, and mastery learning. Among the more widely implemented of these approaches are the many variations of the Keller system or the personalized system of instruction (PSI) (Keller, 1968; Keller & Sherman, 1974; Nelson & Scott, 1972; Stice, 1975). The application of these techniques has done much to improve the quality and efficiency of instruction. Generally, these approaches do organize instruction more skillfully and deliberately than more traditional programs. However, in most cases, the overall goals and intent have not changed greatly from those of the more traditional approaches. The primary concern usually is still the students' mastery of certain information, concepts, and relationships without much specific attention to the explicit teaching of process skills. This set of techniques and methods which originated in the 1930s and 1950s (Keller, 1975; *PSI Newsletter,* 1975) has recently been widely implemented to achieve the traditional set of goals with greater success and certainty. Sometimes PSI and related approaches to instruction have been referred to as "process" programs because greater care is taken to plan, manage, and evaluate the learning behavior of students. In this sense the term "process" refers to the systematic management of instruction toward maximizing student learning. While this is a noble tactic that ought to be widely encouraged, it is not a process education approach to instruction within the usual definition of the theory. The criteria for determining whether PSI or similar approaches to instruction can be legitimately considered process approaches are the same as those described for conventional programs. Judging from their published descriptions, most courses which have adopted PSI or related instructional management strategies have retained a content rather than a process skills orientation (Menges, 1972; Nelson & Scott, 1972; Terrill, Berger, & Mulgrave, 1973).

Self-Directed Learning Approaches

Individually guided education (IGE), sometimes also referred to as individually guided learning (IGL), is an instructional system first introduced by the Wisconsin Research and Development Center for Cognitive Learning for use in public school instruction (Klausmeier, Morrow, & Walter, 1968; Klausmeier & Ripple, 1971, pp. 228–237). IGE approaches formulate an individual set of instructional objectives for each student. Within each student's program of objectives, appropriate topics, materials, and learning activities are selected to achieve the particular outcomes stated for each child. There are planned variations in what each student learns, how he goes about learning it, and the rate at which he progresses. The IGE approach is different in two important ways from the more common individually prescribed instruction (IPI) and programmed instruction. Generally, IPI approaches have individualized primarily the rate of instruction (Bolvin, Lindvall, & Scanlon, 1967; Lindvall & Cox, 1970). As is usual in PSI approaches, each student studies the same content in the same order or sequence as all the other students. There is little or no variation in objectives, course content, and sequence from one student to another.

IGE approaches to the teaching of educational psychology were implemented at Cornell University by Richard Ripple and his students (Ripple, 1971).[1] Different objectives were specified for different students resulting in individually planned courses of study with differences in what students learned, how they learned, and the time required to complete their objectives. Subsequently, Treffinger and Davis (1971, 1972) refined and formalized the IGE approach for teaching educational psychology courses. One important change introduced to IGE strategy by Treffinger and Davis was teaching the learner to identify, define, and operationally state his own learning objectives. Given this initial task, the resources of the course materials and instructor are then organized by the student with assistance from the instructor toward achieving the self-specified learning outcomes. These outcomes are products or performances that can be and are evaluated by both the student and the instructor. This approach has come to be known as Learner Controlled Instruction (LCI) (Treffinger & Johnsen, 1973).

LCI approaches, as they have been described and implemented, are indeed process oriented. The acquisition of content, though not overlooked, is not the primary concern. Content is sampled from among the wide array available because of its utility in helping students achieve self-selected and personally relevant goals. The chief process goals for LCI approaches appear to be the skills of: (*a*) identifying, clarifying, and stating in an achievable form various personal goals related to concerns in the domain of teaching and learning, (*b*) identifying, selecting, and using appropriate resources and knowledge in achieving those goals, and (*c*) determining how successfully those goals have been achieved by evaluating the performance or products that result from the effort. These are highly generalizable skills. They should be of great value to teachers who will face numerous problems in their future professional activity. These real-life problems also usually require self-identification and formulation, the gathering and selection of resources appropriate to their solution, and shared judgment of effectiveness of action taken toward their resolution. These strategies or skills, unlike the particular content of a given textbook chapter which may or may not

---

[1] Personal observation of the Cornell courses by Professor Cole and personal communication from Professor Ripple.

be studied by a particular student, cannot be looked up later if not learned initially.

Group Process and Human Relations Skills Approaches

Teacher training courses concerned with developing human relations, communication, value clarification, group decision making, and problem-solving skills have been developed and widely implemented in the past decade (Chesler & Fox, 1966; Eberlein, 1972; Fox, Luszki, & Schmuck, 1966; Gazda, 1971; Guggenheim, 1968; Menlo, 1971; Miles, 1965; Raths, Harmin, & Simon, 1966; Schmuck, Chesler, & Lippitt, 1966; Schmuck, 1970; Simon, Howe, & Kirschenbaum, 1972). Many of these programs and methods can indeed be considered as process approaches, not simply because they deal with group processes and human relations skills but because they do set forth some broad process skill categories as the primary goals of instruction. Frequently these programs have been prepared especially for counselors, teachers, or administrators to teach them to facilitate the development of human potential and effectively and humanely manage student social behavior within schools and classrooms. A number of programs have combined humanistic and behavioristic theories and development into training activities deliberately designed to teach important process skills such as recognizing, resolving, and dealing with conflict, or building and maintaining interpersonal regard with peers and students (Carkhuff, 1969, 1971a, 1972, 1973; Sydnor, Akridge, & Parkhill, 1972).

Generally, these process oriented training programs have not been introductory courses in educational psychology. Rather, they have typically been short-term, experiential workshops primarily concerned with developing techniques and methodology by which more skillful human relations may be practiced in the classroom or elsewhere. Frequently, these types of courses have been offered outside the usual academic structure of college or university teacher training programs as weekend workshops, in-service training for practicing teachers, or ancillary activities to regular courses. When such programs have been offered for regular course credit they have usually been considered as mental hygiene, human relations, or counseling courses and not as educational psychology courses. Concern with specific techniques and skills has displaced broad conceptual and theoretical principles usually regarded as the core content of educational psychology.

As with PSI approaches, group process and human relations programs have contributed a great deal to the preparation of teachers in important skills. However, many of the principles and concepts of educational psychology, which are the logical basis for skillful interpretation and understanding of human motives and behavior, recognition and accommodation of individual differences, design and management of instruction, and assessment of performance and learning, are not the goals in human relations and group process approaches and are therefore ignored. Yet, it is precisely the interpretative and applicative use of these basic theories and concepts, as well as the use of human relations skills, that is the logical purpose of educational psychology courses for teachers (Neisser, 1975; Samuels, 1975). Klausmeier (1970) identified the substantive content areas of educational psychology as human learning, human development, individual differences, instructional programming, and interactions among students, teachers, and others. Because of their more narrow objectives, the majority of group process and human relations process approaches have appropriately been restricted to the promotion of those skills that have their logical and theoretical roots in only the last substantive area.

Ideal Process Approaches to Teaching Educational Psychology

Having discussed some of the more common approaches to the teaching of educational psychology and their compatibility with the theory of process education, some characteristics displayed by ideal programs or courses of study will now be considered. The characteristics examined will include the various levels and functions of course objectives, the relation of the broad process skill areas or domains to disciplines and fields other than educational psychology, the specification of a core content of theory and technique, and the use of the broad process skill domain objectives and core content to make functional decisions about course management and operation.

Levels and Functions of Objectives

The proper design of any course or curriculum and the execution of instruction require moving through a descending set of abstractions from statements of generic skill domains, which describe highly generalizable performance capabilities, through intermediate statements of competencies or skills sampled from within the larger domain, down to specific behaviorally stated outcomes that are to occur under certain specified conditions and in certain contexts (Krathwohl, 1965, p. 85). All of these various levels of objectives are needed to guide the planning and progress of instruction. The higher order and more generic objectives provide the guidelines for sampling the particular array of intermediate objectives and the highly specific behavioral objectives from among the infinite possibilities. These higher order objectives provide the means for making decisions about which particular topics, instructional materials, and methods comprise a sample of activities likely to result in the attainment of the process goals. It is this variety in types and functions of objectives discussed by Burns (1972),

Eisner (1969), Glaser (1973, pp. 557–566), Klausmeier and Ripple (1971, pp. 117–127), Tyler (1964), and others that is the basis for any process approach to instruction.

Within the specific structure of a course these principles translate into the following guidelines. The course should have stated objectives consisting of the several types and levels described by Krathwohl (1965) and Klausmeier and Ripple (1971). First, there should be broadly stated process skill outcomes that are designed to convey to students, instructors, and the public the general performance capabilities to be achieved by the course or program of study. There should be relatively few of these objectives. Their purpose is primarily to inform, influence, and direct the behavior and choices of teachers and students into appropriate areas of activity, study, and application of theory and technique. The second or intermediate level of objectives should be much greater in number and specificity. These objectives should define areas of competence as clusters or domains of process skills that are quite performance-specific but situation-generalizable. The third and final level of objectives should be large in number, quite highly performance- and situation-specific, and different for different students. These specific behavioral or performance objectives should be selected as a sample of a finite number of possible objectives within a universe of acts or performances which might reasonably be inferred to foster the intermediate and broad skill objectives (Cole, 1973). Perhaps an example will illustrate how these levels of objectives operate to plan and define instruction.

Suppose a teacher education course has as one of its broad process-skill domain objectives, "the development of the person's capacity to exhibit interpersonal regard and empathy for his peers, superiors, and subordinates in task oriented (work) social settings." An intermediate objective might be "the person shows respect for other people's rights, property, feelings, and ideas, especially his students'." Another intermediate objective might be, "the person can adopt and play the role of a peer, superior, or subordinate and describe and enact the feelings, mannerisms, and actions normal to that role in a variety of given situations involving conflict and cooperation."

There are many other intermediate objectives that could be stated. Let us, however, continue with the one that concerns showing respect for others. The course designer must ask himself what are some ways in which people show respect for others. He can identify and watch persons who exhibit the skill, think reflectively, and gather information from many sources toward beginning to list a number of specific activities which indicate respect for others. Some of the activities the person might list could be sharing, listening, helping, waiting for and being patient with others, caring for property of others, complimenting others, being tactful, asking others for their opinions or advice, and so on. He can, armed with his list, begin to conceptualize, identify, and select a multiple but finite set of activities, topics, situations, and materials for instruction that allow the person to engage in these specific performances (skills within a larger skill domain). Thus, he or she may generate an entire series of activities within a given unit or lesson that illustrate and provide opportunity for practicing the broad and intermediate skills which are the major goals of instruction. He can also stage later lessons for the further practice and generalization of the skill in new and more complex contexts.

Suppose "sharing" is one activity which the course designer feels is particularly important to developing the intermediate goal of "respect for others." He may then generate a whole list of sharing activities. First, the designer may ask what things should or do people share with one another when they respect each other, especially as teachers and students?" He or she might list ideas, friends, feelings, responsibility, decisions, experiences, fears, material objects, and tools, such as crayons, scissors, money, wheelbarrows, ladders, teaching techniques, and concepts. The course designer might then decide to construct n number of lessons around the topic (or skill) of sharing. He could choose those activities involving sharing that are most related to developing interpersonal regard in teaching. The activities should be interesting to students and encourage their enthusiastic participation. Within the context of a particular course and unit or lesson, the course designer might want to arrange for students to examine the advantages and disadvantages of sharing and engage in and experience actual sharing in multiple ways. Specific activities might be concerned with sharing ideas, observations, and inferences about one's students with them and other teachers. Activities related to sharing feelings, friendship, ideas, information, influence, responsibility, worries, and concerns, and classroom—corporate—community resources and services might be appropriate areas of practice and inquiry for preservice teachers. Different students would engage in different learning activities by virtue of their special needs and interests, but all would work toward developing the same basic process skills. Given the broad process skills, which are the main objectives of instruction, the course designer can select particular learning activities or materials appropriate for different groups of students and different courses.

Behavioral Objectives within Process Goals

Recent emphasis upon behavioral objectives, while useful in clearly identifying specific performance outcomes to be learned, has also been damaging in some respects. There is currently a tendency in many competency approaches to the training of teachers and other professionals to prepare huge lists of highly specific objectives that students are to master. Such an approach is unachievable in the final analysis since there is an infinity of precisely stated behavioral objectives for any content, discipline, or skill area. Logically and practically, however, courses and programs are designed to teach only a few generalizable classes of skills. If the curriculum designer ignores these important broad skill outcomes and fails to use them logically to organize instruction, if he writes only large sets of very precise behavioral objectives, then the course that has been designed and the instruction that is offered may become a collection of unrelated and poorly articulated specifics. The students he teaches end up being victimized by his own instructional technology of behavioral objectives in the absence of broad process goals.

Interdisciplinary Nature of Process Skills

The basic process skill outcomes that ought to serve as the broad goals of any educational psychology course are not unique to any one field or discipline. Table 12.1 lists and presents a brief rationale for seven highly generalizable and somewhat related process skill domains that have been logically generated as the broad goals of an educational psychology course (Cole, 1973, 1974). These skills are not completely independent; they represent what McClelland (1973, pp. 9–11) calls "clusters of life outcomes." In McClelland's words, they are operant thought or skill patterns with maximum generalizability to various action outcomes important to teachers and other helping professionals (1973, p. 12). These process skill domains have also been determined empirically to underlie effective professional performance in a wide range of fields in the helping professions, as judged by a sample of 250 professionals. Professionals making the judgment included persons in teaching, counseling, school psychology, social work, physical therapy, community health, nutrition, dentistry, and consumer advocacy (Cole & Lacefield, 1975).

There are other process skill domains that could serve as basic educational outcomes for persons in the helping professions (Bowles, 1973; Carkhuff, 1971b; Cooper, Jones, & Weber, 1973; Henderson & Lanier, 1973; Wynn, 1974). Some of the process skills that have been suggested for teachers and counselors, such as verbal communication skills (Flanders, 1973) and instructional design skills (Popham, 1974, 1975), are narrower and more focused than those listed in Table 12.1. Yet, these skills are indeed process skills defining effective areas or domains of performance that apply across disciplines and fields. There are also many other ways to label, cluster, and describe the process skills listed in Table 12.1. However, it is apparent that skills of this type are appropriate broad educational goals, not only for educational psychology courses, but for any course within a teacher training program as well as courses within many other programs in the helping professions outside of teaching. It is also apparent that, by themselves, these process goals do not comprise a set of workable guidelines for the design and management of any course. Broad goals of this type ought to be used to direct the making of informed choices by students and instructors in sampling and assembling a particular finite and carefully specified set of learning activities, topics, and materials which are likely to lay the conceptual, affective, and experiential basis required for strengthening performance in each broad skill domain. The particular content and activities of instruction would be expected to vary across disciplines such as educational psychology, sociology, and philosophy. Yet, the general process skill goals remain as a worthy general framework to guide instruction in each discipline area.

Given such a broad set of process skill goals, IGE and LCI approaches make a great deal of sense, since each broad skill category defines a performance-specific but situation-generalizable skill. Virtually any particular activity or situation that provides practice for the use of that performance can be judged as appropriate. Ensuring that each skill domain is practiced in diverse contexts and situations is likely to result in learning the skill as a generalizable schema or strategy. This is the theory that underlies the teaching and learning of such high order skills (Bruner, 1968, 1973; Gagné, 1970; Gagné & Briggs, 1974; Piaget, 1973).

Nature and Role of Core Content

Given the overall process skill domains as educational goals, is there any body of content that should serve as a common core across introductory educational psychology courses for teachers? Although the process skill domains listed in Table 12.1 apply to fields such as physical therapy and dentistry, no one would argue that there is not in addition a large and acceptable body of specific knowledge content and technical skill that is basic to competent performance in these fields. This basic knowledge and technical skill is taught through a combination of many didactic and practicum courses in the allied health fields. Students study and learn the basic nomenclature, structure, concepts, and theories of bacteriology, chemistry, anatomy, and physics, not as ends in themselves but *because* some of this knowledge content is a useful framework for describing, observing, thinking about, interpreting, and explaining the situations encountered in practice. The wide range of organized knowledge in disciplines basic to informed practice enables the practitioner of physical therapy or dentistry to be more than simply an automaton who performs some standard techniques on patients. Proper conceptual and theoretical training provides the practitioner with wisdom.

In teaching, there are also many problems that can be solved more adequately if the teacher has an appropriate base of theoretical and technical knowledge. Just as a framework of broad process skill goals is needed to direct the planning and management of instruction, another framework consisting of the most useful knowledge and theory basic to informed teaching is also needed. Some knowledge and theory in educational psychology provide a useful conceptual basis for recognizing, defining, and solving certain problems.

Despite past difficulties in specifying a common basic content for introduc-

TABLE 12.1

Process Skill Domains as General Goals for the Helping Professions

Name	Description	Rationale
1. Achieving, exhibiting, and maintaining competence in the academic content of one's discipline or profession.	Being expert in the organized knowledge and practice of one's field or discipline.	Essential to the self-esteem of the individual, his ability to serve well and inspire others, and the esteem which his clients, and colleagues may exhibit toward him.
2. Cogent and accurate verbal communications (semantics).	Being able to recognize and construct precise and unambiguous statements which accurately describe some action, event, idea, or situation (operational definitions and communications).	Essential to efficient, clear communication with others as well as to logical, consistent, and organized thinking and reflection by self.
3. Making observations, constructing inferences, and distinguishing between the two.	Describing objectively. Forming reasonable hypotheses about what course of action to take (decision making). *Not* confusing inference with observations (hypotheses with facts).	Essential to fair, rational, and impartial thought and evaluation. Needed to avoid stereotypic, judgmental thinking which can impose self-fulfilling prophecy situations on others and self.

		Essential to *not* becoming a "true believer" who dogmatically fixates upon and applies one set of constructs to all situations, becoming blind to many other interpretations with equal or greater potential as explanatory constructs.
4. Using multiple theoretical–conceptual frameworks to observe, infer, and explain behavior, events, and situations.	Being able to explain a given situation, event, or instance in multiple ways with different accepted theories with differing assumptions, biases, and implications.	
5. Showing and maintaining respect and regard toward others, especially one's clients, or students.	Being able to exhibit nurturance and esteem toward others, to recognize their competence and worth to whatever degree these qualities are present.	Essential to establishing a supportive environment where the helpee can profit from the nurturance and direction of the helper and will be likely to implement the action prescribed by the helper.
6. Value clarification	Recognizing, questioning, and clarifying one's own beliefs, values, and preferences toward judging their effects on habits, perceptions, biases, actions, and interactions with others. Being able to express what one values and to judge which theories, techniques, or methods agree or conflict with those values. Comprehending and respecting habits and values different from one's own.	Essential to consistent, wise, compassionate, and mature behavior in areas of personal integrity, ethics, and morals in professional practice.
7. General fluence and flexibility of thought, perception, and response.	Being able to break set in one's ideas, observations, feelings, actions, and responses. Being able to see things from multiple perspectives, to respond to given situations in multiple and diverse ways.	Essential to adaptive behavior and problem solving in true problem situations, be they rational, emotional, social, personal, or corporate, because this basic divergent thinking capability results in multiple potential solutions to any given problem.

tory educational psychology courses (Grinder, 1970; Yee, 1970), a strong case can be made that the substantive content of the field of educational psychology as it pertains to teaching and learning includes the areas listed in Table 12.2. Support for these core content areas is evident in the thoughtful reflections of many active educational psychologists who have long been engaged in teacher education as well as theory development and research (Gagné, 1971; Glaser, 1973; Glock & Wilkins, 1971; Klausmeier, 1970; Neisser, 1975; Wynn, 1974). Another source is the perceptions of preservice teachers concerning an "ideal" educational psychology course (Feldhusen, 1970). Still another source is the perceptions of experienced teachers who have some practical idea of what theory and concepts they need to know more about in order to carry out their instructional duties more adequately (AESP, 1975, p. 11; Frey & Ellis, 1966).

TABLE 12.2

Appropriate Core Content Areas for Introductory Educational Psychology Courses

---

Basic Theory

Theories of learning as they explain:
  Varieties and conditions of learning
  Transfer of learning
  Cumulative learning

Theories of development as they explain:
  Cognitive and intellectual development
  Personality development and adjustment, social, emotional, moral, character and motive
    systems development
  Environmental influences upon development

Theories of motivation as they explain:
  Relationships among the constructs of learning, performance, and motives
  Influence of motives on learning, performance, and personality
  Environmental influences on motives and motive systems

Basic Technique

Recognizing and dealing with individual differences:
  Theories of individual differences
  Implications of individual differences for growth, learning, and instruction

Designing and managing instruction and learning:
  Formulating various types of objectives with specific functions
  Selecting and designing topics, materials, and activities appropriate to objectives
  Psychological basis for various modes and methods of instruction

Assessing student learning, performance, and abilities and the effectiveness of instruction:
  Basic assumptions and techniques of measurement
  Standardized measures of student interests, need and abilities; their uses and abuses
  Classroom measures and means for assessing student learning and performance
  Judging the effectiveness of instruction

From these and other efforts it is possible to specify a few core areas as reasonable, appropriate, and fairly well accepted content for introductory educational psychology courses. Six such core content areas are summarized in Table 12.2. They reflect the major content areas usually identified as basic to understanding the teaching-learning activity.

The *purpose* of teaching this core content is to better prepare teachers to both understand their own behavior and to interpret and explain the behavior, events, and situations they will encounter in teaching. Psychology and educational psychology contribute to the practice of teaching mainly through explaining behavior, not predicting and controlling it (Neisser, 1975). The content that is most useful are those concepts, theories, and principles that have the greatest utility as explanatory constructs. Instruction ought to be designed to provide for practice in the interpretive and applicative use of these core knowledge constructs in ways similar to those described by Cole and Musser, 1973; Cole, 1974; Cole, 1975; Glock and Wilkins, 1971; Neisser, 1975; Treffinger and Davis, 1971; Treffinger and Johnsen, 1973, among others. It is very useful for teachers to understand widely applicable concepts, such as the Maslow's needs hierarchy and Murray's needs list, so they can use these constructs to recognize, explain, and deal with observed differences in individual student behavior patterns. It is much less useful for teachers to learn and remember the details and results of a particular psychological study which shows the experimental effects of three manipulated model characteristics on aggression in children of ages 5 to 7 in a controlled environment. The latter information may be useful and even necessary in making some point in the course of instruction. However, the former is a much broader generalization that has direct utility in many situations while the latter is very limited indeed in its generalizability. The former, once learned, will probably be remembered and used for a long time, particularly if specific provision is made for transfer of the construct. The latter will almost certainly be forgotten. Tyler showed this empirically with similar concepts many years ago (Gage & Berliner, 1975, p. 143).

Process Objectives and Course Management

Many professors would agree that the process outcomes listed in Table 12.1 are worthy goals and that they attempt to achieve them. However, lip service to process goals does little to help ensure they are modeled for students by the instructors themselves and encouraged as a main objective for student learning through providing the conditions for their appropriate practice.

If taken seriously, broad process objectives similar to those listed in Table 12.1 provide guidelines for the course management system that is implemented. Thus, the overall classroom climate is directly influenced. For example, if the process objective of enhancing the skill of interpersonal regard is taken seriously, the common adversary relationship between instructor and students would be viewed as a means—ends conflict. Yet, this adversary relationship is clearly evident in reports of and recommendations for teaching, such as McKeachie's (1969) *Teaching Tips.* Serious pursuit of this process skill outcome dictates that the classroom climate and management of instruction be based upon principles of mutual respect and trust among instructors and students. Furthermore, instructors could be expected to make more use of referent and expert power to influence student behavior and less use of coercive and legitimate power. The classroom climate and management system most appropriate to fostering this particular process skill of interpersonal regard is the "need for achievement" climate described by Alschuler (Alschuler, 1968, pp. 313, 325—327; Gage & Berliner, 1975, pp. 312—313). This approach is characterized by a set of rules designed to elicit high performance from students who are free to set their own individual goals within the broad structure and to act with initiative, responsibility, and self-direction to achieve these goals. Instructors relate warmly to students, but within the context of achieving the course goals, not simply to meet affiliation needs. Rewards are emphasized over punishments but are contingent upon good performance. Conflicts between students and the instructor are ignored unless they interfere with achieving particular important course goals. This ideal arrangement and the climate it fosters sounds much like the LCI approach described earlier. This pattern is not common in most traditional approaches to instruction that generally may be more appropriately categorized as exhibiting the characteristics of Alschuler's "need for power" climate. Here emphasis is upon many rules and regulations, the achievement of the same specific objectives by everyone in the same sequence and manner, little student initiative in choice of learning, equal use of rewards and punishment, and student compliance to the authority of the system, which is impersonal and treats everyone exactly alike. Interestingly, many human relations and group process approaches to teaching, as they are reported, appear to fall into Alschuler's third climate category, "need for affiliation," which is mostly concerned with affiliation needs and mutual respect, but little concerned with structure, content, skilled performance, and achievement.

Another example of how broad process goals can influence the operation of a course can be seen in the objective in Table 12.1 concerned with the use of multiple conceptual and theoretical frameworks to explain and interpret observed behavior and events. If this process goal were taken seriously, no introductory course or textbook would seek to present only one theoretical position at the expense of others. Yet, such highly biased introductory textbooks and courses are common, and sometimes their goals seem to be to indoctrinate students with certain theories and conceptualizations rather than to present a more widely based set of multiple constructs and theories with greater collective explanatory utility across the range of situations encountered in teaching. This does not preclude an intensive study of a single theory, provided other theories are not ignored.

Similarly, the process category concerned with recognizing and constructing cogent and accurate verbal statements and descriptions, if taken seriously, would dictate that both students and instructors should use precisely stated objectives or operational statements in the specification of particular learning tasks to be undertaken among the general content and process skills framework for the course. These operational statements could be much like those currently used in LCI and PSI approaches in their statements of learning objectives and contracts.

The skill domain concerned with general fluency and flexibility of thought, perception, and response requires that instruction should be arranged to encourage both students and instructors to solve individual problems in multiple ways and to explain individual situations from many conceptual perspectives. This would be true in instructional tasks, lecture material, test items, and real-life or simulated teaching situations. In carrying out such activity the value clarification skill domain would dictate that students examine alternate conceptualizations, interpretations, and solutions to problem situations, freely choose what they will believe or elect to do on an informed basis, and publicly affirm and defend their choice among their peers. In examining, choosing, planning, and explaining a course of action or decision in an instructional or teaching related situation, both the student and instructor would also be expected to make appropriate observations, to construct good and reasonable inferences, and to clearly distinguish between the two, recognizing that inferences are always tentative and open to reformulation with additional data.

If the process goals in Table 12.1 or other similar process goals were used to guide the design and management of instruction in educational psychology courses, performances similar to these would not only be deliberately planned, but would also be evaluated and viewed as evidence of learning rather than accepting the usual acquisition of knowledge of facts and information as sufficient evidence for transfer of training to teaching related tasks. Evaluation of student performance should be deliberately designed to measure student competence in the process skill domains that are the basic purpose of instruction. The general procedures for translating such constructs into valid measuring instruments are well known (Fiske, 1971, Chap. 6). The need to evaluate process skill outcomes by assessment procedures designed to measure extent and generalizability of process skills is strongly supported by McClelland (1973) and demonstrated in his own work.

Courses that claim to be process oriented but ignore the conditions that process skill categories place on instructional management and operation are, in fact, in opposition to stated process goals. In these cases, inappropriate means may negate important process skill outcomes.

SUMMARY

The objective of process education is to teach highly generalizable skills or strategies that enable the learner to solve a wide variety of problems and to cope effectively with a changing world. In order to be considered a process approach a course in educational psychology must have broad objectives concerned with the development of the students' competency in these or some other broadly adaptive and highly generalizable skills. Thus, traditional approaches to teaching educational psychology and some of the more innovative techniques of individualization of instruction, such as programmed learning, criterion-referenced testing, and mastery learning, are not process approaches. Group process and human relations approaches to teaching educational psychology are process approaches, but they are limited in scope in that many of the theories and concepts necessary for skillful interpretation and understanding of human behavior are not included. Learner Controlled Instruction (LCI) programs do meet the criteria for process approaches, but they should also define a core of basic content expertise to be mastered as well as the process skills which serve as the main objectives.

An ideal process approach to teaching educational psychology would require that the course have broadly stated process skill outcomes, intermediate level objectives that are performance-specific but situation-generalizable, and a third level of objectives that are performance- and situation-specific and different for different students. The broadly stated basic process skill outcomes which are selected should be appropriate not only for educational psychology but also for teacher training programs and for the helping professions in general. To better prepare teachers to understand their own behavior and to interpret and explain the behavior, events, and situations they will encounter in teaching, a body of content should serve as a common core for introductory educational psychology courses for teachers. To avoid means–ends conflicts, the broad process objectives presented in this paper or similar paradigms should also provide guidelines for the course management system which is implemented. The functional behavior of the instructor and the operation of the course should all be directly influenced by the overall process goals.

REFERENCES

Alschuler, A. S. How to increase motivation through climate and structure. Cambridge, Massachusetts: Achievement Motivation Development Project, Graduate School of Education, Harvard University, 1968, Working paper No. 8.

Appalachian Education Satellite Project (AESP). Proposal for the Appalachian Teacher

Corps Project. Submitted to Teacher Corps, U. S. Office of Education, DHEW, by the University of Kentucky, January, 1975.

Aspy, D. N. An investigation into the relationship between teachers' factual knowledge of learning theory and their classroom performance. *Journal of Teacher Education* 1972, *23*(1), 21–24.

Bolvin, J. O., Lindvall, C. M., & Scanlon R. G. *Individually prescribed instruction.* A manual for the IPI Institute. Pittsburgh, Pennsylvania: Learning Research and Development Center, University of Pittsburgh, 1967.

Borton, T. *Reach, touch and teach.* New York: McGraw Hill, 1970.

Bowles, F. D. Decision making in instruction. *Journal of Teacher Education,* 1973, *24*(1), 38–40.

Bruner, J. S. On going beyond the information given. In R. J. C. Harper, C. C. Anderson, C. M. Christensen, & S. M. Hunka (Eds.), *The cognitive processes: Readings.* Englewood Cliffs, New Jersey: Prentice-Hall, 1964.

Bruner, J. S. *Toward a theory of instruction.* New York: W. W. Norton, 1968.

Bruner, J. S. *Beyond the information given: Studies in the psychology of knowing.* New York: Norton, 1973.

Burns, R. W. The central notion: Explicit objectives. In W. R. Houston & R. B. Howsam (Eds.), *Competency-based teacher education, progress, problems, and prospects.* Chicago: Science Research Associates, 1972.

Carkhuff, R. R. *Helping and human relations: A primer for lay and professional helpers* (Vols. I and II). Chicago: Holt, 1969.

Carkhuff, R. R. Helping and human relations: A brief guide to lay helpers. *Journal of Research and Development in Education,* 1971, *4*(2), 17–27. (a)

Carkhuff, R. R. Training as a necessary precondition for education. *Journal of Research and Development in Education,* 1971, *4*(2), 3–16. (b)

Carkhuff, R. R. *The art of helping: A guide for developing helping skills for parents, teachers, and counselors.* Box 222, Amherst, Massachusetts: Human Resource Development Press, 1972.

Carkhuff, R. R. *The art of problem solving: A guide for developing problem solving skills for parents, teachers, counselors, and administrators:* Box 222, Amherst, Massachusetts: Human Resource Development Press, 1973.

Chesler, M., & Fox, R. *Role playing methods in the classroom* Chicago: Science Research Associates, 1966.

Cohen, S. J. Educational psychology: Practice what we teach. *Educational Psychologist,* 1973, *10*(2), 80–86.

Cole, H. P. *Process education.* Englewood Cliffs, New Jersey: Educational Technology, 1972.

Cole, H. P. *Approaches to the logical validation of career development curricula paradigms.* Carbondale, Illinois: Career Development for Children Project, Southern Illinois University, 1973.

Cole, H. P. *Teaching as communication.* Unpublished paper (mimeo). University of Kentucky, Lexington, Kentucky, 1973.

Cole, H. P. Theories of educational innovation applied to teacher education programs. In R. J. Seibel (Ed.), *Trends in teacher education.* Bloomington, Indiana: Indiana University Press, 1974.

Cole, H. P. Evaluative indices for curriculum materials and educational programs. *Teacher Education Forum,* 1975, *9*(3), 1–64. (Whole issue.)

Cole, H. P., & Lacefield, W. E. *Skill domains for the helping professions: A conceptual and empirical inquiry.* Preliminary report of a study funded by a grant from Educational Testing Service and the Carnegie Foundation as part of the Cooperative Assessment of Experiential Learning Project. University of Kentucky, Lexington, Kentucky, July, 1975.

Cole, H. P., & Musser, L. *Field activities selected by preservice teachers in traditional and experiential programs.* Paper presented at the meeting of the American Educational Research Association, New Orleans, 1973.

Cooper, J. M., Jones, H. L., & Weber, W. A. Specifying teacher competencies. *Journal of Teacher Education,* 1973, *24*(1), 17–23.

Eberlein, L. A process approach to teaching teachers. *Improving College and University Teaching,* 1972, *20*(2), 154–157.

Eisner, E. W. Instructional and expressive educational objectives: Their formulation and use in curriculum. In R. E. Stake (Ed.), *Instructional Objectives.* AERA Monograph Series on Curriculum Evaluation (Vol. 3). Chicago: Rand McNally, 1969.

Feldhusen, J. F. Student views of the ideal educational psychology course. *Educational Psychologist,* 1970, *8*(1), 7–9.

Fiske, D. W. *Measuring the concepts of personality.* Chicago: Aldine, 1971.

Flanders, N. A. Basic teaching skills derived from a model of speaking and listening. *Journal of Teacher Education,* 1973, *24*(1), 24–37.

Frey, S., & Ellis, J. Educational psychology and teaching: Opinions of experienced teachers. *Teachers College Journal,* 1966, *38*(3), 88–91.

Fox, R., Luszki, M. B., & Schmuck, R. *Diagnosing classroom learning environments.* Chicago: Science Research Associates, 1966.

Gage, N. L., & Berliner, D. C. *Educational psychology.* Chicago: Rand McNally 1975.

Gagné, R. M. Psychological issues in *Science: A process approach.* In *Psychological bases of Science: A process approach.* Washington, D. C.: American Association for the Advancement of Science, 1965.

Gagné, R. M. *The conditions of learning.* New York: Holt, 1970.

Gagné, R. M. Contributions of psychology to educational research. *Educational Psychologist,* 1971, *8*(2), 30–31.

Gagné, R. M., & Briggs, L. J. *Principles of instructional design.* New York: Holt, 1974.

Gazda, G. M. Systematic human relations training in teacher preparation and inservice education. *Journal of Research and Development in Education,* 1971, *4*(2), 47–51.

Glaser, R. Educational psychology and education. *American Psychologist,* 1973, *28*(7), 557–566.

Glock, M. D., & Wilkins, W. E. A course in educational psychology for prospective teachers. *Educational Psychologist,* 1971, *8*(3), 46–47.

Grinder, R. E. The crisis of content in educational psychology courses. *Educational Psychologist,* 1970, *8*(1), 4.

Guggenheim, F. An integrative approach to the teaching of educational psychology to teachers. *Peabody Journal of Education,* 1968, *46*(1), 34–38.

Henderson, J. E., & Lanier, P. E. What teachers need to know and teach (for survival on the planet). *Journal of Teacher Education,* 1973, *24*(1), 4–16.

Keller, F. S. "Good-bye, teacher. . . ." *Journal of Applied Behavioral Analysis,* 1968, *1*(1), 79–89.

Keller, F. S. Letter to the editor. *PSI Newsletter,* 1975, *3*(3), 6.

Keller, F. S., & Sherman, J. G. *The Keller plan handbook: Essays on a personalized system of instruction.* Menlo Park, California: W. A. Benjamin, 1974.

Klausmeier, H. J. The education in educational psychology. *Educational Psychologist* 1970, *8*(1), 1–3.

Klausmeier, H. J., Morrow, R., & Walter, J. E. *Individually guided education in the multiunit elementary school: Guidelines for implementation.* Madison, Wisconsin: Wisconsin Research and Development Center for Cognitive Learning, 1968.

Klausmeier, H. J., & Ripple, R. E. *Learning and human abilities.* New York: Harper & Row 1971.

Krathwohl, D. R. Stating objectives appropriately for program, for curriculum and for instructional materials development. *Journal of Teacher Education,* 1965, *16*(1), 83–92.

Lindvall, C. M., & Cox, R. C. *Evaluation as a tool in curriculum development: The IPI evaluation program.* AERA Monograph Series on Curriculum Evaluation (Vol. 5). Chicago: Rand McNally, 1970. Whole issue.

Maslow, A. H. *Toward a psychology of being.* Princeton, New Jersey: Van Nostrand, 1962.

McClelland, D. C. Testing for competence rather than for intelligence. *American Psychologist,* 1973, *28*(1), 1–14.

McKeachie, W. J. *Teaching tips: A guidebook for the beginning college teacher.* Lexington, Massachusetts: D. C. Heath, 1969.

Menges, R. J. Freedom to learn: Self-directed study in a required course. *Journal of Teacher Education,* 1972, *23*(1), 32–39.

Menlo, A. Enhancing perceptions of self and others through classroom learning experiences. *Educational Psychologist,* 1971, *8*(2), 31–34.

Miles, M. B. Changes during and following laboratory training: A clinical experimental study. *Journal of Applied Behavioral Science,* 1965, *1*(3), 215–242.

Neisser, U. Self-knowledge and psychological knowledge: Teaching psychology from the cognitive point of view. *Educational Psychologist,* 1975, *11*(3), 158–170.

Nelson, T. F., & Scott, D. W. Personalized instruction in educational psychology. *The Michigan Academician,* 1972, *4*(3), 293–302.

Parker, J. C., & Rubin, L. J. *Process as content: Curriculum design and the application of knowledge.* Chicago: Rand McNally, 1966.

Piaget, J. *To understand is to invent.* New York: Viking Press, 1973.

Popham, W. J. Minimal competencies for objectives-oriented teacher education programs. *Journal of Teacher Education,* 1974, *25*(1), 68–73.

Popham, W. J. Applications of teaching performance tests in preservice and inservice teacher education. *Journal of Teacher Education,* 1975, *26*(3), 244–248.

Postman, N., & Weingartner, C. *Teaching as a subversive activity.* New York: Delacorte Press, 1969.

PSI Newsletter. Editor's note, 1975, *3*(3), 6.

Raths, L. E., Harmin, M., & Simon, S. B. *Values and teaching.* Columbus, Ohio: Charles E. Merrill, 1966.

Ripple, R. E. The teaching of educational psychology: Freedom to choose. *The Journal of Teacher Education,* 1971, *22*(4), 395–399.

Roberts, J. Curriculum development and experimentation. *Review of Educational Research,* 1966, *36*(3), 353–361.

Rubin, L. J. (Ed.), *Life skills in school and society.* Yearbook 1969. Washington, D. C.: Association for Supervision and Curriculum Development, 1969.

Samuels, S. J. The enemy within: Threats to educational psychology from within and outside the field. *Ideas and Views, New Directions in Educational Psychology.* Newsletter of AERA's Special Interest Group, Summer, 1975, 3–4.

Schmuck, R. A. Helping teachers improve classroom group process. In M. W. Miles & W. W. Charters (Eds.), *Learning in social settings.* Boston: Allyn and Bacon, 1970.

Schmuck, R. A., Chesler, M., & Lippitt, R. *Problem solving to improve classroom learning.* Chicago: Science Research Associates, 1966.

Schroder, H. M., Karlins, M., & Phares, J. O. *Education for freedom.* New York: Wiley, 1973.

Seferian, A., & Cole, H. P. *Encounters in thinking: A compendium of curricula for process education.* Buffalo, New York: Creative Education Foundation, Occasional paper No. 6, 1970.

Simon, S. B., Howe, L. W., & Kirschenbanm, H. *Values clarification: A handbook of practical strategies for teacher and students.* New York: Hart, 1972.

Stice, J. E. Progress report on the PSI project at the University of Texas at Austin. *PSI Newsletter,* 1975, *3*(3), 4–5.

Sydnor, G. L., Akridge, R. L., & Parkhill, N. L. *Human relations training: A programmed manual.* Minden, Louisiana: Human Resources Development Institutes, 1972.

Tanner, D. Curriculum theory: Knowledge and content. *Review of Educational Research,* 1966, *36*(3), 362–372.

Terrill, A. F., Berger, V., & Mulgrave N. W. The application of a modified mastery approach to the teaching of graduate educational psychology. *Psychology in the Schools,* 1973, *10*(2), 253–258.

Treffinger, D. J., & Davis, J. K. *Educational psychology: A self directed course of study.* Minneapolis: Burgess, 1971.

Treffinger, D. J., & Davis, J. K. Instructional innovation in educational psychology: The search for "relevance." *Educational Psychologist,* 1972, *9*(2), 21, 27–28.

Treffinger, D. J., & Johnsen, E. P. On self-directed learning: When you say Hello, do they write it in their notebooks? *Liberal Education,* 1973, *59*(4), 471–479.

Tyler, R. W. Some persistent questions on the defining of objectives. In C. M. Lindvall (Ed.), *Defining educational objectives.* Pittsburgh: University of Pittsburgh Press, 1964.

White, R. W. Motivation reconsidered: The concept of competence. *Psychological Review,* 1959, *66,* 297–333.

Wynn, C. Teacher competencies for cultural diversity. In W. A. Hunter (Ed.), *Multicultural education through competency-based teacher education.* Washington, D. C.: American Association of Colleges for Teacher Education, 1974.

Yee, A. H. Educational psychology as seen through its textbooks. *Educational Psychologist,* 1970, *8*(1), 4–6.

13

Teaching for Personal Growth and Awareness

DOUGLAS J. STANWYCK

Georgia State University

Give me a fish, and I eat for a day;
Teach me to fish, and I eat for a lifetime
—Ancient proverb

Can a course in educational psychology be taught in such a way that its students gain not only a mass of information, but grow personally in the process? In the first section of this chapter, some evidence is reviewed to support the idea that such a marriage of content and process is desirable for preservice teachers. A few general guidelines are then proposed to assist the instructor with selection and evaluation of course strategies designed to contribute to the personal growth of students. Several strategies used by the author are described briefly in the third section; finally, the fourth section sets forth some enabling conditions and touches briefly on a few common problems that may arise as a function of the approach offered here for your consideration. The constraint of space prevents this chapter from being comprehensive or exhaustive; it presumes to be neither. It is offered, rather, in the hope that it will stimulate the kind of instructional thinking, planning, and execution that will bear fruit in the lives of educational psychology students—and, eventually, in the lives of their students as well.

WHY CONSIDER "PERSONAL GROWTH AND AWARENESS"?

An instructor of educational psychology must make many difficult decisions about course content and structure, including, for example, decisions about which of the many legitimate topics and subtopics should be "covered" in the course; how thoroughly each topic should be dealt with; how many and what kind of tests or other evaluation procedures should be used. The suggestion that those who struggle heroically with such problems ought additionally to consider "teaching for personal growth and awareness" is apt to be met with more resistance than eagerness. Some may assert that they are already too busy dealing with the more important cognitive objectives of the course; others may refer more tellingly to the general lack of clear empirical evidence that affective characteristics of teachers are related to student achievement. The requirements of fully convincing research—clear operational definitions, rigorous methodology, well-validated instrumentation, and so on—have so far proven difficult, if not impossible, to satisfy in approaching questions about the relationship of teacher effectiveness and teacher affective characteristics.

The same situation is true, of course, with respect to questions about the relationship of teacher effectiveness and, say, teacher exposure to an educational psychology course, or to teacher education in general (see e.g., Gage, 1972). However, in light of the growing body of evidence that is available, it is reasonable to conclude that teacher attitudes and values must be considered to be important influences on what happens in classrooms.

Schmuck and Schmuck (1974), for example, have approached the analysis of classroom dynamics with a "social systems" perspective, looking not only at teacher behaviors with individual students, but also attending to the complex interactions and interpersonal systems existing within the learning group. On the basis of their studies of teachers, students, and schools, they assert that "teachers whose classrooms have favorable climates . . . differ cognitively, attitudinally, and behaviorally from teachers with less favorable climates [p. 110]." More specifically, Schmuck and Schmuck report that teachers who establish favorable climates

> tend to see many more of the complexities of the interpersonal world and to understand how they might affect student behavior and academic learning For another, [they] tend to adopt a democratic and equalitarian relationship with their students. They ask for suggestions, listen carefully to ideas, and react generally with respect and evidence of caring [They] talk often with a wide variety of students, encourage students to talk and to influence one another, use a great deal of praise and are honest about their personal values and preferences . . . . In contrast teachers of classes with less favorable social climates typically talk with only a few students (implying favoritism), rebuke students publicly, and are not as generous with their praise [p. 110].

The Florida Studies of the Helping Professions

What is it that distinguishes "good" teachers from "bad" ones, effective teachers from ineffective ones? The *Florida Studies in the Helping Professions* (Combs, Soper, Gooding, Benton, Dickman, & Usher, 1969) explored the question of effectiveness in several helping professions, including teaching. Their findings led to the conclusion that while subject-matter knowledge and method-ological expertise are *necessary* for effective teaching, differences in these areas were not *sufficient* to account for differences between effective and ineffective teachers. Differences in effectiveness were reported to be most clearly explicable in terms of attitudinal and perceptual variables—"belief systems." "What we *believe* to be important *inevitably determines* the methods we use in dealing with other people [Combs, Avila, & Purkey, 1971, p. 8; italics added]."

There are several categories of important beliefs that are influential in interpersonal relationships: belief about one's subject; beliefs about others; beliefs about onself (i.e., one's self-concept); beliefs about the purposes of helping; and beliefs about approaches to one's particular task. With respect to beliefs about others, according to the *Florida Studies,* effective teachers believe that, in general, people have the ability to deal with and to solve their own problems; that people are basically friendly and well-intentioned; that people have personal dignity and integrity that requires that they be valued and treated with respect; that people are inherently creative and internally motivated; and that people are potentially sources of satisfaction rather than of frustration for the teacher.

The *self*-beliefs of an effective teacher include the belief that he or she is related to others, rather than separate and alienated from them; that he or she is essentially adequate and competent to deal with his or her own problems; that he or she is personally responsible and trustworthy; that he or she is likeable, attractive to others as a person, and accepted rather than rejected by them; that as a person he or she possesses inherent worth, dignity and integrity and therefore that he or she is important and should be treated with respect by others.

It seems fairly obvious that a personal philosophy that includes the beliefs listed here will inevitably have important consequences for a person's view of the purposes of his or her own behavior, which will in turn lead to differences in actual behavior relative to the behavior of those who do not hold such beliefs In their summary of findings of the *Florida Studies,* Combs *et al.* (1971) report differences between effective and ineffective helpers in terms of their percep-tions of the *purposes* of the helper role and in terms of observed *approaches* to their professional behavior. While their report uses the word "helper," since several professions were studied, the following summary descriptions were found to hold true for effective teachers:

Freeing–controlling. Helpers perceive their purpose as one of freeing rather than controlling people—that is to say, the helper sees the purpose of the helping task as one of assisting, releasing, and facilitating rather than as a matter of controlling, manipulating, coercing, blocking, or inhibiting behavior.

Larger issues—smaller ones. Helpers tend to more concerned with larger than with smaller issues. They tend to view events in a broad rather than a narrow perspective. They are concerned with the larger connotations of events and with more extensive implications rather than with the immediate and specific. They are not exclusively concerned with details, but can perceive beyond the immediate to the future.

Self-revealing–self-concealing. Helpers are more likely to be self-revealing than self-concealing. They are willing to disclose the self. They can trust their feelings and shortcomings as important and significant rather than hide or cover them up. They seem to be willing to be themselves.

Involved–alienated. Helpers tend to be personally involved with rather than alienated from the people they work with. The helper sees his appropriate role as one of commitment to the helping process and willingness to enter into interaction as opposed to being aloof or remote from interaction.

Process-oriented–goal-oriented. Helpers are concerned with furthering processes rather than achieving goals. They seem to see their appropriate role as one of encouraging and facilitating the process of search and discovery as opposed to promoting or working toward a personal goal or preconceived solution.

People–things. The basic approach of the helper is directed more toward people than things—that is to say, his [or her] orientation is human rather than with objects, events, rules, regulations, and the like.

Perceptual–objective. Effective practitioners are more likely to approach their clients subjectively or phenomenologically. They are more concerned with the perceptual experience of their subjects than with the objective facts [pp. 15–16].

Examination of these descriptions of effective teachers reveals that none of them is methodologically specific—they refer to the dynamics of teacher–student interaction rather than to curricular strategy. This is not to say that such strategies are unimportant; only that they are not enough. Good, Biddle, and Brophy (1975) summarize their extensive review of research on teaching behavior with the succinct statement: "Simply put, the call is for teacher behavior that says *I see you and you're okay* . . . [p. 206]."

Developmental Concerns of Teachers

Another group of studies relevant to the issues of personal growth and awareness of teachers was carried out by the late Frances F. Fuller and her associates in the Research and Development Center for Teacher Education, at the University of Texas (Austin). These studies centered around the investigation and analysis of the issues of most concern to preservice and inservice teachers. The group of concerns found to be dominant for the preservice teachers—those students who enroll in teacher education courses—have been called *survival* concerns, and include concerns about personal and professional adequacy and survival as a teacher, and about being liked and approved by supervisors by pupils. They are concerned about the adequacy of skills and knowledge they may, in fact, already possess, but that have not yet been tested on the "front lines" of the classroom.

It has not been long for most prospective teachers since they themselves were students in schools like the ones they are now preparing themselves to staff. In their visits to schools (generally infrequent, except for those enrolled in "field-based" programs such as are offered at the University of Houston and the University of Maryland Baltimore County) it is easy for them to align themselves emotionally *with* pupils and *against* teachers; they have not yet carried the responsibility of the classroom teachers they observe. Later—during student teaching, and at the beginning of professional employment—the dominant concerns of these students shift to worries about classroom control, content mastery, and the evaluations of their supervisors. While these concerns may be viewed as situational in nature, it is this writer's experience, based on conversations with many young teachers, that concerns about survival as a teacher are deeply involved with concerns about adequacy as a person.

When these early concerns have begun to be dealt with in a way that reduces their overwhelming dominance, additional concerns emerge: concerns about the *teaching situation* include growing awareness of the need for methodological and subject-matter competence—methods, materials, and facts. The last group of concerns to emerge—but only when some resolution of prior concerns has been achieved—is the group of *pupil* concerns: concerns about dealing with the social and emotional needs of pupils, about individualization of curriculum materials, and about personalization of the instructional process. Preservice teachers, as well as inservice teachers, express such concerns about pupils, but "flooded by feelings of inadequacy, by situational demands and conflicts, they may have to lay aside these concerns until they have learned to cope with more urgent tasks, such as being heard above the din [Fuller & Bown, 1975, p. 39]."

If the prospective teacher is to be equipped to do more than merely survive in the teaching profession, to become personally and professionally competent and effective and adequate to the complex and often conflicting demands of being a "good" teacher, then his or her self-awareness and personal growth needs must be more adequately provided for by programs of teacher education. As Fuller and Bown assert, "increasing the teacher's awareness (not merely exposing her to information) is an important role for teacher education. Such awareness, both affective and cognitive, is a worthy behavioral objective [1975, p. 44]."

Beginning with Educational Psychology

For several years it has been the author's practice to meet students at the first session of every course with the statement: "The way to become an effective *teacher* is to become an effective *person*!" This statement is a personal conviction, based on experience in the processes of helping with teachers and counselors and fortified by the writings of Carl Rogers (see, e.g., Rogers, 1966, 1967), among others. The evidence in support of such assertions is increasing and should no longer be ignored or given lip service by those whose business it is to prepare persons to be effective teachers.

Educational psychology courses provide the ideal context in which the implementation of processes that provide for some of the personal growth and awareness needs of prospective teachers can be begun. Some educational psychology courses are little more than collections of disconnected pieces of other courses—child development, learning theory, instructional methodology, etc. Such courses are often "taken" reluctantly by students because of program or certification requirements. The "pieces," however, may be connected by introducing a concern for the *person* of the prospective teacher without becoming (as many seem to fear) less academically or professionally legitimate. In fact, when instructors of educational psychology courses become more concerned with the needs of their learners, the courses may become not only more popular, but more professionally relevant as well.

THINKING ABOUT TEACHING FOR PERSONAL GROWTH AND AWARENESS

Furth and Wachs (1975), in illustrating Piaget's concept of equilibration, use the example of a plant. If you want a plant to grow, you place it in nutritious soil, water and spray it at appropriate intervals, and expose it to reasonable amounts of sunlight. And that is about all you can do (although some insist that plants will grow better if you talk to them and play the right kind of music for them). If you pull on the leaves or stem in order to "make it grow faster," the leaves are likely to fall off and the plant will die. Obviously, people are not plants; yet in considering personal growth, the analogy is useful. A teacher cannot "make" a student learn or grow; he can only create conditions under which learning and growth are most likely to occur, or under which certain behaviors are likely to increase in frequency. The task of teaching would doubtless be far easier than it is if this were not the case—if the teacher could make a few adjustments in the child, turn some valves and push some buttons and make learning and growth happen. The children who seem to be most frustrating for teachers to deal with are those who, actively or passively, refuse to cooperate with the teacher's goals. When a child says, "You can't make me do it," as Dreikurs, Grunwald, and Pepper (1971) have pointed out, he is correct: He or she cannot be "made" to do it.

College students have professional goals that public school students often do not, so that they usually do cooperate with the teacher's goals, even if reluctantly and sometimes resentfully. Ultimately, however, the situation is the same: They cannot be "made" to do anything. Attempting to force personal growth precludes, or at least severely inhibits, the very growth that is seen as desirable. Instructors can at best create the conditions in which growth is likely to occur, and they can do this by establishing a positive climate between teacher and students, and then by offering students the opportunity and the invitation to make meaningful decisions.

The Teacher as Decision Maker

A useful way to view the teacher's role is as that of a *decision maker*. Two decades ago Stephens (1956) acknowledged the constant need for teachers to make decisions when he proposed that the teacher attempt to combine a *theorist* role with a *practitioner* role. The teacher as theorist develops hypotheses, assesses conditions and relevant factors, and tests and retests the hypothesis. Once a decision is made, however, the teacher as practitioner surrenders tentativeness and carries out the decision with confidence. Stephens suggested that it is most appropriate for the teacher as theorist to suspend his or her feelings, wishes, and personal goals in favor of scientific and objective contemplation of the facts of the situation.

The view proposed here, however, is that the teacher's feelings, wishes, and goals are themselves important facts which are integral to every decision he or she makes, and that any decision is likely to be appropriate to the degree that it takes into account *all* relevant factors. The teacher makes decisions continually, in the midst of complex pressures and realities—community, parents, administration, curricula, students, and self. Out of this perspective, Seaberg (1974) has proposed a fourfold model of the teacher's role: the teacher is Relator (facilitating growth through interpersonal relationships); Mediator (structuring learning experiences by bringing together students and curricula); Diagnostician (analyzing the students' needs, potentials, and impediments); and Choreographer (creating an esthetically pleasing environment which integrates all roles). Seaberg argues, as we do, that the teacher is a professional decision maker functioning in a complex social system. It follows that the teacher's effectiveness is a direct result of his or her competence to make the most appropriate decisions possible, in all roles, in light of the immediate and remote needs and goals, resources, and constraints of the situation. A useful way, then, to look at the meaning of "personal growth" in the context of "teacher as decision maker" is that *personal growth is the increase of a person's competence to make appropriate decisions in all aspects of experience.*

Offering Growth Choices

How can a prospective teacher be helped to become more competent in decision making and to increase the area of choice possibilities for which he or she undertakes to make responsible decisions? Maslow (1968) proposed that choices that are likely to lead to growth involve some degree of risk, and that choices which are made in order to avoid risk are unlikely to lead to growth. Choices involving risk are those in which outcomes are not totally predictable, and an important consequence of making risky choices is that they contribute to the accumulation of new information for the chooser, on the basis of which future choices may be made with more predictability, i.e., with greater probability of success. If a teacher continually makes "safety" choices, as opposed to the more risky "growth" choices, he or she may be numbered among the "others" referred to in the aphorism: "After 20 years, some teachers have 20 years' experience; others have 1 year's experience repeated 19 times!"

Persons are likely to make relatively fewer safety choices and more growth choices, when they become aware of the ways in which they rationalize their risk-avoidance behavior. Risks tend to be avoided in three ways: by a devaluation of potential gains (the sour grapes syndrome); by overestimation of the potential costs (developing unrealistically ominous expectations of choice consequences); and by the underestimation or denial of one's power to make any choice at all ("playing helpless"). The condition most likely to result in reduction of risk-avoidance behavior is the increase in awareness of reality; in other words, a more realistic evaluation of one's power to choose and of the potential consequences of a choice.

More realistic evaluation of potential gains is often brought about by the accumulation of more evidence, for example, hearing others say things like, "I did something like that and it worked for me." Reevaluation of potential costs, as well as of potential gains, may also result from more thorough analysis of the anticipated consequences of the choice. Tenured teachers, for example, have been heard to explain that they "can't" make a suggestion to their principal because they "might get fired." Analysis of such a rationale often leads to its abandonment in favor of other more realistic ones (e.g., "The principal might get angry"; or "He might not approve my request for something else").

The third rationale for avoiding risk in decision making—the underestimation or denial of one's power to choose—is often not an excuse, but a realistic and appropriate description of the student's circumstance in a college course. In many college courses, including courses in teacher education programs, students have little or no power to make choices about any part of the course—structure, process, content, or evaluation. College students frequently exhibit a great reluctance to make meaningful decisions about their own course participation.

Such reluctance is the inevitable result of their long experience of virtually total passivity and lack of influence in their own schooling—their teachers have made, and continue to make, all the important decisions. Ironically, at the end of the certification process, these students are deemed ready to teach on the basis of their having satisfied subject-matter and methodological course requirements, and are expected to make sound decisions about the schooling of others without their ever having had opportunity to make meaningful decisions about their own schooling! This is unfortunate and unnecessary, since competence in decision making can be strengthened through the utilization of opportunities to make meaningful decisions, and such opportunities can be provided in teacher-education courses, including Educational Psychology.

The Decision Making Process Matrix (Figure 13.1) represents a useful way for an instructor to consider how best to provide opportunities for student growth. The columns in the matrix represent major components of a decision and may be used for analyzing the decisions underlying course development. Selection of the contents of each component can be arrived at by a questioning process:

Goal: What do I want? What do I need? What is expected of me? Considering my overall goal structure, what is a realistic next objective?

Strategy: How can I best achieve the goal I have selected? What resources are available to me? What constraints?

Evaluation: How will I know when, and how well, I have achieved my goal? How well did the selected strategy work? What have I learned about myself? My world? What modifications might now be appropriate for my overall goal structure? What are the incidental outcomes of my behavior?

The rows of the matrix represent several possibilities for the division of responsibility between teacher and learner in terms of (*a*) the generation of alternatives in a given decision process; and (*b*) the selection of the alternative most likely to succeed. The responsibility for either may be taken totally by the teacher; partially by the learner under the direct guidance of the teacher; by the learner with the teacher as resource; or totally by the learner.

Much of the process of schooling, at all grades including graduate school, is at Level 0, wherein the learner's only decision is whether to comply and cooperate with the teacher's decisions about goals, strategies, and evaluation procedures. Level 4 may be seen as the level which is most desirable for the learner who is graduating from a teacher education program, for at this level the learner-now—teacher will have developed a substantial degree of expertise and competence in the decision making process, and will be in an ideal position to assist others in

DISTRIBUTION OF RESPONSIBILITY	DECISION COMPONENTS		
	Goal	Strategy	Evaluation
Level 4 Alternatives: S(T) Selection: S			
Level 3 Alternatives: T/S Selection: S(T)			
Level 2 Alternatives: T Selection: S(T)			
Level 1 Alternatives: T Selection: T/S			
Level 0 Alternatives: T Selection: T			

Figure 13.1. Decision Making process matrix. Alternatives are generated and final selection of an alternative is made for each Decision Component, by: teacher alone (T); student, under the direct guidance of the teacher (T/S); student, with teacher as available resource (S(T)): or by student alone (S). [From V. M. Howes, *Informal Teaching in the Open Classroom.* Copyright © 1974, Macmillan, New York. Reproduced by permission.]

the process of their growth (as well as to continue her own growth process). Growing means moving from Level 0 to Level 4, as the learner gradually accumulates experience in exercising his personal responsibility over his own behavioral choices, and in interpreting and dealing with their consequences.

The primary advantage to the teacher of operating at Level 0 would seem to be that, *if* the teacher selects the best goals and strategies for a well-motivated learner, the probability of the learner's failure is minimal. This advantage however, is purchased at great cost, namely, that the learner's dependence on the teacher is perpetuated and the learner's personal growth is inhibited; the situation further works against the learner when he is later held culpable for not having learned how to make appropriate behavioral choices. This became clear to the author one day in a class of teachers and administrators, as the conversation turned to the problems of a local "open-space" middle school to which a number of the class members were assigned. "This open-space business is a lot of nonsense," ran a typical comment. "Those kids just can't handle all that freedom. Nothing got done at all until I lowered the boom and laid down the law. We're getting something done now, but it's not being done the open-space way!" Further conversation revealed that the dominant mode of operation at the schools from which the "irresponsible" students had come was at Level 0, while the original structure and curricula of the middle school were at Levels 3 and 4.

When teachers and administrators do not attend to the process (or lack of it) by which students learn to make responsible decisions, it is natural for them to assume that when students consistently make inappropriate decisions something is wrong either with the "free" approaches or with the students (or parents!), and that teachers can do nothing about the situation except to return to Level 0 functioning. Similar bitterness has been experienced by many college and university instructors who "threw open" their course structure only to return to the old ways when students floundered. The point here is that personal growth is more likely to occur in small increments than in large ones. Expecting students to respond appropriately in situations requiring far more maturity than they have yet achieved leads, more often than not, to their confusion, anxiety, and failure.

The Role of Awareness

The role of awareness in the personal growth process may be summarized in a sentence: With each new unit of information about himself, a person is able to make more appropriate decisions. The probability that a decision outcome will be successful is enhanced when the person making the decision possesses maximum information about all relevant aspects of that decision—the more you know, the better decision you can make. Goal selection, for example, is not merely, "Is

X an appropriate goal?" It also includes the subjective question, "Is *X* an appropriate goal *for me at this time*?" Likewise, the strategy question is not simply: What is the best strategy for achieving *X*? A crucial additional question is: Is this a strategy *that I can use effectively,* given what I know about myself?

A teacher makes many decisions in the classroom and often experiences great frustration and confusion with the unsuccessful results of strategies (especially in the area of classroom management) that some respected book or professor or colleague has presented as "the way" to deal with the situation. Often, the reason for lack of success is not the fault of the particular strategy; rather, it is that the teacher has not adequately adapted the suggested strategy to his or her own personal "style" of functioning. There is probably no strategy that works exactly the same in all respects for any two people. It follows that in the selection and execution of any strategy, the strategist must consider the potential effect of his or her own values, attitudes, habits, and skills. In order to make good decisions, the teacher needs to be aware of himself or herself as well as of other components of the decision making situation.

An additional benefit of personal awareness is that it often leads almost "automatically" to changes in behavior. In conjunction with a project with which the author was affiliated, teachers were asked to make a list of their students, and then, for one complete day, simply to tally the number of times they provided individual students with positive feedback about student behavior; they were asked further to try not to change their normal patterns of behavior as they did so. At their next meeting, many of the teachers reported surprise at the results of the assignment. They were somewhat dismayed by the discovery that they had given positive feedback and reinforcement much more frequently to some students than to others. The "others," to whom little or no positive feedback had been given, turned out to be the students whom the teachers identified as presenting them with relatively more problems. After having discussed their reactions, the teachers were requested to repeat the assignment in a few weeks. Without either admonition or suggestion by the program leaders, the teachers' second tallies showed a more even distribution of positive feedback instances—and the teachers declared they had had fewer problems with their "problem students" than ever before. In this case, as is possible in many others, increased awareness of their own behavior enabled these teachers to make more appropriate decisions about that behavior. The program leaders did not even provide the information, but instead, simply invited the teachers to look at their behavior in a new way. Similarly, students in the educational psychology classroom may be invited to look at their behavior from a different perspective.

Some Guidelines

Instructors who wish to consider developing and using opportunities to contribute to the personal growth and awareness of their students need first to attend to their own growth and self-awareness, so that the messages transmitted by what they do are congruent with the messages conveyed by their verbal communications. It may be true, as some have said, that teachers are more likely to teach the way they were *taught* than the way they were *told* to teach. Many an educational psychology student has listened patiently to lectures about the disadvantages of the lecture method or obediently answered a test question about the advantages of pretesting without ever having been given a pretest. "You can't give what you haven't got," or teach what you haven't learned—students, like others, tend to rely more on what their instructors do, than on what they say, as the ultimate test of truth.

Because of the wide variety of approaches used by instructors of educational psychology, it is unlikely that a list of specific instructions for teaching for personal growth and awareness would be helpful. Some general guidelines, however, may be proposed.

1. Since different students are likely to be functioning at differing levels of awareness and growth, some degree of flexibility within course structures is appropriate so as to allow personalization of the course experience. This does *not* mean that everyone "does his own thing"; it *does* mean that basic course structures can be established (the fixed limits of the course), with substructures provided that allow for, or require, student decision (e.g., projects, assignments, test format and scheduling, etc.).

2. Decision opportunities offered to students need to be meaningful to them, rather than trivial. The question of when or whether to take a class break during a long class session may be referred to students in order to accommodate their comfort, but such a decision is not meaningful in terms of its growth-inviting potential.

3. Instructors should be willing to invite negotiation and to respond seriously to student requests for negotiation during the course itself. Once having agreed on a course of action, it is crucial to his or her credibility that the instructor not renege.

4. Activities should be provided regularly for students to relate course concepts to their own experience, and should be carefully scrutinized for personal growth and awareness potential. Carefully selected activities, assignments, projects, etc., in addition to their growth and awareness potential and motivational function, may also increase retention of course concepts.

5. The personal privacy and integrity of the student must be respected at all times. When a student feels embarrassed, or that his "personal space" has been invaded, growth possibilities are diminished severely, and awareness is likely to be rejected.

6. A growth-inviting climate is one in which teachers view students *positively* rather than *negatively,* and in which persons are dealt with in *freeing* rather than in *restricting* ways. In a negative and restricting climate, personal growth and

awareness will not occur, either for students or for instructor. It is the positive attitude of the instructor toward his or her students which forms the basis for the interpersonal climate in which growth is possible.

TEACHING FOR PERSONAL GROWTH AND AWARENESS: "HERE'S WHAT I DO!"

In this section I will describe some things I do as an instructor of educational psychology courses. Since such a presentation is on the order of a "testimonial," I will use the first person throughout the descriptions. A second reason for using this more personal style here is that I do not intend to imply that other instructors should do these particular things, or that they are especially "good." Rather, I am saying, "Here are some things that work for me—you might consider doing them, too, or doing some things like these, according to what fits your style and your personal criteria for the course." I believe these activities have been effective in encouraging the personal growth and awareness of students—they have said so, they have shown it in their behavior, and I believe them.

Belief Systems

During the first class session of each quarter I make the following assignment: "Before the next meeting of the class, your assignment is to write your responses to three questions. Think about the questions between now and the time you sit down to write, then write for not more than about 10 minutes in response to each question. The questions are: (*a*) What do I believe about kids? (*b*) What do I believe about schools? and (*c*) What do I believe about myself?" I indicate to the students that this assignment is required but will not be graded, and that I will read their responses without commenting on them.

After I have collected the responses at the next class session, I read them and file them away. On the next-to-last class session of the quarter, I repeat the assignment, but do not collect responses at the last session. Instead, I return to each student his or her earlier responses with a dittoed suggestion: "Sometime today, reread what you wrote at the beginning of this quarter, and then reread what you wrote this week. Take a few minute to consider these questions for yourself: Have your beliefs changed? How? Do you feel more confident now about any of your earlier statements? Why? How do your beliefs show in your behavior? Are there some new things you could start to do now, that would be consistent with what you believe?"

Project

After having spent several class sessions discussing "Educational Psychology as a Discipline" and presenting an overview of the course, I distribute Project

Proposal forms (Figure 13.2), and discuss the primary criteria for the student's selection of a project to undertake. *My* criteria are that the project must be relevant to the discipline and that the Proposal form must be submitted by a given deadline (usually 7 to 10 days) for my feedback and approval. I suggest to students that they choose a project that is genuinely interesting and meaningful to them and that is likely to be useful to them after the end of the course. I mention some kinds of projects that have been done in the past and encourage

---

1. THE QUESTION (What do you want to find out?):

2. MEANINGFULNESS (How is your question important to you?):

3. PROCEDURES (How do you anticipate approaching an answer to your question? What will you read? To whom will you talk? What will you do?):

4. FEEDBACK (Leave blank—I'll write here!):

- -

IF your project will require the use of institutions other than GSU (schools, etc.), *exactly* what will you want it or them to do for you?

"Bearer may carry out the project described above in (Institution)_____

_____." Date:_____

Official signature:_____

Position:_____

Figure 13.2. Project proposal form.

students to do something other than a traditional term paper (although term papers are also acceptable), and if possible, to do something with children in an educational setting. I do not distribute lists of projects done by former students (although this is usually requested)—my experience has been that many students will evade their own decision making by simply choosing a project on the list. I further encourage students to use brainstorming and questioning techniques as they consider project ideas and to submit more than one Proposal if they wish.

When the Proposal forms are submitted, I critique them carefully, indicating any resources I believe to be appropriate. When the final project report is ready, I request that a new Project Proposal form be completed for the same project idea, but modified on the basis of the student's experience (e.g., What is a better question to start with? What could you do to get better answers?).

I *do* make myself available to students for discussion, at any time, of their project ideas or progress; I do *not* select a project for any student. As a last resort for those who report they "just can't decide what to do," I work to discover their areas of interest within the discipline, and then offer at least three topics for their choice (Level 2 of the Decision Making Process Matrix, Figure 13.1). I allow students to make "mistakes" unless I believe that what they propose to do is unethical or will present serious blocks to their learning experience.

Moral Reasoning

As a part of a unit on development, I present students with a moral dilemma of the type suggested by Kohlberg (1966, 1969), and ask them to respond to it with a judgment and a reason. I collect and shuffle the index cards I have given them for their response, then redistribute them for small group discussion and identification of the moral reasoning stage represented by each one. (When I instruct for the group task, I add a request that students treat all responses with respect even though they may personally disagree with the values and reasons involved.) After allowing time for group discussion, the stage assignments are tallied on the chalkboard; we then discuss implications of the entire process for teacher behavior in classrooms, and for personal growth and awareness possibilities for the students themselves.

The Star Track

During a unit on learning, I present students with a dittoed blind-tracking course in the shape of a five-pointed star. Students are grouped in threes, and each student in turn attempts to follow the track with a pen or pencil while his eyes are closed. A second student provides one of three conditions: (*a*) nonspecific reinforcement ("Yes," "Good," etc.); (*b*) nonspecific punishment ("No," "Wrong!," etc.); or (*c*) specific information feedback ("Move to your left," "You've gone too far."). I allow from 3 to 5 minutes for each "round" of blind tracking; most students will not complete the track in this amount of time.

I then solicit reports of the personal feelings of students under the various conditions, both as "teacher" and "learner," and the conditions are discussed in terms of instructional applications and effects. In addition, I invite students to examine, consider, and discuss their own tracking behavior in terms of its relation to their risk-taking behavior. Some questions I may use here are: What does your performance on the star track tell you about your own risk-taking behavior? Did you use small pen movements in order to avoid failure? If you used bold movements, were they within realistic limits? Can you think of something you've done in the last day or so that is consistent with the risk-taking you've shown here? How can you develop more useful risk-taking behavior? How can you help your students to do so?

Level of Discomfort

Near the beginning of the quarter I distribute copies of the Decision Making Processes chart (Figure 13.1), and discuss it briefly. I ask students to place an E (for Experience) in the matrix boxes which best describe their schooling experience in the past; a C (for Comfort) in the boxes which represent the level with which they are most comfortable; and a star in the boxes at the level they see as ideal for themselves. We discuss briefly the discomfort associated with decisions having growth potential, and I request that the students consider committing themselves to functioning in the course at the level next above that indicated as most comfortable to them. I collect the charts and reconsider my instructional decisions in the light of the information they provide.

Process Evaluation

Periodically during the progress of the course I invite verbal or written responses to questions about their course experience: "Given your experience up to now, what changes in the course structure might help you to learn more effectively? What would be more interesting?" I modify my planning and behavior as much as possible in line with students' suggestions, unless to do so, in my estimation, would violate my academic standards for the course, in which case I state my objections and the degree to which I am willing to negotiate. For example, one of the most frequent suggestions from students is that tests be discontinued. I acknowledge that tests are often unpleasant experiences, but that I must have a demonstration of student performance relative to course content objectives in order to assign a meaningful grade. The usual outcome of such discussions is that we continue to have tests, but that students now begin to see the tests as opportunities for the demonstration of learning, rather than as unreasonable impositions on them by the instructor. When the testing issue is resolved, I solicit discussion about their new insights or attitudes about the function of classroom evaluation procedures, in terms of implications for their own future teaching behavior.

Self-Evaluation

At the beginning of each quarter, while obtaining information from students about prior exposure to education or psychology courses, etc., I ask students to list briefly what they want from *this* course in terms of their personal and professional goals. Near the end of the quarter, I return each student's list with a list of self-evaluation questions (Figure 13.3) to which a written and signed response is required from each student. The grade they assign themselves after consideration of the questions contributes a proportion of their final course grade (the exact amount is determined by negotiation at the beginning of the quarter). This process allows students to evaluate their own course-related behavior and to report direct and incidental learnings which my tests have not allowed them to demonstrate.

CONDITIONS AND PROBLEMS

Teaching for personal growth and awareness is a delicate business for all persons concerned and requires continual monitoring of the goals and strategies employed. The instructor needs to be sensitive to the possibility that on occasion he or she will ask students to function in ways for which their previous experience has not adequately prepared them. When this occurs, students may express confusion and hostility; they may intensify direct or indirect demands that the instructor make decisions on their behalf; or they may reduce their discomfort by withdrawing investment and involvement from course activities.

Student responses to the instructor's occasional solicitation of course process evaluation (see the section entitled Process Evaluation) can serve to alert the instructor to the possibility that the students are not prepared to deal with the requirements or imposed structures in the way the instructor hoped for. A crucial condition for constructive coping with such events is that the instructor possess effective personal and interpersonal sensitivity and skills. It is perhaps natural for us to react with defensiveness and resentment when students criticize or fail to respond in desired ways, after we have spent many hours planning the best course experience for them that we can. It is easy for us to become personally identified with the goals and strategies on which we have decided. An instructor who is concerned about teaching for the personal growth and awareness of his students must therefore work continually to increase his or her own personal awareness and personal growth status, as well as his or her interpersonal and communication skills.

[NOTE: The "Final Statement" (item 8) *must* appear at the end of your self-evaluation report, and *must* be signed.]

1. What did I want from this course, professionally and personally?

2. To what extent did I get what I wanted?

3. To what extent am I personally responsible for getting—or for not getting—what I wanted? (Note: Explicit sentences can be helpful for this, e.g.: "I got X because I . . ."; and "I might have gotten Y if I had . . .")

4. To what extent did I invest myself in course requirements and activities?
   a. Did I do more than "minimum-to-get-by"? How? How much?
   b. When—and how seriously—did I begin carrying out my Project?

5. What, if anything, have I gained from this course experience which I did not expect? To what extent are these incidental gains the result of *my* investment? How?

6. In what ways, if any, have my ideas changed about:
   a. Education?
   b. Teaching?
   c. Children?
   d. Myself?

7. What, if any, changes do I expect (or plan) to make in my professional and/or personal *behavior* as a direct or indirect result of this course experience? When?

8. Final Statement:
   "On the basis of my serious and honest consideration of the above question, and/or other questions as indicated, I hereby assert that I deserve a grade of _____ for aspects of my course performance which are not otherwise evaluated."

   (Signed) _____

Figure 13.3. Suggested questions for self-evaluation.

Occasional or regular participation in off-campus growth opportunities can be extremely helpful for the instructor's own personal development. Useful information about how one "comes across" can be gained in a situation in which the instructor can be seen apart from his professional role, and in which colleague relationships and "academic politics" do not play a part. Such opportunities can be found in most urban areas, at low cost, through community service agencies and professionally approved "growth centers."

Colleagues can also be an important source of informative feedback for the instructor. When good relationships exist with peers, they can be invited to attend a class or two, and then to report and discuss their observations and impressions of the instructor's classroom behavior as it related to climate and process as well as to content. Obviously, in this case the peer relationship needs to be an honest, trusting, and respectful one so that constructive critique, rather than destructive criticism, can be given. (It was through peer observation that I discovered my tendency during class to face more often to the left side of the room—the side with the windows—than to the right side, and also became aware of some trivial but distracting physical mannerisms.)

An essential ingredient of the instructor's interpersonal effectiveness is the ability to communicate effectively. It is useful to consider the process of communication to be not so much "telling and being told" as "hearing and being heard." Teacher skill in hearing is a sine qua non of personalized instruction in any setting, in order for that instruction to be "relevant to the learner's inner personal goals and needs. Personalization helps the learner to become aware of his personal needs, potential, and limitations, and it offers instruction that is sequenced according to [his or her] 'concerns' [Hall & Jones, 1976, p. 136]."

The instructor may equip himself to hear more effectively by attending skills development workshops in communication, by auditing the classes of colleagues, or by working through one of the many helpful books available (see, e.g., Gordon, 1970, 1975; Gorman, 1974; Kraft, 1975). Participation in such programs will also contribute to skill in "being heard," as participants become more aware of their attitudes, values, and feelings, and learn to take appropriate risks of self-disclosure.

Despite the instructor's careful planning and conscientious preparation to include students' personal growth and awareness as an instructional concern, this is, after all, a human endeavor, and success is not guaranteed. Students appreciate the acceptance and respect accorded to them in the process, but they may also become confused, hostile, or withdrawn as a result of the anxiety they experience when they are challenged to grow in all respects rather than simply to learn information and instructional methodologies.

Confusion is not "all bad." It may serve to disrupt some "hardening of the categories" which results in the rejection of new information that threatens to change opinions and attitudes. On occasion it may be appropriate to introduce confusion as an instructional strategy; from such tactics students may discover the benefits of occasional reconsideration of their opinions, and may also find useful new ways to work at resolving their own confusion constructively. Sometimes, however, confusion may arise which seems unhelpful or contributes to overanxiety; if so, the instructor may help by identifying the source of the confusion through discussion (skill in hearing is important here), then by clarifying his own communications, or by referring students to other resources (e.g., to other students who are less confused).

In dealing with student *hostility*, the instructor needs first to separate the student's hostility from his or her own possible defensiveness so that the student will feel heard. If the instructor finds this impossible, it is best to refer the student—and himself or herself—to a receptive third party. Constructive discussion and resolution of the issues involved will not be possible until the angry student feels that he or she has been heard and accepted. Again, the instructor's skill in listening nonjudgmentally is critical, since paraphrasing (reflective listening) invites expression of the anger without implying approval of the opinions and judgments being expressed. When it seems inappropriate to invite full expression of hostility during a class session, it is wise to do so as soon as possible afterwards. A simple, "You seemed upset today; I'd like to hear about it," spoken after class, can be the first step toward establishing a new level of understanding and cooperation between teacher and student. Skills in interpersonal problem solving and conflict resolution will also be quite helpful.

Withdrawal behavior is minimized when students feel influential in their own learning process, and when they feel free to express their dissatisfactions and confusions; nonetheless, withdrawal behavior does occur. Since the decision whether (and how much) to participate in the course is the student's and not the instructor's, it is usually not helpful for the instructor to attempt to force a student to become more fully involved in the course activities. When the instructor becomes aware of withdrawal behavior (seen in poor attendnace, attending behavior during class, test performance, etc.), it may be useful to issue a gentle invitation (written or verbal), e.g.: "If you think it would be helpful to talk about what's happening for you in the course, let's make a date." Specific behavioral feedback may also constitute an invitation, e.g.: "I've noticed that you've missed a few classes . . . . " It is important to note here than when an instructor offers invitations—to talk, to learn, to grow—he or she must be willing to allow students the *freedom to decline* the invitation, to say "No!"

Dependent behavior is perhaps the most difficult to perceive and to deal with, for at least two reasons. First, teachers usually see themselves as helpers, and often feel most helpful when others depend on their knowledge, wisdom, and guidance. Second, many dependent behaviors appeal directly to the instructor's need to feel competent, and are thus apt to be extremely seductive. When a student says something like, "You know so much more about this than I can ever hope to, so won't you please . . . ?" it is very difficult for the instructor to avoid feeling just a little more important in the scheme of things and consequently responding to the request that he made a decision on behalf of the student. The instructor can take several measures to keep from falling into the "dependency trap," the most important of which is to develop sensitivity to his own need system and find ways to meet his needs without using students. He may also find it helpful to clarify for himself (and sometimes for the student) the established or agreed-upon distribution of responsibility for making the decision requested by the student. Another useful procedure is to assist the student to make the decision himself by "sidestepping" the overt request and directing attention to the student's own decision-making process, e.g.: "What do you need to know (or, What do you need me to do) to help you make the decision?"

The instructor of educational psychology has a unique opportunity to apply his "whole person" to the task of assisting students to gain understanding of the psychology of the educational process. He or she can do so in a way that contributes to the "whole person" education of students by giving serious consideration to the potential consequences of his or her instructional behavior to the personal growth and awareness needs of his students. It is the author's belief that, in turn, his or her students will be more effective teachers as they bring to their future classroom and students not just their subject-matter competence and methodological expertise, but their human attitudes and concerns as well. They will be able to personalize, not simply individualize, the process of education. If this occurs, it will obviously not be solely the result of their experience in one course in educational psychology. The subject matter of educational psychology, however, seems ideally suited for adaptation and application to student needs and concerns; through it, the lifelong process of personal growth can take root and be nourished.

REFERENCES

Combs, A. W., Soper, D. W., Gooding, C. T., Benton, J. A., Jr., Dickman, J. F., & Usher, R. H. *Florida studies in the helping professions.* University of Florida School Science Monograph No. 37, Gainesville, Florida: University of Florida Press, 1969.

Combs, A. W., Avila, D., & Purkey, W. W. *Helping relationships: Basic concepts for the helping professions.* Boston: Allyn and Bacon, 1971.

Dreikurs, R., Grunwald, B. B., & Pepper, F. C. *Maintaining sanity in the classroom.* New York: Harper & Row, 1971.

Fuller, F. F., & Bown, O. H. Becoming a teacher. In the *Seventy-fourth Yearbook of the*

National Society for the Study of Education. Chicago: The National Society for the Study of Education, 1975.

Furth, H. G., & Wachs, H. *Thinking goes to school.* New York: Oxofrd, 1975.

Gage, N. L. *Teacher effectiveness and teacher education: The search for a scientific basis.* Palo Alto, California: Pacific, 1972.

Good, T. L., Biddle, B. J., & Brophy, J. E. *Teachers make a difference.* New York: Holt, Rinehart & Winston, 1975.

Gordon, T. *Parent effectiveness training.* New York: Wyden, 1970.

Gordon, T. *Teacher effectiveness training.* New York: Wyden, 1974.

Gorman, A. H. *Teachers and learners: The interactive process of education* (2nd ed.). Boston: Allyn and Bacon, 1974.

Hall, G. E., & Jones, H. L. *Competency-based education: A process for the improvement of education.* Englewood Cliffs, New Jersey: Prentice-Hall, 1976.

Howes, V. M. *Informal teaching in the open classroom.* New York: Macmillan, 1974.

Kohlberg, L. Moral education in the schools: A developmental view. *School Review,* 1966, *74,* 1–30.

Kohlberg, L. Stage and sequence: The cognitive–developmental approach to socialization. In D. Goslin (Ed.), *Handbook of Socialization Theory and Research.* Chicago: Rand McNally, 1969.

Kraft, A. *The living classroom.* New York: Harper & Row, 1975.

Maslow, A. H. *Toward a psychology of being* (2nd ed.). Princeton, New Jersey: Van Nostrand, 1968.

Rogers, C. W. *Freedom to learn.* Columbus, Ohio: Charles E. Merrill, 1966.

Rogers, C. W. The interpersonal relationship in the facilitation of learning. In R. R. Leeper (Ed.), *Humanizing education: The person in the process.* Washington, D.C.: Association for Supervision and Curriculum Development, 1967.

Schmuck, R. A., & Schmuck, P. A. *A humanistic psychology of education: Making the school everybody's house.* Palo Alto, California: National, 1974.

Seaberg, D. I. *The four faces of teaching: The role of the teacher in humanizing education.* Pacific Palisades, California: Goodyear, 1974.

Stephens, J. M. *Educational psychology* (2nd ed.). New York: Holt, 1956. Cited in R. F. Biehler, *Psychology applied to teaching* (2nd ed.). Boston: Houghton Mifflin, 1974.

Part IV

SUMMARY: UNDERGRADUATE
AND GRADUATE LEVELS

14

Issues in Teaching Undergraduate Educational Psychology Courses

JOHN FELDHUSEN

Purdue University

Educational psychology is a fluid field and the teaching of educational psychology is an ill defined and uncertain professional endeavor. We remain uncertain about the scope and nature of the discipline of educational psychology and are the victims of numerous definitions or pronouncements concerning the content or nature of this field. Thus, it is not surprising that instruction in the area of educational psychology is also subject to assorted views, beliefs, and inclinations. Of course, instruction is also an ill defined activity in all disciplines in higher education. Thus, the teaching of educational psychology is subject dually to the uncertainties of the discipline in particular and of instruction in general.

The indefiniteness of instruction in educational psychology is reflected in the issues that constitute our major concerns as educational psychologists. These issues give some focus to our discussions and to our efforts to define the field and appropriate teaching strategies. The issues provide direction for those who seek to understand the field. They also identify anchor points which teachers of undergraduate educational psychology courses can use to examine and clarify their own positions.

Thus, this chapter is devoted to a presentation of some issues in the teaching of educational psychology at the undergraduate level. An effort will be made to discuss issues at a general level and not at the level of specific content or

313

procedures in teaching. However, there will be some references to specific procedures or content, such as PSI (personalized system of instruction, Keller, 1968) or behavioral objectives as illustrations in developing the chapter.

APPROPRIATE GOALS

Goals are inescapable (Feldhusen, 1972). There is no way of teaching educational psychology that does not reflect someone's choice of goals. A specific teacher of an educational psychology course might slavishly follow a course outline, course objectives, and/or methods in teaching which reflect no deliberation, judgment, or selection on his or her own part. But someone has made choices, and the instructor who follows slavishly (as many or most do) has already made the big choice of acquiescence.

Goals are the broad, subsuming, value-laden indicators of what is important, what is worthwhile, what ends should be pursued, and what means should be employed (Feldhusen, 1972). There are two kinds of goals: process and content. *Process goals* focus on ways to achieve some ends while content goals focus on the end product. "To use problem-solving techniques in all aspects of teaching" is a process goal. "To help all students learn the basic principles of test theory" represents a *content goal*, even though the goal statement speaks of the process of "helping all students."

What goals are appropriate for an undergraduate educational psychology course? Should all of the goals reflect the learning of some cognitive content? Or should the goals relate chiefly to the learning of skills necessary in teaching? Should the goals reflect social values? Should the goals relate to philosophical issues? A cognitive goal would be "to help students learn how to use Piagetian concepts in analyzing and interpreting various types of classroom behavior." A skill goal might be "to help students learn to how write the various types of test items they will use in teaching." A goal reflecting a social values' orientation would be "to help students learn how to analyze their own biases and prejudices and overcome or control them in teaching." A goal reflecting philosophical concerns would be "to help students develop a general set of values concerning ethical issues in teaching about racial characteristics and the problems of minority and economically disadvantaged children."

Goals should be distinguishable from behavioral objectives (Kryspin & Feldhusen, 1974b). They are broader; they need not reflect the specific performance, skill or behavior to be learned. But goals can (or should) be used to generate instructional or behavioral objectives. Realistic goal statements can be linked to the specifics of instruction. Of course, some or many statements of goals are mere window dressing and reflect no discernible influence on the aims or directions of a course of instruction. When asked to state goals many instructors also state vague, idealistic ambitions which may never be explicitly pursued in planning or conducting a course of instruction.

A uniform set of goals cannot be defined for all instructors of undergraduate educational psychology courses in all places. Here are the goals that we formulated for a course of instruction at Purdue University:

1. Learn a set of basic concepts, principles and theories
2. Develop higher cognitive abilities
3. Learn how to apply knowledge to realistic professional problems
4. Become self-directed learners
5. Appreciate the course as a model of instructional design
6. Experience personal relevance in the course experiences
7. Develop competence in working with others on professional problems
8. Learn to help one another achieve course goals (Feldhusen, Ames, & Linden, 1974).

Instructors in other colleges or universities might formulate completely different lists.

What can be specified is the need for instructors of educational psychology courses to spend some time examining their goals. Those who are designing new courses or are just beginning to teach should most emphatically begin with attention to goals. Procedures for goals analysis are set forth by Mager (1972) and Feldhusen (1972). The results of the efforts should then be used as fundamental guides in developing objectives, instructional activities, and evaluation procedures. Content goals and some process goals translate easily into behavioral objectives, but some goals that reflect attention to social concerns or to philosophical issues may be translated only into broader considerations in the design of instruction. The goal "to provide varied experience in working with minority students" might not be reflected in any behavioral objectives. Instead, it might be the case that a number of practicum experiences would be arranged in schools enrolling large numbers of minority students. Evaluation of some goals, such as this illustration, might also be carried out only in terms of presence or absence of the experience, not as quantification of student performance on some specific test or student project.

Goals determine the content, processes, and direction of all instruction in undergraduate educational psychology courses. They should be developed as an explicit activity in the design of a course or they should be carefully examined in retrospect. Either way, they should be linked to the activities of a course of instruction. Without attention to goals, courses become mindless activities leading we know not where.

THE PROBLEM OF RELEVANCE

The major concern of students in educational psychology courses seems to be the relevance of what is learned (Feldhusen, 1970). Relevance may mean the students' perceptions of the correlation between course goals or objectives and the students' current views of the knowledge or skills they will need on the job. Of course, in a phenomenological sense it could also refer to the student's perception of the meaningfulness of the course in relation to his or her current views of self and personal needs. Relevance is, in any event, a perceptual problem.

Few students have any clear idea of what knowledge or skill they will need on the job. Very few students can know what the job will be. The demands of a given job (e.g., third grade teacher) differ tremendously from school to school. Very few reports of task analysis of specific teaching jobs have appeared in the literature. Instructors in educational psychology courses rarely have close contact with real classroom situations in public schools and many have had no prior experience in teaching there.

So what is relevance? How is it defined? Who can define it? Is it at all desirable for a course to be relevant in the sense of providing specific training in skills that will be needed on a job? Might not such training better fit technical and vocational schools rather than college or university education for a profession?

Undoubtedly task analyses could be carried out to identify some specific skills and knowledge needed in various types of teaching situations. It is equally certain that specific educational activities could be designed to help students learn those skills and that knowledge. But the task would be formidable, both from the standpoint of analysis of the many varied patterns prevailing in the schools and from the standpoint of designing instruction to fit all the contingencies.

So the relevance issue in designing undergraduate courses of instruction in educational psychology may never be solved. It seems likely that students really mean that they want to learn about the broader and more obvious skills of teaching when they call for relevance (e.g., how to handle discipline problems, how to prepare a lesson, how to write a test). To this end, the new competency-based programs of teacher education might be especially appropriate.

The problem of relevance is also probably exacerbated by the tendency of educational psychologists (as reflected in texts and in teaching) to stress the theoretical and cognitive side of teaching. Teaching basic information and skills is the hallmark of many public school teachers, but both are apt to be played down in texts, while concept learning, creativity, and inquiry are stressed. Theories of learning are also popular in texts and among educational psychologists. Arguments run long and hard among instructors about the value of good theory. But Jackson's (1968) analysis of teachers on the job indicated that they retained or used few of our theories or principles once they get on the job. Jackson (1972) described our teaching focus on theories and principles as analogous to "stalking beasts and swatting flies." The swatting may represent the true impact of our efforts.

Treffinger and Davis (1972) have developed a system of instruction for educational psychology courses that strives for relevance by making students active participants in the selection of goals, objectives, and course activities. Students are urged to tailor the course to meet their own needs, interests, and current states of development.

Relevance for the present is a knotty problem complicated by students' perceptual difficulties, the tendency of texts and instructors to rely on lofty theoretical positions and esoteric educationese or jargon, the development of undergraduate specializations in education without teacher certification (Ripple & Ayabe, 1975), and the complexity and diversity of real teaching situations. Students may push for relevance. Instructors may resist or they may strive for relevance. But all are enmeshed in an ill defined morass of uncertainty. For the present, the instructor might best be advised to avoid preoccupation with theories, and stress practical problems of teaching and students' personal needs as prospective teachers.

APPROPRIATE CONTENT

What content, what information, what knowledge, what skills are appropriate to be taught in an undergraduate educational psychology course? What topics should we "cover"? Content most often refers to bookish subject matter to be presented in text material or lectures. It is also the "stuff" on which students are tested in our typical "multiple guess" tests. At its best it refers to concepts, principles, and theories presented and tested at levels one and two of the Bloom taxonomy (1956). Rarely is content regarded as the information that students must know and understand as a prelude to analyzing and/or solving problems, synthesizing complex solutions, and judging or carrying out realistic projects related to teaching.

If content is an end in itself, as it is much of the time in educational psychology courses, selection of appropriate content is relatively easy. The most widely accepted view of appropriate content, in fact the dictator or definer of appropriate content, is the typical educational psychology textbook. Most texts cover a standard set of topics. As the basis for a survey, I reviewed 30 educational psychology texts and found that there is a recurring set of topics (see Figure 14.1). Of course, each instructor will also have his or her own favorite topics to be stressed and possibly some that he or she dislikes and/or omits from the course. Since it appears that students retain little of content

On the line to the left of each numbered topic rate its importance or value for inclusion in an educational psychology textbook or course. Use this scale:

3 = Absolutely necessary and important
2 = Moderately necessary or important
1 = Unnecessary, unimportant

Under many of the numbered topics subtopics are given. Please check (X) those which should be covered if you rated the main topic 2 or 3.

	Frequency		
	3	2	1
1. Affective Processes	17	11	3
2. Personality Factors	8	14	9
3. Character, Values, Moral Development	7	16	9
4. Measurement, Testing	22	7	2
5. Social Factors	14	16	0
6. Learning Disabilities	7	15	8
7. Learning Processes	23	7	1
8. Memory, Retention, Transfer	14	11	6
9. Learning Outcomes	24	5	2
10. Mental Hygiene	10	11	10
11. Development	11	16	4
12. Abilities	17	10	4
13. Motivation	22	9	0
14. Teaching and Instruction	24	5	2
15. Educational Psychology As A Discipline	8	9	12
16. Goals, Objectives	9	14	5
17. Individual Differences	15	10	4
18. Research Methods	2	10	19
19. Discipline, Behavioral Control	16	13	2
20. Special Groups: Gifted, MRs, Disadvantaged, Handicapped	7	12	10

Figure 14.1. Ratings of importance of topics for an educational psychology textbook.

anyway, (Jackson, 1968) it really makes little difference what we teach. Indeed, as Treffinger and Davis suggest (1972), students might as well be encouraged to select their own goals and objectives. They might find the course more personally relevant and interesting that way.

Of course, there is sometimes the problem that instructors in subsequent courses in the teacher education curriculum voice expectations of what should be learned in the educational psychology course. "Why in the world aren't they teaching Havighurst's developmental tasks?" "Why aren't they teaching classical conditioning paradigms?" "How come they aren't teaching interaction analysis?" On and on it goes. The rationale is clear. Professor X learned about these topics when taking an educational psychology course 20 years ago, liked them, and now feels that all subsequent students should learn them.

There is another approach, alluded to earlier, to the selection of content. That view, as set forth by Feldhusen, Linden, and Ames (1975), is to select content as a basis for higher level (cognitive) learnings and professional applications. Gagné's (1970) concepts of hierarchical structures of learning can be studied and then used as a theoretical guide in learning how to design real instructional materials for classroom use. Principles of reinforcement can be learned as a prelude to designing behavioral management approaches to classroom discipline problems. The rationale for content selection then is based upon goals that specify the higher level learnings to be achieved. The higher level goals hopefully are related to real abilities potentially applicable in teaching. The ultimate extension of this approach might be a course in behavior modification in which the student learns a highly specific set of skills for classroom behavioral management.

I conducted a survey among teachers of educational psychology and solicited their views of what should be taught in educational psychology courses. The teachers were given an outline of potential content or topics and asked to rate the importance of the proposed topics. The outline topics were drawn from an analysis of the 30 major educational psychology texts. The survey instrument is presented in Figure 14.1. Thirty-two teachers from 32 different institutions responded. They rated the topics on a 1 to 3 scale in which a 3 rating was described as "absolutely necessary and important," 2 as "moderately necessary or important," and 1 as "unnecessary, unimportant." The most highly rated topics were "measurement and evaluation in the schools," "learning processes," "learning outcomes," "motivation," and "teaching and instruction." The middle level of importance was assigned to "affective processes," "social factors," "retention and transfer," "development," "human abilities," "individual difference," and "discipline." Low ratings were given to the topics "research methods," "special groups," "goals and objectives," "personality," "educational psychology as a discipline," "mental hygiene," "learning disabilities," and "character, values, and moral development."

Appropriate content will nevertheless be dictated by the popular texts. Teachers of educational psychology may make an effort to secure material to teach topics not covered in the standard texts. But they will be the exception. Few will be forced to first identify competencies and then select appropriate content for those competencies. In fact, Samuels (1975) has recently suggested that in competency-based teacher education programs educational psychology may be displaced or eliminated. So for the present, viable, clear-cut alternative approaches are not on the horizon. We will probably keep teaching the texts, although some pioneers may endeavor to select content that helps students achieve higher level goals and abilities for professional applications.

OBJECTIVES

Even though educational psychologists give low ratings to the importance of goals and objectives as topics for courses, educational psychology texts usually include a chapter on behavioral objectives. Several major educational psychology texts also have stated objectives at the beginning of each chapter (Galloway, 1976; De Cecco & Crawford, 1974; Klausmeier & Goodwin, 1975). Furthermore, modular instruction in educational psychology is almost always based on stated objectives, PSI courses (Keller, 1968) in educational psychology always include statements of objectives, and competency-based programs always include statements of objectives for competencies related to or derived from educational psychology. Thus, in one way or another, educational psychologists must be concerned with behavioral objectives.

Statements of objectives for textbook chapters are usually focused on content, information, or the knowledge level. The same is often true of objectives stated for PSI courses. Objectives at the higher cognitive levels of analysis, problem solving, divergent thinking, and evaluation rarely appear in statements of objectives for educational psychology courses. It is difficult to formulate the higher level objectives, difficult to design instruction to achieve them, and difficult to develop tests to assess student attainment of the objectives.

There are numerous guides for the writing of objectives (Bloom, 1956; Gronlund, 1970; Harrow, 1972; Kibler, Cegala, Barker, & Miles, 1974; Krathwohl, Bloom, & Masia, 1964; Kryspin & Feldhusen, 1974b; Mager, 1975; Vargas, 1972). All stress the importance of specifying observable behaviors, performances or products. Components of the statements may vary from one (behavior) to five (behavior, audience, conditions, standard or level of performance, and result or product), (Kibler *et al.*, 1974). Thus, a statement of objectives may be as simple as

To be able to define creativity

or as complex as

> The educational psychology students will be able to write a definition of creativity which is identical to the text definition.

There continues to be much argument concerning the values or dangers of stating and using objectives in teaching (Popham, Eisner, Sullivan, & Tyler, 1969; Tennyson & Tennyson, 1975). Will they block creative thinking? Will they limit intellectual explorations? Will instruction become too narrow? Many of the questions sound like rationalizations for those who have not gotten around to the task. The arguments would be most convincing if they came from those who had a substantial experience in writing and using objectives in teaching. Even if not used directly as guides in teaching, objectives seem to be invaluable as one dimension of tables of specification in test development (Kryspin & Feldhusen, 1974a).

Ideally the sequence of events in formulating objectives might be as follows:

1. State broad goals for the course.
2. Formulate instructional objectives based on the goals.
3. Design instruction to provide the necessary information, models, practice, feedback, and reinforcement to help students achieve the objectives, and design measures to assess student attainment of the objectives.

This is the technological approach to teaching. It does not close the door to artistry and histrionics nor to all the rich extensions of other goals which might also be pursued. But it does assure a core of specifiable learnings for a large number of students. Hopefully more and more educational psychology courses will be designed according to this model.

Who Should Teach Educational Psychology Courses?

The people who teach educational psychology courses come from infinitely varied backgrounds. Some are well trained in educational psychology. Others have barely a course or two and are otherwise trained in guidance, counseling, school psychology, or other related fields. Concern has been expressed by members of Division 15 (Educational Psychology) of the American Psychological Association. A Committee of the Division chaired by David Ausubel studied the problem and made the following recommendation:

> Division 15 of the APA views with concern the assumption that is prevalent in many teachers colleges and departments of education, that any person with a degree in education is competent to teach educational psychology courses. An ethical respect for the standards of educational study demands the teaching of educational psychology content be restricted to persons who hold themselves professionally as

educational psychologists, who are members of psychological groups identified with educational psychology, and with adequate academic background in educational psychology [*Educational Psychologist*, 1968, p. 11]!

While the Ausubel committee stressed the importance of having educational psychologists teach educational psychology courses, it is not clear that they are really any better prepared for the task than people from other related disciplines. The graduate programs for educational psychologists frequently stress training in research and theory and neglect training for teaching. Thus, it may only be in the areas of content and research methodology that the educational psychologist is better prepared. For the present it seems likely that faculty from other related disciplines might be appropriate teachers of educational psychology courses, especially if they have had *some* training in the area of educational psychology and good experience or training in teaching education courses.

EVALUATING RESULTS

As with objectives, evaluation is something educational psychologists teach about but often fail to do in relation to their own courses and teaching. There is little evidence in the literature of systematic efforts to evaluate educational psychology courses (Feldhusen, 1966). Such efforts might focus on particular models or designs for educational psychology courses and might assess student achievement and attitudes and the long-range impact on the students' performance in subsequent teacher education courses and on-the-job in teaching. Does anything worthwhile flow from the undergraduate educational psychology course?

Student pessimism about the relevance of educational psychology courses (Feldhusen, 1970) and the evidence that they retain little of our jargon and few of our concepts (Jackson, 1968) suggest that more systematic investigation might turn up discouraging evidence.

New models for educational psychology courses have been presented in the journals, *Teaching of Psychology* (Chandler, 1976; Saxon & Holt, 1974) and the *Educational Psychologist* (Newson & Gaite, 1971; Knief, 1972; Sattler, Woehlke, & Grinder, 1972; Cohen, 1973), and in *Teaching Educational Psychology, Proceedings of The First Annual Midwestern Conference on the Teaching of Educational Psychology* (Feldhusen, 1973). The reports have included some evaluation evidence for end-of-course achievements and attitudes. Some reports have also focused on evaluation of particular components or innovations in a course.

An effective evaluation program for educational psychology courses ought to include assessment of the following:

1. an assessment of student needs based on task analyses of teachers' performance on the job
2. an input evaluation of all the possible resources and approaches which might be used (Samuels, 1971)
3. a formative assessment of the operations of the course and its components once it is implemented
4. an evaluation of student achievement of the goals and objectives of the course
5. an attitudinal evaluation of students' views of their own growth as prospective teachers, the course, and the discipline as presented in the course
6. a longitudinal analysis of the impact of the course on students' performance in subsequent teacher education courses and on the job as teachers

RELATIONSHIP TO THE TOTAL TEACHER EDUCATION PROGRAM

It is a frequent complaint that the different courses in an undergraduate teacher education curriculum tend to go separate ways without coordination and without consideration of ways to improve the overall program through cooperation. Educational psychology courses are often theory and research oriented, while methods and curriculum courses are viewed as excessively practical, cookbookish, or Mickey Mouse in their orientation.

The ideal program is probably one that combines knowledge input (knowledge of theory, research, basic principles, and essential information) with subsequent attention to competencies appropriate for the teacher. Ideally, both would be organized on the basis of task analysis of the knowledge and competencies teachers need on the job. Of course, a certain amount of idealism would be appropriate as input too. Even though teachers do little on the job to use higher level questions in discussions or fail to teach creative thinking and problem solving, teacher educators might well introduce some of these topics into the teacher education curriculum. The problem is now that this idealism often dominates the teacher education curriculum.

In the ideal, well organized, and coordinated teacher education program, educational psychology might better be included as a series of modules rather than as a one- or two-semester course. Some of the modules most appropriate for educational psychology to provide would include

1. writing objectives
2. developing classroom tests
3. using standardized tests
4. cognitive aspects of development
5. teaching creativity and problem solving

6. teaching information, concepts and principles
7. verbal learning
8. learning theories applied to teaching
9. principles of classroom management
10. motivation and guidance of learning
11. moral development, attitudes, and values clarification

The educational psychology courses developed by Treffinger and Davis (1972) and by Sattler *et al.* (1972) are both modular in design and include modules for a number of these topics.

It seems entirely inappropriate for an educational psychology course to be relegated to the beginning or end of the teacher education course sequence and to try to cover all the topics in one concentrated semester. A series of modules, spread out over the entire program and combined with appropriate field or teaching experiences, would seem to make much more sense. Students might be able to select modules in a sequence which would best fit their own individual programs and development, or the faculty might prescribe sequences to fit different groups of students in particular curricula. Ideally, student teaching would not be run as a block at the end of the program, but it too might best be broken up into smaller sequences interspersed among the educational psychology modules.

RELATING TO THE DISCIPLINE OF EDUCATIONAL PSYCHOLOGY

Most educational psychology text writers assume that students in teacher education should learn about the discipline of educational psychology, its history, its tenets, and its research orientation. For the most part, undergraduates could not care less! At the worst, the text and course introduce the student to the discipline at the beginning of the text or course before the student has any idea of the substance or structure of the discipline. Thus, the experience is necessarily doomed to be meaningless.

Ideally this attempt to teach something about the discipline ought to be dropped and reintroduced, if at all, in masters' level courses for teachers. If it must remain in the undergraduate curriculum it should probably be offered as an elective or optional module titled "The Discipline of Educational Psychology." Since most undergraduates know little about academic disciplines, a few may elect the module erroneously assuming that it has something to do with classroom discipline.

Educational psychology is essentially a research oriented discipline. Methodology still dominates our thinking. As noted in an earlier section, we do not have a well defined set of information, concepts, and principles that can be organized and held out as representing the discipline of educational psychology.

We do have a popular and somewhat standardized set of broad subsuming topics that are traditionally addressed in educational psychology texts and courses. But the material covered under those subsuming topics can be almost infinitely varied. Thus, the best we can probably do in teaching about the discipline of educational psychology is to reveal our research strategies and the tentativeness and variety of most of our knowledge. Neither of these topics is likely to be of much interest or value to undergraduates or masters' degree candidates, but doctoral candidates may profit from learning about them.

RAISING STANDARDS IN RELATION TO THE NEW TEACHER MARKET

With the vast oversupply of new teachers, a shortage of jobs, and economic hardships in most schools of education, the time seems propitious to raise our standards for admission, performance in courses, and graduation in teacher education (Klees, 1975). Our teacher education graduates rate low in abilities as compared with graduates of other professional schools (Educational Testing Service, 1971). Similarly, within colleges and universities, teacher education students are often viewed as the least able among students in the various disciplines. Professors of education are even wont to complain about the low levels of motivation, performance, and professional ambitions of many of their own students. Obviously there is substantial room for improvement.

Educational psychologists, by themselves, are not, of course, in a position to set or change admission or graduation criteria in schools of education. At most, they can work with others to effect changes. However, since educational psychologists are frequently measurement and research specialists, they are in a unique position to evoke their expertise in relation to the development of admission and graduation criteria. Both involve measurement problems and both call for validation and reliability research. Professors of education in other areas often express despondence or gross pessimism concerning the reliability of admission procedures and graduation criteria, but the problems are probably no more unsolvable than similar problems in other professional fields. Educational psychologists should provide leadership in finding new solutions.

In their own courses, educational psychologists need to reexamine their grading, testing, and evaluation procedures. Do the procedures result in valid and reliable assessments of student performance? Within the last decade there has been a substantial increase in grade level across all course work (Scully, 1975). Educational psychology courses probably suffer from the same grade inflation. Satisfactory performance (not excellent) is coming to be defined as a grade of "A." Some instructors dream of a new grading scale which like the Standard and Poor's bond rating system includes grades of "A," "AA," and "AAA."

It is possible that the increase in the use of student ratings of instruction has paralleled the rise in average grade level (Scully, 1975). Have professors unwittingly become victims of student rating systems? Are they massaging students through easy evaluation and grading systems in order to be massaged by students at rating scale administration time? Recent work by Frey (1973) and by Rodin and Rodin (1972) suggests that grades and ratings may be highly correlated.

Now this leads back to the educational psychology course, the instructor, and the evaluation procedures used. The general topic under consideration is standards of student performance, especially in a changed teacher market. Have standards been lowered substantially just at a time when they should be going up? Is the whole situation confounded by the conditions in many institutions in which there is a real threat of lower enrollments and lost jobs for professors of education? Does the latter situation lead to an effort to retain as many students as possible, standards notwithstanding? These questions will be very difficult to answer.

Educational psychologists need to reexamine the standards of performance, evaluation procedures, and grading practices in their courses. The several problems that have developed during the last decade relevant to student evaluation along with the general problem of oversupply of teachers lead to a need to reexamine our procedures for evaluating student achievement and progress. Greater rigor in evaluation procedures and more severe grading practices may be called for.

SYSTEMS VERSUS AD HOC APPROACHES TO COURSES

The systems approach to instructional development has been widely accepted by educational technologists (Davis, Alexander, & Yelon, 1974), but there is little evidence that it has "caught on" among educational psychologists. Knief (1972) described the development of a course in educational psychology using a systems approach at the University of Arizona. Systems approaches probably will afford the possibility of improvement in our courses, and they merit consideration by coordinators of undergraduate courses in educational psychology.

The following are probably critical elements in a systems approach to the organization of a course:

1. Planning begins with a careful needs assessment of the students and task analyses of the work situation for which they are to be prepared.
2. Broad goals of the course are formulated.
3. Specific instructional objectives are written.
4. Constraints on instructional design are specified.
5. Instructional resources, media and personnel are identified.
6. Student characteristics and/or entering behavior are assessed.

7. Instructional materials and activities are planned in relation to objectives, goals, student characteristics, and constraints.
8. Instructional materials and activities are examined and developed as they relate to, interact with, or complement one another as a total system.
9. Instruments and procedures are developed to monitor student achievement and progress.
10. Principles of learning are carefully considered in developing instructional materials and activities.
11. Formative and summative evaluation procedures are used to assess operations and the short- and long-range impact of the course.
12. Personnel resources and personnel training procedures are carefully considered throughout the course development and implementation.

The author and several colleagues have carried on an extensive systems approach to the design of the undergraduate educational psychology course. Results have been reported in a series of articles (Feldhusen, Ames, & Linden, 1973, 1974; Feldhusen, Linden, & Ames, 1975). Treffinger and Davis (1972) and Knief (1972) have reported similar systematic approaches to the design of educational psychology courses. We conclude that a systems approach can be fruitful in bringing our knowledge of instructional psychology to bear on course development. Ad hoc approaches, in which there is little thought to course design, in which each instructor "does his thing," and in which outcomes or effects are never assessed, create a severe contradiction. Most educational psychology courses present content to students from which at least a quasi-systems approach as the best way to organized instruction is implied. Use of a systems model can make the educational psychology course more consistent with the message "preached" in the course (Cohen, 1973).

USE OF PROCTORS, TUTORS, COURSE ASSISTANTS

The opportunity of educational psychology courses to provide a greater variety of learning activities and experiences can probably be enhanced substantially through the use of teaching aides, course assistants, proctors, and/or tutors. Trowbridge (1970) described such an arrangement for an undergraduate educational psychology course at Drake University. Linden, Ames, and Feldhusen (1975) have also described such a plan for the undergraduate educational psychology course at Purdue University. Proctors and tutors are almost always used in PSI (personalized system of instruction) organized under the Keller Plan (Keller, 1968).

Course assistants are most frequently selected from recent enrollees in the course for which assistants are wanted. Students who have performed well and show an interest may be invited to apply for positions as course assistants. At most institutions it has been the case that more students will apply than can be accommodated.

At Purdue University, divisions of the undergraduate educational psychology course are taught by faculty and graduate students in classes enrolling 30 to 40 students each. Undergraduate course assistants are assigned to individual instructors. They participate in orientation sessions at the beginning of the semester and meet weekly throughout the course to discuss ongoing problems of course design and management. They may be enrolled for credit in an educational practicum course for one to three credits while they are serving as course assistants.

Course assistants can be used in the following ways in undergraduate educational psychology courses:

1. Administer tests, score them and provide feedback to students (the proctor role).
2. Tutor students who are having trouble understanding some course content.
3. Lead or guide small groups of students who are working on projects.
4. Assist in the design of new instructional materials for a course.
5. Participate in discussion and resolution of course design or management problems.
6. Perform routine clerical tasks such as typing and collating materials.
7. Assist in course record keeping procedures.
8. Serve as tryout "guinea pigs" for new course materials.

Undergraduate course assistants can extend the capability of a course immensely, but their usefulness is not without a price. Someone must select, train, and supervise them. The experience must also be viewed as a learning experience for the assistants with identifiable goals and purposes. When properly planned and administered, such a program can be of great value to students in the course, the course assistants, and to the faculty who are responsible for the course.

USE OF THE COURSE FOR RESEARCH AND A DATA BASE

Educational psychologists are renowned for conducting research with their own students (college level) and attempting to generalize to all levels of students. The average undergraduate in university courses in educational psychology and in introductory psychology is probably overexposed to research so that even his value as a subject is somewhat questionable.

The research uses of students have been relatively sporadic, unplanned, and frequently not closely related to the content of the courses in which the research is conducted. Thus, an alternative approach may be considered in which research data gathering in the educational psychology course is planned as a systematic and continuous procedure and is tied as closely as possible to course content and topics as a learning experience for students. The data base might be developed as a continuous or longitudinal store that can be added to from semester to semester so that longitudinal studies may be undertaken with shorter time lags. Accumulated data may also be useful as a source of information about student traits or characteristics for researchers in subsequent courses who wish to study trait–treatment interactions.

Such a storehouse of information about students in the current courses might also be invaluable for studies of the retention and transfer effects of learnings in educational psychology courses on performance and learning in subsequent teacher education courses or on the job as a teacher. There is an urgent need to assess the impact of educational psychology courses since at present our courses, like most teacher education courses, must stand on faith alone.

Of course, all such systematic data gathering, if it is undertaken, must be conducted within the framework of guidelines for protection of human subjects in research. This means that researchers must develop written plans for their research, impartial committees must judge the degree of risk to subjects, subjects must be fully informed of the research purposes and procedures prior to giving their signed consent to participate, and after completion of the research, subjects must be debriefed and given a report of the research findings.

Research data gathering in educational psychology courses, if systematic, well planned, and conducted with due regard for student rights, can provide a valuable source of information for a variety of studies on basic learning and personality variables, instructional conditions, and the impact of educational psychology courses.

CONCLUSIONS

In this review of issues in teaching undergraduate educational psychology courses, a number of major concerns, developments, and problems have been identified and discussed. They include (a) appropriate goals, (b) problems of relevance, (c) appropriate content, (d) objectives for educational psychology courses, (e) qualifications of instructors, (f) evaluating courses, (g) relating to teacher education, (h) relationships with the discipline of educational psychology, (i) raising standards for student performance, (j) systematic approaches to the course, (k) use of student assistants, and (l) research with students as subjects. In some cases solutions have been proposed. As teacher education undergoes critical examination and retrenchment in the latter part of the 1970s and 1980s, educational psychologists must take the lead in studying their own courses, in initiating change or innovation when it seems appropriate, and in conducting research evaluations as documentations of their successes and failures. Perpetuation of the status quo and failure to undertake critical examination of our courses and efforts will lead to our demise as a part of the teacher education curriculum.

REFERENCES

Bloom, B. S. *Taxonomy of educational objectives, cognitive domain.* New York: McKay, 1956.

Chandler, T. A. Utilization of contract options in teaching educational psychology. *Teaching of Psychology*, 1976, *3*(1), 26–28.

Cohen, S. J. Educational Psychology: Practice what we teach. *Educational Psychologist,* 1973, *10*(2), 80–86.

Davis, R. H., Alexander, L. T., & Yelon, S. L. *Learning system design.* New York: McGraw-Hill, 1974.

DeCecco, J. P., & Crawford, W. R. *The psychology of learning and instruction.* Englewood Cliffs, New Jersey: Prentice-Hall, 1974.

Educational Psychologist, Minutes of the business meeting of Division 15 (Educational Psychology) of the American Psychological Association, 1968, *6*, 11.

Educational Testing Service. *GRE, guide to the use of GRE scores in graduate admissions.* Princeton, New Jersey: Educational Testing Service, 1971.

Feldhusen, J. F. Focus on educational psychology. *Educational Psychologist*, 1966, *3*, 10.

Feldhusen, J. F. Student views of the ideal educational psychology course. *The Educational Psychologist,* 1970, *8*, 7–9.

Feldhusen, J. F. *A logical approach to curriculum development and revision.* Paper presented at the annual meeting of the Midwestern Pharmacy Association, West Lafayette, Indiana, 1972.

Feldhusen, J. F. (Ed.). *Teaching Educational Psychology, Proceedings of the First Annual Midwestern Conference on The Teaching of Educational Psychology.* West Lafayette, Indiana: Purdue University, Department of Education, 1973.

Feldhusen, J. F., Ames, R., & Linden, K. The Purdue three-stage model for a college course. *APA Division 2 Newsletter,* October, 1973, 5–6.

Feldhusen, J. F., Ames, R. E., & Linden, K. W. Designing instruction to achieve higher level goals and objectives. *Educational Technology*, 1974, *14*, 21–23.

Feldhusen, J. F., Linden, K. W., & Ames, R. E. Using instructional theory and educational technology in designing college courses. *Improving College and University Teaching Yearbook 1975.* Corvallis, Oregon: Oregon State University Press, 1975.

Frey, P. W. Student ratings of teaching: Validity of several rating factors. *Science,* 1973, *182*, 83–85.

Gagné, R. M. *The conditions of learning.* New York: Holt, Rinehart & Winston, 1970.

Galloway, C. *Psychology for learning and teaching.* New York: McGraw-Hill, 1976.

Gronlund, N. E. *Stating behavioral objectives for classroom instruction.* Toronto: Macmillan, 1970.

Harrow, A. J. *A taxonomy of the psychomotor domain.* New York: David McKay, 1972.

Jackson, P. W. *Life in classrooms.* New York: Holt, Rinehart & Winston, 1968.

Jackson, P. W. Stalking beasts and swatting flies: Comments on educational psychology and teacher trainiing. In J. F. Feldhusen (Ed.), *Teaching educational psychology.* Proceedings of the First Annual Midwestern Conference on the Teaching of Educational Psychology, Purdue University, West Lafayette, Indiana, 1972.

Keller, F. S. Goodbye teacher. *Journal of Applied Behavior Analysis,* 1968, *1,* 79–89.

Kibler, R. J., Cegala, D. S., Barker, L. L., & Miles, D. T. *Objectives for instruction and evaluation.* Boston: Allyn & Bacon, 1974.

Klausmeier, H. J., & Goodwin, W. *Learning and human abilities, educational psychology.* New York: Harper & Row, 1975.

Klees, S. J. The role of colleges of education in a time of teacher surplus: An economist's perspective. *Educational Perspectives,* 1975, *14,* 4–9.

Knief, L. M. A systematic approach to educational psychology courses. *Educational Psychologist,* 1972, *9*(2), 21, 23–26.

Krathwohl, D. R., Bloom, B. S., & Masia, B. B. *Taxonomy of educational objectives. Handbook II: Affective domain.* New York: David McKay, 1964.

Kryspin, W., & Feldhusen, J. *Developing classroom tests: Writing and evaluating test items.* Minneapolis: Burgess, 1974. (a)

Kryspin, W., & Feldhusen, J. *Writing behavioral objectives: A guide for planning instruction.* Minneapolis: Burgess, 1974. (b)

Linden, K. W., Ames, R., & Feldhusen, J. F. *The role of the undergraduate course assistant and the instructional team in an educational psychology course.* Unpublished paper available from the first author, at Educational Psychology Section, Purdue University, West Lafayette, Indiana, 1975.

Mager, R. F. *Goal analysis.* Belmont, California: Fearon, 1972.

Mager, R. F. *Preparing instructional objectives* (2nd ed.). Palo Alto: Fearon, 1975.

Newson, R. S., & Gaite, A. J. H. An evaluation of two approaches to the teaching of educational psychology. *Educational Psychologist,* 1971, *9*(1), 14–16.

Popham, W. J., Eisner, E. W., Sullivan, H. J., & Tyler, L. L. *Instructional objectives.* Chicago: Rand McNally, 1969.

Ripple, R. E., & Ayabe, H. I. Undergraduate specialization in education: One alternative role for faculties of education. *Educational Perspectives,* 1975, *14,* 22–24.

Rodin, M., & Rodin, B. Student evaluations of teachers. *Science,* 1972, *177,* 1164–1166.

Samuels, S. J. Thirty-two ways to teach educational psychology. *Educational Psychologist,* 1971, *8,* 42–45.

Samuels, S. J. The enemy within: Threats to educational psychology from within and outside the field. *Ideas and Views, New Directions in Educational Psychology,* newsletter of AERA's Special Interest Group, Summer, 1975, 3–4.

Sattler, H. E., Woehlke, H. L., & Grinder, R. E. An empirical assessment of preference for the modular program in educational psychology. *Educational Psychologist,* 1972, *9*(3), 38–40.

Saxon, S. A., & Holt, M. M. Field placement as an adjunct experience for developmental psychology students. *Teaching of Psychology,* 1974, *1*(2), 82–83.

Scully, M. G. Crackdown on grade inflation. *The Chronicle of Higher Education,* 1975, *11*(15), 1, 12.

Tennyson, C. L., & Tennyson, R. D. Instructional objectives–Who needs them? *Improving Human Performance Quarterly,* 1975, *4,* 12–16.

Treffinger, D. J., & Davis, J. K. Instructional innovation in educational psychology: The search for relevance. *Educational Psychologist,* 1972, *9*(2), 21, 27–28.

Trowbridge, N. An approach to teaching a large undergraduate class in educational psychology. *Educational Psychologist,* 1970, *7,* 3–6.

Vargas, J. S. *Writing worthwhile behavioral objectives.* New York: Harper & Row, 1972.

15

Graduate Training in Educational Psychology

JOHN P. DE CECCO
San Francisco State University
and
ARLENE K. RICHARDS
New York City

PRESENT STATUS

As a graduate discipline, educational psychology is currently in crisis. The concern for the future of this field was indicated by the inclusion of two symposia on graduate education in educational psychology in the program of the annual meeting of the American Psychological Association in Chicago in August 1975. Participants expressed their lack of satisfaction with current graduate training programs and suggested ways in which graduate programs could be changed to make them more useful to students and more productive for professors. It is our contention that graduate eduation in educational psychology can remain vital only if the needs of a third constituency are considered in planning and carrying them out. This third constituency is the public which employs educational psychologists.

Aversano (1975), who is completing doctoral studies, described some of the difficulties the graduate student faces during the training period. The diverse and constantly changing subject matter, the difficulty in forming close working relationships with professors, and the confusing nature of the relationship between the scientific discipline and classroom applications were cited as the major difficulties. He believed that close relationships with faculty members was the most valuable part of his own graduate education. Aversano's experience is corroborated by the findings of various investigators.

Holmstrom and Holmstrom (1974) found that contact with faculty was a determinant of success in graduate school. They postulated that women had special difficulty in graduate school. Based on their reports from over 13,000 doctoral students in many universities, they concluded that graduate education is more stressful for women than for men. They found that women reported more difficulty in making informal contact with faculty members and that emotional strain and doubts about completing their work was exacerbated by the lack of encouragement from faculty members. This finding supports the idea that graduate education depends on personal relationships between students and faculty.

Widlak and Garza (1975) found that minority graduate students perceived the university environment as being less friendly and encouraging than did majority students. Faculty contact, friendliness, and encouragement appear to be special needs of minority students. A connection between graduate student satisfaction and degree of contact with faculty members was found in graduate education courses by Rugg and Norris (1975). They showed that student rating of supervisors in a graduate education course was proportional to the amount of time students spent in direct contact with their faculty supervisors.

Contact with faculty was shown to be the most important factor in student ratings of an effective university instructional climate by Romine (1974). He found that both students and faculty in undergraduate and graduate programs rated the effectiveness of instruction in terms of the perceived interest in and respect for students on the part of faculty members. Presumably, student judgments of faculty interest in them would be proportional to amount of faculty time spent with students.

Contact with faculty has another dimension. According to Mathews and Reed (1974) novice educational researchers find their first jobs through faculty and friends at the school where they receive their graduate training. Finding a job is a major need for all graduate students. In a study of recent employment patterns of new holders of the doctoral degree in education, Higgins (1973) found that too many degree holders were being produced to fill currently available positions on the doctoral level. He found both university and nonuniversity jobs were decreasing in all the traditional areas. Hynes (1975) found that present graduates in educational psychology are competing for jobs in a market that has room for only half as many people as complete their doctorates each year. The needs of graduate students to find jobs, when met successfully, usually brings them into faculty positions. A different set of needs emerges for faculty members attempting to enlarge and pass on a coherent discipline to new graduate students.

New departures in graduate education in educational psychology may be signaled by the methods training sessions for educational psychologists offered at the meetings of the American Educational Research Association. If the courses offered to practicing educational psychologists are taken as an indication of the interests of those in the field, they can point the way for graduate training. In 1973, seven sessions were offered. In 1974, three, in 1975, four. Thus, there was a decrease in the anticipated demand for courses among those offering them. The content of the courses changed as well as the quantity. Instead of the computational formula oriented courses, current offerings focused on alternative methodologies for research and testing which are individual rather than normative. Thus, the field of educational psychology is responding to the demands of the larger society that attention be paid to the development of the individual to accord with potential rather than merely the development of standards by which to select or reject individual achievement.

In a survey of interests of members of APA Division 15, Frasi and Schwartz (1975) found a great diversity of 25 topics, with measurement the most central interest. They found a focus of interest to be individuals. The overriding implication of their findings is a need to avoid narrowness in an extremely diverse field.

Page (1975) argued that educational psychology must retain a distinct body of knowledge about how to make curricular and methodological decisions. He felt that the unique contribution of the educational psychologist to the schools was in providing mathematical models for such decision making. He emphasized the need for good data as input for these models. We conclude that educational psychologists must be trained to work closely with school people to get such data as well as to communicate the results of their analyses to the school people once they have been found.

Eye (1975) claimed that while many researchers with good research skills were currently on the scene, too few people capable of synthesis and application of research findings were available to put all the research knowledge available to use in educational settings.

Suppes' (1974) statement that more attention to theory and less to hardware would be more productive in training educational researchers supports the conclusion that the field would benefit from more attention to "soft" thinking and integration of current findings than from a proliferation of data generated by investigators working in isolation.

Taking into account the third constituency, the consumers of educational psychology, leads to new definitions of the discipline as well as new training at graduate levels. Replying to Gagné's (1975) suggestion that the training of educational researchers be curtailed to fit the decreasing demand for them in the current job market, Guba and Clark (1975) argued that current educational researchers have failed to build support for their field. They advocate building constituencies in geographical areas, among minority groups and addressing current problems as ways of expanding the scope of research. Their suggestion implies that new researchers be trained to do applied research in school settings rather than continuing on the old course of laboratory research directed at subjects of interest to researchers.

Byers (1975) pointed out that current and projected decreases in growth of school populations at all levels make for fewer new faculty members in schools, thus shifting training needs from the preservice undergraduate teacher preparation to in-service graduate courses aimed at upgrading skills for currently practicing teachers. Such teachers, he suggested, are less interested in theoretical than in practical knowledge. Educational psychologists will thus be forced to communicate with people outside the field of educational psychology and to convince them of the value of our discipline by showing them the value of its practical applications. We infer that the training of educational psychologists must take into account their necessary contact with the public.

Austin (1975) reported on a panel at the 1975 AERA on federal policy issues for which research is needed. The panel addressed these current issues: long-range school finance, desegregation, and education for the disadvantaged, including the crippled. The participants mentioned declining enrollments in schools and the need for effective collective bargaining procedures among the issues to be dealt with in the near future. Commentators on the panel stated that mistrust between the educational research community and most U. S. politicians was a barrier to effective use of educational research in the schools.

Competency-based teacher training was cited by Treffinger (1975) as a challenge to the educational psychologist to show how what is taught in the educational psychology courses adds to the effectiveness of the classroom teacher. He suggested that learning to find and solve problems was the major learning that must be provided to students. Rather than courses in which groups of people were strangers to each other, he suggested that programs in which people who worked together in a school setting be offered in order to maximize the mutual reinforcing potential of students with a common goal. On the graduate level, this suggestion would imply that graduate students must learn how to teach in action oriented groups rather than in conventional classrooms. Davis (1975) suggested a differentiation of course work in educational psychology for elementary and secondary schoolteachers. He introduced the idea that educational psychology turn its attention to classroom management. This suggestion directs efforts of educational psychologists toward meeting immediate and specific needs of teachers and away from general questions of philosophical interest.

The symposium presented by graduate students focused on what the students felt their training had not yet provided them and on what they had learned from incidentally that could be incorporated in the curriculum to strengthen it. Among the suggestions were: informal evaluation of research and teaching competencies; training in multivariate research design appropriate to school settings; faculty involvement in research; training in research early in the graduate program; and involvement in professional societies at an earlier level of training. Froman (1975) and Kallsnick (1975) suggested that graduate students become involved in the schools in order to research topics of potential value to schools rather than, as is presently the case, topics of value only to their advisors. Lutz and Ramsey (1974) called for more thorough preparation of researchers in anthropological methods to be used in educational research. These methods involve going out to the schools and using teachers and learners as sources of knowledge about how learning takes place. They contrast with the more traditional model of educational research as bringing knowledge from the laboratory into the classroom. Thus, they respond to the school's need for practicable educational methods.

Building bridges between schools, graduate students, and practicing educational psychologist is the future challenge of the discipline. Aversano (1975) suggested that courses in the history of educational psychology and in grant proposal and paper writing would be helpful. He saw a history course as useful in systematizing what educational psychology had been in the past and suggesting future directions. The course in grant and paper writing was his solution to the difficulty in making contact with the classroom for research and application of the results of research. His suggestions for building bridges between scientific educational psychology and the classroom included: providing graduate students with experience in teaching at all school levels; a teaching apprenticeship for undergraduates in educational psychology; experience in teaching educational psychology to undergraduate education majors; experience teaching an educational psychology graduate course to in-service teachers and administrators; and participating in a research project as an on-site supervisor.

Pulling together findings on the research skills in demand for educational researchers from three USOE task forces, Worthen (1975) concluded that responding to needs for research in the schools required that the research community must provide 25 specific skills. Such skills as obtaining information about areas in need of research, using formal research procedures, using libraries and the ERIC system, and identifying and contacting other workers in the same area were cited as essential. Making recommendations as a result of evaluation and translating data into calls for action were emphasized. He concluded that his list was already dated as a result of new interests in anthropological, economic, linguistic, historical, and philosophical approaches to educational problems.

In another session on the future directions of educational psychology at APA in Chicago in 1975, a call for suggestions was made. Recognizing that educational psychology was in danger as a discipline unless it could meet the challenges of the new realities in education, members of the panel agreed that finding the new directions could be an energizing challenge.

PROFESSIONAL SERVICES

The categories of services educational psychologists can provide have not changed much since 1948, as outlined in the report of the committee on the function of the Division of educational psychology of the APA. The report describes six functions: (1) teaching at the college level; (2) directing and interpreting research; (3) serving as a personnel worker or expert by (a) training counselors and school psychologists, (b) counseling at the college level, and (c) providing psychometric services at the college level; (4) providing psychotherapy, especially for children and young adults; (5) consulting in industry and the armed forces; and (6) constructing and evaluating measuring instruments.

Although the functions of the educational psychologists have not changed in the last 20 years, the settings in which these functions are performed have drastically changed.

Teaching

Teaching remains a major function. With the general decline in college enrollments and the trimming back of college teaching positions, fewer and fewer educational psychologists can expect to teach in college.

Cuca (1975) reported the employment status of 1975 doctorates in the various subfields of psychology. The numbers are based on responses from 74% of the psychology departments in the nation which grant doctorates in psychology. Fifty percent of the educational psychologists were employed in academic positions. This is well above the average (36.9%) for all fields combined. Since doctorates in educational psychology are granted in education departments that are not devoted exclusively to educational psychology, the figure may be somewhat misleading.

There is also a trend in several states to cut back on educational psychology as a requirement for the teaching credential. This reduction or elimination of the educational psychology requirement deprives departments of educational psychology of their chief source of consumers.

There are increasing opportunities for educational psychologists to provide short-term training functions in workshops that have specific purposes. There are workshops on new curricular materials and teaching techniques, on diagnosing and dealing with reading disabilities, on new techniques of evaluation such as

TABLE 15.1

Employment Status of 1975 Doctorates by Subfield

Subfield	No Position		Postdoctoral Study		Nonacademic Position		Academic Position		Total	
	N	%	N	%	N	%	N	%	N	%
Clinical	106	15.1	37	5.3	402	57.3	156	22.2	701	34.1
Counseling	17	11.0	9	5.8	61	39.6	67	43.5	154	7.5
Developmental	19	13.6	13	9.3	30	21.4	78	55.7	140	6.8
Educational School	7	14.6	3	6.2	14	29.2	24	50.0	48	2.3
Experimental	68	24.9	40	14.0	56	19.6	121	42.5	285	13.9
Comparative	4	26.7	5	33.3	1	6.7	5	33.3	15	0.7
Physiological	30	21.3	56	39.7	13	9.2	42	29.8	141	6.9
Industrial	5	8.8	1	1.8	24	42.1	27	47.4	57	2.8
Personality	9	17.6	3	5.9	10	19.6	29	56.9	51	2.5
Social	47	20.8	9	4.0	50	22.1	120	53.1	226	11.0
Psychometrics	10	41.7	1	4.2	3	12.5	10	41.7	24	1.2
Other	76	49.7	2	1.3	21	13.7	54	35.3	153	7.5
	404	19.7	180	8.8	712	34.7	757	36.9	2,053	100.0

criterion-referenced measures, on new counseling techniques and measuring devices, and on new research designs and procedures such as multivariate analysis.

The settings for these workshops are increasingly varied. They can be a series of weekend workshops offered on a college campus or at some convenient airport hotel. They can be held on site, at the places of work of the personnel to be trained. These training sites can be public schools and classrooms, offices in business and industry of managerial and supervisory personnel, and various community settings, such as recreational centers, church halls, private homes, and so on. There are advanced professional seminars held before and after meetings of such organizations as the American Educational Research Association and the American Psychological Association. Workshops are increasingly incorporated within convention formats and, to some extent, are replacing sessions devoted to the presentation of papers.

In summary, there may be a trend to move the teaching of educational psychology off the college campus to the site where the training can be conveniently provided for a diverse group of participants. These new sites are sometimes the places where what is learned can be immediately applied.

Directing and Interpreting Research

The direction of research in the past was mostly on university campuses. The majority of research grants in educational psychology were made to investigators who were professors in schools of education and departments of psychology. For educational psychology the grants in recent years have focused on establishing new learning objectives, new teaching and curricular materials, new teaching methods, and new ways of assessing individual and even school performance. There has been great concern with teaching of mathematics and reading and with teaching children and adults who have a variety of learning disabilities.

The direction of research involves the successful submission of a proposal, the setting up of the research staff, the development of the research and evaluation instruments, the collection, summary, analysis, and interpretation of data, and the preparation of research reports.

The interpreting of research is a necessary function of those doing research and of those who synthesize research knowledge in review articles, monographs, and books. It is important for an investigator to understand the theory and findings of the research area in which she or he is working. It is also important to have broad syntheses of previous research to maintain research focus and to move research in a given field ahead. Textbooks can be syntheses that can be used to introduce students quickly to the major knowledge corpora of educational psychology.

On the university campus the direction of research includes the supervision of masters' theses and doctoral dissertations. Graduate students sometimes do their research under grants directed by professors who are also their theses or dissertations supervisors.

As in the teaching of educational psychology, research increasingly is moving off campus to new research sites. Perhaps more research in educational psychology is done in private research corporations than on university campuses. Examples of major research corporations are the Educational Testing Service, the American Institutes of Research, the Psychological Corporation, and the Stanford Research Institute. There are smaller research corporations throughout the nation that serve as conduits for proposal writing, submission, funding, and administration. The Educational Testing Service directed the development, research and evaluation of the television program for children, *Sesame Street*. The American Institutes of Research have been directing the longitudinal study of high achieving students known as Project Talent. The Stanford Research Institute has been involved in evaluating the effects of school integration and desegregation and of the voucher system.

In the future it appears that an increasingly large proportion of educational psychologists will be employed by private research corporations, mostly on a contractual basis, whereby their services are tied to particular research projects. By looking for new projects as old projects are ending, they will act as professional entrepreneurs.

Many educational psychologists will continue to work for local school systems as research and evaluation specialists. As research specialists they prepare proposals that enable their districts to take advantage of the federal grant money available under the titles established by Congress for use of the Department of Health, Education and Welfare. They often administer the grant money given the district by apportioning it to schools throughout the district, supervising its expenditure, and supervising the evaluation of the new programs for which the money is spent.

With the growth of public interest in professional accountability of school officials and teachers, many educational psychologists were involved in the overall evaluation of student performance in critical subject matter and skill areas in particular schools and school districts.

Increasing numbers of educational psychologists are employed for their skills in research and evaluation by professional schools of nursing, medicine, dentistry, and public health. In these positions they do longitudinal and follow-up studies of graduates, evaluate the effects of such instructional innovations as computerized and programmed instruction, use of new audiovisual instructional materials and procedures, and performance-based programs of student evaluation. They also prepare proposals that initiate and sustain these investigations. Some of these psychologists become involved in epidemiological research on the community health needs for which their institutions must ultimately provide professional services.

Educational psychologists working in state and federal government are frequently in positions to influence research emphases and directions. They have served as heads of governmental divisions concerned with research in such areas as special education, child development, curricular development, and teacher training. Working with political leaders, professional groups, and various minority and geographical communities, they develop research priorities, guidelines, timetables, and review committees that must determine the particular investigators and what the particular projects will be. Some of these educational psychologists become tenured civil service employees of the government. Others are top-level administrators who serve short periods of time to formulate and implement research innovations.

Some educational psychologists serve in quasi-governmental positions. They work for research and development centers that are primarily supported by federal funds. Examples of these centers are the various regional laboratories established throughout the nation. One example is the Far West Laboratory. Educational psychologists in this laboratory are engaged in research activities connected with the development of new forms of teaching and community outreach. For example, they have studied the effects of a program to train tutors to teach children how to read. They have studied developmental problems in reading associated with various ethnic minorities. They have studied the relationship of such personality variables as internal/external locus of control to educational aspirations and achievements of children of various ethnic backgrounds.

Other sites for research by educational psychologists are industry and the military. Some of the most basic research on learning has been carried on by educational psychologists working at the Bell Telephone laboratories. Basic research on task description, task analysis, and skill learning has occurred in the military and in aerospace programs.

In summary, it appears that research is a primary function of educational psychologists and in time may become the major demand for their professional services.

Program Development

The research functions described earlier are frequently part of efforts to develop new training programs, materials, and procedures. The trend in federal funding requires the development of new programs and products to be followed by evaluation of their effectiveness. If this trend in funding continues, educational psychologists can expect to find positions that will require skills in designing as well as evaluating educational innovations.

They may also find themselves involved in training personnel to carry out a new teaching technique. For example, they may have to train professors of dental surgery to demonstrate a surgical intervention in a way that enables students viewing a TV monitor or videotape to understand what is crucial. They may need to train teachers to train their paraprofessional aides in ways that make them most useful. In these ways the educational psychologist is involved in both the design and introduction of independent variables (i.e., training variables) as well as evaluating dependent variables (i.e., outcomes).

Program development in the future may be the function of educational psychologists working in the public school system. Some of the major innovations in curriculum in the 1960s in the physical and biological sciences, in social studies, and in mathematics were the joint efforts of subject matter specialists and educational psychologists. To implement these new curricula, educational psychologists often trained teachers and supervised the use of the materials in classrooms. Educational psychologists are needed to help curriculum supervisors and teachers design and implement new courses of study in public schools. Their help can result in more explicit and focused objectives, careful preparation and selection of materials, clear and realistic timetables, more varied adaptations to different student interests and abilities, and careful evaluation of outcomes. They could work with teachers in the same close professional relationship that teachers need to work with students.

Psychometric Services

There are two categories of psychometric services: (*a*) constructing and evaluating measuring instruments and (*b*) providing psychometric services for school districts, state departments of education, and colleges and universities.

The construction and evaluation of measuring instruments are often the work of educational psychologists working for the commercial test publishers and carrying out university research that requires new instrumentation. Many of the standardized tests of achievement in the various skill and content areas are the work of educational psychologists. They have also been leaders in constructing and revising intelligence tests, college and university qualification tests, graduate record examinations, qualifying tests for professional schools, vocational aptitude tests, and so on. In carrying out their own research they constructed innumerable cognitive and attitudinal measures to obtain evidence on the effectiveness of a wide range of independent variables.

Providing psychometric services is a very old function of educational psychologists. They are employed by school districts to supervise the administration, scoring, and reporting of tests required by federal, state, and local regulations. In these districts they often head divisions of pupil services. In this supervisory capacity they are responsible for all standardized or district-wide tests used by teachers, counselors, school psychologists, special education teachers, and so on. To varying extents they are also involved in pupil placement in special classes. Standardized testing includes both intelligence tests and the state achievement tests. To the extent that results have become political issues in most states and districts, educational psychologists, as chief psychometricians of their districts, become involved with the press, the community, local school boards, and state departments of education. What once was a purely technical function appears now to become a highly volatile political issue.

Educational psychologists sometimes head testing programs for entire states. At this level they occupy very responsible positions since appropriations of state funds to schools are often tied to level of pupil performance on state tests. Some educational psychologists in these positions have pointed out the assets and liabilities of norm-referenced as compared with criterion-referenced tests. Some states under the leadership of educational psychologists have instituted curricular reforms that require teachers in districts to state course and curricular objectives in performance terms so that testing can be criterion-referenced. These curricular reforms have been efforts to make schools more "accountable" for the services made available to students and community. Educational psychologists have played important roles in the accountability movement of the late 1960s and early 1970s.

Educational psychologists often work as psychometricians in college and university offices of evaluation. In this capacity they may construct tests conjointly with professors who are the subject matter and skill specialists. Educational psychologists take charge of the technical development of the test by performing item analyses and reporting results to department heads and deans. Some university evaluation services are also responsible for constructing and administering English language tests for graduating seniors, for bilingual students, and for entering freshmen. Some are in charge of examinations in foreign languages, statistics, and computer science for advanced degrees. Some are in charge of selection and administration of test batteries that include scholastic achievement, personality measures, and occupational preference. These results are provided the university counselors who interpret them for guidance of the student–counselees.

Many of the educational psychologists who work as evaluation specialists on university campuses are often involved in research on test construction, item innovation, scoring techniques, and so on. Some also teach educational psychology and measurement on their campuses. The contributors to the major journals on educational measurement are frequently educational psychologists who are employed as university psychometricians.

Psychotherapy

Educational psychologists do psychotherapy in several settings. Some work with young children in nursery schools, incorporating learning principles into their milieu for strengthening the integrating, decision-making, and reality-testing functions of the ego. Others engage in private practice, helping older children and adults achieve these ego functions where developmental and experiential events have prevented satisfactory ego development.

Such therapists are called educational therapists, child psychologists, or remedial learning specialists. They have many theoretical orientations, ranging from behavior modification (mainly used in institutions for the severely retarded and hospitals for the severely regressed) to intrapsychic dynamics. Some have become involved in biofeedback. Functioning as psychologists, they have obtained advanced training at the postgraduate level in internships, supervised practice, and seminars with colleagues. The special conditions of private practice require lifelong education and stimulation through seminars. All private practitioners must deal with clients, insurance agencies, federal and state licensing agencies, and peer review.

Special Education

Remedial treatment of learning disabilities has begun to occupy the work time of educational psychologists. Such remedial work is done in special schools for children and adults who are handicapped by blindness, deafness, mental retardation, aphasia, cerebral palsy, speech impediments, and emotional disturbance. Residential institutions serving these handicapped people use remedial learning specialists to devise and modify the curriculum to meet their special needs. Learning specialists may function as teachers and administrators of special schools or residential institutions.

Some remedial specialists work in private practice, treating youngsters whose handicaps are not so severe that they must be placed in special schools, yet are too difficult to be treated even in a special classroom in a regular school.

Whether in private practice or special schools, these specialists must deal with state legislators who control appropriations for expensive special education programs.

Remedial learning specialists often work in university departments of special education. In these positions they train graduate students for remedial work with people who have a particular class of handicap. They also supervise graduate research at the masters and doctoral levels. This research is both basic and applied. As basic research it deals with the etiology and developmental history of particular disabilities and syndromes; as applied research it deals with new methods and materials of remedial teaching and learning. Much of the research on applications of behavior modification to learning disabilities has been done by educational psychologists working in special education departments.

Consulting Services

The 1948 report referred to the consulting educational psychologists do in industry and the armed forces. The range of this consulting has greatly expanded in the last 20 years to include more direct work with schools and school districts, health services, and minority communities. It may be that industrial and applied engineering psychologists have taken over much of the consulting previously done by educational psychologists in industry and the armed forces. It may also be that social psychologists will take over much of the community involvement of educational psychologists.

Consultation is usually provided when institutions and communities face new problems for which they have little knowledge and experience to solve. Schools, for example, are experiencing a great escalation in violence, vandalism, and suspensions. The cultural heterogeneity of the school has increased awareness of how much conflict a school and classroom can face in one day and how a major professional responsibility of teachers and administrators is to deal with conflict in ways that are educative for students who must learn to live in a democracy. Since most educators are taught how to use negotiation to resolve conflict with colleagues, students, and superiors, schools must hire consultants to speak with and to train their staffs in the use of negotiation.

Similarly, schools have hired educational psychologists who were specialists in human relations training to set up training groups of officials, teachers, and students to improve informational and affective communication and thereby their ability to deal more directly and productively with each other.

Whenever there have been problems arising from the need to deal with children with particular learning disabilities or new legislation requiring curricular and testing innovations, educational psychologists have been used as consultants. Some psychologists have set up consulting firms for schools, other institutions, and communities need the specialized services offered by their staffs. There are or have been consulting firms on performance objectives, school crisis intervention, reading innovations, drug usage, and so on.

In summary, we have described many professional services educational psychologists can provide: teaching, research, program development, psychometry, psychotherapy, special education, and consultation. We have described many sites where these services can be performed: colleges and universities, private research corporations, local communities, local school districts, in federal and state government, and in industry and the armed forces. With the rapid expansion in adult education in community groups and in institutions like the church, social and recreational clubs, and senior citizen communities, we can expect that the number of sites will multiply in the years ahead.

Of all the functional described the three that appear to apply most generally in the various sites are research, development, and training. It may be that educational psychologists should prepare themselves for the complicated work involved in developing new programs, providing the necessary new training, and carrying out the evaluative research to determine degrees and foci of change and success.

TRAINING

To train graduate students for a wide variety of services is the new challenge of professors and programs of educational psychology. Graduate programs that prepared students only for university teaching and research are probably too narrow in focus, experience, and content to provide the training presently needed.

We suggest the following guidelines for training graduate students in educational psychology. They are based on our view of the current status of graduate training and the variety of services educational psychologists can now provide.

First, the programs should be flexible enough to build on current interests and talents of the graduate students. There are two reasons to base programs on current student interests: (1) These interests, when operationally defined, may point to the areas of research, development, and training where change is needed and most possible and (2) They can be the basis for students' creative work in educational psychology.

There can also be more program response to individual talent since the variety of services is rapidly expanding to meet educational needs of peoples who, in the past, have been left undereducated: the preschoolers, the disabled, the incorrigible, the minorities (both sexual and ethnic), and the middle-aged and old. Surely a variety of talents is needed to reach a diverse group of students.

Second, programs should provide training for institutions that are requiring new skills and content. Public schools are providing new content and skills in the physical, social, and behavioral sciences, in art, drama, music, and the humanities, in recreation, and in community outreach that considerably stretch the limits and teaching methodologies of the older curricula. Graduate students in educational psychology may have to learn enough about these new content and skills required in such areas as ecology, dietary changes, music, urban renewal, museum art, political reform, and minority politics to know what is relevant to study about learning, development, measurement, and research. To assure that they are learning the content and skills that are needed, graduate students should have opportunities from the very beginning of their graduate work to deal with the new subject matter and skill needs of the public schools.

Almost all institutions have had to expand their educational functions as changes in technology, the economy, the family, interpersonal relationships, the community, and the nation have occurred. Almost all social agencies, welfare, control, and health, have had to train personnel to deal with new people and new problems. Police, for example, have had to be trained to deal with minority communities, high school students, and the rise in violence and vandalism. Rising insurance rates for doctors have required hospitals to raise the level of personnel training and patient protection and care. Rehabilitation agencies have had to train personnel to deal with clients whose experience and educational levels keep them unemployable. The clergy have to be trained in pastoral counseling of children, parents, couples, and individuals facing breakups in traditional relationships. Welfare and health agencies dealing with older men and women have had to teach personnel about the changes that occur in old age and the capacities for learning that remain.

Educational psychologists, therefore, must be prepared to work in institutional settings in which education may be the subordinate rather than the major function.

Third, graduate programs should place greater emphasis on fieldwork as compared with classroom or laboratory training. The reason for this guideline is clear. Most educational psychologists will be working in the field (i.e., off campus) during most of their professional careers. On-campus training tends to emphasize theory, laboratory research, precise measurement. Although some training in these areas is crucial, its preponderance will deny students the experience of learning in the field—both the limitations and appropriate use of what was learned on campus and new theories, hypotheses, facts, and interventions that not even their professors know.

The field training can take the form of supervised internships. The supervision can be contractual arrangement between the on-campus professor, the field professionals, and the graduate student. The professor must take responsibility for the student's learning and the preparation and completion of studies based on the field experience. The field professional is responsible for finding opportunities for graduate students that enable them to deliver a service to the agency while allowing them to learn at a professional level. There is a delicate balance that must be reached by not reducing an agency to a graduate school laboratory and not reducing the graduate student to a clerk.

Fourth, graduate students should learn to work as members of teams. The reason is that most fieldwork involves working as a member of staff developing, implementing, and evaluating new programs. The federal government requirements for integration of personnel, both ethnic and sexual minorities, employed in programs receiving federal funds, will increase demands for teamwork. Members of teams will be culturally and socially heterogeneous. Educational psychologists will need experience in dealing with a wide range of cultural traditions, points of view, value systems, and personalities in order to learn effective teamwork.

Fifth, graduate students should have opportunty to interrupt graduate training and return to it at appropriate times. The reason is that field opportunities may materialize that are professionally profitable to pursue. To take these opportunities may require commitments of time, energy, and mobility that would undermine commitments to on-campus work.

Sixth, graduate programs should allow students who cannot or do not obtain doctoral degrees to complete significant amounts of training at the master's or special credential's levels. Such training is adequate for programs in early childhood education, junior college teaching, school psychology, and positions as research associates.

Finally, graduate programs in educational psychology should allow students to develop as individuals who have their own sensibilities, values, and priorities. Perhaps the best way to foster this growth is a colleagueal relationship of professors with students and students with students that is embodied in cooperative projects that are creative, satisfying and productive for all participants.

REFERENCES

Austin, G. H. Federal perspectives on education. *Educational Researcher, 1975, 4,* 7–8.
Aversano, F. M. Faculty–student interaction–A re-emphasis. In A. J. H. Gaite (Chair), *Graduate training in educational psychology: Definition, direction, and development.* Symposium presented at the meeting of the American Psychological Association, Chicago, 1975.
Byers, J. L. Interdisciplinary research and training in educational psychology. In A. J. H. Gaite (Chair), *Graduate training in educational psychology: Definition, direction, and development.* Symposium presented at the meeting of the American Psychological Association, Chicago, 1975.

Cuca, J. Survey shows deterioration of job market for new doctoral psychologists. *APA Monitor,* November 1975, 11.

Davis, J. K. Current status of teaching educational psychology for undergraduates. In L. Stolurow (Chair), *Status and future of educational psychology as a discipline.* Symposium presented at the meeting of the American Psychological Association, Chicago, 1975.

Eye, G. G. Many researchers but few synthesizers. *Journal of Educational Research,* 1975, *68,* 294–299.

Frase, L. T., & Schwartz, B. J. Survey of interests of Division 15 members. In L. Stolurow (Chair), *Status and future of educational psychology as a discipline.* Symposium presented at the meeting of the American Psychological Association, Chicago, 1975.

Froman, R. Educational psychology and graduate student preparation and participation. In D. J. Treffinger (Chair), *Graduate student views of future directions for educational psychology.* Symposium presented at the meeting of the American Psychological Association, Chicago, 1975.

Gagné, R. M. Qualifications of professionals in educational research and development. *Educational Researcher,* 1975, *4,* 7–11.

Guba, E. G., & Clark, D. C. The configurational perspective: A new view of educational knowledge production and utilization. *Educational Researcher,* 1975, *4,* 6–9.

Higgins, A. S. Present employment patterns of new education doctorates. *Educational Researcher,* 1973, *2,* 9–13.

Holmstrom, E. I., & Holmstrom, R. W. The plight of the woman doctoral student. *American Educational Research Journal,* 1974, *11,* 1–17.

Hynes, K. Placement services and job-seeking graduates of educational psychology. In D. J. Treffinger (Chair), *Graduate student views of future directions for educational psychology.* Symposium presented at the meeting of the American Psychological Association, Chicago, 1975.

Kallsnick, L. R. Destination points in educational psychology programs. In D. J. Treffinger (Chair), *Graduate student views of future directions for educational psychology.* Symposium presented at the meeting of the American Psychological Association, Chicago, 1975.

Lutz, F. W., & Ramsey, M. A. The uses of anthropological field methods in education. *Educational Researcher,* 1974, *3,* 5–9.

Mathews, W. M., & Reed, C. R. How do novice educational researchers find jobs? *Educational Researcher,* 1974, *3,* 13–14.

Ory, J. C. Educational psychology: What needs to be done? In D. J. Treffinger (Chair), *Graduate student views of future directions for educational psychology.* Symposium presented at the meeting of the American Psychological Association, Chicago, 1975.

Page, E. B. Training in educational psychology: New disciplines for a scientific elite. In A. J. H. Gaite (Chair), *Graduate training in educational psychology: Definition, direction, and development.* Symposium presented at the meeting of the American Psychological Association, Chicago, 1975.

Romine, S. Student and faculty perceptions of an effective university instructional climate. *Journal of Educational Research,* 1974, *68,* 139–143.

Rugg, E. A., & Norris, R. C. Student ratings of individualized faculty supervision: Description and evaluation. *American Educational Research Journal,* 1975, *12,* 41–53.

Suppes, P. The place of theory in educational research. *Educational Researcher,* 1974, *6,* 3–10.

Treffinger, D. J. Educational psychology and the classroom teacher. In A. J. H. Gaite

(Chair), *Graduate training in educational psychology: Definition, direction, and development.* Symposium presented at the meeting of the American Psychological Association, Chicago, 1975.

Widlak, F. W., & Garza, R. T. *Determinants of Chicano and Anglo perceptions of university environment.* Paper presented at the meeting of the American Psychological Association, Chicago, August, 1975.

Worthen, B. R. Competencies for educational research and evaluation. *Educational Researcher,* 1975, *4,* 13–16.

Index

A
B 7
C 8
D 9
E 0
F 1
G 2
H 3
I 4
J 5